Mother,
Behold Your Son

Mother, Behold Your Son

ESSAYS IN HONOR OF

EAMON R. CARROLL, O.CARM.

EDITED BY

DONALD W. BUGGERT, O.CARM.

LOUIS P. ROGGE, O.CARM.

MICHAEL J. WASTAG, O.CARM.

The Carmelite Institute

WASHINGTON, D.C.

2001

We gratefully acknowledge permission to reprint previously published or copyrighted material.

Edinburgh University Press and Polygon for excerpts from T. O. Clancy and G. Markus, O.P., *The Earliest Poetry of a Celtic Monastery.* Copyright © 1995, Edinburgh, EH8 9LF.

Harcourt, Inc. for excerpts from "East Coker in Four Quartets" by T.S. Eliot, found in *The Complete Poems and Plays.* Copyright © 1958, Orlando, Florida.

ICS Publications for excerpts from *The Collected Works of St. John of the Cross,* translated by Keiran Kavanaugh and Otilio Rodriguez. Copyright © 1979, 1991 by Washington Province of Discalced Carmelites, 2131 Lincoln Road, N.E., Washington, D.C., 20002-1199.

ICS Publications for excerpts from *The Selected Poetry of Jessica Powers.* Copyright © 1999, Carmelite Monastery, Pewaukee, Wisconsin.

Scripture quotations are for the most part from the New Revised Standard Version, copyright © 1989 by the Division of Christian Education of the National Council of the Churches of Christ in the United States of America and used by permission.

Library of Congress Cataloging-in-Publication Data

Mother, behold your son : essays in honor of Eamon R. Carroll /
    Donald W. Buggert, Louis P. Rogge, Michael J. Wastag, editors.
        p. cm.
    Includes bibliographical references.
    ISBN 0-9656910-2-0 (pbk.)
    1. Mary, Blessed Virgin, Saint. 2. Carmelites—Spiritual life.
    I. Carroll, Eamon R. II. Buggert, Donald W., 1940- III. Rogge, Louis
    Philip. IV. Wastag, Michael J., 1955-
BT613 .M67 2001
232.91—dc21

                                                            2001004155
                                                            CIP

Published by The Carmelite Institute
1600 Webster St., N.E.
Washington, D.C. 20017

Printed and bound in the United States of America

Contents

PART I: INTRODUCTION

Letter from the Prior General
      Most Rev. Joseph Chalmers, O.Carm.   3

Letter from the Prior Provincial
      V. Rev. Leo McCarthy, O.Carm.   4

A Tribute to Eamon
      Most Rev. Kilian Healy, O.Carm.   5

Foreword
      Donald Buggert, O.Carm.   9

PART II: ESSAYS

Eamon R. Carroll, O.Carm.: Theologian Specializing in Marian
      Studies: His Contribution to a Deeper Understanding
      of the Marian Reality
      George F. Kirwin, O.M.I.   13

Eamon Carroll and the National Shrine
      Leopold Glueckert, O.Carm.   39

Carmelite Marian Shrines and Images
      Joachim Smet, O.Carm.   51

Devotion to Our Lady at the Beginnings of Carmel
      Emanuele Boaga, O.Carm.   81

Arnold Bostius' *Collectarius parvus*: Historical Notes
      on the Carmelite Order
      Richard Copsey, O.Carm.   103

Chants, Feasts and Traditions: The Liturgical Celebration
      of the Virgin Mary in the Carmelite Rite
      James Boyce, O.Carm.   137

Mary and the Saints in Early Scottish Poetry
      John Macquarrie   159

The Honor of Our People: Mary and the Lay Carmelites
    Patrick McMahon, O.Carm.   173

A Changed Context for Marian Doctrine
    Thomas Thompson, S.M.   195

Blessed Among Women
    Carlos Mesters, O.Carm.   215

Overshadowed by the Holy Spirit
    Louis Rogge, O.Carm.   231

The Ordination of Women, Gender Symbolism
    and the Blessed Virgin Mary
    Edward Yarnold, S.J.   247

Preaching on the Feasts of Mary
    James Wallace, C.Ss.R.   267

Our Lady of Mount Carmel, Pray for Us! The Scapular Promise
    and the Garbage Pickers at the Nejapa Dump
    David Blanchard, O.Carm.   289

The Ecclesial Presence of Our Lady and Our Alliance with Her
    Theodore Koehler, S.M.   309

The Biblical Blend of Speech and Silence
    Roland E. Murphy, O.Carm.   325

Carmelite Spirituality: Enduring Themes
    John Welch, O.Carm.   339

A Spiritual Reading of the "Dark Night"
    Ernest Larkin, O.Carm.   357

Theotokos Yesterday and Today
    Donald Buggert, O.Carm.   373

PART III: BIBLIOGRAPHY

Bibliography of Eamon Carroll, O.Carm.
    Joachim Smet, O.Carm. and
    Donald Buggert, O.Carm.   407

List of Contributors   441

Mother,
Behold Your Son

PART I

INTRODUCTION

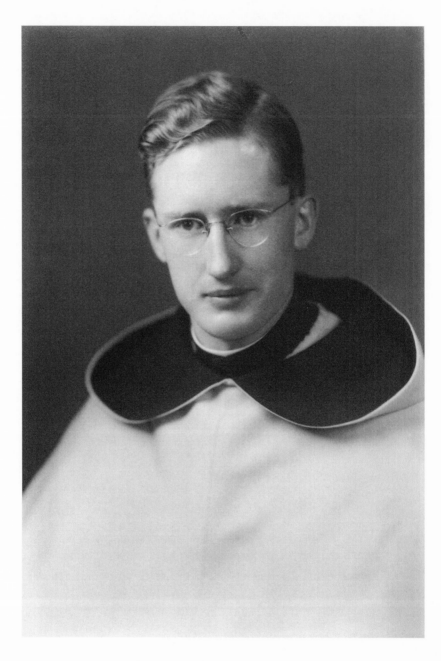

The New Priest at Ordination
June 8, 1946

PRIORE GENERALE DEI CARMELITANI
VIA GIOVANNI LANZA, 138
00184 ROMA - ITALIA

September 23, 2001

Rev. Eamon Carroll, O. Carm.
Carmel at Mission Valley
955 Laurel Road, East
Nokomis, FL. 34275-4507

Dear Fr. Eamon,

It is a great pleasure for me to contribute to this publication in your honour. You have been one of the great Marian scholars of our age and you have made a profound contribution to the renewal of Marian devotion. You have lectured in universities and written in scholarly journals but you have been able to combine this with work at the popular level.

Your love for Our Lady comes across very clearly in all your writings and talks. Because this love is firmly based on sound theological principles, you are able to see clearly her role in God's plan of salvation for the whole of humanity.

For the Carmelite Order, Mary has always been a very important figure. She is looked upon by all Carmelites as Patroness, Mother and Sister; she is the perfect disciple of her Son Jesus and is our constant companion on our journey towards the holy mountain. Over the centuries the Order has produced men and women whose profound meditation on the Gospel has led them to a new appreciation of the place of Our Lady in the Christian mystery. You have enriched the Order and the Church by your studies and your desire to spread the love and knowledge of Mary.

I pray that you will be able to continue far many more years to bear witness to the maternal presence of Mary and that, through your example, many others may come to know and love her.

Sincerely,

Joseph Chalmers O. Carm

Joseph Chalmers, O. Carm.
Prior General

ORDER OF CARMELITES

September 23, 2001

Rev. Eamon Carroll, O.Carm.
Carmel at Mission Valley
955 Laurel Road, East
Nokomis, FL 34275-4507

Dear Eamon,

It has been many years since you first arrived at Niagara's Mount Carmel as a boy! Since then you have spent your life witnessing to your love for Mary, the Order of Carmel, and our Church. That is one reason why your friends and colleagues tip their hats to you through this *Festschrift*.

I sincerely hope that as you read these pages, you will see them as a reflection of the appreciation which so many men and women have for you. Without a doubt, the number whom you have touched through your written and spoken word is myriad. The authors of the articles within this book honor you today on behalf of all of them.

Mary, the mother and queen of Carmel, has been the focal point of much of your energy over the years. For that reason, you have every right to revel in the recognition which is being paid to you within the covers of this book. You have been an inspiration to many of us, and helped us to appreciate the Mother of Jesus and her place in salvation history.

Praying that Our Lady will continue to intercede on your behalf, I remain,

Your brother in Carmel,

Leo McCarthy, O.Carm.
Prior Provincial

1317 Frontage Road • Darien, Illinois 60561-5376
Telephone (630) 971-0050 • Telefax (630) 971- 0196

A Tribute to Eamon

Eamon and I have been friends for over fifty years. Our friendship began when we were members of the Carmelite community at Whitefriars Hall, Washington, D.C., in the 1940's. It matured during our teaching days at St. Albert's International College in Rome in the 1950's. Since that time we have lived in different communities but have remained in constant communication. During all these years I have come to admire Eamon as a wholesome human being, a dedicated Carmelite, and a zealous priest.

On his 80th birthday, however, I would like to salute Eamon the Mariologist.

While it is true that he has taught several tracts of Patristic and Dogmatic Theology not only in various Carmelite houses, but also at The Catholic University of America, at the University of Dayton, and at Loyola University in Chicago, he has never wavered in his devotion to Mariology. In fact, he chose as his doctoral thesis at the Pontifical Gregorian University in Rome the Marian Theology of the English humanist and Carmelite, Arnold Bostius. An extract of his dissertation appeared in *Carmelus* entitled "The Marian Theology of Arnold Bostius, O.Carm. (1445-1499)."[1] Eamon's interest in Bostius continues to this day: together with Father Richard Copsey, O.Carm., he is preparing a critical edition of Bostius' *De Patronatu Mariae*.

For many years Eamon has promoted the devotion of the Brown Scapular of our Lady of Mount Carmel. There is no doubt that his interest in Bostius has had a profound influence on his

5

presentation of the Scapular devotion through his homilies, conferences, essays and pamphlets.

In 1950 he had written an essay entitled *Arnold Bostius and the Scapular.*[2] The occasion was the international celebration of the seventh centenary of the gift of the Scapular to Saint Simon Stock. To celebrate this event Pope Pius XII had written an Apostolic Letter, *Neminem profecto latet,* in which the Holy Father reaffirmed the traditional Scapular promises and encouraged the devotion. Citing the importance of this letter Eamon declares: "The papal teaching is the 20th century repetition of the theology of the Scapular which Arnold Bostius set down in ardent words in 1479.[3] Eamon without hesitation affirms that Arnold Bostius is one of the great Mariologists of the 15th century, and all promoters of the authentic Scapular devotion "walked in his footsteps."

Eamon's interest in Mariology ranges far beyond the borders of Carmel. He has been an ardent active member of the Mariological Society of America (MSA), and each year since 1967 he has written a survey of recent Mariology for *Marian Studies,* the yearly publication of the Society. One year, 1972, the survey was omitted, but in its place he provided a report on the 1971 International Mariological Congress held in Zagreb.[4]

On the occasion of the 50th anniversary of the MSA, celebrated May 25-28, 1999, in Washington, D. C., Eamon gave the keynote address: "A Survey of 50 Years of Mariology."[5]

The Ecumenical Society of the Blessed Virgin Mary (ESBVM), founded in England in 1967, includes leaders of the Anglican, Catholic, Methodist and Orthodox Churches; a branch of the Society was established in Washington, D.C., in 1976. Eamon, who is recognized as one of the founders of ESBVM, U.S.A., invited me to the first meeting of this Society and we both remain active members to this day.

Since 1950 the International Mariological Congress, held every four years in different countries, has been most influential in fostering studies on Marian doctrine and devotion. Eamon has attended many of these meetings and has made significant contributions. In 1967 the Congress encouraged ecumenical round table discussions. Eamon participated in them and has provided a survey of them along with his own personal insights.[6]

If we turn our attention to the classroom, the lecture hall, and the pulpit, who can measure Eamon's impact? Not to be forgotten is that he was an adviser to the American Catholic Bishops in the composition of their influential and memorable pastoral letter *Behold Your Mother* published in 1973, simultaneously in English and Spanish, followed by French and Italian translations.

In 1970 Eamon, encouraged by the publisher Michael Glazier, undertook the role of General Editor of the Marian Library, a project to promote interest in the Blessed Virgin Mary. The first in the series was his own book *Understanding the Mother of Jesus*.[7] It was not intended to be a full scale study of the Blessed Virgin: his hope, he tells us, was "to open doors, to indicate lines of further inquiry, to stimulate interest in the Mother of Jesus."

Down through the years Eamon has written scholarly and popular articles on various Marian themes. One of his special interests has been Mary in the communion of saints. In 1966 his presidential address at the annual meeting of the American Theological Society of America was entitled: "The Mother of Jesus in the Communion of Saints."[8] He returns to this theme time and again. In a remarkable essay commemorating the 30th anniversary of two capital documents of the Second Vatican Council (*Lumen gentium* and *Unitatis redintegratio*) delivered before members of the ESBVM, U.S.A., he speaks of future hopes for Christian Unity, through devotion to Mary.[9]

In offering this tribute to Eamon I have depended on memory of many enjoyable discussions with him, and on some of his writings that he sent me down through the years. Today, in judging his position in the field of Mariology I find myself in agreement with the late eminent scripture scholar, Raymond E. Brown, who, in a personal letter, once referred to Eamon as the outstanding American Mariologist.

St. Therese of the Child Jesus once said to her sister Genevieve (Celine): I have always dreamed of saying in a song to the Blessed Mother everything I think about her. In the declining months of her short life she wrote the lovely poem "Why I Love You, O Mary." It would give me great pleasure if one day Eamon would write his story of love for Mary. It would be the story of his life. For she is the woman who has been his constant companion on his journey to the summit of the mountain, Jesus Christ.

Kilian J. Healy, O.Carm.

Endnotes

1.   *Carmelus* 9 (1962), 197-236.
2.   *Sword* 14 (1950), 342-355.
3.   *Ibid.*, p. 355.
4.   "Report on the Zagreb Mariological Congress." *Marian Studies* 23 (1972), 113-132.
5.   "Evolution in Mariology, 1949-1999." Keynote Address to the Mariological Society of America. *Marian Studies* 50 (1999), 139-145.
6.   "Ecumenical Roundtables and International Mariological Congresses." *Marian Library Studies* 17-23 (1991), 566-577.
7.   Wilmington, Delaware: Michael Glazier, Inc.
8.   "The Mother of Jesus in the Communion of Saints - Challenge to the Churches." *The Catholic Theological Society of America Proceedings* 21 (1967), 249-265.
9.   See *Hope and Visions* No. 1 (August, 1996).

Foreword

I first met Father Eamon Carroll, O.Carm., in 1963. He was one of my professors of systematic theology and my first Christology professor. Among many things which I learned from Eamon as a young student of theology, the most significant was the importance of the history of theology and doctrine. As I plowed through one of Eamon's favorite texts, Aloys Grillmeier's classic work on patristic-conciliar Christology entitled *Christ in Christian Tradition,* I began learning that "truth," even revealed truth, is always embedded in and hence also limited by the finitude and opaqueness of history, language and consciousness. I was also beginning to learn that this same finitude and opaqueness of history, language and consciousness gave rise to a developing and self-correcting tradition. Eamon was one of my first professors to alert me to the need to find theology, *theo-logos,* God-talk, in the very feeble but inescapable locus of history, since that is where we are and what we are. We are our histories and our narratives. As important as speculative theology may be, it must always be rooted in scholarly historical theology. Thank you, Eamon Carroll.

Although throughout his academic career, Eamon taught various courses in systematic theology, e.g. Christology, soteriology, the theology of creation and grace, and eschatology, he has distinguished himself as a theologian primarily in the field of Mariology. The bibliography found in this volume quickly reveals that reflection on Mary, at various levels, is what has occupied Eamon's heart and mind for over fifty years. This comes as no surprise. Eamon is a Carmelite, a religious Order within the Catholic Church dedicated to Mary from its very origins in the early thirteenth century.

Recognizing Eamon's immense contribution as both scholar and Carmelite priest to Mariology and Marian devotion, Rev. Leo McCarthy, prior provincial of the Carmelite Province of the Most Pure Heart of Mary and himself a former student of Eamon, most graciously and enthusiastically approved funding for the writing of this *Festschrift in* honor of Eamon Carroll in November of 1998. The whole Province now presents it to our brother, Eamon, upon the occasion of his eightieth birthday in gratitude for all that he has done for his brother and sister Carmelites as well as the larger Church. We hope that it pays him fitting and deserved tribute. How fortuitous that this Carmelite friar's eightieth birthday happens to fall in the year of the seven-hundred and fiftieth anniversary of the brown scapular of Our Lady of Mount Carmel, symbol of the mutual dedication of Mary and the Carmelite Order.

Since this volume is intended to be a sign of gratitude and acknowledgement from Eamon's Carmelite brothers, the contributors to it are for the most part Carmelites. However, given Eamon's participation in and contribution to Mariological scholarship at both the national and international levels for over forty years, colleagues and friends of his from the larger academy were also asked to contribute to this volume.

Many words of gratitude are in order. First, to all the authors, who generously and enthusiastically responded to the invitation to contribute to this volume. Second, to Joachim Smet, O.Carm., for his assistance in constructing Eamon's bibliography. Third, to my associate editors, Louis Rogge, O.Carm., and Michael Wastag, O.Carm., whose work not only made this *Festschrift* possible but also fitting. Finally, a special word of gratitude to John Welch, O.Carm., President of the Carmelite Institute, for the publication of this work.

Donald Buggert, O.Carm.
Editor

PART II

ESSAYS

Fr. Eamon with Joseph Cardinal Bernardin
and Fr. Eamon's brother, Kevin
January 7, 1984

Eamon R. Carroll, O.Carm.

Theologian Specializing in Marian Studies:

His Contribution to a Deeper Understanding of the Marian Reality

I choose this title in an attempt to express our admiration for the work of Father Eamon during this past half-century. It will be difficult to capture in words the vitality of his thought and especially the spirit which has animated him to devote a major part of his life as professor, preacher and scholar to what I call "the Marian reality." It is something which must be experienced first hand. And personally it has been experienced time and time again as Eamon delivers what is called "A Survey of Recent Mariology" as the concluding talk each year for the annual meeting of the Mariological Society of America. If one is limited to the written text, one is impressed by the scholarly detail and the precise analysis offered for a great variety of writings on Mary. But if one is present to hear his presentation, one has the added pleasure of experiencing the energy and one can say, at times, the passion which courses through the paper. We could almost say that he is preaching to us as he exhorts us to read this article and to pay particular attention to sections of that book.

Father Eamon is first and foremost a theologian, former president of the Theological Society of America, professor of systematic theology at Catholic University in Washington and more recently at Loyola University in Chicago. For many years he has been a professor at the International Marian Institute for Research at the University of Dayton. His Marian writings come out of a broad theological background which lends credence to his animated expression of the truth about Mary.

It is appropriate that he was asked to give the keynote address to the Mariological Society of America on the occasion of its celebration of fifty years.[1] He was so in touch with the accomplishments of the Society over those years that he was able to weave quite effectively a pattern of an evolving theology of Mary together with other strands which we might call suggestions for further development. He deliberately chose as his title "Evolution in Mariology, 1949-1999" to highlight in a positive way the recent advances in Marian thought supported by and, in fact stimulated by, the second Vatican Council. At the same time he balanced this with the sobering fact that some of the expected results had not yet been realized, that rich veins of Marian doctrine recently uncovered by Conciliar scholarship were still untapped and in some cases left dormant. This critique, forceful yet gentle, is typical of Father Eamon's style. He constantly prods for more scholarly work on a given point, yet he seems to understand that this will take time and much energy and perhaps even a little luck.

It is his theme of evolution which I should like to use as a guide for our reflections upon his own work in the field of Marian studies. In an earlier study[2] he had used the term "revolution" to describe the changes which had taken place in Mariology over the years immediately preceding the Council and thereafter. He touches upon some of the same issues, though in his later reflections he approaches them with a great sensitivity to the workings of the Spirit in the process of growth.

Perhaps we can best appreciate his personal contribution to the Marian reality by examining some of the themes to which he returns time and time again over the years. The first of these–which I consider to be foundational–is his concern for an on-going dialogue with his fellow theologians and scripture scholars. This reflects his awareness of an isolation which has taken place between those who specialize in the study of Mary and other scholars whose concerns are broader than what they consider to be the narrow field of Mariology.

In an address to the International Mariological-Marian congress held in Santo Domingo in 1967 he gets to the nub of the problem in his opening remarks:

> Mariology seems to be the one where differences between dogma and scripture are most manifest. For example, it is hard to imagine any area where doctrinal development enters more strikingly than in the dogma of the Assumption and where our present knowledge of a scriptural witness to this revealed truth is less satisfactory.[3]

And after reflecting upon the issue and offering some insights into a possible solution he concludes with a plea to both dogmaticians and exegetes.

> Again, some of us seem wed to the certainty of definitions, and anxious for more definitions .... Would we not do better to seek a deeper understanding of the truths we possess, being content to explain, without having to 'demonstrate,' without campaigning for stronger '*notae theologicae*'?

And to the exegete:

> please, judge dogmatic theology by the best examples, not the worst. Above all, do not judge us

> by mediocre manuals, or perhaps by diminishing personal memories of old seminary courses. Recent years have seen great progress in dogmatic theology and even though it may not yet have reached the level of public interest and overall quality that distinguish recent Catholic exegesis, it is of high caliber. Our own good spokesmen would not think of taking as representative of current exegesis outmoded scripture textbooks, neither should you in examining our views.[4]

Here we find the balance prerequisite for dialogue and an invitation to it which is not difficult to accept.

Concomitant with his overall concern for dialogue among specialists there are his own attempts to be clear and precise in analyzing current or recent trends in the field of Marian studies. On numerous occasions he was asked by the editors of professional theological journals to address the issue of "what is happening in the field?" He might choose one particular author, for example, Herbert Richardson, a Protestant theologian who had been offering some rather new insights into the Marian reality from a less traditional perspective,[5] or he might cover a series of developments taking place throughout the field, analyzing now one now another doctrinal issue, highlighting some hopeful signs for progress, criticizing others for their too narrow perspective. And always in these he encourages and supports honest attempts at scholarly work, even as he is pained by some of the erroneous conclusions produced.[6]

I believe that one of his greatest contributions in the area of dialogue with fellow theologians comes in the presidential address which he gave to the Theological Society of America in 1966. The title of the address was: "The Mother of Jesus in the Communion of Saints—Challenge to the Churches."[7] It was actually a challenge issued to his fellow theologians, Catholic and non-Catholic alike. It is a subject to which Eamon has alluded on many other occasions, almost as a plea that someone do a study on the doctrine of the Communion of Saints as a stimulus to dialogue and a means to help us all appreciate the profound meaning of Our Lady's Assumption. The key issue to be discussed is the relationship between the Church in heaven and the Church on earth. He points out that the veneration of the saints and especially of Mary by the Church is not simply in remembrance of their (her) fidelity to Christ; it is based on a conviction of faith that they (she) are actively involved with Jesus in the continuing work of redemption. This, of course, raises the whole issue of the role of any creature in his/her salvation. It also demands that we use language which will better express the link between time and eternity, language which comes out of a better grasp of that mysterious reality. Though it is difficult work, Eamon insists that it must be undertaken in order to bring clarity to our understanding of our present situation vis-à-vis our eternal destiny.

And so the issues he raises in that address have far-reaching ramifications both for Christian unity and practical spiritual living. He feels, rightly so, that we can no longer neglect this investigation of the real meaning of the communion of saints. To do so would be to leave unanswered a number of important questions which have a real impact upon Christian living. The motivation is not to add to the luster of Mary's crown; rather it is to deepen our awareness of what it means to have been brought into the drama of salvation as an active, cooperative participant.

One of the greatest insights of the participants in the second Vatican Council was their grasp of what has been called "the Mary-Church Analogy." It comes as the fruit of many years of study by the experts in the field, both ecclesiologists and Mariologists. On the one hand, it might seem quite logical to devote a section of the document on Mary to the issue of her relationship to the Church since the chapter on Mary was situated within the document on the Church ; on the other hand, initially this approach was a great threat to those who had been accustomed to a deductive, privilege-based Mariology.

In an article written before the document had been composed Eamon gave a good summary of the scriptural-traditional material relating Mary to the Church.[8] At the conclusion of his article he asks: what will the Council say about Mary? While he has no direct information, he finds a good hint at things to come in the already accepted document on the liturgy which speaks clearly of Mary as a model of the Church, perfectly united to Christ's saving work. And then he shows his pastoral concern for the faithful when he concludes by saying:

> While waiting for the further action of the Council on Mary and the Church Catholics should deepen their own understanding of Mary. The great doctrines the Church teaches about her–Mother of God, ever-Virgin, Immaculate, in heaven body and soul–should be appreciated far more than they are. The same is true of the Catholic conviction that Mary is the spiritual Mother of all the brethren of Christ, and that God's gift of grace is given to us through our Lady's intercession. In this time of the council Catholics are called to enter into the conciliar task of 'renovation,' in a spirit of patient willingness to accept the ancient truths about Mary in a way adapted to the modern needs of the Church and in a manner appealing also to other Christians.[9]

He speaks this strongly because he realizes that even among Marian theologians there was much tension about this new direction in which Mariology seemed to be going. For his part, he makes the choice to support these further developments, even as he understands the caution demanded for a balance between the exaltation of Mary as an individual and the appreciation of her role of personification or "personalization," as some would later call it.

In a straightforward way he addresses the issue: "What is the utility of the Mary-Church analogy?

> Mary is not compared to the Church in its external operations, that is, in its hierarchical and sacerdo-

tal aspects, but she is likened to the Church in its inner life of grace. We have seen briefly the ancient comparisons of virginity, maternity and holiness. In all these respects Mary is the prototype of the Church, the first and most perfect realization of what God expects from his Church and from its members. A basic relationship of Mary to the Church is that she is spiritual Mother of the Church. This was implicit in her ancient title of 'new Eve.' Mary is 'mother of the living' because she is Mother of Christ.[10]

Yet, he cautions wisely, there are limitations to the analogy:

A danger exists of being so captivated by the comparison between Mary and the Church that the central doctrine about Mary slips out of focus, the truth that this humble maid of Nazareth is the Mother of the God-man, Christ the Redeemer. No sound Christian outlook on Our Lady can fail to give full importance to this primary revealed truth of the divine motherhood.[11]

Another hazard is to get so involved in 'types, figures, prototypes and archetypes' as to forget that

Mary was and is a human person, whose relationship with God and with each of us is an intensely personal one, while the mystical body, the Church, is a moral body, an organism consisting of many people. We must beware of turning the handmaid of the Lord, the Mother of Jesus and our mother, into an idea, an abstraction, a personification at the expense of her personality .... This typology rests on her historical role as Mother of Christ.[12]

For Eamon, Mary is the prototype of the Church insofar as she is the perfect Christian. "What God did for Mary is a sign of his intention for all people through the Church."[13] We have become so accustomed to these distinctions and this terminology that we could fail to appreciate the pioneering efforts of those who willingly took this path to a more profound awareness of who this woman of faith is.

One of the aspects of Eamon's contribution to our understanding of the Marian reality which might easily be missed is the fact that his material appears in a variety of journals, both professional and more popular, yet always with an emphasis upon the theology which is developing.

In a 1969 article in the *American Ecclesiastical Review* Eamon points to the larger perspective, the ecclesial presentation of the mystery of Mary within the body of believers, with a special sensitivity to other Christians and the still smoldering polemics about Mary's meaning.[14] A shift has taken place from a historical-speculative study of Mary's mediation and co-redemption to a scriptural, patristic, ecclesial orientation.

Commenting upon the three-volume work by J. B. Carol, O.F.M.,[15] and his own contribution to this work, Eamon says:

> Were I to rewrite my own early article, 'Mary in the Documents of the Magisterium,' I would nuance more carefully the papal citations, and then take into consideration the point made by the decree on Ecumenism of Vatican II about the 'hierarchy of truths' (no. 11; cf. also no. 30). Certain aspects of the mystery of Mary as experienced by the Church, even if never proposed by the magisterium as formal doctrine, may be more meaningful than dogmatically defined truths. The relationship between Mary and the Church would seem to be such an experienced truth, concerning which we are attaining an explicit awareness in our day.[16]

Eamon goes on to say: "The Mary-Church relationship is not an accidental extra, it is a central element in both the mystery of the Church and the mystery of Mary."[17] Referring to the document on the liturgy which speaks about the cult of Mary, Eamon says it is one of the best kept secrets of the Council. It sums up Mary's role. He calls this a marvelously exact cartoon of the mystery of Mary a full year before they executed the large scale Chapter VIII of *Lumen Gentium.*[18]

Further insights regarding this analogy continue to flow from his pen. The original papal definitions of the Immaculate Conception and papal infallibility were issued with an air of triumph. The Church was under siege by the State and this was a way of showing the power of the papacy. Now, since Vatican II, the Immaculate Conception and the papal office are seen to underline the servant character of the Church. Mary, the all-holy one, was made so by God to serve God's plan of salvation. The Pope's role is that of servant in guarding the word of God, hearing it and keeping it. It is in continuity with these thoughts that he mentions in passing the significance of Mary's virginity. As such she remains faithful to her Lord. The oldest comparison between Mary and the Church is in terms of their virginities and their maternities. He concludes: "All Christians and all theology have a stake in the virginity of Mary–from the redemptive virginity of the Annunciation to the exaltation of the Virgin Mary at the side of the virginal Christ who sits at the right hand of God the Father."[19]

After the Council, again in an article in *The Marian Era,*[20] he develops his thought regarding the benefits of the analogy: "Whenever we talk about Our Lady, we are ultimately talking about ourselves, for we are members of the Church, and talk about Mary is a proclamation of the Christian ideal of humanity."[21] "She is the Church made perfect in a single individual."[22] "God created the first Eve with the intention of creating the second, the new Eve, who is at once Mary and the Church."[23] "At Cana Mary (as Church) was also asking her Son to enter upon his missionary career of accomplishing His Father's work."[24] He concludes with a reference to the liturgical prayers which portray

Mary as model and figure of the Church; he cites the preface for the Marian mass, "Mary, Mother of the Church," as an exemplification of the meaning of this analogy. The liturgy becomes another means to inculcate these new insights

In still another periodical in 1986 he underlines the contrast in the approach to Mary which has arisen since the Council because of the emphasis being placed upon the relationship between Mary and the Church: "Mediatrix" vs. "Model."[25] The renewed liturgy has supported the developing sense of the analogy as witnessed by the new prefaces for the Immaculate Conception and the Assumption. Another aspect of this analogy which he sees as enriching Ecclesiology is that while

> the scriptural, patristic and liturgical insights on the Church as 'bride of Christ' need still to be recovered, yet the council did at least tap this rich vein of Christian tradition by way of Mary's Assumption, the Church-Bride rejoining Christ the Bridegroom in the heavenly nuptials of his royal resurrection.[26]

What needs to be grasped more fully is Augustine's idea of Mary as a woman of faith–the perfect exemplar of bringing Christ forth in faith, the apostolic task to which we, as church, are called.[27]

It is an acknowledged fact that the ecumenical dialogue which began before the Council and which has continued since then has forced both sides to do their homework. Time after time it became apparent that there were misconceptions about what the participants in the dialogue actually believed concerning a particular truth, and even more often there was misunderstanding concerning the background out of which they were coming to the discussion. As the dialogues continued it became more clear what the central, neuralgic issues were. And quite often these had a direct relationship to beliefs and practices regarding Mary. It was imperative that the specialist in Mariology become engaged in the dialogue for the sake of clarity and with the hope for progress.

Eamon has devoted his time, energy and talents to this task in a number of ways: by direct involvement in ecumenical discussions (referred to as ecumenical roundtables) held for the past several years during the International Mariological-Marian Congresses; by addressing the ecumenically sensitive issues in his talks and articles and personal conversations; and I would say that his greatest contribution has been his constant, faithful reporting of what is happening in this area of Marian interest. He himself has said more than once that the most important ingredient in this dialogue is truth and clarity.

I believe that he has been most effective through his yearly survey of Mariology which has become a staple in the meetings of the Mariological Society of America since 1967. There is hardly a book, an article or an event of ecumenical import which goes unreported. And there is always that precise analysis and above all that encouraging note of hoped-for results.

Each survey has a special section entitled "Ecumenism" and each time he begins with information concerning the latest meeting of the Ecumenical Society of the Blessed Virgin Mary, whether in England or the United States. He analyzes the papers, pointing to hopeful signs for agreement where possible, and yet realistically indicating the areas of disagreement. He himself has become personally involved in many of the meetings both here and in England. Reading his reports, one sees that his heart is very much into this aspect of scholarly discussion. Without fail he reports the addresses of the offices for these societies, the cost of membership, and the availability of papers delivered at the meetings. He has been a constant, faithful spokesman and friend for them.

What I find particularly important is the dissemination of information regarding the scholarly writings of non-Catholics who are partners in the dialogue. Eamon is not only clear; he is sympathetic to their approach without compromising any Catholic belief. He always encourages further investigation and more discussion and writing.

In a talk given at Seton Hall University in 1995 and printed in the periodical *Ecumenical Trends*,[28] he indicates the primary sources of difficulty for the dialogue: the relationship between scripture and tradition and the Church's teaching authority; Mary's role as the exalted model of the Church which makes both her and the Church human cooperators in salvation; Catholic devotion to Mary involving her intercession. And he indicates the context of these difficulties: "Protestants find unbiblical, even anti-scriptural, Catholic claims that there are binding revealed truths not contained in the Bible."[29] For Barth, the fact that we believe that Mary cooperates with grace gravely endangers Christian faith in the all-sufficient saving grace of God alone. When the Council called Mary the model of the Church, according to Barth, "the humble woman of the gospels was being changed into the figure of the Church cooperating with grace and thereby meriting salvation."[30]

> The thorny problem is Catholic devotion to Mary in all its forms, both liturgical and popular. The technical term for praying to Mary is invocation. Invoking Mary and the saints has been forbidden from the start of the Reformation because calling on Mary, praying to her, meant diminished confidence in Jesus Christ, the one Mediator.[31]

Father Eamon responds to each of these difficulties from a Catholic perspective. Then he indicates three signs of real hope: a common study of the Scriptures; the mutual discovery of the early Christian authors, our common patrimony; the Marian writings of the Reformers themselves. He cites some good examples of real progress made in this common scriptural study, not the least of which was the ecumenical study, *Mary in the New Testament*, the result of the collaborative effort of several outstanding Catholic and non-Catholic scripture scholars.

In relation to the second issue, the study of the Fathers, he mentions several studies recently undertaken by Protestant scholars, notably Jaroslav Pelikan, which consider Marian themes in the Fathers. Some of the writings of the original Reformers have been rediscovered lately (namely on the occasion of the 450th anniversary of the posting of the theses by Luther). These contain clear references to praise and honor to be accorded to Mary, something which had been totally neglected by the Reformed tradition. A reinvestigation of these writings might well stimulate further dialogue.[32]

In his concluding remarks Eamon finds some room for hope in emphasizing the need for a thorough, prayer-filled study of the doctrine of the communion of saints. This will involve reflection upon the ways in which Mary (and the saints) have responded to God on their faith journey towards Him. He returns to this theme frequently, even as he rejoices in the progress being made through the dialogues between theologians of international renown. In his report on the International Congress held in Saragossa, Spain, in 1979[33] he writes:

> It is a painful paradox that divided Christians are in basic agreement, at times strongly so, on three of the four aspects, i.e., veneration, praise, imitation. They do not agree on 'invocation,' even when there is some admission of a possible heavenly 'intercession' by the Mother of the Savior.[34]

Again:

> To praise God in his saints, indeed particularly in St Mary, is truly Christian and not contested. This was her prophecy in the Magnificat. But as Protestant scholars admit, even the praise has been greatly muted over the polemic centuries, apart from hymns. Both Luther and Calvin preached imitation of the holy Virgin. The great Protestant formularies of faith reject calling on the saints in prayer (i.e., 'invoking' them, even St Mary) as prejudicial to confidence in Christ, the one Mediator.[35]

Yet he goes on to say:

> In my judgment, Saragossa is the high point of
> these agreed statements. It concentrated on the
> place of the Blessed Virgin in the communion of
> saints, setting forth calmly and clearly agreements
> and disagreements. Among the 'common convic-
> tions,' certainly 'more indeed than they could have
> expected,' the group described the praise of Mary
> as Mother of God as essentially giving glory to God;
> for God in glorifying the saints crowns his own gifts
> (from the preface of the Roman liturgy). Such
> praise 'has become an urgent question for all
> Christians.'[36]

In regard to the topic of invocation, it was considered
against the background of the doctrine of the communion of
saints. A fairly strong statement was made with an added *cautela*:
"As a Christian can and should pray for others, we believe that the
saints who have already entered into the fullness which is in
Christ, amongst whom Mary holds the first place, can and do pray
for us sinners (implicit evocation of the second part of the Hail
Mary?), who are still struggling on earth." "The one and unique
mediation of Christ is in no way affected by this," a point made
strongly by the Second Vatican Council. A remaining difficulty is
stated simply and frankly: "The meaning of the direct invocation
of the saints who are alive in God, an invocation which is not
practiced in all the Churches, remains to be elucidated."[37]

In his talk about the fifty years of existence of the
Mariological Society, Father Eamon mentions once again the
need to relate chapter 8 of *Lumen Gentium* more closely to chapter
7 in order to promote a clearer understanding of Mary's place
within the communion of saints. This remains a key issue in the
dialogue which needs to be settled.[38]

Another important question which is at the heart of the
ecumenical discussion was taken up by Eamon in 1975. It was an

address he gave entitled, "Papal Infallibility and Marian Definitions, Some Considerations."[39] He spoke at the Lutheran-Roman Catholic Consultation in September of 1975. His comments on that meeting and his participation in it are insightful:

> The experience of the meeting was pleasant and interesting, but I came away convinced that a better ecumenical introduction to the Mother of Jesus would be to stake out possible common ground first and only then to take up the peculiarly difficult doctrines of Mary's freedom from original sin and her Assumption to full union with the Risen Christ with the further complication of the papal definition of these doctrines in 1854 and 1950. Both the Immaculate Conception and the Assumption are bound to seem arbitrary unless one is first convinced of Mary's place in God's merciful plan of salvation and her abiding union with her glorified Son in the communion of saints.[40]

After addressing the history of these two definitions, one taking place in 1854 and the other in 1950, he considers the Vatican Council's statement concerning the hierarchy of truths. In some detail, and with his usual precision, he discusses the approaches taken by several theologians in an attempt to find a way for groups of Christians to be in full union with the Catholic Church while not accepting these two Marian dogmas. He does not profess to have found a solution to the problem, but he is open to listening to and engaging in the discussion. This is another instance of his ecumenical sensitivity which endears him to those who are vitally interested in this aspect of Church life.

In his concluding remarks relative to the ecumenical situation Eamon quotes John Wesley as writing: "... if we cannot as yet think alike in all things, at least we may love alike." This is a fitting description of Eamon's approach to ecumenical issues.

In his yearly survey of Mariology Eamon is fond of the expression, "potpourri," something which he uses to link together a number of different items, none of which would merit a separate treatment. I will use this method in a concluding section of this tribute, realizing that I may be failing to pay sufficient attention to one or other "piece of the puzzle" which constitutes the Marian reality.

As I have indicated before, I believe one of the major contributions made by Eamon is his ability to analyze and then to synthesize a particular discussion that is taking place among scholars. While most often his reflections appear in a scholarly periodical, still he disseminates this material through a variety of magazines which are more popular in style. It is his way of getting the word out to those who need to hear it. It serves as an added stimulus to devotion, to a devotion that is well rooted in the scriptures, the liturgy and the teaching of the Church.

In 1985 we find evidence of such an approach in a talk given to a gathering of the Western Region of the Mariological Society.[41] He emphasizes the foundational truth:

> More than ever the conviction that Mary is the Mother of God is necessary, absolutely indispensable for current understanding of the Incarnation, of the saving truth that the Son of God became man. It is impossible to exaggerate the incarnational doctrine that the Blessed Virgin is the Mother of God become man, our brother in the flesh.[42]

And he adds:

> With sovereign freedom the Father sent his Son on earth as the true child of Mary, our brother human being, with the conception occurring, not by agency of a human father, but by the power of the Holy Spirit .... The Church's conviction of Our Lady's perpetual virginity rests on its own Spirit-guided intuition, which came to the surface in the 4th

century after the Roman persecution ended, when many Christians took up lives of consecrated virginity and celibacy.[43]

It is in that context of the incarnation that he explains the consecration of the world made by Pope John Paul II as one linked to the self-consecration of Jesus to the Father: "And I consecrate myself for them, so that they also may be consecrated in truth" (Jn 17:19). Through this consecration we are entrusted to Mary in order to be joined to Jesus' self-consecration to the Father.[44] The Christological focus of our devotion to Mary could not be expressed more forcefully or clearly. The emphasis is upon the realism of Jesus' birth from Mary because there were some who were so spiritualizing the humanity of Jesus that the reality of the coming to be of God's Son was not considered to be a true incarnation but rather a symbolic statement. This would totally undermine the Christian doctrine of redemption.

His Carmelite Brothers certainly appreciate his tireless investigation of their common Marian roots. Eamon's doctoral thesis was completed in 1951 in Rome. It focused on the writings of Arnold Bostius, a 15th century Carmelite, especially on his work entitled: *De patronatu et patrocinio Beatissimae Virginis Mariae in dedicatum sibi Carmeli ordinem.*[45] Bostius had written extensively to explain and to defend the Marian roots of the order. The Rule of Carmel is proposed as the mirror of Mary's life on earth: "Life in Carmel is walking to God hand in hand with Our Blessed Mother."[46] One can feel the emotional attachment to this subject which defines his own life. In a series of articles through the years Eamon has explained and extolled for the benefit of his brothers the meaning of the scapular: it is a gift given by Mary for protection; it is the sign of a covenant, a reciprocal spiritual love and consecration. "A child of Mary will not perish." "We cannot find Christ except where the Wise Men found him–with Mary, his mother.[47] A splendid title for a book about our Blessed Mother would be 'the woman who is real.'"[48] She is indeed that for Eamon.

This latter phrase could well have been taken from the writings of St. Thérèse of the Child Jesus.[49] "For a sermon on the Blessed Virgin to please me and do me any good, I must see her real life and not her imagined life."[50] Two women Carmelite Saints, Teresa of Jesus and Thérèse of the Child Jesus, were subjects about whom Eamon often wrote.[51]

Ever concerned to help ordinary people understand the vicissitudes of post-Vatican II Marian devotion, he offers some suggestions in his article on "What Happened to Devotion to Mary?" "I will offer two suggestions on what must be done to restore and renew authentic devotion to Our Lady: The two suggestions will be, firstly, knowledge, secondly, courage."[52] He gives a very pastoral analysis of the situation and a concrete solution: we must get to know Mary from what the Council teaches, especially through imitation: she was a listener to God's word, she prayed, and she is a mother. Courage means preaching Mary with patience and inventiveness. He himself exemplified this approach in a novena given in preparation for the feast of the Assumption in 1964: "During the novena I would like to dispel false fears, and help you understand Our Lady's true and lasting place in the Church and in our lives."[53] He preaches out of scripture and the liturgy as primary sources. He makes a series of suggestions to his fellow priests in an article in the *Homiletic and Pastoral Review*: "For men of our day the good news begins with Mary."[54] He begins with what he calls "the allusive theology" of Matthew and Luke–their references back into the Old Testament for insights into the meaning of Jesus' coming among us. The Ark of the Covenant as applied to Mary by Luke; Mary as Figure of the Church. "Mary's presence at Cana contains many possible meanings–her compassionate intercession, her sensitivity to the sudden need and her fear for the embarrassment of the young couple. All of this should not be passed over."[55] Mary as a symbol of the Synagogue and the Church: initially at Cana she does not understand Jesus' words: "Woman, how does this concern of yours affect me?" Then, following his command to the wine-stewards, she understands his intentions and believes as the Church : "Do whatever he tells you." She represents the Bride greeting the Bridegroom and it is at her request that the new wine is supplied.

On Calvary she is the Daughter of Sion, the Church bringing forth new Christians in pain. Mary's faith should be compared to that of Abraham as its fulfillment. These and many more insights are shared, to be used by those whose mission it is to preach the good news.

At prayer with Mary is one of his favorite themes.

> The most frequent reminder that the Church at prayer is one with Mary is the prayer of community remembrance, the '*communmicantes*' in the eucharistic liturgy. The underlying doctrine is of great ecumenical importance as well as of pressing pastoral significance, the communion of saints. The presence of the Mother of Jesus with the Risen Lord is the warrant for confidence in her heavenly intercession on behalf of the still earth-bound pilgrims; she shares in the unending mediation of Christ, the eternal high priest who lives forever to make intercession for us.[56]

This is an excellent reflection upon the Apostolic letter *Marialis Cultus*. It makes the purpose of the letter come alive.

Eamon enters into the arena of charismatic prayer with an address to the Ecumenical society of the Blessed Virgin Mary.[57] He sees Mary's charisms as mainly three-fold: a) the gift of praise which she exercised on many occasions, particularly through the Magnificat– it was her ability to address God spontaneously and exuberantly; b) the gift of tongues–her presence at Pentecost guarantees her that gift–fundamentally a new way to praise God; c) the gift of intercession which is more than petition on behalf of others but it also involves an intimate association with Jesus' self-consecration to the Father, a gift that makes great demands upon its recipient but also empowers her to do heroic things for God's glory.

In a chapter on Marian spirituality which he contributed to a book entitled: *Spiritual Traditions for the Contemporary Church*[58] he describes Mary's spirituality as that of the faithful disciple, while he continues to insist upon her role as intercessor within the communion of saints. He highlights once again her important place in the anaphora within the liturgy and concludes with a reflection upon the developing dialogue with Protestants concerning prayer "to" Mary. His words are intended to provide the basis for a common ground for Marian prayer among Christians:

> The basic raison d'être of true Marian spirituality is paschal spirituality. For Mary personally, and for all who are influenced by her–in whatever positive manner– the Paschal Mystery is the criterion for authentic spirituality. The suffering, death, and resurrection of Jesus are at the heart of all Christian spirituality. In her life on earth Mary was, like all of us, a pilgrim, discovering ever-new dimensions of the mystery of her Son.[59]

Perhaps the greatest tribute to Eamon's scholarly reputation was paid by the American Bishops when in 1971 they invited him to be the "anchor man" for the team of theological experts who would help to compose the now famous pastoral letter, *Behold Your Mother*.[60] His was the guiding hand for the composition of the letter and it certainly reflects his awareness of what was needed on the American scene to promote a better understanding of the Vatican Council's document on Mary, and to stimulate Marian devotion which would avoid both the excesses of an emotional piety and a sterile, abstract approach to this Woman of Faith, as she was called in the letter.

> Towards the end of the letter there is a reflection upon Mary and the priesthood: As Our Lady's *fiat* at the Annunciation was consummated in her total surrender to the Father's will at the foot of the

cross, so too through Mary's inspiration and intercession the priest is offered the grace of Christ to
give of himself, in union with the Eucharistic
victim, for the salvation of his fellow-men.[61]

Through his tireless zeal for preaching and teaching what we have
called, "the Marian Reality" Eamon has lived that ideal to an
exemplary degree. Those of us who have been guided by his
wisdom and support are forever in his debt. May his Immaculate
Mother, and ours, continue to protect him from all harm and bring
him one day into the full presence of her Son in perfect communion with all the Saints! Surely, "a child of Mary will never be lost!"

George F. Kirwin, O.M.I.

Endnotes

1. Eamon R. Carroll, O.Carm., "Evolution in Mariology," *Marian Studies* 50 (1999), 139-145.

2. Eamon R. Carroll, O.Carm., "Revolution in Mariology," in *The Land of Carmel: Essays in honor of Joachim Smet, O.Carm.*, edited by Paul Chandler, O.Carm., and Keith Egan (Rome: Institutum Carmelitanum, 1991), 451-465.

3. Eamon R. Carroll, O.Carm., "Reflections of a Dogmatic Theologian about Exegesis," in *Maria in Sacra Scriptura: Acta Congressus Mariologici-mariani in Republica Dominicana anno 1965 celebrati*, II:29-66.

4. *Ibid.*, 64-65.

5. Eamon R. Carroll, O.Carm., "Mariology and Theology Today," *Ephemerides Mariologicae* 20 (1970), 137-151.

6. Maria Warner, "Alone of her Sex," Knopf Publications, 1976. Cf. Eamon R. Carroll, O.Carm., *The Catholic Historical Review* 64 (1978), 102-103: "In one sense everything in the book is right, with evidence adduced for even the oldest aberrations in devotion to Mary; in another sense everything is wrong, so distorting are the spectacles through which she views the Marian scene. Are Catholic attitudes toward the Virgin Mary still so arcane and repulsive to others that Maria Warner's beautiful and bitter book can be hailed as truly representative of the religious convictions of so many millions of Catholics in the United States and elsewhere?"

7. Eamon R. Carroll, O.Carm., "The Mother of Jesus in the Communion of Saints," *Proceedings, Catholic Theological Society of America* 21 (1967), 249-265.

8. *The Marian Era* V (1964), 18-22, 107-110.

9. *Ibid.*, 110.

10. *Ibid.*, 108.

11. *Ibid.*, 108-109

12. *Ibid.*, 109.

13. *Ibid.*
14. Eamon R. Carroll, O.Carm., "Mary and the Church," *American Ecclesiastical Review* 160 (1969), 291-311.
15. Juniper B. Carol, O.F.M., *Mariology* (Milwaukee: Bruce, 1955-1961), 3 volumes.
16. Carroll, "Mary and the Church," p. 298.
17. *Ibid.*, 304.
18. *Ibid.*, 305.
19. *Ibid.*, 311.
20. Eamon R. Carroll, O.Carm., "Our Lady and the Church," *The Marian Era* XII (1979), 23-25.
21. *Ibid.*, 23.
22. *Ibid.*, 24.
23. *Ibid.*
24. *Ibid.*
25. Eamon R. Carroll, O.Carm., "Mary and the Church: Trends in Marian Theology since Vatican II," *The New Catholic World* 229 (1986), 248-260.
26. *Ibid.*, 252.
27. *Ibid.*, 254.
28. Eamon R. Carroll, O.Carm., "Mary in Ecumenical Perspective," *Ecumenical Trends* 26 (1997), 65-73.
29. *Ibid.*, 66.
30. *Ibid.*, 67.
31. *Ibid.*
32. *Ibid.*, 67-69.
33. Eamon R. Carroll, O.Carm., "Ecumenical Roundtables at International Mariological Congresses," *Marian Library Studies*, 17-23 (1991), 566-577.
34. *Ibid.*, 571.
35. *Ibid.*
36. *Ibid.*, 572.
37. *Ibid.*
38. Eamon R. Carroll, O.Carm., "Evolution in Mariology," *Marian Studies* 50 (1999), 139-145. Keynote Address to the Mariological Society of America.

39. Eamon R. Carroll, O.Carm., "Papal Infallibility and the Marian Definitions: Some Considerations," *Carmelus* 26 (1979), 213-250.

40. Eamon R. Carroll, O.Carm., *Understanding the Mother of Jesus* (Wilmington, Delaware: Michael Glazier, Inc., 1979), p. 42.

41. Eamon R. Carroll, O.Carm., "Mary: the Woman Come of Age," *Marian Studies* 36 (1985), 136-160.

42. *Ibid.*, 140.

43. *Ibid.*, 143.

44. *Ibid.*

45. Eamon R. Carroll, O.Carm., *The Marian Theology of Arnold Bostius, O.Carm. (1445-1499): A Study of His Work, "De Patronatu et patrocinio Beatissimae Virginis Mariae in dedicatum sibi Carmeli ordinem,"* Roma, 1962.

46. Eamon R. Carroll, O.Carm., "Carmel and Our Lady," *The Sword* 19 (1956), p. 151.

47. *Ibid.*

48. Eamon R. Carroll, O.Carm., "The meaning of Mary to the American Catholic," *The Sword* 23 (1963), 11.

49. Eamon R. Carroll, O.Carm., *Thérèse and the Mother of God* (Washington, New Jersey: AMI Press, 1994).

50. *Ibid.*, 2.

51. Suffice a few examples: "St. Thérèse, the Little Flower of Our Lady of Mount Carmel," *Our Lady's Digest* 16 (1961), 43-50; "St Teresa of Avila: Daughter of Our Lady of Mt Carmel," *Our Lady's Digest* 37 (1982), 4-9; "The Saving Role of the Human Christ for St. Teresa," *Carmelite Studies* III (Washington, D.C.: ICS Publications, 1984), 135-152.

52. Eamon R. Carroll, O.Carm., "What Happened to Devotion to Mary?" *The Sword* 29 (1969), 40-53.

53. Eamon R. Carroll, O.Carm., "Preachers, Pulpits and People," *The Sword* 25 (1965), 79-80.

54. Eamon R. Carroll, O.Carm., "Preaching the Good News about the Mother of Jesus," *The Homiletic and Pastoral*

Review 73 (1975), 11.

55. *Ibid.*, 14.
56. Eamon R. Carroll, O.Carm., "Mary in the Western Liturgy: Marialis Cultus," *Communio* 7 (1980), 140-156.
57. Eamon R. Carroll, O.Carm., "New Testament Charisms of the Blessed Virgin Mary," *One in Christ* 72 (1986), 356-364.
58. Robin Maas and Gabriel O'Donnell, O.P., *Spiritual Traditions for the Contemporary Church* (Nashville: Abingdon Press, 1980), pp. 365-379.
59. *Ibid.*, 375.
60. *Behold Your Mother, Woman of Faith.* A Pastoral Letter on the Blessed Virgin Mary of the National Conference of Catholic Bishops, November 21, 1973. (Washington, D. C.: United States Catholic Conference, 1973).
61. *Ibid.*, n. 120.

Eamon Carroll
and the National Shrine

When it comes to expressions of faith, brick and mortar have a way of outlasting most other tributes. The National Shrine of the Immaculate Conception is not only one of the world's largest churches, but a truly unique compilation of religious art, expressing the great variety of belief and devotion of America's Catholics. In a very substantial way, Eamon R. Carroll contributed to the ornamentation of this stunning basilica during its most significant period of adornment, the years of 1957-80.

Even in the early years of the twentieth century, there were plans for some sort of tribute to the national patroness. The design began to take form in detail with the blessing of the foundation stone in 1920. Work proceeded briskly during the 1920's as contributions flooded in. The building of the Crypt Church outlined the contours of a great structure, but work had to be suspended in spring of 1933 because of the overall lack of funds. It was not until after World War II that the American bishops decided to complete the church, authorizing collections and sponsorship for the remaining work. Archbishop O'Boyle commissioned the detailed plans for the Great Upper Church in 1951.[1]

Work finally resumed in 1954, the Marian Year, to complete the remainder of the Shrine. But a multitude of serious questions about exterior decoration crowded the architect's desk and mind. Even the best church builders have to admit that they deal with stone, brick, and structural steel, not concepts. This church had to be different. The broad lines of its construction would indeed proclaim the love which millions of Americans felt for Mary. But when it came to *what* those same people believed, the builders knew they needed help from others who understood the richness of Marian heritage.

The principal architect was Eugene F. Kennedy, Jr., of the firm of Maginnis and Walsh and Kennedy, Boston. At his request, Archbishop Patrick O'Boyle assembled an ad hoc Iconography Committee to review plans and suggest forms of decoration which expressed the best understandings of Catholics in America. The National Shrine was intended as more than just a believers' act of faith; it had to *proclaim* that same faith in terms best understood by teachers and scholars.[2]

As artistic consultant, Archbishop O'Boyle selected a seasoned artist, John H. de Rosen, who had designed both murals and stained-glass windows in 1925-37 for the Armenian Catholic Cathedral in Lvov, Poland, as well as the decoration for the Pope's chapel at Castel Gondolfo in 1933. That work made him the first layman to embellish a Pontifical chapel since Michelangelo decorated the Sistine. De Rosen was born in Warsaw in 1891; his father had been court painter to Russian Czars Alexander III and Nicholas II. He served in the French and Polish national armies during World War I, then continued his studies in liturgical art. He emigrated to the United States in 1937 and became an American citizen. He taught at The Catholic University of America during the war years (1939-46) while occupying the Chair of Liturgical Art.[3]

Catholic University would provide the other consultants. To head the Iconography Committee, O'Boyle appointed Monsignor Joseph Fenton, editor of the *American Ecclesiastical Review*. He would be assisted by Edward P. Arbez, S.S., a scripture scholar, and Theodore C. Peterson, C.S.P., a dogmatic theologian. These would serve on a voluntary basis. O'Boyle named artist de Rosen to be "Consultant on the Iconography of the National Shrine" and authorized that he be paid $1000 per month for the period between October, 1954, and March, 1955.[4] At the time, that span of time looked like quite enough to do the job at hand.

Throughout this short period, the Committee members met weekly, and worked mightily to decide the details of the Shrine's exterior. In over forty separate meetings they debated and decided the particulars for the front facade, the main entrance, the side porches, the mosaics of the tympanum areas over the doors, and the statues on the upper walls. One practical example of the Committee's work involved the great northern apse beyond the main altar.

The architect had originally proposed a large rose window in this space. But after spirited discussion, de Rosen and his colleagues concluded that the window would blind worshipers during the day, and contribute unattractive dead space at night. They suggested a large mosaic instead.[5]

Although the pace of their work had been demanding, nearly everyone involved agreed that the final result represented both pleasing artistry and solid theology. With a sigh of relief, the first Iconography Committee declared its work complete, and disbanded itself in mid-1955.[6]

However it did not take long before architect Kennedy began to realize that the scholars' work for the Shrine was just beginning. The vast interior of the church represented a bare but intricate labyrinth of vaults and domes, together with large and small chapels. Each would need its particular embellishment and accent.

The fund-raising requirements of the enterprise encouraged religious orders, together with fraternal and ethnic groups, to "adopt" and sponsor their own particular chapels or sections within the shrine. Although the response was spirited, it was taken for granted that those same patrons would have vastly different visions of what their particular sectors would look like, and how they would express their own proper Marian devotion.

De Rosen felt that there was a compelling need for a guiding vision that would direct the teaching mission of the Shrine. When the entire job was complete, the religious iconography had to present a unified lesson in Marian theology (although in many facets), rather than a chaotic series of impressions seasoned by popular piety. He believed strongly that the first eighteen centuries of Christianity had created a rich corpus of imagery, still useful for teaching. With so many ethnic groups presenting their particular visions and traditions, there was the classic danger of "too many cooks" who might damage this unified ideal. The Committee favored authorizing a handful of first-rate artists to work in relative freedom, but always with the gentle, guiding hand of the theologians to direct their work.[7]

In order to maintain some semblance of harmony, Eugene Kennedy asked Archbishop O'Boyle to re-activate the Iconography Committee this time with no end date in sight. It would function as both a friendly resource for planners, and also a cultural watchdog, with a very low profile.

Bishop Bryan J. McEntegart, Rector of Catholic University, had suggested that the membership should include the young Marian theologian Eamon R. Carroll, O.Carm. In a letter of May 3, 1957, O'Boyle told McEntegart that the trustees agreed that Eamon Carroll should be added, as well as the Shrine Director Thomas J. Grady. Grady had been appointed in 1956, and would shepherd the Shrine through its most crucial phase of growth. O'Boyle added that Fenton should reconvene his Committee by October. In another letter of July 3, O'Boyle urged Fenton to act quickly; he knew that Fr. Carroll was at home, because he had just phoned to arrange Mass at the Shrine for July 16.

As things turned out, the October deadline proved to be too ambitious, so the Committee reconvened in November, 1957, and has not disbanded since. O'Boyle also authorized a renewal of the $1000 per month fee for artist John de Rosen, with no termination date.[8]

As a steady contributor to the work of the Committee, Eamon Carroll had the benefit not only of solid Marian theology, but of his own travels and observations of much of the early Christian art which inspired the Shrine. From frescos in the catacombs, through Constantinian basilicas and Byzantine mosaics, to medieval stained glass and Renaissance oils, Eamon knew first hand what dogmas had been taught, and by what artistic medium. If beauty is the currency of good liturgical art, then bad art also teaches badly. So his efforts to research carefully and choose wisely were to translate bit by bit into a magnificent structure which was itself a fine lesson in stone and glass.

The new Committee was not required to meet with the architects as frequently as the old one had. On an average of one meeting every two months, they would submit suggestions to the Executive Committee which, more often than not, approved them and passed them on to the artisans. With a much longer view, they would be able to delve into their own rich trove of ideas and images, and produce a more unified and systematic result than any other group or party was likely to suggest.

Among their first daunting tasks were decisions about the most appropriate biblical texts and symbols for the great northern apse where the rose window would have gone. The final result was an awe-inspiring Christ Pantocrator. Since the overall design of the Shrine was Byzantine, it was appropriate to follow the tradition established by such great Greek triumphs in Sicily as Cefalù and Monreale, as well as countless others in Greece and Asia Minor.

In the large flanking apses on either side, there would be mosaics of the Woman of Revelation (west), and St. Joseph, Patron of Workers (east). In harmony with the Church's best teachings, the Shrine of Our Lady was to be presented under the auspices of Christ and the Holy Trinity. Plans for chapels representing the Mysteries of the Rosary would fall under the same umbrella.[9] Further down the path, Committee members would make decisions for a variety of vaults and domes, as well as for the Blessed Sacrament chapel and the sacristy.[10]

In a report to the Executive Committee (June 19, 1958), Monsignor Grady gave a hint of the massive workload of the Iconography Committee. He reported that recently they had been meeting every week, and hoped to finish their current tasks in July. The interior finish was to be buff-colored brick. He described the mosaics in the three large apses, and added that the narthex would show scenes related to John the Baptist. The seven domes in the interior ceiling would depict: 1) the Triumph of the Lamb, 2) the Incarnation, 3) Redemption, 4) the Trinity with angels and saints, and 5-7 still to be determined.[11]

Beneath each of those large apses there were plans for a series of saints (as yet unspecified) flanking apsidal chapels, with five small altars, for each of the three groups of the Mysteries of the Rosary. Each Mystery is to be presented in a clear and familiar form. Together with them are to be figures from the Old Testament which prefigure the Mysteries: clearly an intricate construction of astute theologians, who had spent more than an afternoon on their work. It is no accident that Elijah in his fiery chariot is the pre-figure for the Ascension of Jesus. One of the figures who watches Jesus rise into heaven is a semi-Carmelite, whose scapular is not brown but white, and tied in a knot at that. But the Carmelite connection is there (and the source of the idea is not hard to infer).

Another ironic twist is found in the choice of the saints for the Glorious Mysteries chapel, below the Pantocrator mosaic. The other two chapels were adopted and generously funded by the Jesuits and Franciscans, who selected some of their own fine saints to flank the altars. But the Catholic Daughters of America had donated the central chapel, and they were not committed to any favorite saints. So by default, the Iconography Committee chose the figures for that area, people intentionally selected for their humility and privation. They are Gemma Galgani, a lifelong invalid; the beggar, Benedict Joseph Labre; country priest John Vianney; Margaret of Cortona, a repentant sinner; monastery doorkeeper Conrad of Parzham; and Zita, a domestic servant. This very public chapel turned out to be a fine instruction on Jesus' statement: "The first shall be last, and the last first."

The frantic work to construct and embellish the upper church of the Shrine finally bore fruit on November 20, 1959, the formal Day of Dedication. Although by no means complete, the imposing church now loomed over the crypt, thanks to the herculean efforts of the past five years. Most of the interior chapels, in fact, were still in the planning stages, and they would require another decade to complete. But at least the outer shell of the great upper structure was up and roofed over, and much of the scaffolding was finally removed to make room for pilgrims.[12]

In January of 1960, while these decisions were being finalized, Monsignor Fenton's notes included references to the ill health of Fr. Petersen, and the resignation of Fr. Arbez due to many other commitments. Archbishop O'Boyle reluctantly accepted the loss of these two fine men and immediately set to work to find competent replacements. He wrote to Monsignor Grady to find an outstanding scripture scholar to replace Arbez immediately; he suggested either Patrick W. Skehan, or Roland Murphy, O.Carm. Monsignor Skehan accepted before the end of February and was welcomed into the Committee.[13]

During the Committee's early years, one powerful element was always the personality of the chair, Monsignor Fenton. His position as Professor of Ecclesiology at Catholic University and editor of *The American Ecclesiastical Review* made him a formidable figure who disliked opposition of any kind and did not tolerate those who might rock the boat. As always, Eamon Carroll came to meetings with reams of notes and armloads of well-marked books, brimming with ideas to share. Fenton often dismissed the contributions of the young friar and referred to him as "boy." On one occasion, when the chair had gone beyond the bounds of rudeness, he was quickly told by his mark to mind his manners.[14] The offensive behavior was not repeated.

Yet another example of the benefit of the Iconography Committee is the issue of the Joyful Mysteries chapel in the west apse. Originally the Dominicans had been approached as likely patrons, but their vision of the central figure was that of St. Dominic receiving the Rosary from Mary. This would be a clear mismatch for the apse's major mosaic, the Woman of Revelation. So the Dominicans moved their offering to the east side of the nave, where they contributed one major chapel of Our Lady of the Rosary, flanked by two minor chapels of St. Dominic and St. Catherine of

Siena, all completed by 1970. The Jesuits then adopted the west apse, and made their own generous endowment.[15]

One source of great personal satisfaction for Fr. Eamon was the completion of the chapel of Our Lady of Mount Carmel in September of 1964. Located in a very prominent place in the west transept, the chapel is a paragon of simple beauty. The central figure is a large statue of Mary and Jesus, both holding the Scapular. Surrounding the center are smaller figures of favorite Carmelite saints: Simon Stock, Teresa of Avila, Andrew Corsini, Mary Magdalene de Pazzi, John of the Cross, and Thérèse of Lisieux. The white statues are set off against a blue mosaic background. The chapel was formally dedicated in May of the following year.

Beginning in 1965, the Iconography Committee set to work on the Blessed Sacrament chapel, one of the Shrine's most important components. As the special gift of the bishops, priests, and seminarians of the United States, the chapel was to have a eucharistic motif which departs to some degree from the Shrine's overall Marian theme. Coming at the time it did, the discussion of the chapel's design was often spirited, as committee members tried to follow the developing eucharistic theology just emerging from the Second Vatican Council.

A detailed memo from Monsignor Grady to Eugene Kennedy (dated May 24, 1965) lists several options regarding the facing and number of altars (one or two), and the placement of the tabernacle, as well as the usual questions about artistic themes and texts. Later communications indicate that both Fr. Eamon and Monsignor Skehan strongly favored a single altar, facing the people, with the tabernacle under a small dome with skylight. That format was ultimately adopted, although the final plans were not completed until 1968. Several notes from 1967 explore the decorative options of mosaics: Mary holding wheat, the wedding at Cana, an Orante, a Tree of Life, Jesus washing the apostles' feet, and the Manna in the desert.[16]

In the finished version, completed in June, 1970, the tabernacle under the skylight resembles the Ark of the Covenant, with twin angels above it. The mosaic of the dome shows a Crucifixion scene, with twenty people from various times and places standing there, a reference to the doctrine of the Mystical Body of Christ. Other mosaics show both the Last Supper and the Multiplication of Loaves and Fish. And naturally, eucharistic symbols are everywhere.

The pace of the work kept Committee members, and everyone else, quite busy. Although the Upper Church got most of the attention, work also continued on neglected parts of the Crypt. A note in the Executive Committee minutes (dated June 13, 1967) authorized a review of artist's sketches for the Crypt narthex as soon as possible.[17]

The prolonged deliberation over the Blessed Sacrament Chapel highlighted the need for additional minds and voices on the Iconography Committee. One of the early additions was William F. McDonough, who subsequently became director of the Shrine after June, 1967, when Thomas Grady was named Auxiliary Bishop of Chicago. His departure was somewhat precipitate, forcing many of the Shrine's organizers to scramble to keep services on schedule. Bishop Grady had presided over some of the Shrine's most significant turning points, and there was no easy way to see him go. Other new colleagues of the Committee included Fathers John J. Murphy, Frederick McManus, and Kevin Seasoltz, O.S.B.[18]

Beginning in 1968, Fr. Eamon took a sabbatical in Burlingame, California. Monsignor McDonough sent him a note on May 15, 1968 in which he assures him that the work at the Shrine was proceeding well. He told him to enjoy the sabbatical, but also requested that he help artist Millard Sheets, of Claremont, California, with the plans for several projects.[19] Sheets' earliest masterpiece was the "Triumph of the Lamb" inside the main sanctuary dome. Based on John's vision in chapters 5 and 6 of the Book of Revelation, the central figure is the Lamb of God, who was slain, but who lives forever. The Lamb is surrounded by four groups of elders, and by creatures symbolic of the four evangelists. These themes are truly ancient, appearing in the basilicas of Torcello, near Venice, and San Vitale in Ravenna. The brilliant colors of the central design are enhanced by use of Venetian glass, and the overall impression is indelible.[20]

In the overall context of the Shrine, much traditional Marian devotion had been called into question since the conclusion of the Second Vatican Council. The American bishops saw a need to clarify and amplify Mary's part in the Church and in human salvation. Early in 1971, Monsignor McDonough began a discussion with Cardinal Carberry which ultimately led to the first ever pastoral letter by the American hierarchy on Mary's place in human spirituality. A committee of bishops drew up a first draft, which was then revised many times by Eamon Carroll to produce a much amplified second draft. This was sent to the National Conference of Catholic Bishops for final approval; it was promulgated under the title "Behold Your Mother" on November 14, 1973. The overall effect was to re-locate Marian veneration within God's plan of salvation.[21]

From about the middle of 1970, a discussion began on the themes of the six interior tympana over the side doors. Since the doors were triples, each transept would have a semi-circular tympanum over each door, with a global theme of the development of Marian doctrine. The minutes of the meeting of June 30, 1970, state that, although neither was present at that meeting, the help of Eamon Carroll and Kevin Seasoltz would be essential for this imposing task. In the same folder is a long and closely typed (though undated) memo from Eamon presenting his detailed suggestions. He proposes that the six tympana display: 1) Mary's perpetual virginity via the Synod of Milan, 2) Ephesus and the title Mother of God, 3) the Second Council of Nicea and Light of the Nations, 4) Queen of Nations, already suggested by Monsignor Skehan, 5) a combined group: the Immaculate Conception and the Assumption, and 6) Mother of the Church.[22] In the end, nearly all his suggestions came to pass. Second Nicea was not in fact used, and the vacancy was filled instead with the Vatican Council title, Mother of Holy Hope. But his other suggestions were followed in meticulous detail.

Early in 1980, Fr. Eamon submitted his resignation from the Committee, in anticipation of his transfer to Chicago and his acceptance of a position at Loyola University. Except for architect Kennedy, he was the longest-serving member of the Iconography Committee. It seems especially appropriate that the final major project which drew his attention was the chapel of Our Lady Queen of Ireland, which was dedicated in November of that same year.[23]

One final and very appropriate footnote was the decision to award Eamon the Shrine's Patronal Medal in September of 1989. That tradition began 15 years before, with a medal which honored Fulton J. Sheen. Since that beginning, subsequent awards had acclaimed fellow Committee members Kennedy and Grady.[24] For Fr. Eamon, the Medal was a source of singular pride, symbolizing as it did, a job well done.

Very well indeed!

Leopold Glueckert, O.Carm.

Endnotes

1. Gregory W. Tucker, *America's Church; The Basilica of the National Shrine of the Immaculate Conception*, Huntington, Indiana: Our Sunday Visitor, 2000, pp.276 f.
2. Washington, D.C.: Archives of the National Shrine of the Immaculate Conception (NSIC), C-1 (Iconography Committee).
3. NSIC. C-1, "John H. de Rosen" personal resume'; and Tucker, *America's Church*, p.134.
4. NSIC, C-1, Letter of 11/4/54.
5. Tucker, *America's Church*. pp.137-139.
6. NSIC, C-1, Letter of 6/16/55.
7. Tucker, *America's Church*, pp.139-141.
8. NSIC, C-1.
9. Frank DiFederico, *The Mosaics of the National Shrine of the Immaculate Conception, Washington*, D.C.: Decatur House Press, 1980, pp. 9 f.
10. Tucker, *America's Church*, pp.144 f.
11. NSIC, C-1, Iconography Committee report to Executive Committee.
12. Tucker, *America's Church*, pp.153-160.
13. NSIC, C-1, several documents of January and February, 1960.
14. An unnamed but unimpeachable source, present at the time.
15. Tucker, *America's Church*, p. 185.
16. NSIC, A-15 (Blessed Sacrament Chapel), various communications from 4/65 through 10/17/67.
17. NSIC, B-2 (Executive Committee).
18. NSIC, A-15, several communications, dated 9/12/66 to 1/17/68.
19. NSIC, A-15.
20. DiFederico, *Mosaics*, pp. 15 f.
21. Tucker, America's Church, pp.207-209.
22. NSIC, B-23 (Iconography Committee).
23. Tucker, *America's Church*, pp.231-233.
24. NSIC, C-1.

Carmelite Marian Shrines
and Images

Considering the life-long dedication to the study of Marian doctrine of my confrere and long-time friend, Eamon Carroll, as well as his contribution to the National Shrine of the Immaculate Conception in the nation's capitol, an article on Carmelite Marian shrines seemed a *sine qua non* in a *Festschrift* in his honor.

While there are not lacking in the history of Carmel theologians who contributed to Marian doctrine and mystics who experienced Mary's presence and maternal love, perhaps the Order's characteristic contribution to Catholic life lies in the field of popular devotion.

Eamon's career reflects this historic parameter. Not to be minimized are his contributions to scientific journals and the decades he devoted to the teaching of systematic theology in the Carmelite theologate in Washington, D.C., the Catholic University of America in Washington, D.C., and Loyola University in Chicago; yet perhaps his most valued service to his heavenly Mother lies in less esoteric realms. Through innumerable conferences, retreats, cassettes, video tapes, and articles in popular religious journals, he undertook (successfully) to "sell" Our Lady to a somewhat confused laity of the immediately post-conciliar years. His simple message, presented with theological competence, was that the Second Vatican Council had not "downgraded" Mary, but had bestowed a new splendor on her name.

In the history of the Church, Marian shrines and images have played a significant role as rallying points of popular devotion. As befitted a Marian Order, Carmelite churches were often dedicated to Our Lady of Mount Carmel or to Mary under one of her other titles. Even when the patron of a church was a saint, it would contain a Marian shrine which attracted the devotion of the faithful. The focus of Marian churches and shrines was the image of Our Lady , sculptured or painted, usually of some antiquity, deemed miraculous either because of its origin or because of the graces and favors obtained through the intercession of the Blessed Virgin (*Gnadenbilden*).

Francesco Voersio (1562-1634), secretary to the prior general, Enrico Silvio, whom he accompanied on his canonical visitations throughout the Order, attested:

> Because the Order bears the title and name of Our
> Lady, all Carmelite churches are frequented by the
> people with great devotion in every part of the
> world; nor is there a church of the Order in which
> there is not a chapel or altar of this Mother of God,
> cared for with great reverence."[1]

The destruction wrought in the Order in the course of time also destroyed most of its Marian shrines. Only a few of the more important surviving shrines and images can be considered here.

La Bruna

No particular image is the official representation of Our Lady of Mount Carmel, but if any were to be considered such, it would be the Madonna, called "La Bruna," of the *Carmine* of Naples, unequaled for fame and popularity. In his time, Juan Bautista de Lezana (1602-1654), theologian and Marian writer, long resident in Rome, ranked it second only to Our Lady of Loreto among famous images of Mary in Italy.[2] In the Byzantine style, the life-size painting on wood was claimed to be the work of St. Luke, brought to Naples by the Carmelites emigrating from Palestine, but it probably originated in Tuscany in the 13th century. Our Lady in a blue mantle and reddish brown tunic is pictured from the waist upward, holding the Child Jesus, who presses his cheek to hers. In 1580 the picture was enshrined in a marble altar in the Renaissance style, thought to be the work of the Cimafonti brothers. The painting was restored with indifferent success by, among others, Francesco Solimena (1699).

Carmel's most famous Madonna is called *La Bruna* from the color of her skin and that of her Child. In an unconsciously humorous passage, the 18th century Roque Faci indignantly protested that he who deigned to become her Son could only have given Mary a skin whiter than snow.[3]

During the Jubilee Year of 1500, the tanners of the quarter around the *Carmine* carried their Madonna to Rome, where it was exposed for some time in St. Peter's Basilica. This act of faith— commemorated in a painting by Luca Giordano, today in the church of Donna Regina in Naples—caused Mary, in St. Gregory's phrase, to open her "miracle workshop" (*officina miraculorum*), and the flow of graces and favors continued during the years that followed. Dearly beloved by the people of Naples, the *Madonna della Bruna* has also been the object of devotion of rulers, popes, and saints. Wednesday is the day dedicated in her honor.[4]

Our Lady of Trapani

The choice between La Bruna and Our Lady of Trapani for preeminence among Carmelite Madonnas is a difficult one. Not so, however, if artistic quality is the primary consideration. This life-size marble statue of the Blessed Virgin has awakened universal enthusiasm over its beauty. "Most precious pearl of our Order," cries Faci in an apt figure of speech recalling the translucent quality of the marble.[5] "He who would see her more beautiful must go to heaven to see her," exclaimed the Viceroy of Sicily, Diego Enríquez de Guzmán.[6]

Mary is standing and holding the Child, whose right arm is laid on her breast, his left hand placed in her right. Mother and Child regard each other smilingly. Our Lady's smile is one of those miracles of art that occur only in an occasional Mona Lisa. According to the legendary account of its origin, discounting variant versions, the statue was brought to Trapani in the 13th century by Pisans fleeing from the Saracens. Dr. Maria Pia Sibilia Cosentino rejects such legends and, basing her judgment on stylistic features alone, assigns the statue to Giovanni Pisano (1245-1314).[7] On the other hand, Hanno-Walter Kruft avails himself of the legendary data (even obtaining the services of an expert to decipher the alleged Syrian inscription on the statue) to conclude that the figure did indeed originate in the East in the middle of the 14th century, probably the work of a Pisan sculptor on Cyprus.[8]

Francesco Laurana (d. 1502?) and Domenico Gagini (d. 1492) head the list of artists commissioned to copy the much admired statue. Later, smaller copies for uses of personal devotion were made of alabaster, terra cotta or wood. "Many buy the image carved in alabaster and take it along to their native land," writes William Gumppenberg; "There are forty workshops of able sculptors who, except for work in coral, do nothing but make alabaster statues of St. Mary of Trapani."[9] It comes as no surprise that today copies are especially abundant in Spain, long master of Sicily.

In the Carmelite church of the Annunziata, the Madonna of Trapani is enshrined in a richly ornamented chapel which one enters through the fine marble portal of Antonello Gagini. There, writes Dr Cosentino, "the people of Trapani have venerated her for centuries, heaping treasures on her with oriental fanaticism, proud of her, jealous of her, casting at her feet everything good and everything bad."[10] The many copies of the Madonna attest the fact that not only the people of Trapani but persons of all nations have been given an inkling of the beauty of Mary through "this stupendous work of art which providentially found a home in Trapani."[11]

Madonnas in the Byzantine Style

Byzantine Madonnas, or in the Byzantine style, held to have been brought by the early Carmelites from the Holy Land, usually represent the longest traditions of Marian devotion in the Order.

The image venerated in the church of Traspontina in Rome was solemnly transferred there in the 15th century from the original foundation in Rome, to be moved again in the relocation of Traspontina nearer the Vatican. At the request of Theodore Straccio, the icon was crowned by the Vatican Chapter in 1641, the first of the Carmelite Madonnas to receive this distinction. In 1674, it was enshrined over the main altar under the baldachin of rare marbles designed by Carlo Fontana. Lezana, a member of the community, in 1648 witnesses to the many votive tablets around the Virgin, attesting to favors received.[12]

Another Byzantine Madonna, allegedly brought by the Carmelites from Palestine, is the Madonna del Popolo, a 13th century painting of the Tuscan School venerated in the *Carmine* of Florence. Only in heaven is Our Lady more gloriously enthroned: the Madonna del Popolo is framed by the Brancacci chapel.[13]

The *Carmine* of Siena, best known for its altar-piece by Pietro Lorenzetti, is not listed by the old authors as a place of particular Marian devotion, but it possessed a genuine Byzantine Virgin, as usual said to have been brought by the Carmelites from the East, besides another 13th century Gothic Madonna "of the Mantellates" (*dei Mantellini*). The *Carmine* of Siena was lost to the Order, suppressed by Napoleon in 1810.[14]

Another genuine Byzantine Madonna, dated by art experts in the 9th to the 11th century, is found in remote Sorbo, near Rome. It is not clear how this precious work of art found its way to such a rustic church, since 1425 in charge of the Carmelites, or what is its relation to Mary's appearance in a service tree (*sorbo*) to a swineherd, which gave rise to the popular devotion.[15] At present, the convent is in ruins; the painting is preserved in the parish rectory of Canpagnano Romano.

Marian Shrines in Sicily

Sicily, where hundreds of churches are dedicated to Our Lady of Mount Carmel, may itself be called her shrine.

In the *Carmine Maggiore* of Palermo is the Madonna painted around 1492 by Thomas de Vigilia, noted artist of the same city.[16] The life-size figure, shown in the act of suckling the Christ Child, is framed by eight smaller vignettes representing episodes of Carmelite history and the scapular devotion. The historian of Sicilian art, Joachim di Marzio, notes "the profound expression of majesty and tenderness" of the Virgin.[17] The picture forms the altar-piece of the altar in the left transept of the church, framed by a grandiose arch supported by four spiral columns in the style of Bernini, the creation of the Serpotta brothers, Joseph and James. Philip Meli finds in it "admirable qualities of a solid and constructive art, which in the subsequent artistic production of Sicily will cease to give signs of life."[18] An identical Madonna by Thomas de Vigilia is found in the Carmelite church of Corleone; it is not clear which came first.

In the style of the Madonna of Palermo is that in Catania painted by Antonio di Viterbo, called *Il Pastura*, in 1501. Beside Our Lady nursing the Child stand Sts. Elijah and Berthold. Eight vignettes likewise recount the favors of Mary. The painting remained intact in the rubble of the church after the earthquake of 1693, but only in 1932 was it restored to the present church. This grandiose structure, built under the aegis of the reform of Santa Maria della Scala, which had taken over the convent in 1729, conceded the place of honor in the Lady Chapel to the painting of Our Lady of Mount Carmel by Sebastian Toccarini (1703-1773) reflecting the style of Guido Reni. Crowned by the Vatican Chapter in 1833, this image of Mary attracted the devotion of the faithful in later times.[19]

Contemporaries do not fail to mention the devotion of the people of Messina to the miraculous image of Our Lady of Mount Carmel venerated at the *Carmine* and reputed to have been brought from Mount Carmel to this very early settlement of the

Order in Europe. The painting, in fact of the 15th century and attributed to Polidoro di Caravaggio, is a mantle Virgin, flanked by Elijah and Elisha, who is shielding the Carmelites and their affiliates under her mantle from the wrath of Christ threatening famine, pestilence, and war. Polidoro might have added earthquakes, three of which (in 1693, 1785, and 1906) the painting survived to find refuge in the Museo Nazionale of Messina.[20]

The old authors record a fresco of Our Lady of Grace venerated in the Carmelite church of Noto. The friars had brought it with them in 1586, when they moved from their original site outside the city. This image of the Virgin did not survive the terrible earthquake of 1693, which leveled the entire city. The better known Madonna of the Ladder to Paradise (*Scala del Paradiso*) had at some remote time been painted on the rock face of a cliff in the "Valley of the Cattle." The hermit, Jerome Terzo, settled beside it and, around 1713-1714, had it removed and transferred to the chapel of the hermitage on the hill opposite. The hermitage was subsequently enlarged into a convent and aggregated to the Carmelite Order. After the suppression of religious Orders and the departure of the Carmelites in the last century, devotion to Our Lady of the Ladder to Paradise did not lag. The painting was crowned by the Vatican Chapter in 1831. Today the church is the center for diocesan pilgrimages. In 1963, Pope Paul VI declared Our Lady of the Ladder to Paradise co-patroness with St. Conrad of the diocese of Noto.[21]

Valletta, Malta, possesses a treasured Madonna, from which "originated in the faithful hearts of the Maltese people that special affection they have for the Mother of Carmel."[22] The painting, by an unknown hand (ca. 1600), shows the Virgin bestowing the scapular on St. Simon Stock. On the right is St. Agatha, much venerated in Malta, holding her severed breasts on a platter.[23] The picture was crowned by the Vatican Chapter in 1881.[24]

Shrines on the Italian Peninsula

Among famous Marian shrines of the Order, Lezana rates
Padua in the Venetian province second only to Naples and
Trapani.[25] The devotion of the people to Our Lady of Lights was
stimulated by her miraculous intervention in the pestilence
which devastated all of Italy in 1576. At that time, the picture was
transferred to the Carmelite church. Attributed to Stefano
dall'Arzere, disciple of Tiziano, the oval-shaped painting shows
Mary holding out her Child for the adoration of the faithful.[26]

The 15th century fresco by an unknown artist of Our Lady
of Grace at San Felice del Benaco shows Mary clothed in brown
tunic and white mantle, seated on a throne, with Sts. Albert and
Angelus at her side. The Child Jesus lies in her lap with a swallow
perched on the thumb of his left hand.[27]

The Byzantine Madonna and Child attributed to St. Luke
was placed in the *Carmine* of Brescia in 1437 by the prior general
Christopher Martignoni. The altar, in the Venetian style, which
enshrines it, is the work of G. M. Morlaiter (1737).[28]

A *Madonna "della Guardia"* of Bologna was reputed by
17th century writers to have been brought from Mount Carmel.[29]
In the church today, there is a fresco attributed to Lippo Dalmasio
(1352-1410), showing the crowned figures of Our Lady and the
Child. Likewise, there is a 14th century fresco attributed to
Simone da Bologna of Our Lady nursing the Child and surrounded by angels. Later devotion centered around the statue of
Our Lady of Mount Carmel carved in wood by Guglielmo
Borgognone and colored while kneeling by Guercino (1644) who
lived nearby. It was crowned with extravagant pomp in 1704 and
again in 1939, after the crown had been stolen two years
previously. The statue is enshrined in the richly baroque Lady
Chapel, given its present form by Alfonso Torreggiani in 1753.[30]

In the monumental *Carmine* of Pavia, no longer possessed
by the Order, Our Lady of Grace became the subject of devotion
after a crippled woman was instantaneously cured in 1597. Faci
records the many cures effected during a pestilence around the

same time.[31] The fresco in a rich baroque frame represents the Virgin with the Infant on her lap. In her right hand she has a rose. The Child Jesus is holding an open book. Beside them in black habits are St. Julius d'Orta and St. Anthony the Abbot. The Lady Chapel contains a lovely marble figure of Our Lady of Mount Carmel by John Angelo Giudici (1699).[32]

At Cervia in Romagna , the miraculous image of Our Lady of the Pine, said to have been found affixed to a pine by wood gatherers, is of the Venetian school of the 15th century and shows Mary seated on a throne and nursing the Infant. The painting became the object of special devotion to the lay-brother, Jerome Lambertini, who settled down by it to live as a hermit. Before his death (ca. 1515), a church and convent had risen to accommodate the devotion of the people. Suppressed by Innocent X in 1652, the remote convent was subsequently torn down, but the little Romanesque church and its Madonna survived, to be masterfully restored in 1972.[33]

The Madonna of the Virgins of Macerata is a mantle-virgin shielding young people of both sexes, hence her title. It is said to have been painted in 1533 by a local artist, Lawrence, called Juda, of Matelica. A product of the Renaissance at its height, the work nevertheless breathes an old-fashioned air of the naif. Among the curious favors attributed to the Madonna is the salvation of a child from a crocodile, the skin of which hangs to the left of the Lady Chapel.[34]

Devotion to Our Lady of Grace in Jesi (Romagna) began when the liberation of the town from pestilence in 1454 was attributed to a fresco of the Virgin painted on the wall of a farmhouse. In 1458, the Carmelites took charge of the sanctuary which arose. The Lady Chapel was incorporated into the present church, the work of the architect Nicholas Majolatesi. Begun in 1709, the altar-piece of the chapel is a mantle-virgin shielding men and women of every condition. Two angels hold a crown over Mary's head, others kneel in reverent prayer. The Child is pictured in her womb, blessing the world. The 14th century painting,

attributed to Lippo di Dalmazio of Bologna, was crowned by the
Vatican Chapter in 1745.[35]

The church of Santa Maria in Monte Santo is the left of the
twin churches in the Piazza del Popolo in Rome. The Madonna of
Monte Santo was painted, according to the legendary account, by
a fifteen-year old girl who, on being unable to do the face of the
Virgin, fell asleep, to find on awakening that it had been miraculously completed. Mary, seated on a cloud, holds the Child and the
globe of the world. Above her are the heads of two angels and the
Holy Spirit pictured as a dove. Her halo is studded with twelve
stars. The Child holds the cross and a scepter. At the bottom of
the picture is a harbor scene that would seem to recall the legend
of St. Mary dell'Indirizzo in Catania. This Madonna was crowned
by the Vatican Chapter in 1659.[36] Authorities have proposed
various hypotheses regarding the origin of the picture. It corresponds to the description of the Madonna of Monte Santo in the
church of the reform in Messina, allegedly painted by Giovanni
Simone Comande and lost in the earthquake of 1908, but
described by the contemporary Placido Samperi.[37]

For some reason, contemporaries do not commemorate the
Madonna of Mesagne in Puglia, painted by Francis Palvisino around
1650. It may have heen executed on the occasion that the city chose
Our Lady of Mount Carmel as its patron (1651). In 1914, the figures
of Virgin and Child were crowned by the Vatican Chapter.[38]

Sardinia hardly yields pride of place to Sicily as an island
devoted to Our Lady of Mount Carmel. The Carmelite church of
Cagliari in Aragonese Gothic style was destroyed in a bombard-
ment of 1943, but the miraculous image of Our Lady of Mount
Carmel, remembered by contemporary authors, survived. A 16th
century figure, carved of cedar of Lebanon and elaborately clothed
"in Spanish style," shows Mary holding the Infant and the
scapular of the Order.[39]

The following is a list of places in Italy, some of them
already referred to above, with images of Our Lady of Mount
Carmel crowned by the Vatican Chapter: Accadia, Ariano Irpino,
Avigliano, Bologna (S. Martino), Cagliari, Calvenzano di Vergato,

Capannori, Catania, Curinga, Desenzano al Serio, Ferrara, Forlì, Genoa, Jesi, Laurenzana (santuario diocesano), Lugo, Lana, Mesagne, Montefalcone, Valfortore, Naples (*Carmine*), Noto, Nocera dei Pagani, Palmi, Polla, Randazzo, Riccia, Rionero in Vulture (*Collegiata S. Marco*), Roma (Monte Santo), Roma (Transpontina), Roma (San Martino), San Felice del Benaco, Scalea, Sorrento, Trisulti di Collepardo, Valetta (Malta).[40]

Marian Shrines and Images in Spain

The Marian devotion of Spain and Portugal is proverbial; no small share of it relates to Our Lady of Mount Carmel. Unfortunately, in this case, time has treated less kindly the objects of popular devotion. Spanish and Portuguese Carmelites, unlike their Italian confreres, have few ancient Madonnas about which to center their devotion to Mary. Only their memory remains in the fervent pages of Carmelite chroniclers, especially of that great devotee of Mary, Juan Bautista Lezana. In many cases, these images seem to have been of great antiquity: their style was Gothic and their legends often tell of discovery underground, where they were allegedly hidden in Moslem times.

Castile

A relic to survive to modern times is the statue in wood of Our Lady of Mount Carmel in the former Carmelite church of Madrid, today the parish church of San Luis. The work of Juan Sánchez Barba (1654), it is enshrined in the retable of the main altar, executed by Sebastian Benavente. Originally, the Virgin was shown bestowing the scapular on St. Simon Stock, but the figure of the latter was subsequently destroyed. The noble ladies of the court vied with each other in providing rich garments for the image.[41]

Requena honored still another Virgin *Soterrana,* hidden during the Moslem Conquest and later discovered by an humble shepherd. Today, Our Lady as represented by this statue, is the patroness of the town.[42]

Aragon and Catalonia

In the Carmelite church of Onda was the image of Our Lady of Hope, or Expectancy, reputed to antedate Moorish times. In 1561 the pestilence suddenly ceased at Our Lady's intercession. In 1751 a new and sumptuous *camarín* was inaugurated, on which occasion Master Peter Nicholau preached the sermon (Valencia, 1751).[43] Jerome Caset, known for his piety and close friend of the Carmelite spiritual writer, John Sanz, attributed to this Madonna of Onda his escape unharmed after a fall from a great height onto a stone pavement.[44] Spared from the fire that destroyed the church in 1835, the statue was restored in 1887 to the new church constructed by the Carmelites after their return in 1880.[45]

In the province of Catalonia, the faithful of Lérida found comfort during years of wars and destruction in recourse to Our Lady of Mount Carmel. The Gothic image, which had formed the principal feature of the stone retable of the main altar in the original church, showed the Virgin and Child characteristically wearing crowns. On visits to Lérida, St. Vincent Ferrer never failed to show reverence to this image. In the third church of the Carmelites, completed in 1766, the statue was placed over the main portal, where it can be seen today, though the church is no longer administered by Carmelites.[46]

The miraculous image of the Virgin in Manresa was discovered during excavations in the church in the 14th century. In Lezana's time, it was over the main altar (*capella maior*).[47] This is no doubt the statue preserved today in the *Museo Municipal* of Manresa.[48]

A Gothic Virgin and Child from the *Carmen* of Barcelona, the early object of Carmelite devotion, is in the *Museo Provincial* of Barcelona.[49]

No Carmelite was more devoted to Our Lady of Mount Carmel than the diocesan priest, Francis Colmenero, author of *El Carmelo ilustrado*. During parish missions conducted in a dozen dioceses of Castile, Galicia, Asturias, Aragon, and Portugal, he caused 760 images of the Mother of Carmel to be placed in the parishes in which he preached.[50]

Andalusia

Jerez de la Frontera in the province of Andalusia treasures an historic image of Our Lady, today the most famous Carmelite Virgin in Spain. This lovely 16th century statue, measuring 1.75 meters, probably arrived with the Carmelites from Seville in 1586. In her right hand the Virgin holds a scepter, in her left the Infant. The latter, added to the figure a century later, is attributed to Luisa Roldán (*La Roldana*). "In this statue," wrote Fr Barbero Moreno, "antiquity, art, beauty, devotion, and charm form a combination so happy, so harmonious, so perfect as to cry out for crowning by the Holy See," a distinction conferred in 1925.[51]

During the renovation in 1428 of the sanctuary of the church of the *Carmen* of Seville, an ancient statue of the Virgin was unearthed. Measuring about four and a half feet, the figure, stated by Faci to be of white marble, represented the Virgin at full length, her features and those of the Child of a swarthy hue. On the pedestal were the figures of a kneeling religious and an *Ecce homo*. The ladies of Seville clothed the statue in rich garments and a large scapular. The statue, actually of alabaster, in modern times found its way to the church of St. Laurence.[52]

The feast of the Immaculate Conception was celebrated with special solemnity at the *Carmen* of Seville, thanks to a legacy of Juan Ponce, Count of Medellín.[53] In this connection, Faci mentions a "most beautiful" picture venerated by the faithful, which, however, he admits not having seen. It would indeed have been beautiful, if it is the painting of Mary Immaculate by

Velásquez, formerly of the *Carmen* of Seville, now in the National
Gallery in London.[54]

A painting of Our Lady of Mount Carmel with St. Simon
Stock and St. Teresa (School of Seville), now in the Church of St.
Stephen, may be provenant from one of the Order's convents in
Seville, possibly the College of St. Teresa. That it is not of
Discalced origin is evident from our Lady's brooch.[55]

The statue of Our Lady of Mount Carmel in the Carmelite
church in Granada was located on the right side altar. Noble
ladies of the Third Order adorned it with elaborate clothing
studded with precious stones of great value. The many votive
tablets attesting to favors received were removed in 1740, when
church and chapel were renovated.[56] Today, the statue is found
in the cathedral.[57]

The history of the monastery of Carmelite nuns in Madrid
is closely bound up with its miraculous image of Our Lady of the
Marigolds (*de las Maravillas*); in fact, the building was the gift of
Philip IV in gratitude to this Virgin for recovery from illness (1646).
The figure was about four and a half feet high. Mary supported the
Child and held a flower in her hand. The nuns managed to
safeguard their treasure during the vicissitudes of the 19th
century, but in the civil war (1936-1939) the Reds discovered it in
the patio of the monastery and burned it.[58]

Marian Shrines and Images of Brazil

More fortunate than the mother province of Portugal,
Carmel in Brazil today cherishes its three centuries' old statue of
Our Lady of Mount Carmel at Recife (Pernambuco). The Virgin,
larger than life size, holds the Child in her left hand, a scepter in
her right. The statue is exquisitely carved of cedar wood and is
thought to have been imported from Portugal before the occupation of Recife by the Dutch, when it was kept carefully hidden. In
1908, Our Lady of Mount Carmel was declared patroness of the
city; in 1919, the image was canonically crowned, the fourth on

the American continent to receive this honor, after those of Guadalupe (Mexico), Lujan (Argentina), Sao Paulo (Brazil).[59]

Marian Shrines and Images in France

The absence of Carmelites in France since the Revolution makes it difficult to trace evidences of Carmelite Marian cult in that country. Also, the authors who concerned themselves with the subject of Marian shrines are Italians and Spaniards, who had only vague ideas about what went on in the North. Nevertheless, devotion to Mary flourished in the eldest daughter of the Church.

Germain to its devotion to Mary is the Order's devotion to St. Anne. In 1627, the Carmelites were summoned to Auray to take charge of the cult which arose when a simple laborer discovered in a field a statue of St. Anne. Seraphinus of Jesus and three others formed the first community. Hugh of St. Francis wrote the first history of the cult of St. Anne d'Auray; Benedict of St. Peter was the architect of the chapel which became the focus of the devotion until 1866, when the cornerstone was placed on the present grandiose basilica which the Bretons built for their beloved patroness.[60]

The miraculous image of the Weeping Virgin *(Notre Dame des Plaintes)* at La Rochette in the province of Provence happily still exists. The statue was said to have been found by a shepherd who was alerted by the sound of weeping coming from a thorn bush. "There," writes Lezana, "he saw the statue of the Most Blessed Virgin like a lily among thorns." In Lezana's time, the statue was over the main altar of the 15th century church.[61]

The convent of Toulouse had, according to the legend, been founded on land provided by a Jew, converted by a vision of the Virgin. In any case, devotion to Our Lady flourished there and many favors were recorded. By what in the Middle Ages would have been considered a miracle of Our Lady (perhaps it was), a pilgrim's badge of "Blessed Mary of Mount Carmel of Toulouse" (13th-14th cent.) was found in 1982 during excavations for the Swan Lane Car Park, Upper Thames Street, London. The badge reveals that the image venerated in the Carmelite church in Toulouse showed Our Lady seated, with the Child Jesus on her left arm. Both figures wear a crown. The badge further adds examples of miracles worked by the Virgin: a paralytic man and a woman freed from the devil.[62]

La Bruna in Belgium

The Flemish province vied with Naples in devotion to their Madonna. The provincial, Michael of St. Augustine, carried a picture of *La Bruna* with him everywhere and placed it before him wherever he stayed. At his insistence, the annual congregation of 1657 urged superiors to provide their churches and convents with copies of this painting which had come from Mount Carmel. That same year, Brussels set the example, followed by the other houses of the province. The prior of Aalst, Isidore of St. Giles, himself cured of an illness by the *Madonna della Bruna*, not only enshrined her picture in the conventual church but wrote *Enkindling of Devotion to the Miraculous Image of our Blessed Virgin of Naples* (Gent, 1670). At Ieperen, attendance at the Wednesday devotions was so great that the crowd overflowed into the street. At Bruges, many priests were required to hear confessions from five until noon. At the evening devotions, crowds were so dense one could walk over the heads, to use a witness's picturesque expression.[63] At Antwerp, the chapel of Our Lady of Naples in the conventual church was enriched with silver candlesticks and a silver arch over the picture.[64]

La Bruna penetrated even into the inhospitable regions of the Calvinistic North, where Belgian Carmelites were active in the Mission of Holland. When the church of Rukven burned down in 1684, Archangelus of the Holy Spirit, in charge as pastor, installed a Madonna della Bruna in the new building.[65]

Arlon in the Walloon vicariate also venerated *La Bruna*. Philip of the Visitation (Vifquin) wrote the history of her picture.[66]

Nunneries in Belgium

A famous image of Mary is that of Our Lady of Consolation preserved in the monastery of the Carmelite nuns in Vilvoorde. This statue had been venerated in the beguinage of Our Lady of Consolation and was the gift in 1247 of Sophia, Duchess of Brabant, who had received four statues from her mother, St. Elizabeth of Hungary. The other three Sophia gave to her sister-in-law, Mechtilda, who in turn also bestowed one on the Carmelites of Haarlem. "The fair Order of Carmel should rejoice," writes Lezana, "that of four most precious jewels it should have two."[67] The statue was thought to have escaped the suppression of the Haarlem convent in 1578 and in a miraculous manner to have found its way to Brussels. It does in fact seem to have survived, but to have found asylum instead in the beguinage of Haarlem.[68] When the Carmelite nuns took over the beguinage of Vilvoorde in 1469, they also took charge of its miraculous Virgin. In 1579, during the Calvinist reign of terror, the statue was saved by a laysister, Catherine Vayems, who, dressed as a peasant, smuggled it out of the city in a swath of hay on her head. At Mechelen, where the nuns fled, the statue escaped unharmed in the seizure of the city by Olivier van den Tempel in 1580. In 1587, when the *gueux* again sacked Vilvoorde, the statue once more remained intact. During the continual wars of the 17th century, the nuns several times carried their precious treasure to safety in other cities: Brussels, Antwerp, Mechelen. It consists of a bust of the Virgin holding the Infant on her left arm; it is carved from oak and 63 cm. in height. "The features, appropriately colored, have a remarkable expression of tenderness, which reassures and consoles."[69]

Treasured in the monastery of Sion in Bruges was the Virgin painted by Gerard David in 1509, today in the museum of Rouen.[70]

Marian Shrines and Images in Germany

Undoubtedly one of the most famous Marian shrines of the Order north of the Alps was that of Our Lady of the Nettles *(Nesselmutter)* located at Heilbronn in the Upper German province. It was found in 1442 by a devout couple, Albert and Kunigunda, in a niche in a wall overgrown by nettles. Pilgrimages began to the spot (since it proved mysteriously impossible to move the statue), and in 1448 a Carmelite convent was founded there. The noted Benedictine polymath, John Trithemius (1462-1516), wrote the first history of the devotion, *De laudibus et miraculis B. Mariae in urticeto factis*.[71] During the Reformation, the statue fell into Protestant hands and was lost; the present statue is a copy made in 1550. After various peregrinations, in 1661 it found a final resting-place in the scapular chapel in the Carmelite church of Straubing, where it has since been cherished with uninterrupted devotion. Our Lady of the Nettles is a wooden *pietà* or *Vesperbild*, showing the Virgin holding the body of her Son after his crucifixion. "Artistically, it is of mediore quality," writes Fr Hatzold, "but so much the greater is its value for the veneration of the faithful."[72]

Straubing had, possibly from the time of its foundation from Regensburg in 1367, its own *Gnadenbild*, today preserved on the altar of St. Sebastian. The statue, popularly called "The Growing Virgin," shows Mary seated on a throne and smiling at her Child whom she supports with her left hand and who is holding a round object. Both figures are crowned. That of the Virgin is lacking its right arm. The title alludes to the legend that the figure of the Infant grew on the arm of its mother. The other name for this image, "Our Lady of the Snow," refers to the snowy landscape on the retable of the altar on which it stands.[73]

Marian Shrines and Images of Eastern Europe

Carmel in Eastern Europe, appropriately enough, possessed a number of famous Marian shrines. A few have survived in modern Poland.[74]

Cracow's Virgin *in Arenis* attracted the devotion of the faithful in 1587, when the image was found intact among the ashes, after the suburb was put to the torch for the defense of the city. The wall to which the painting was attached also outlasted the destruction wreaked on the church by the Swedes in 1655. With the establishment of peace in 1657, the church was rebuilt, and devotion to Our Lady *in Arenis* resumed, all the more fervently for the trials of the past. The Virgin, shown in half-figure, wears an expression rather of concern and sadness. The child on her arm holds a book in his left hand, while his right rests on a round object offered by his mother. The picture was crowned by the Vatican Chapter in 1883.[75]

When Obory was founded from Bydgoszcz in 1605, the friars brought with them a miraculous statue, a *pieta,* one of two statues which the mother house possessed, the other being of Our Lady of the Scapular. Already the source of many miracles, Our Lady of Sorrows continued her benevolent ministry in this new location, as many votive tablets attested.[76] This statue, too, was crowned.[77]

The Carmelites settled in Wola Gulowska (also known as Gulowska Wola) in 1633. The convent was suppressed during the political vagaries of the 19th century, but the Carmelites were able to return in 1924 and reopen their Marian sanctuary.[78] The Virgin of Wola Gulowska is pictured offering an apple to her child, who raises his right hand in blessing. In this attractive picture, Mary's veil and mantle and the Child's tunic are of a dusky color with gilt borders. In 1981, the image was crowned by Pope John Paul II.[79]

Danzig (Gdansk), founded in the 14th century, perished in the course of Poland's troubled history. The Carmelites returned in 1947, not to their original site, but to the church of St. Catherine.[80] When Bogszowice (founded 1620) was abandoned sometime previously, Danzig inherited its 17th century painting of Our Lady and the popular devotion attached to it. Mary wears a garment of rich material and is seated, holding the standing Infant before her. The Infant holds a round object. Both figures had been crowned in 1777.[81]

New Marian Shrines

Aylesford in Kent, England, founded in 1242, can hardly be considered a new foundation. Suppressed by Henry VIII in the 16th century, its remaining medieval buildings were repossessed by the Carmelites in 1949. Although Aylesford was not known as a focus of Marian devotion during its pre-Reformation existence, a shrine to Mary in the mystery of her Assumption was added upon its recovery, which today vies with Walsingham as England's most visited place of pilgrimage. The statue of the Glorious Virgin of the Assumption over the altar of the main chapel is by Michael Clark. The larger-than-life gold-leafed wooden figure shows Mary standing, her hands lifted in prayer.[82]

While Palmi in the province of Reggio Calabria, like Aylesford, is not a new foundation, the devotion to a miraculous statue of Our Lady of Mount Carmel developed during the absence of the friars. Founded in 1540, the convent in 1652 fell victim to the suppression by Pope Innocent X of small convents, but the devotion to Our Lady continued. Only in 1892 was a statue of Our Lady of Mount Carmel rescued from obscurity in the sacristy and given place of honor over the main altar of the church. Two years later, Mary was seen by many to blink her eyes, as if in anticipation of a catastrophe. During a procession of the statue, which led the populace into the countryside, an earthquake took place, leveling the town. Since then, Our Lady has been credited with saving the people from an earthquake. In 1896, the statue was crowned by the Vatican Chapter. The polychromed wooden image of Mary measures 1.5 m., including the base. She is seated, holding the Child on her lap and resting her feet on a globe. Five angels form a circle at her feet. The provenance of the statue is not known, but its baroque style dates it to the 17th or 18th century. In 1927, the Carmelites returned to a new convent and the imposing church built in 1733.[83]

Caivano, six miles north of Naples, is the site of a shrine of great antiquity, dedicated to Our Lady of Graces, better known as Our Lady of Campiglione. In 1560, the shrine was given to the care of the Dominicans,[84] who remained in charge until the suppressions of the nineteenth century. In 1912, the church, in considerable disrepair, was taken over by the Carmelites, who restored it to its present condition in 1939.[85] The devotion to Our Lady's image arose in 1483, when a mother won the acquittal of her son condemned to death for a crime he did not commit. The Virgin, to whom the mother had recourse, is said to have bowed her head in assent to her prayers, and in fact, the head of the Virgin is somewhat inclined to her right. The fresco, painted on an apse-like structure (*la Cona*) behind the main altar of the church, is dated 1419 and is attributed to Colantonio Fiore (1352?-1444). Our Lady is surrounded by the twelve apostles, all standing. The figure was crowned by the Vatican Chapter in 1804.[86]

The shrine of Our Lady of the Ox is situated on a height overlooking the bay of Naples in Vico Equense (south of Naples). According to legend, in 1458, a farmer had an image of Our Lady painted in a grotto in his olive grove. In the course of time, the grotto was covered with undergrowth and the painting of Mary was forgotten, but a certain ox was seen to genuflect every time it passed the cave. Then a crippled girl, told in a vision of the Virgin to visit the hidden cave, was completely cured. Other favors followed, and in 1500 the present church was built. In 1576, the Theatines took over the care of the church until the suppressions by Napoleon in 1807. From 1603 to 1652, the Carmelites also had a convent and church in the same town, dedicated to Our Lady of Peace. After the departure of the Theatines, diocesan clergy were in charge and fostered the devotion, but in 1933, the Carmelites took over its care. In 1972, the last of a series of restorations brought the church to its present state. In a niche behind the main altar, a fresco in Renaissance style depicts a seated Virgin holding the Child with St. Bernardine of Siena at her side.[87]

Joachim Smet, O.Carm.

Endnotes

1. Francisco Voerisio, *Breve relatione della vita et gesta del Reverendissimo Padre Maestro Enrico Silvio* (Asti, 1613), p. 182.

2. Juan Bautista de Lezana, *Maria patrona* (Romae, 1648), p. 129.

3. Roque Alberto Faci, O.Carm., *Carmelo consagrado con santíssimas imágines de Christo y de María santíssima* (Pamplona, 1759), p. 173.

4. For this account of *La Bruna*, see Pier Tommaso Quagliarella, O.Carm., *Guida storico-artistica del Carmine Maggiore di Napoli* (Taranto, 1932), pp. 48-65.

5. Faci, *Carmelo consagrado*, p. 234.

6. Gabriele Monaco, O.Carm., *Notizie storiche della Basilica-Santuario della Madonna di Trapani* (Trapani, 1950), p. 15.

7. Dr. Cosentino's essay is published as an appendix in Monaco, *Notizie storiche*, pp. 37-55.

8. Hanno Walter Kruft, "Die Madonna von Trapani und ihre Kopien," *Mitteilungen des Kunsthistorischen Institutes in Florenz* 14 (1970), 297-322.

9. William Gumppenberg, *Atlante mariano* (3d ed., München, 1657), quoted by Kruft, "Die Madonna von Trapani," p. 305.

10. In Monaco, *Notizie storiche*, p. 38.

11. Cosentino, in Monaco, *Notizie storiche*, p. 55.

12. Lezana, *Maria Patrona*, p. 131. For this paragraph, see Alberto Martino, O.Carm., "Santa Maria in Traspontina, Roma," *La Madonna del Carmine* 26 (1972), 60-66.

13. Alberto Martino, O.Carm., "La Basilica del Carmine di Firenze," *ibid.*, 218-225.

14. V. Lusini, *La chiesa di S. Nicolò de carmine in Siena* (Siena, 1907), pp. 23-24, 72.

15. Paolo Cajoli, O.Carm., "Di una antica immagine bizantina della Madonna venerata nel santuario del 'Sorbo' de' PP. Carmelitani," *Il Monte Carmelo*, 1 (1915), 339-343.

16. Carmelo Nicotra, O.Carm., *Il Carmelo palermitano, tradizione e storia* (Palermo, 1960).

17. Quoted by Nicotra, *ibid.*, 107.

18. Quoted by Nicotra, *ibid.*, 99.

19. Carmelo Nicotra, O.Carm., *Il Carmelo catanese nella storia e nell'arte,* (2nd ed., Messina, 1977, Catania, 1977), pp. 117-123, 161-166.

20. Carmelo Nicotra, O.Carm., *Il Carmelo messinese, tradizione e storia* (Messina, 1974), pp. 50, 69-72.

21. Salvatore Guastella, *Il cammino della Chiesa Nettina nella storia del suo santuario diocesano; conversazione mariana* (Scala di Noto, 1979).

22. Anastasio Ronci, O.Carm., *Brevi cenni sul santuario e sull'augusta icone della prodigiosa Vergine sotto il titolo del Carmelo, venerata nella città Valletta, e ricordi storici alla solenne incoronazione di Lei avvenuta il dì 15 luglio 1881* (Malta, 1883), p. 12.

23. Lorenzo M. Sammut, O.Carm., *Breve storia della devozione di Maria SS. del Carmine nell'Isola di Malta* (Valletta, 1951), pp. 17-18.

24. Ronci, *Brevi cenni*, pp. 15-43.

25. Lezana, *Maria patrona*, pp. 130-131.

26. Cesira Gasparotto, *Santa Maria del Carmine di Padova* (Padova, 1955), pp. 187-208.

27. Gherardo M. Fadalti, O.Carm., and S.M. Pizzol, *Guida storico-artistica del santuario del Carmine, S. Felice del Benaco* (Vittorio Veneto, n.d., but 1964).

28. Antonio Fappani and Giovanni Vezzoli, *La chiesa e il convento del Carmine, note di storia e d'arte* (Brescia, 1975).

29. Juan Bautista Lezana, O.Carm., *Annales sacri, prophetici, et Eliani Ordinis Beatissimae Virginis Mariae de Monte Carmelo* (Romae, 1645-1656), II:204-205; IV:53-54.

30. Angelo Raule, *San Martino Maggiore in Bologna* (Bologna, 1970).

31. Faci, *Carmelo consagrado*, p. 349.

32. Fausto Gianani, *Il Carmine di Pavia, storia e guida del grande monumento* (Pavia, 1962).

33. Umberto Foschi, *Il santuario della Madonna del Pino di Cervia* (Ravenna, 1972).

34. Ludovico Saggi, O.Carm., *Il tempio di S. Maria delle Vergini in Macerata* (2nd ed., Macerata, 1974).

35. Anonymous, *Il santuario di Maria SS. delle Grazie in Jesi* (Roma, 1934).

36. Alberto Martini, O.Carm., "La basilica di S. Maria in Monte Santo a Roma," *La Madonna del Carmine* 26 (1972), 389-394.

37. *Iconologia della Beata Maria*, Messina, 1644, p. 291; quoted by Faci, *Carmelo consagrado*, p. 176. On the church of Santa Maria di Montesanto in Messina, see Nicotra, *Il Carmelo messinese*, pp. 239-245, 251-254.

38. Elia Biscosi, O.Carm., "La chiesa e il convento del Carmine in Mesagne," *Il Monte Carmelo* 1 (1915), 80-83.

39. Alberto Martino, O.Carm., "Santuari carmelitani a Cagliari," *La Madonna del Carmine* 26 (1972), 299-305.

40. Information kindly provided by Fr. Alberto Martini, O.Carm.

41. Faci, *Carmelo consagrado*, pp. 166-167; Juan Fernández Martín, O.Carm., *Apuntos y documentos para la historia del Carmen Calçado en Madrid* (Madrid, 1950), pp. 38, 50; Balbino Velasco, O.Carm., "El convento del Carmen de Madrid," *Anales del Instituto de Estudios Madrilenos* 14 (1977), 116, 145.

42. Lezana, *Annales*, IV, 451; Ignacio de la Eucaristía, O.C.D., "La iconografia primitiva del Carmen en España," *El Escapulario del Carmen*, no. 2 (1950), 89-90 and fig. 10, who gives other versions of the legendary origins of the statue.

43. Faci, *Carmelo consagrado*, pp. 297-299.

44 Juan Pinto de Vitoria, O.Carm., *Hierarchia carmelitana y gloria de los santos de Monte Carmelo, con sermones para los dias de sus fiestas* (Valencia, 1626), p. 378. On Caset, see Pablo Garrido, O.Carm., "El Carmelita Juan Sanz (1557-1608), promotor de la oración metódica y aspiritiva," *Carmelus* 17 (1970), 28.

45. Un devoto de María santísima del Carmen, "Restitución de la milagrosa imágen de N.S. de la Esperanza a la iglesia de

los Padres Carmelitas de Onda," *Revista carmelitana* 11 (1887), 21-26, 32-33.

46.   José Lladonosa Pujol, *El Carmelo en Lérida* (Lérida, 1953), pp. 8,10.

47.   Lezana, *Annales*, IV, 477.

48.   Ignacio, "La iconografía primitiva," p. 89 and fig. 9.

49.   *Ibid.*, 88 and fig. 1.

50.   Francisco Colmenero, *Carmelo ilustrado con favores de la reyna de los ángeles* (Valladolid, 1754), pp. 333-386.

51.   Miguel Barbero Moreno, O.Carm., *La imagen de la Virgen del Carmelo, coronado de Jérez y su basílica* (Jerez de la Frontera, 1970), p. 14.

52.   Alonso Morgado, "Imagen de N.S. del Carmen, célebre por su antiguëdad en Sevilla," *El Santo Escapulario* 16 (1919), 68-73. See also Luis J. Pedregal, "Grandezas y historia de la Orden carmelitana en Sevilla," *ibid.* 38 (1941), 136, 137-138.

53.   Lezana, *Annales*, III, 274-275; IV, 1049.

54.   Faci, *Carmelo consagrado*, p. 267. Ismael Martínez, O.Carm., "La Imaculada y los Carmeltas Sevillanos," *Escapulario del Carmen* núm. 888-889 (1972), 223-230.

55.   The painting is reproduced on the cover of the September issue of *El Santo Escapulario* 45 (1949). See also the inside cover of the February issue, 67 (1971).

56.   Faci, *Carmelo consagrado*, pp. 157-158.

57.   See the reproduction on the back cover of the July issue of *El Santo Escapulario*, 47 (1951).

58.   Balbino Velasco, O.Carm., "Il convento de las Carmelitas de Nuestra Señora de las Maravillas de Madrid," *Carmelus* 23 (1976), 142-148.

59.   *Convento e basílica do Carmo do Recife, a trisecular imagen de N.S. do Carmo, que se venera na mesma igreja*, por um devotado filho do Carmelo (Recife, 1939), pp. 17-18, 27-55.

60.   Max Nicol, *Saint Anne d'Auray, histoire du pèlerinage* (Paris, 1877).

61.   Lezana, *Annales*, IV, 962-963, 969.

62. Adrianus Staring, O.Carm., "The Miracles of Toulouse," *Carmelus* 38 (1991), 128-154.

63. Valerius Hoppenbrouwers, O.Carm., "De vereering van O. L. Vrouw van Naples in de Nederlanden," *De Standaard van Maria* 22 (1946), 276-292.

64. Marcellinus Klaver, O.Carm., "Stichting en bouw van het Carmelieten-klooster te Antwerpen," *Documenta carmelitana neerlandica, Bijdragen* I, 77.

65. Hoppenbrouwers, "De vereering van O.L.Vrouw," 292.

66. Cosmas de Villiers, O.Carm., *Bibliotheca carmelitana* (2 vol. in 1, Aurelianis, 1752); offset edition (Roma, 1927), II: 655.

67. Lezana, *Annales*, IV: 321.

68. Norbertus a S. Juliana, O.Carm., *Batavia desolata carmelitana*, ed. in *Analecta Ordinis Carmelitarum* 8 (1932), 377-378.

69. H.P. Vanderspeeten, S.J., *Notre Dame de Consolation* (Bruxelles, 1878), p. 24.

70. Lezana, *Annales*, IV:967; *Enciclopedia italiana*, XII:415.

71. John Trithemius, *Opera*, ed. J. Busaeus, S.J. (Mainz, 1604), pp. 1131-1215.

72. Gundekar Hatzold, O.Carm., *Das Karmelitenkloster Straubing* (Straubing, 1947), p. 98. See also Adalbertus Deckert, O.Carm., *Karmel in Straubing* (Rom, 1968), pp. 208-215.

73. Hatzhold, *Straubing*, p. 27; Deckert, *Straubing*, pp. 208-209.

74. On the Marian shrines in Poland, see *Z dawna Polski ty królow ; przewodnik po sankatuariach maryjnych* (Szymanów, 1983), 2 vols.

75. Janina Bieniarzówna and Antoni Tomasz Piotrowski, *Sanktuarium Maryjne w ko ciele. Karmelitów "na Piasku" w Krakowie; dzieje kultu i kaplicy* (Kraków, 1983); Michal Rozek, *Koscio OO. Karmelitów "na Piasku" w Krakowie, przewodnik dla zwiedzajacych* (Kraków, 1990); Witold Malej, "Regina Poloniae majestas in iconibus observata," *Marianum* 23 (1961), 319.

76. T. Chrzanowski, "Rze ba pieta z klastoro Karmelitów w Oborach w ziemi Dobrzy skiej," *Nasza Przesz o* 38 (1972), 55-83. See also this author's article on the same subject in the review, *Miesiecznik Pasterski Plocki* 60 (1975), 375-400. Add Andrzej Malicki, "Cudowna figura Matki Bo ej bolesnej w Oborach, dzieje kultu," *Miesiecznik Pasterski Plocki* 61 (1976), 112-128.

77. W. Gapi ski, "Koronacja cudownej figury Matki Bo ej bolesnej w Oborach," *Miesiecznik Pasterski Plocki* 61 (1976), 453-476.

78. Zofia Walczy, Sanktuarium Maryjne w Woli Gu owskiej (Kraków, 1984).

79. *Analecta Ordinis Carmelitarum* 35 (1981), 153-154.

80. *Vinculum Ordinis Carmelitarum* 1 (1948/49), 9.

81. On Danzig, see Andrej Januszajtis, *Ko cio wi tej Katarzyny w Gdansku* (Gdansk, 1989). On Bogszowice, Franciszek Bizsak, O.Carm., *O cudownym obrazie iko ciele Matki Boskiej w Bogszowcach z dodaniem i wiadomo ci o szkapuleru w* (Lwów, 1907).

82. *The Friars, Aylesford* (Aylesford, 1981); *Image of Carmel: the Art of Aylesford* (Aylesford, 1974).

83. Agostino Poci, O.Carm., *Cenni storici sulla miracolosa immagine della B.V.M. del Monte Carmelo* (Bari, 1974).

84. Giuseppe Maria de Nigris, O.P., *Origine e fatti della miracolosa immagine di Maria delle Grazie, volgarmente detta S. Maria a Campiglione e del suo convento de' PP. Predicatori della Terra di Caivano* (Benevento, 1729), pp. 27-31.

85. Angelo Massaro, "Artistici restauri nel Santuario di Campiglione a Caivano," *Il Monte Carmelo* 25 (1939), 49-54.

86. *Breve notizia della sacra immagine di S. Maria delle Grazie a Campiglione nella Terra di Caivano. Quarta edizione uniforme alla prima dell'anno 1791* (Napoli, 1838); Giovanni Scherillo, *La Terra di Caivano e Santa Maria di Campiglione. Con un breve commento su di una lettera di S. Gregorio*

Magno intorno alla chiesa di Santa Maria di Campisone, e due divinazioni delle etimologie di Caivano e Campisone (Napoli, 1852); *La Madonna di Campiglione* (Caivano, 1993).

87. Anastasio M. Ruggiero, O.Carm., *Santa Maria del Toro, brevi notizie e pie tradizioni* (Napoli, 1933); Ferdinando Sorrentino, O.Carm., *Santa Maria del Toro, leggenda, storia, arte* (Vico Equense, 1993).

Devotion to Our Lady
at the Beginnings of Carmel

Introduction

A distinctive element of the spirituality of Carmel is the vital and deep influence which the presence of the Blessed Virgin Mary has played, to the point that the Order has been described as "wholly Marian," an eminently Marian Order. It may therefore come as a surprise that in the *Formula vitae* given by St Albert, Patriarch of Jerusalem, to the group of Latin hermits living on Mount Carmel–from which the Order of Carmel originates–Our Lady is not mentioned. A recent study addresses itself to this lack of Marian data in view of the particular nature of St Albert's intervention: Albert's document appears more a practical confirmation of the basic "proposal" of the Latin hermits' lifestyle than a detailed, theoretical exposition of the principles of their way of life. The author seeks to confirm his assertion by comparing Albert's *Formula* with the Rules of other monastic or canonical institutes, also known for their Marian charism. At the end of his study he draws this conclusion:

> Devotion for the Blessed Mother, rather than being imposed ... by legal prescriptions–not excluding their Rule–flourished in their spirits in the warmth of their faith–in their naturally Christian, and inseparably Marian, soul.[1]

But is the Marian dimension truly present from the very origins of the Order? Experts in this area have conducted studies of the experience of the first generations of Carmelites and the presence of certain elements which, in the medieval mentality, gave a characteristically Marian nature to an association or religious order. They have answered that the Marian element is present from the beginnings of the Order, as evidenced by means of the dedication to Mary of the group's first chapel on Mount Carmel and by the resulting patronage of Mary in favor of the Order.[2]

The feudal concept of patronage explains the first Carmelites' choice of Mary and their attitude toward her: they see in her the "lady of the place" in the land of their Lord Jesus, in whose service they intend to live, and they consider themselves bound to her service and under her protection. This feudal concept of the bond between Carmel and Mary is further developed and confirmed in the course of the 13th century. In fact, this sense of the Order's special dedication to Mary appears in documents of the time and is very clearly expressed in the acts of the general chapter of Montpellier in 1289, which stated that the brethren gathered there ask the prayers of the "*gloriosae virginis Mariae, matris Iesu, in cuius obsequio et honore fundata est nostra religio de monte Carmelo.*"[3] With the passage of time, there was an ever increasing awareness of her patronage over the Order and of the Order's Marian nature, until eventually its principles and practices merged, forming a living dimension that we today call the Marian spirituality of Carmel.[4]

Over and above these generally accepted components of the Marian origins of the Order, there is another series of questions which demands an adequate reply. What was the background of those who formed that first group of Latin hermits on Mount Carmel? What was it that led them to dedicate their first oratory to the Blessed Virgin? Is it sufficient to center the explanation of this Marian choice on the fact of the "title" of the church to which they committed their service (*manicipati*) as an essential condition for the group's official recognition, even if only by a bishop? In the medieval mind is it sufficient to consider only the relationship between those "vowed to service," *mancipati,* and the Patroness, with its resulting Marian orientation?

For an adequate reply it is necessary to frame and analyze this gesture of the Latin hermits of Mount Carmel by which they dedicated their first oratory to the Blessed Virgin Mary, not only in the context of the feudal "service" (*mancipatio*), but also within the more general context of Marian devotion in the West, and of the specific Marian devotion in the Holy Land at the very beginnings of the Order.

Marian Spirituality and Devotion in the West

First of all, by means of a brief panoramic view, we wish to see the Marian ambience of the Western world, from which the first Latin hermits on Mount Carmel came.[5]

In Europe, in the 9th century and even more in the 11th and 12th centuries, the theological view of Mary was developed within the framework of Christology, basing it on the relationship between Mary and Christ the God-man, and on Mary's role in the work of salvation. The Marian questions which were dealt with most often were the doctrine of the Assumption and that of the Immaculate Conception. Reflection on the divine motherhood came to stimulate speculation on the maternal figure of Mary with regard to the individual members of the faithful, and conjecture about her mercy and mediation of grace. Also current were the Marian themes of the new Eve, of Our Lady both as a type of the Church and as the Woman of the Apocalypse.

Marian devotion integrated the liturgy and popular devotion. The favorite theme was that of Mary's joy in her election as Mother of God, and of the delight experienced when reminded of that election. There was more sharing in the joys than in the sorrows of Mary, even though the theme of her compassion is not absent. From the 10th and 11th centuries on, one of the most venerated of Marian mysteries was the Annunciation; this is reflected in various systems of reckoning dates adopted by many states.

In context, reference to divine motherhood within the feudal framework of service to Christ the Lord produces a relationship on both descendant and ascendant levels:

– the motherly mediation of Mary (i.e., protection), the descendant aspect;

– the virtues of the devotee of Our Lady (i.e., the "laudes": trust, supplication, "service" or *mancipatio*, the ascendant aspect).

St Bernard summarizes and propagates medieval Marian devotion, as it is deeply rooted in service, along three lines:

1) to honor Mary, the Mother of God: our praises will never be adequate; we must take as our model Jesus himself, who placed in her all fullness of good;[6]

2) to pray to Mary with great confidence: Bernard bases himself on the doctrines of mediation and of patronage, which he amply illustrates:[7] all creatures look to Mary, invoking her and obtaining her aid; Mary is an advocate with her Son; her goodness leads to trust in her role as dispenser of graces. This doctrine, already taught by St Cyril of Alexandria[8] and by St John Damascene,[9] St Bernard amplifies, specifies and diffuses.[10]

3) to imitate the virtues of Mary: this, together with prayer, is the best way to enjoy her protection.[11]

In the witness of St Bernard we find the whole gamut of tender sentiments medieval man had for Mary.

Quite current among those devoted to Mary, especially in France and in religious Orders, was the teaching of Guerricus d'Igny (+1157) on Mary as the spiritual model for every soul. In the moral and mystical conception of Christ present in her virginal and pure heart, the soul advances with Mary in love.[12]

In Europe of the 12th and 13th centuries, spirituality was oriented towards Christ in his humanity in a much more marked way than previously. This Christocentric tendency led to contemplation of the infancy of Christ, of the Redeemer on the Cross, and consequently also of the Virgin in these mysteries of the Lord: at the manger and during the other mysteries of his infancy, of his public life, and of his passion. Prayers are addressed to Mary as

Mother of mercy, Queen of the universe, Lady in heaven seated at the right hand of the Son.

In the context of the "service of Mary" there was a flowering of liturgical texts, prayers addressed to her, collections of "miracles" and "examples." A privileged place was reserved for the Mother of God in various artistic forms. There was an ever-growing number of monasteries, hospitals, churches, cathedrals dedicated to her. Many of the religious Orders of recent institution followed this example. Within both the monastic Orders and the new religious institutes, there was a diffusion of characteristically Marian expressions, both in the liturgy and in private devotions. In the ambit of monastic and mendicant Orders, the religious habit was interpreted in a Marian sense. Already in the 11th century monastic reforms, imitated later by the mendicants, there was a strong link between Marian devotion and the "reform of the Church;" this was often expressed by introducing the name of Mary into the formula of religious profession. Thus the Mother of the Lord appeared as the means, the guarantee, and the prototype of reformed life in the Church.[13] It would be quite interesting to verify how the name of Mary entered into the profession formula of Carmelites in the 13th century, and its probable link with the reform of the Church. Unfortunately, the documentary evidence we have on hand offers no basis for such a study.[14]

Finally, we must note the phenomenon of medieval knighthood which developed from the middle of the 12th century. It was an element dominant in the current culture of the people, the bourgeois and courtly circles, with significant and relevant impact on the literature of the time.[15] It influenced religious expression as well. In this context there arose an authentic "Marian knighthood," whose members considered themselves ministers and servants of Mary, whose colors they bear.[16]

In the East, during the 12th and 13th centuries, Marian devotion flourished especially in liturgical celebrations, and consequently it remained in harmony with the mysteries of Christ. Recurring Marian themes are those of the Mother of God, of the Virgin, of the All-holy One. With regard to the intercession of Mary, there is talk of her graces but not of her mediation. Abundant expressions of Marian veneration are to be found in the liturgy, in prayers addressed to her, in acts of respect, and in the veneration of icons.

Marian Devotion of the Crusades

Directing our attention now to the ambience of the Crusades and the Holy Land, the most comprehensive documentation about Marian devotion is presented by literary sources known as the *Itinera ad loca sacra*, namely, accounts of trips written by pilgrims in the medieval period. They take the form of guidebooks for the Holy Land and they reveal what struck the pious pilgrim about Mary.[17]

The principal references to Mary in these *Itinera* are: Mary was reputedly born in Magdala and lived in Jerusalem for three years in the place where the Church of St Anne now stands. Her home in Nazareth was transformed into a basilica. The seat on which she was sitting at the moment of the Annunciation was preserved at Diocesarea, where one could also view her *amula* (jars) and a *canistellum* (basket). At Nazareth a pilgrim found the fountain at which the Virgin Mary had drawn water. There too were two churches dedicated to the Mother of God. One could view the rock on which Mary, on her way to Bethlehem, sat when she dismounted from her donkey; the rock had been blessed by Mary. At Bethlehem, the pilgrim saw the table at which Mary had sat with the Magi. During the flight into Egypt, a font of water appeared at the place where she took a rest. Her Egyptian residence was in Menfi. In Nazareth one could view a beam on which Jesus the child had played in the synagogue. In Cana the wine jars which had contained the miraculous wine were shown. In Jerusalem were preserved the pin and the ribbon which the Virgin Mary used for her hair. Mary was supposed to have woven a linen cloth with the articles of the Creed as the Apostles recited it, and also an image of Our Lord.[18] For the medieval pilgrim this "reference" was very important; it spoke to him of the values which Mary had lived out. Without a doubt, theirs was a very different sense of history.

In the *Itinera* there is also reference to various churches and altars built in Mary's honor.[19] These churches and altars are to be found linked especially to various Gospel episodes, as for instance, the altar of the Sorrowful Mother on Calvary, of Our Lady in the grotto at Nazareth, in the grotto of the Annunciation, in the grotto of Bethlehem, in the choir of the Holy Sepulcher. There are other churches linked with facts recorded in the Gospels (the Annunciation at Nazareth and at Acre and on Sinai; the Visitation at Ain Karim; the Feeding at Nazareth; Our Lady of the Sighs on the Way of the Cross; Our Lady on the Pinnaculum) or acquired by tradition (e.g., the Dormition of the Virgin on Mount Sion, Our Lady of the Milk, and the Tomb of Our Lady in the Valley of Jehoshaphat). Besides these, many other churches were dedicated to Mary in Jerusalem, in Acre, and at various places in Palestine (Tyre, Sidon, Tortosa, etc.) with legendary references and accounts about the life of Mary.

We must note, then, that the dedication of a place to Mary in the Holy Land was always made with a geographic link to some biblical episode, or to some local tradition, sometimes of a legendary nature.[20]

At all these Marian sites, alongside the manifold aspects of worship of the Lord that an altar or a church involved, there was also veneration of Our Lady in a European framework, especially with the prevailing new forms of devotion and prayer. The *Ave Maria*, the *Salve Regina* (in embryonic form), the *Angelus Domini*, and the litany (which later became the Litany of Loreto) were recited in these Palestinian shrines. There they acquired a spiritual worth from their immediate association with the sacred place which recalled an episode from the life of Mary, and from their significance in the daily life of the pilgrim.[21]

A study of the *Itinera*, then, gives evidence of the interest of pilgrims in the places and objects linked with Our Lady. In their visits to the places sanctified by Jesus, Mary as Mother of God was always seen in intimate union with her Son. This is confirmed by Arab accounts from the 12th and 13th centuries, in which there is explicit reference to Christians' devotion to Mary, the Mother of the "Spirit and Word of God, the Mother of Light."[22]

Other testimonies of Marian devotion during the time of the crusades include the liturgical recurrence of feasts, some of which were not yet officially approved for the universal Church. There is also an abundance of testimonies on stone epigraphs, of graffiti and of images of Our Lady both in mosaic, in paintings and on seals.[23] These testimonies provide abundant examples, sometimes with tender nuances, of prayers trustfully addressed to the Mother of God and of the pilgrims' awareness of her mediation. Nor are examples lacking of how the Blessed Mother was understood to be a model of one who prays. Marian themes that appear frequently in these images are the Annunciation, Mediation, Dormition, Assumption.

Given our present knowledge of Marian devotion during the period of the crusades in the Holy Land in the 12th and 13th centuries,[24] we can draw the following conclusions:

a) Marian devotion among the crusaders was intense. The contents of this veneration and its theological references were those proper to the medieval mentality which obtained in Europe: it was decisively "Latin" and "Western." At present it can be no more than a hypothesis to speak of the influences, or better of the stimuli, which may have been experienced by reason of contact with Eastern Christians, among whom veneration of Mary was as strong as in Europe. Moreover they had very ancient traditions, particularly about the sites which pertained to the life of Mary.

b) Mary is always seen in intimate union with her Son. Veneration of Mary invariably leads to Christ.

c) The Marian "mysteries" most in evidence are: Annunciation, Mediation, Dormition, and Assumption. Both epigraphs and paintings provide evidence that the "mysteries" are always linked to Christ. Perhaps this link derives. as references to the Incarnation sometimes indicate, from their wish to make clear the total fulfillment of God's plan with regard to Mary and her pilgrimage, from beginning (Annunciation) to end (Assumption), when she is completely transformed.

d) The sources and the evidence from the environment of the crusades refer to Mary's "presence" on three levels:

– the experience of geographic contact with the site of the *memoria*, guaranteed by a Gospel account or by a local tradition. Consequently, it was a reference to values noted in this type of experience.

– the prayer of intercession and the awareness of the mediation of Mary, because she was the Lady, the Patroness. Consequently, there was imitation of her virtues.

– Marian inspiration which touches one's own life, based on considerations of generic or epochal nature.

The Dedication of the Oratory on Mount Carmel

It is in this context of facts, spiritual dynamism, and orientation of Marian devotion that we should situate the dedication of the first oratory on Mount Carmel by the Latin hermits. This will lead to an understanding of this gesture's profound meaning.

As has already been abundantly stressed, the fact of the dedication of the first oratory to Our Lady cannot be doubted: it is attested to by numerous sources and writings of the 13th century which refer to it. Later the event was embellished by our writers with arbitrary and legendary details, as for instance, the date of its construction in the year 83 A.D., and the claim that it was the first church in all of Christianity to be dedicated to Our Lady.[25]

As we find this dedication within the crusade environment, we admit that, both from a juridical standpoint and on a spiritual level, it exercised a fundamental impact on the development of the Marian spirit of the Order. However, it was not a cause of this Marian spirit, but rather its effect.

The pre-existing cause must be found in the devotion to the Mother of God that the first hermits already nurtured in their hearts because of the religious framework not only of the times but more especially of the Holy Land, particularly during the era of the Crusades. It was doubtless this devotion, first lived in Europe and then filtered through the context of the crusades, that led the hermits on Mount Carmel to the choice of Mary as their Patroness. The Latin hermits were children of the 12th and 13th centuries, living in and reacting to the spirit of their times. This factor ought never be forgotten.

The dynamics of the Marian dedication of churches in the Holy Land, as we have seen, is tied to an affirmation—we are not judging whether it is valid today or not, just that it was valid for that time—of a "presence" or "link" between Mary and the place dedicated to her. Did this also happen in the case of the first Carmelites?

The whole of Mount Carmel and the *wadi 'ain es-Siah*, in which the first Carmelite monastery was built, were immersed in an aura of sacred traditions with reference to Elijah and to Mary.

With regard to the relationship of Mary to Carmel, biblical references already existed before the arrival of the crusaders, and it had been maintained by several writers. These affirmations were well known at the time to both pilgrims and Christians living in the Holy Land. There are two biblical passages applied to Our Lady: *Caput tuum ut Carmelus* ("Your head rises like Carmel" Sg 7:6), and Elijah's vision on Carmel of the small cloud rising from the sea (1 Kgs 18:41-45). To give but a few examples, in the case of the first citation, we have the beautiful paraphrase by Honorius of Autun: "Blessed is your head, which as often as you bend over to kiss the Son of God, is like Carmel, i.e. dazzling in virtue."[26] In the 12th century, the text of Philip of Harveng[27] is based on his Marian interpretation of The Song of Songs 7:5, on the patristic explanation of "Carmel" as knowledge of circumcision.[28] To be noted is the link between the Marian interpretation and the spiritual dynamic of the circumcision of one's vices, ascending gradually from virtue to virtue, as this is applied to Carmel. Mary's life is the example of this: she is thus the most beautiful flower of Carmel, according to the above-mentioned Marian interpretation. Such were the sentiments of the pilgrim, nurtured with a devout and reverent spirit, as he followed the paths of the mountain in search of venerable places to visit. Curiously the application of the text of Isaiah 5:2 to Mary, Beauty of Carmel, does not seem to be present to the crusaders, although it was known in Europe.[29]

Regarding the second biblical passage, that of the small cloud, it is interesting that one of the correctors of the *Formula vitae* of St Albert, Cardinal Hugh of St Cher, maintains the Marian interpretation.[30] Before him several fathers of the Church express the same idea.[31]

There were, then, biblical references, noted by those who visited and lived on Mount Carmel, which implied a "presence" of Mary. This "presence" spoke to their hearts of spiritual values and teachings. It is easy to understand how–given the mentality of the times, quite different from ours–various gentle, expressive legends came to be formulated to supply for the lack of direct biblical references.

Thus, in the medieval era a legendary tradition was formed that asserted how, following the sacrifice and the defeat of the followers of Baal, Elijah prayed near the font of *wadi 'ain es-Siah*, and the small cloud appeared to him. This legend was then taken up by Ribot in his famous collection of texts.[32] Unfortunately, until now, I have not been able to determine the exact time when this legendary account originated.

It is interesting to note that the biblical passages quoted above, with their Marian interpretation, are adopted by Carmelite writers of the 13th and 14th centuries, in particular by Baconthorpe and Ribot. From them they flow into the subsequent tradition of the Order, becoming a *de rigeur* point of reference for Carmelites.[33]

These legendary elements presuppose a personal contact of Mary with Mount Carmel. In the language of medieval "examples," they were rather significant for a person sensitive to the symbolism, overladen with spiritual meaning, expressed by them.[34]

We might also add that among the Carmelite writers of the 13th and 14th centuries we find another series of legendary references to the relationship between Mary and Mount Carmel. One such legend, with all its accompanying symbolism, asserts that the angel of the Lord transported the child Mary from the Temple to Mount Carmel, where she consecrated her perpetual virginity to God; in another Mary visits Carmel and is welcomed by the hermits; again, Mary stays with the hermits, with other virgins, her companions.[35]

It would be interesting to investigate the origins of such Carmelite legends and the possibility of discovering some elements that even pre-existed the Latin hermits.[36] For example, the last of these legends, which describes the meeting of Mary with her virgin companions on Mount Carmel, finds at least indirect verification in an observation contained in the *Itinerarium* of Pseudo-Antoninus of Piacenza (6th cent.): the Hebrew women of Nazareth are the most beautiful of the whole region, and it was said that this was granted them by Our Blessed Lady, who claimed them as her relatives.[37]

Besides the biblical references and their interpretation, there is also an historical reference which links Mary more properly to the *wadi 'ain es-Siah* on Mount Carmel. Today we know with certainty that before the Latin hermits, there was a Byzantine *laura* in the *wadi*, and that originally what had been considered to have been the stables of the monastery was its cave-chapel.[38] It is presupposed that it was a "Marian chapel."[39] It is known that there was a custom among hermits to dedicate their chapels to the Blessed Virgin. With regard to the affirmation of the Marian dedication of the Byzantine *laura*, Friedmann observes:

> If that were the case, then the fact that, in the course of time, the Latin hermits of Mount Carmel were so to dedicate their own oratory in Wadi 'ain es-Siah, takes on, a new dimension.[40]

From what we have said so far, it seems to me sufficiently clear what this "new dimension" is. At the basis of the choice made by the Latin hermits with their gesture of a Marian dedication of their oratory, besides the feudal choice of Mary as the Patroness of their oratory, there is evident the Marian "presence" or link with the first and second levels indicated in our synthesis of the Marian ambience of the Crusades; we could also form a hypothesis even about the third level.

The dedication of the oratory, then, shows how the first hermits were men of their times, and they fully lived their Marian devotion in its Bernardine, medieval and crusader dimensions. They looked to Mary, the Mother of God, with an awareness of her role of mediation. They saw in her a model for their own life of ascent of the mount of perfection. To my mind, this is the vital dynamism that emerges from the origins, and constitutes the basis of later developments, together with the contents and perspectives of the patronage of Our Lady.

A Generic or Specific Marian Title?

The dedication of their oratory to Mary posits another question. The earliest documents (from the first half of the 13th century) that speak of the title of the little church, affirm that it was dedicated to *Our Lady*.[41] The title, Saint Mary of Mount Carmel, on the other hand, is later; it is found, very probably, in papal documents as early as 1246, with the addition of a reference to the virginity of Mary, and certainly in 1263 and 1264. Apart from its presence in papal documents, the Marian title of the Order seems already to have appeared in 1246 or 1247 in England, and certainly in 1249 and 1250 in Pisa and Trapani.[42]

It is legitimate to ask, then, to what Marian mystery did the Marian title of the oratory refer? Was it a generic or a specific title? Faced with a lack of documents, we can only suggest a hypothesis with a certain foundation.

Without doubt, some specific assertions about the title (e.g., the Assumption) presented by our authors from the 14th century onwards, are to be rejected, because they are clearly based on subsequent developments. These developments were due to the reflection undertaken by the Order, especially in the controversy on the Marian title, and stimulated by this title.[43]

In the context of the crusades, the Marian title "Our Lady" and "Holy Mary" always refers to Christ and therefore it is understood to refer to the Mother of God. Moreover, in the title "Our Lady" is included the "Lady of the place" with her patronage.[44] And to these specifications can be added another element, the *Mariae Virginis* of the above-mentioned papal document of 1246, which does not seem to have been added by the Carmelites themselves.[45]

For the meaning of "Holy Mary" there is also another connotation, noted by St Thomas Aquinas: "blessed" and "holy" applied to Mary mean the same thing, and they are linked to the question of the sanctification of Mary; and in the line of St Bernard of Clairvaux there is "the way of beauty" in the title "holy Mary".[46] This nuance may have been a factor at the choice of the title by the first hermits.

A confirmation that the title "Our Lady" and "Holy Mary" should be understood as specifically referring to the "Mother of God" comes from the most ancient iconography of the Order. In fact, the most ancient images of Mary, from the 13th and 14th centuries, preserved in Carmelite churches, present the iconographic type of the Mother of God known as the *Eleusa*, and all of them are linked with the legend that they derive from Mount Carmel.[47] The symbolic language of such legends is clear. In Eastern iconography, there existed legends of the images of Mary painted by St Luke, while in the West they were described as being the product of angels (achetype images).[48] In this context, to affirm that our images came from Mount Carmel indicated, by the iconographic choice of the *Eleusa*, a single-minded motivation that is tied to the origins of referring to and contemplating Mary as the Mother of God.

Conclusion

At the origins of the Order, then, I think we meet a Marian presence, fed by biblical references, by local traditions, and by the awareness of the role of Mary in the mystery of Christ and of the Church. The dynamic values behind the dedication of the first oratory doubtlessly refer to the Mother of God, along with references to the patroness and to the "Lady of the place."

From this original humus in harmony with the feudal and crusader ambience, there follows a process of idealizing one's origins. This led to the development of a rapport laden with affection, cordiality, tenderness, and of intimate familiarity with Mary, which will take on new dimensions and new nuances.

Emanuele Boaga, O.Carm.

Endnotes

1. N. Geagea, O.C.D., *Maria Madre e Decoro del Carmelo. La pietà mariana dei Carmelitani durante i primi tre secoli della loro storia* (Roma, 1988), pp. 75-77. Cf. also: L. Saggi, O.Carm., *Santa Maria del Monte Carmelo* (Roma, 1986), pp. 7-8. In a recent study an effort was made to find traces of Marian devotion in the *Formula vitae* of St Albert (cf. A. Scapin, O.Carm., "Tracce di devozione a Maria nella Regola del Carmelo" in *Presenza del Carmelo* [Supplemento n. 25, 1981], pp. 61-69).

2. Cf. Saggi, *Santa Maria*, pp. 6-9; V. Hoppenbrouwers, O.Carm., "Come l'Ordine Carmelitano ha veduto e come vede la Madonna," in *Carmelus*, 15 (1968), 209-210; *idem.*, "Carmelitani, Vita mariana," in *DIP* II: 507-508. Not likely is the opinion of C. Kopp, *Elias und Christentum auf dem Karmel* (Paderborn, 1929), pp. 106-122, who holds that there was no Marian element in the origins of the Order.

3. A. Staring, *Medieval Carmelite Heritage. Early Reflection on the Nature of the Order.* (Critical Edition with introduction and Notes. Roma, 1989), p. 61.

4. On the Marian elements present in the Order in the 13th century, see Geagea, *Maria Madre e Decoro del Carmelo*, pp. 59-120, 522-533; Saggi, *Santa Maria*, pp. 6-18; E. Boaga, O.Carm., "Carmelite Devotion toward Our Lady," in *Carmel in the World* 28:1 (1989), 10-17.

5. For this paragraph, see G. Besutti, O.S.M., "Alcune caratteristiche della pietà mariana negli Ordini religiosi dalla riforma gregoriana alla metà del Duecento, in *Alle origini dei Servi* (Monte Senario, 1979), pp. 59-74; *idem* and J. Gribmont, "Maria," DIP V:915-923; Th. Koehler, O.S.M., "Storia della Mariologia," *Nuovo Dizionario di Mariologia*, a cura di S. De Fiores and S. Meo (Cinisello

Balsamo, 1985), pp. 1391-1396; *idem*, "Marie," *Dictionnaire de Spiritualité, Ascétique et Mystique* X:440-454.

6. S. *Bernardi Opera*, ed. By J. Leclercq (Roma,1957-77), *Dominica infra Octavam Assumptionis* 1-2, in V:262-263; cf. *Super "Missus est"*, homilia II, 3, *ibid.*, V:321-322.

7. S. *Bernardi Opera*, *Dominica infra Octavam Assumptionis*, 1-2, V:262-263); cf. *In Nativitate B.V.M.*, 7, *ibid.*, V:279; *Super "Missus est"*, homilia II, 3; *In Adventu*, sermo II, 5, *ibid.*, IV:174).

8. Cf. Cyril of Alexandria, *Homilia XI* (PG 77:1033).

9. John Damascene, *Homilia I in Dormitione B.V.M.* (PG 96:701).

10. S. *Bernardi Opera*, *In Nativitate B.V.M.*, 3, 4, 7, 8, 9 etc. V:276-288; *In vigilia Nativitatis Domini*, III, 10, *ibid.*, IV:219; *In Dominica I post Epiphaniam*, II, 3, *ibid.*, IV:321-322); *Super "Missus est"*, homilia II, 7, *ibid.*, IV:25; *In Assumptione B.V.M.*, IV, 8, *ibid.*, V:249-250.

11. Cf. *Sermo "Missus est"*, homilia II, 7, *ibid.*, IV:25.

12. See especially *Sermo 2 in Assumptione* (PL 185:190-193); *Sermo 192*, 2 (PL 38:1012); *In Lucae evangelio*, 1 (PL 92:320b).

13. Cf. DIP, V:918-919.

14. For other Marian implications of a feudal character in the profession formula used by the Carmelites, see Geagea, *Maria Madre e Decoro del Carmelo*, pp. 544-552.

15. D. Delcorno Branca, *Il romanzo cavalleresco medievale* (Firenze, 1974), pp. 2-7. For a bibliography on the subject, see pp. 46-53.

16. It is significant that St Francis compares his companions "*a Carlo imperatore, a Orlando e Olivieor, e a tutti i paladini e forti campioni che si distinsero in battaglia*", or to the Knights of King Arthur: "*questi sono i miei fratelli, cavalieri della tavola rotonda, che se stanno nascosti in luoghi deserti e solitari per dedicarsi più attentamente alla preghiera e alla meditazione.*" *Speculum Perfectionis*, ed. P. Sabatier (Paris, 1898), capp. 4 and 72; "Intentio Regu-

lae," *Documenta Antiqua Franciscana*, ed. L. Lemmens
(Quaracchi, 1901), p. 90.

17.   See the edition of *Itinera* of the 12th to the 13th centuries
       by S. De Sandoli, *Itinera Hierosolymitana Crucesignatorum*
       (Jerusalem, 1983-1984), III-IV. Other sources are pub-
       lished by: D. Baldi, O.F.M., *Enchiridion Locorum Sanctorum*
       (Jerusalem, 1935). For the itineraries followed by pil-
       grims: M.-H. Vicaire, O.P., "Les trois itinérance du
       pélerinage aux XIIIe e XIVe siècle," *Le pélerinage* (Toulouse,
       1980), pp. 17-41. For this paragraph see also: E. Boaga,
       O.Carm., "La devozione mariana nelle crociate," *La
       dimensione mariana del Carmelo* (Roma, 1989), I: 5-10;
       and the other studies indicated in the following notes.

18.   Cf. D. Baldi, O.F.M., "I santuari mariani in Terra Santa,"
       Studi Francescani Liber annuus 3 (1952-1953), 219-269;
       F.-M. Albel, O.P., "Sanctuaires marials en Palestine," in
       Maria. Études sur la Sainte Vierge, a cura di H. du Manoir,
       S.J., (Paris, 1956), IV:853-866; G. Besutti, O.S.M.,
       "Santuari e pellegrinaggi nella pietà mariana," in *Lateranum*
       48 (1982), 461-463, 471; *idem*, "La storia dei santuari,"
       Liturgia e mobilità urbana (Padova, [1987]), pp. 24-26;
       idem "Santuari," *Nuovo Dizionario di Mariologia*, 1257-
       1259. For the epoch preceding the crusades, see E. Testa,
       O.F.M., *Maria terra vergine*, vol. 2: *Il culto mariano
       palestinese (sec. I-IX)* (Studium Biblicum Franciscanum,
       Collectio Maior, n. 31, Jerusalem, Franciscan Printing
       Press, 1984).

19.   Besides the sources and studies cited in notes 17 and 18,
       see B. Bagatti, O.F.M., "L'apporto degli scavi in Terra
       Santa alla conoscenza di Maria," *Salesianum* 40 (1978),
       151-156; M. Piccirillo, O.F.M., "L'edicola crociata sulla
       tomba della Madonna," *Liber Annuus Studii Biblici
       Franciscani* (Jerusalem, 1972), II:291-314.

20.   Cf. Besutti, *Santuari e pellegrinaggi*, pp. 461-463; *La
       storia dei santuari*, p. 257; *Santuari*, p. 1259.

21.   Boaga, "La devozione mariana nelle crociate," p. 6.

22.   Ibn al-Furat, *Ta'r"ikh al-Duwal wa-al-Muluk* (History of the dynasties and kings), ms Wien Ar. 814, v. VII, ff. 182r-183r. An Italian translation is found in *Storici arabi delle Crociate*, ed. by F. Gabrieli (Torino, 1987), p. 324.

23.   Cf. *Corpus inscriptionum crucesignatorum Terrae Sanctae, 1099-1291*, edited by S. De Sandoli (Jerusalem, 1974), especially pp. LIX-LXI. On this subject see also Boaga, "La devozione mariana nelle crociate," pp. 7-9.

24.   Cf. Boaga, "La devozione mariana nelle crociate," pp. 9-10.

25.   Geagea, *Maria Madre e Decoro del Carmelo*, pp. 522-533.

26.   Honorius of Autun, *Sygillum B. V.M., ubi exponuntur Cantica Canticorum* (PL 172:513).

27.   Philip of Harveng, *Commentaria in Cantica Canticorum* (PL 203:465).

28.   Cf.: Jerome, *Liber de interpretatione Hebraicorum nominum* (CC 72, 92 and 110); St Bede the Venerable, *Capita in Cant. Canticorum* (PL 91:1195); Aimon of Halberstadt, *Expositio in Cant.* (PL 117:344-345); Alan of Lynne, *Compendiosa in Cant. ... elucidatio* (PL 210:100); Smaragdus, *Diadema monachorum* (PL 102:653); Wolberonius, *In Canticum Canticorum* (PL 195: 1233); Thomas Cistercian and John Algrinus, *In Cant. eruditissimi commentarii* (PL 206:721-724); Rupert of Deutz, *In Cant. de incarnatione Domini commentariorum libri VII* (PL 168:946).

29.   Carmelite authors cite do this text of Isaiah in a Marian sense, beginning with Baconthorpe; cf. Geagea, *Maria Madre e decoro del Carmelo*, pp. 457-458.

30.   Cf. ed. *Textum Bibliae postillae* (Parisiis, [1532]), I, f. CCLXX.

31.   This is found already in the 5th century, according to Crisippus of Jerusalem, *Homily on the Holy Mother of God*, 1 (PG 19:293); later, St John Damascene, *Canon of the Most Holy Mother of God*, ode IX, tropari, in *Parakletik* (Roma, 1889), p. 59. The symbolism of the cloud, based especially of texts of Isaiah (19:1 and 45:8) and applied to Mary, Mother of God, virgin and channel of grace, is current in Christian antiquity. So, for example, Pseudo-

Methodius, *Homily on St Simon and Anne*, 7 (PG 18:363), Cyril of Alexandria *Commentary on Isaiah*, 2, 4 (PG 70:452), Pseudo-Epiphanius, *Homily in praise of Holy Mary, Mother of God* (PG 43:485-501), Germanus of Constantinople, *Homily I for the entrance of the Most Holy Virgin*, 14 (PG 98:306), Theodore Studita *Praise for the Dormition of Our Lady, Mother of God*, 4 (PG 99:720-729), Leo VI, *Homily III on the Annunciation* (PG 107:26). In *Speculum carmelitanum*, ed. Daniel of the Virgin Mary, O.Carm. (Anversa, 1680), I:216, the Marian interpretation of the little cloud of Elijah is joined to that based on the texts of Isaiah by Ribot, with references to texts of Jerome, Cyril of Alexandria, Procopius and Ambrose.

32.   Cf. *Speculum carmelitanum* I:240.

33.   Thus, John Baconthorpe, *Speculum de institutione Ordinis Carmelitani*, in Staring, *Medieval Carmelite Heritage*, p. 185; *Laus religionis carmelitanae, ibid.,* 218 ff.); and Felipe Ribot, *De Institutione primorum monachorum*, in *Speculum carmelitanum*, I:235). In his *Maria Patrona, ibid.*, 1730, John Baptist de Lezana cites various authors who admit the Marian symbolism of the little cloud.

34.   On the *exempla* as instruments of teaching and edification, see Cl. Brémond, J. Le Goff, J.-Cl. Schmitt, *L' "exemplum"*, fasc. 40 of *Typologie des sources du Moyen âge occidental*, edited by L. Génicot and R. Bultot (Turnhout, 1982).

35.   Staring, *Medieval Carmelite Heritage*, p. 127-128, 158, 220-221, 373. See also Geagea, *Maria Madre e Decoro del Carmelo*, pp. 458 and 531.

36.   On legends in the Carmelite ambiance cf. E. Carroll, O.Carm., "Legends mariales du Carmel" *Marie*, 5 (1952), 13-15; E. Palumbo, "Le leggende mariane di B. Leersio," *La dimensione mariana del Carmelo*, (Roma, 1989), I:93-97; E. Boaga, *A Senhora do Lugar. Maria na historia e na vida do Carmelo* (Paranavai, 1994), pp. 108-109.

37.   Cf. *Corpus Christianorum, series latina*, 175:129-174.

38. E. Friedman, O.C.D., *The Latin Hermits of Mount Carmel. A study in Carmelite Origins* (Roma, 1979), p. 67.
39. E. von Mülinen, *Breiträge zur Kenntnis des Karmels* (Leipzig, 1908), p. 108, note 1.
40. Friedman, *The Latin Hermits*, p. 67.
41. Cf. De Sandoli, *Itinera Hierosolymitana crucesignatorum*, III, 450, 471; IV, 59, 69.
42. Cf. E. Boaga, O.Carm., "Una lettera 'secreta' di Innocenzo IV a favore dei Carmelitani," *Analecta Ordinis Carmelitarum* 41 (1990), 109-112; the author examines the originals of papal bulls and other 13th century documents referring to the Marian title of the Order.
43. Cf. Boaga, "Carmelite Devotion toward Our Lady," pp. 12-14; *A Senhora do Lugar*, pp. 38-40.
44. Cf. Geagea, *Maria Madre e Decoro del Carmelo*, p. 529.
45. Cf. Boaga, "Una lettera 'secreta' di Innocenzo IV", p. 110.
46. *Summa* III, q. 27, a. 1.
47. Cf. E. Boaga, O.Carm., *La Vergine Bruna e il Carmine Maggiore di Napoli. Fede, Storia, Arte* (Napoli, 1988), p. 3; C. Catena, O.Carm., *Traspontina: guida storica e artistica* (Roma, 1954), p. 51; Saggi, *Santa Maria*, p. 15.
48. Cf. M. Vloberg, "Les Madones dites de Saint-Luc," in *Sanctuaires et Péregrinages* 10 (1964), n. 35, pp. 75-85; Besutti, "Santuari e pellegrinaggi," pp. 479-482; and the word, "Icone," *Nuovo Dizionario di Mariologia*, pp. 672-677.

Arnold Bostius'
Collectarius parvus:
Historical Notes
on the Carmelite Order

Introduction

The following small work, *Collectarius parvus* (a small collection) was found transcribed into one of the notebooks compiled by the English Carmelite, John Bale, during a visit that he made to Northern France and the Low Countries around 1523-1524. The work was brought to my attention by Eamon Carroll whilst he was writing the introduction to our forthcoming edition of Arnold Bostius' *De Patronatu*. At the time, Eamon wished to include in his introduction a reference to the account which Bostius gives of three Franciscans visiting Ghent in 1469 and who recounted to Bostius an attempt made by some Italian Carmelites the previous year to re-establish a community on Mount Carmel. Eamon, though, had mislaid the exact reference and it was only through my trawling through a large number of pages in Bale's notebooks that the story was finally located in chapter twelve of the *Collectarius*. However the search did draw my attention to this small work and to its somewhat unusual contents.

John Bale, to whom we owe the single remaining copy of the *Collectarius*, was an inveterate collector of information about the Carmelite Order; during his trip to the Low Countries he made

103

extensive notes on Carmelite history, on the books that he saw, and on the distinguished members of the Order. Whilst in Belgium, Bale stayed for some weeks or months at Ghent, clearly impressed by its fine library and the number of Carmelite works preserved there which he had not encountered before. He took the opportunity to copy some of the more significant manuscripts that he found, among which were a number of compositions, letters and poems by Arnold Bostius (1445/6-1499), one of the most illustrious alumni of that convent.

The longest and most important of Bostius' works which Bale transcribed was his *De Patronatu*, which Eamon Carroll studied at length in his doctoral thesis and which he and the present author are currently preparing for publication.[1] The manuscript copy which Bale used seems to have been a fair copy of the work which had been prepared for publication after Bostius' death as it includes two epitaphs to Bostius at the beginning. Sadly the *De Patronatu* was never published in its entirety and only reached print in the 17th century in a severely edited edition, lacking one third of its contents, in Daniel of the Virgin Mary's *Speculum Carmelitanum*.[2] Bale's transcription was thought to be the only surviving complete copy of the *De Patronatu*, but an earlier copy, made by a German student in 1485, has recently been identified in Cologne and the readings from this manuscript are now being incorporated into the projected edition of the work.[3]

Other Bostius' compositions copied by Bale whilst he was in Ghent include a copy of *De viris illustribus*, several poems, and a number of his letters.[4] One of the smaller works preserved by Bale is the present *Collectarius parvus* which is a short collection of historical facts about the Carmelite Order never before transcribed or published. Superficially, it resembles another small historical work by Bostius, his *Breviloquium tripartitum*, which survives only in another of Daniel of the Virgin Mary's compilations, the *Vinea Carmeli* (1662).[5] It is hoped to publish the Latin text of the *Collectarius* in an edition of John Bale's Carmelite notebooks and the translation which follows here is taken from the provisional text being prepared for this project.[6]

Dating and Context

It is possible to identify the earliest year for the composition of the *Collectarius* from some internal references to datable events. Bostius mentions a sermon given by Guglielmo di Guidone, the provincial of Sicily, which was preached in Ghent in 1468; the visit of the three Franciscans to Ghent in June, 1469; and he is aware of the death of Françoise d'Amboise which occurred on November 4, 1485. For his information on Françoise d'Amboise, Bostius uses as his source a lost account of her life written by a fellow Carmelite from Ghent who was her confessor, Mathieu de la Croix.[7] Allowing time for Mathieu de la Croix to compile his biography and for a copy to have reached Ghent, Bostius cannot have completed the *Collectarius* before 1486 which forms the *terminus a quo*. Bostius died in 1499 so this provides the *terminus ad quem* for the work.

The context within which the *Collectarius* was written can be appreciated by reference to Bostius' other known historical books, the *Breviloquium tripartita*, *De Patronatu*, two works entitled *De viris illustribus* and his *Speculum historiale*.[8] Whilst the *De Patronatu* can be dated precisely to 1479 from the colophon, the dating of the other works has to be done from internal evidence. In the *Speculum historiale*, Bostius is aware that his fellow countryman, John Beetz, had died on July 17, 1476, and that another, John van Riet (de Arundine), had been consecrated as a bishop in July, 1477. However, elsewhere, the English Carmelite, Walter Hunt, who died on November 28, 1478, is mentioned as still being alive so the work must have been completed not too long after that year.[9] This dates the work probably to the years 1479-1481(?).

It would appear that Bostius composed two works with the same title, *De viris illustribus*. One work survives in full because there is a copy made by Bale in one of his notebooks, but the other is known only because Bale made some brief notes on its contents.[10] That the two works are separate compositions is revealed by the fact that Bale gives them completely distinct *incipits*, and the surviving work has only 44 entries whilst the other appears from Bale's notes to have had more than 85 entries. Dating the surviving work is complicated slightly by the fact that the entries were not all written at the same time. The first 41 entries were completed in 1475 as Bale mentions, at the end of the 41st chapter on Goswin Hex, that he "died last March of the present year", i.e. 1475. The remaining three entries on Walter Hunt, Paul Bisconti and Giovanni Craston were written some time later. Walter Hunt and Paul Bisconti seem to have been added between 1476-1479 as Bostius is aware of Bisconti's death in 1476 but not of Walter Hunt's at the end of 1478. The Giovanni Craston entry is later still as Bostius mentions Bonus Accursius' edition of Craston's Greek *Lexikon* which was not printed until 1483 in Vicenza.

The dating of the larger *De viris illustribus* is more difficult as Bale preserves only the names of the entries and an occasional extra phrase. The latest of the only three dates which Bale copies is 1475, the death of Goswin Hex. However, in this version, Hex is only the 68th entry and, although the names are not in chronological order, there are entries for a number of other younger Carmelites, e.g. Claude Vincent (d.1489) & Nicholas of Alsace (fl.1495). As many of these extra entries are not in Bostius' *Speculum historiale*, it would seem reasonable to conclude that the larger version of the *De viris illustribus* is a later, more mature work and should perhaps be dated to 1485-1490.

Finally, the small *Breviloquium tripartita* is also difficult to date as there are no internal clues as to when it was written. From the style, it appears to be an early work, preceding the larger historical compositions, and hence should probably be dated to the early 1470's. If this is correct, the sequence of Bostius' historical works would seem to be as follows:

> *Breviloquium tripartita* 1470-1475(?)
> *De viris illustribus I*   1475 with additions to 1483+
> *De Patronatu*   1479
> *Speculum historiale*   1479-1481(?)

Collectarius parvus   1486+[11]
De viris illustribus II   1485-1490(?)

Contents

Turning to the contents of the *Collectarius*, the twelve chapters of this work are divided as follows:

Chapter 1:   [Commentaries on the text "Your head is like Carmel"][12]

Chapter 2:   On Elijah and Elisha, the first fathers of the Order of Carmel.

Chapter 3:   On Saint Elijah, first founder of the Order.

Chapter 4:   On Saint John the Baptist and Saint Agabus.

Chapter 5:   On Saint Anthony and the other hermits.

Chapter 6:   On the translation of the bones of Saint John the Baptist.

Chapter 7:   On the cloister of the soul.

Chapter 8:   The witness of Philip of Jerusalem.

Chapter 9:   A wonderful miracle worked by Saint Albert, confessor.

Chapter 10: Of Mount Carmel, from the writings of Ludolph von Suchem and some others.

Chapter 11: On François, sister of the Order of Carmel.

Chapter 12: Of a beautiful miracle and some other events.

From these contents, it is clear that Bostius has not attempted to write a comprehensive history of the Order. There is no systematic account of the development of the Order nor any listing of the important historical milestones. In fact, the impression is of a somewhat random collection of interesting references, historical facts, and recent events of which Bostius has personal experience, arranged in a rough chronological order. In the earlier chapters, there are references to Mount Carmel, Elijah, John the Baptist, etc., which Bostius has traced in works by Bede, Robert

Holcot, Jean Gerson, Hugh of St. Victor, Ulric the Carthusian, Jean Beleth, etc., and to the standard historical works. The later chapters relate some events of which Bostius has personal knowledge, such as the sermon of Guglielmo di Guidone, the visit of the three Franciscans, and the information on Françoise d'Amboise from the life written by a fellow Carmelite from Ghent.

A number of the references or quotations in the *Collectarius* feature in Bostius' other histories. For example, the first quotation from John Cassian (chapter 2) is also cited in chapter 2 of the *De Patronatu*, whilst a shorter account of the miracle attributed to St. Albert and related by Guglielmo di Guidone (chapter 9) can be found in chapter 4 of Bostius' *De viris illustribus*. Similarly, the quotations on the Holy Land (chapter 10) are shorter versions of quotations found in chapter 6 of *De Patronatu*.

In his attribution of the quotations in the *Collectarius*, Bostius has often been betrayed by the sources that he is using. The quote from a supposed letter of Balbinus to the emperor Anthony (chapter 1) is first found in an early manuscript, copied in 1334, of John Baconthorpe's *Compendium*, and the same brief quotation features in many later Carmelite works, from one of which Bostius must have copied it. However, no record of this work survives and it is unknown outside of Carmelite circles. In other instances, Bostius' has misattributed works or made mistakes over their titles. For example, the quotations from Hugh of St. Victor's *De laude patrum* (chapters 2 & 5) turn out to be from his work *De vanitate mundi*. The quotation in chapter 8, supposedly from Philip of Jerusalem's commentary on St. John's gospel, is actually from the better known commentary on the same gospel by Jerome. Robert Holcot, though, is not known to have written any commentary on the Song of Songs, and the source of Bostius' alleged quotation from this work in chapter 1 has not been traced. In fact, it has proved impossible to locate a number of the other quotations which Bostius has cited. All of the texts have been checked in Migne's *Patrologia Latina* using the CD-ROM version and also against the more modern editions contained in the CETEDOC CD-ROM. In spite of using the resources of both the

Queen Mother Library in Aberdeen University and the British Library, a number of Bostius' quotes from fifteenth century writers remain tantalisingly untraceable.

In spite of errors in attribution and a somewhat cavalier attitude to textual accuracy, the breadth of Bostius' reading is impressive, and although not all of the works he quotes would have necessarily been available in the Carmelite library in Ghent, it is clear that the collection there must have been extensive. Sadly, within a few years, the library was to perish in the destruction wreaked by religious zealots during the Wars of Religion.

Purpose of the Work

From the apparently random nature of its contents, the *Collectarius* is clearly not a work designed for someone without any previous acquaintance with the Order's history. The assumption seems to be that the reader is already fairly knowledgeable about the Order and the *Collectarius* is designed to supplement this knowledge with some interesting lesser-known references and accounts of notable events. One might hypothesize that the *Collectarius* was put together for one of Bostius' many correspondants who was already fairly familiar with basic Carmelite history: for instance someone like the Carmelites, John Oudewater (Paleonydorus) or Giles Faber, or the abbot, John Trithemius. All of these persons were friends of Bostius, and each compiled a history of the Order.

Arnold Bostius is one of the outstanding Carmelite writers of the fifteenth century and his writings deserve to be better known. All Carmelite historians owe a debt to Eamon Carroll who, for nearly half a century, has sought to increase our appreciation of Bostius and his writings. However, one of the biggest hurdles has been the lack of availability of texts. Bostius' *De Viris Illustribus I* is the only composition available in a modern edition. Thanks to Daniel of the Virgin Mary, the *Breviloquium, De*

Patronatu and *Speculum historiale* were printed in truncated form in the 17th century. However, all these works remain in Latin and it is a feature of modern-day education that the number of Carmelites who read that language with any facility is fairly small. Only the *De Patronatu* has ever been made available in a modern European language, Spanish. So the following translation of one of Bostius' smaller works is offered to Eamon in appreciation for all his efforts on behalf of this notable Flemish Carmelite and as a small thank you for the many kindnesses which the translator has received.

Richard Copsey, O.Carm.

COLLECTARIUS PARVUS

[fol. 331]

A small collection of some notable facts about the Order of Carmel gathered from various sources by the venerable father Arnold Bostius, a Carmelite of Ghent.

Chapter 1

"Your head is like Carmel" *Song of Songs* 7°.[13] Bede in his commentary of the Song of Songs writes: "The head of the bride is rightly interpreted as the mind of the faithful soul for the members are ruled by the head. Thus the thoughts are disposed by the mind. For what is said of one beloved soul, the prudent reader should realise, is to be understood of the whole church. For though the multitude of believers differ in their merits, they have, however, but one heart and one soul. Insofar as they share one faith, one hope and one love, they all yearn for the same heavenly home. The scriptures relate that on Mount Carmel Elijah prayed on his bended knees. And after a long drought he obtained rains from God. Thus the head of the bride is like Carmel, for the hearts of the elect are lifted up through conversion and they give witness, through the daily practice of virtue, to the Lord, who has himself risen. Elijah, like the Lord God it is said, prayed to the Father for these people and, just as the furrows are opened, he released the rains from heaven, and through this act he encouraged invisibly the worship of God and in response to their prayers and merits often he bestowed his gifts and defended them against the dangers of the world. The name "Carmel" is interpreted as the knowledge of circumcision and is combined with the head of the bride in the mind of the Church, which knows well that it ought to glory not in fleshly but in spiritual circumcision. Of this, the apostle in his letter to the Galatians writes at length and the prophet teaches, saying: 'Circumcise yourselves for the Lord and cut off the foreskin of your hearts'.[14] Thus the Jews shirk this knowledge since for them it was only the external circumcision which they valued, and they did not know about Carmel for they placed their trust in the value of what was the lowest and carnal. Thus, through the voice of the blessed promartyr Stephen, they are rebuked when he says: 'You stubborn people with your uncircumcised hearts and ears, you are always resisting the Holy Spirit.'"[15] Thus writes Bede on the words 'Your head is like Carmel'.[16] Also the abbot of Vercelli explains how these words refer to the high dignity of the Order of Carmelite brothers in his commentary on the Song of Songs, saying thus: "Carmel is luscious and fertile. Carmel because of its height and its fertility and the interpretation of its name (which is the knowledge of circumcision) is called the seraphic order of the bride. For it is the most distinguished of all the other orders and all benefit from its abundance." Thus he writes.[17] And [fol. 331v] Balbinus in his letter to the emperor Anthony: "The mountain called Carmel is where the old religious life and ancient holiness is found. Elijah always offered his sacrifices there. There remain still the remains of an altar for the sacrifices." Thus it is written.[18] Similarly the psalmist: "The mountain in which God is pleased to dwell; for the Lord will live there for ever."[19] "Your head is like Carmel": the *Glosa ordinaria* has: "Your head, that is your mind, which controls the whole body of your thoughts. The mind is lifted up, like Mount Carmel, through the conversion of one's life. And such is the mind which has a knowledge of circumcision not in the sense of a fleshly offering but in an outpouring of the heart."[20] And master Robert Holcot, the English Dominican, in his commentary on the Song of Songs, lecture 7: "Your head, that is the intention that directs a range of actions, just as in the head the collection of members is like Carmel, which is a mountain free from brambles and spines in spite of the terrain. By this is meant that our mind should be lifted up on high through heavenly desires. Carmel is understood as the knowledge of circumcision and signifies an ordered intention towards a right end, through which everything superfluous is pruned and all is done for the honour of God. Thus Jeremiah says: 'Circumcise yourselves for the Lord and cut off the foreskin of your hearts.'[21] By foreskins is meant the worst of the sins that have been cut off from the roots, and thus is the saying of Isaiah fulfilled: 'The glory of Lebanon is bestowed on it, the splendour of Carmel and Sharon.'[22]" Thus he has written.[23] Also, from some other commentary on the Song of Songs: "Your head, that is your intention, should illumine and bring to life the whole body, that is the mass of your actions, like Carmel which is described as a high and great mountain. As if he should say that all your intention should be directed towards the heavens, as directed towards the heavens implies modesty, for the seeker for advancement is hampered by fame. Therefore not by any of the other mountains but by Carmel is meant the intention of the contemplative soul. Thus, Carmel is interpreted as the knowledge of circumcision for all curiosity should be superfluous to the circumcised contemplative mind." Jeremiah chapter 4: "Circumcise yourselves men of Judah, etc." Again the greater and lesser [glosses] on Isaiah chapter 35, 'The glory of Lebanon is bestowed on it',[24] that is, on such a soul for her neck is like an ivory tower and this is the beauty of Carmel, namely, an abstinence from food and drink that pass through the neck, for her head is like Carmel."[25] Master Jean Gerson: "the prelates and rectors of the greater and lesser churches and the doctors ... are called the head on account of their universal governing and influencing power over all spiritual [fol. 332] feelings and emotions, just as bodily nourishment is received from Mount Carmel." This was written by master Jean Gerson, chancellor of Paris, in his commentary on the Song of Songs which begins, "I love your sacred order": he wrote this commentary in Lyons in 1429 and died the same year.[26]

Chapter 2:   On Elijah and Elisha, the First Fathers of the Order of Carmel

"Some make it their whole purpose to aim at the secrecy of the anchorite and purity of heart, as we know that in the past Elijah and Elisha and in our own day the blessed Anthony and others who followed with the same object, were joined most closely to God by the silence of solitude." This is in the conferences of the fathers, chapter 4, the conference of abbot Nesteros on spiritual knowledge, a conference which is well worth noting.[27] Again, he says in his second conference, chapter 3, which is on divine gifts: "And certainly it was not the ostentation of glory but the love of Christ and the good of all the people that wrung from the blessed Elijah the performance of miracles, as the passage in the book of Kings shows us. He asked that fire might descend from heaven on the sacrifices laid on the pyre, for this reason that he might set free the faith of the whole people which was endangered by the tricks of the false prophets."[28] And in the conference of the abbot Theonas, chapter 4, on remission during the fifty days:[29] "so we are sure that Elijah and Jeremiah were not under the law, as though they might without blame have taken advantage of lawful matrimony, yet they preferred to remain virgins. So we read that Elisha and others of the same mode of life went beyond the commands of Moses, as of them the Apostle speaks as follows: 'They went about in sheepskins and goatskins, they were oppressed, afflicted, in want, of whom the world was not worthy, they wandered about in deserts and in mountains and in caves and in dens of the earth.'"[30] Hugh of Saint Victor in his sermon *In praise of the fathers* has: "There arose prophets and diligent men, inspired by the spirit, who prophesied under the influence of the spirit and sought to avert God's anger. And there came Elijah the Tishbite, sealing up the rain in heaven and forbidding the dew to settle. He drew down fire and made flames descend from above manifesting the anger of the Lord's fury, so that he could show righteousness coming from on high. The prophets of Baal ran before him and he overcame them, all alone, in a holy trial, so that he might give glory to God. The dead rose in answer to his prayer as if awakened from sleep,[31] and he was carried up into heaven in a fiery chariot and was never seen again by men on earth.[32] Wrapt in his cloak, Elisha divided the Jordan and crossed over, showing that he had taken his place with a double portion of his spirit.[33] He made the waters drinkable and neutralised poisoned food with seasoning, [fol. 332v] he called back souls which were departing to their graves.[34] He sent an armed force by another route, and in the sight of the king miraculously revealed a multitude of fiery chariots.[35] Micaiah saw the Lord in the heavens and feared not the impious king, constantly reproving him for his abominations.[36] Jonas was swallowed by a whale and then thrown up on dry land so that he should announce, as he had been commanded, the destruction of the Ninevites."[37] All this is taken, word for word, from the sermon in praise of the fathers by Hugh of Saint Victor.[38]

Bede's Commentary on the Song of Songs, on the words "Jealousy as relentless as the underworld":[39] "The jealousy of the faithful, who are pure and devoted to God, is likened to the underworld for, like that place which once it has received someone never releases them, so the tenacity of their fervent zeal never weakens at any time. This is the zeal which filled Phinehas when he threw down the fornicators in the wilderness,[40] the same which consumed Elijah when, after having sealed up the waters in the heavens, three years later he called the heart of the people to turn back to the Lord, crying out: 'I am filled with zeal for the Lord God of hosts because the sons of Israel have betrayed their covenant with the Lord, they have destroyed your altars and they have killed your prophets with the sword.'"[41] Thus he has written.[42]

"Prophecy calls for a supreme elevation of mind to contemplative and spiritual realities. This is indeed impaired by vehemence of the passions and by inordinate occupation with external affairs. So we read that the sons of the prophets, in the 2nd book of Kings, chapter 4,[43] lived together with Elisha–living as it were a solitary life lest they should be impeded in the gift of prophecy by worldly occupations." So writes Saint Thomas in book 2, part 2, question 172, article 4, in the body of the text near the end.[44] Bede in his commentary on Samuel has: "Their possession," that is of the company of scribes and pharisees, "in Carmel, that is the knowledge of circumcision, for although the reading of the law gave them an understanding of the true chastisement, it did not give them a perfect one, for the written word points to what is ordered, however not it but grace gives perfect direction. Therefore, they confirm the chastisement, not perfectly but through knowledge. The pharisee and the legal scribe have possession of the law, for the law and prophecy were given through Moses, but grace and truth came through Jesus."[45]

Chapter 3:   On Saint Elijah, First Founder of the Order

From the legend of saint Abund, priest and monk of the Cistercian Order in the monastery at Villers-La-Ville in Brabant: "This blessed father on one occasion when he was persevering in most devout prayer was caught up in a mystical experience and he became aware of being led by someone dressed in the habit of a monk into a wonderful orchard like a paradise filled with the most beautiful fruitful trees. His guide left him to wander through the orchard and there he found under an arbour [fol. 333] an old man who had a book before him and in which he was writing, gradually and slowly. And this book was full of writing except for the last four pages in which nothing had been entered. Seeing him, Abund addressed the old man in this fashion: 'I beg you reverend father that you would tell me who you are and what is this book, and what you are writing in it, and why you are writing so slowly.' The old man replied: 'I am Elijah who, as sacred

scripture testifies, was lifted up from here in a fiery chariot. This
book is called the book of life, in which the names of all the elect
and the saved are written, and whenever some holy man dies, his
death and his name are revealed to me by the Holy Spirit and then
I write his name in this book. And, as you can understand, I write
so slowly in this book because only a few are saved. When these
last four pages are filled, the world will end and then Christ will
come in judgement and reward each one according to his merits.'"
This is what is there. Thus claims John Belleus in a sermon or
little book on the Assumption of the Virgin, chapter 12, which, at
the request of many devout persons, he wrote in German, and it
is in the house of the holy nuns of St. Agnes in Ghent.[46]

Also John Ballester, in his book *On the last days*, which
was sent to the pope, describes most clearly the six prerogatives
of Elijah that make him so commendable, admirable and most
worthy of imitation, together with other aspects.[47]

Chapter 4:   On Saint John the Baptist and Saint Agabus

"After the ascent of Elijah, his successor Elisha (upon
whom a double portion of Elijah's spirit remained) with the other
sons of the prophets attracted many people through their exemplary lives to live devotedly on the same Mount Carmel. And from
this, it is said that saint John the Baptist was inspired by devotion
to the place to frequent the said mountain and similarly many
other saints." Thus master Grossy, the 22nd prior general.[48] This
is confirmed by the abbot of Vercelli when writing on the text,
"What did you go into the desert to see?"[49] And Dom Ulricus, the
Carthusian,[50] and others with saint Macarius: "Therefore, here
and there, through all the peoples of the nations the divine grace
was already being poured out lavishly, first Cornelius at Caesarea
that great Palestinian city, with all his household, was led by
Peter's ministrations to the faith of Christ. And there were already
many others from the populace in Antioch who came to the faith
drawn by the preaching of those who, fearful after the betrayal of
Stephen, dispersed themselves throughout all the places which

we have mentioned above. Through them a flourishing church was formed at Antioch, [fol. 333v] in which there were many men of the order of prophets, and with them were Barnabus and Paul. All of whom lived equally in the grace of God and in unity, and there, from the everlasting fountain full of words, the disciples were first called Christians."[51]

"At which time, a certain Agabus, from among the prophets who were there, was inspired in prayer to prophesy a great famine. Paul and Barnabus set out with a collection taken up by the brothers for the use of the saints in Jerusalem."[52] Thus Eusebius in the 2nd book of his *History of the Church*.[53] This Agabus was of the order of prophets, that is of the Carmelites, as is clear in the records and as Baptist of Mantua states in his *Parthenice* to the blessed Virgin Mary.[54] "16. Gaius had reigned the kingdom for less than four years when he was succeeded by the emperor Claudius. In his time, a severe famine descended on the whole world. But this had been predicted long before by our holy prophets, as is related in the Acts of the Apostles. A certain prophet, Agabus, had warned of a great famine in the reign of emperor Claudius. And Luke, referring to Agabus, adds:[55] 'Also the brothers who were at Antioch, took a collection from everyone of the men and they sent it, by the hands of Paul and Barnabus, to the saints dwelling in Jerusalem.'" Thus in the same *History of the Church*, book 2, chapter 8.[56]

Chapter 5:   On Saint Anthony and the Other Hermits

"Along the road to Saint Anthony's, we saw castles and fortresses the lords of which as well as they themselves had been struck by lightening for their maltreatment of pilgrims. This was the work of the renewer of life of Elijah who shared his predecessor's holiness and especial powers. Like Elijah, he called down swiftly in vengeance on the rebels the same fire which he extinguished when he healed those who besought his aid." This is in chapter 14 of the fifth book of the legend of saint Hugh, bishop of Lincoln, of the Carthusian Order.[57] The following is by the same Anthony in his life of Pachomius, whose prologue begins "Venerable Lord." "And, at the same time, the life of blessed Anthony was totally dedicated to the imitation of this way of living. And who, being an follower of the great Elijah and Elisha as well as Saint John the Baptist, was extraordinarily devoted to the study of the secrets of the internal hermitage."[58] Of whom saint Athanasius, bishop of the city of Alexandria, gave witness in a fine style; a balanced, worthy observer of the way of life of Anthony and, following the supplication of the brethren, he wrote his life for the help of many and showed how it might be imitated by spiritual men. For example, he has: "He remembered also that Anthony in referring to the saying of the prophet Elijah, 'The Lord lives in whose sight I stand today' explained why the word 'today' was used. It was because Elijah did not count time past [fol. 334] and that it was today that was the time of trial." There follows "therefore reckoning that he ought to be the servant of God, he sought to follow the example derived from the way of life of the great Elijah, and that he ought to mould his life on that model." Thus blessed Athanasius on the life of the abbot, saint Anthony.[59]

And the abbot Piamun in the conferences of the fathers, chapter 6 on the three sorts of monks, says: "Anchorites, that means solitaries, because, being by no means satisfied with that victory whereby they had trodden under foot the hidden snares of the devil while still living among men, they were eager to fight with the devils in open conflict and a straightforward battle. And so they feared not to penetrate the vast recesses of the desert, imitating John the Baptist (who passed all his life in the desert) and Elijah and Elisha and of those whom the Apostle commemorates thus: 'They wandered about in sheepskins and goatskins, etc.'"[60] Thus he writes.

Hugh of Saint Victor in his sermon in praise of the fathers has: "The deserts were turned into fertile places when they received this infusion of heavenly grace, they flourished in happiness. The empty wastes were filled up and floods of grace were poured out on their dryness. Paul and Anthony and Hilarion were like precious stones where there was once no value and beauty, and they built a marvellous structure on the foundation that they had laid, as a house was built a short way into the desert of Lebanon and a short way on Carmel measured towards Lebanon. Macarius and Pafnutius and Arsenius and Pastor, joined with Moses in the same spirit and virtue, led many people to God, to the promised land through the age-old desert, and with these, all those named, holy and elect men, powerful workers of miracles, passed." Thus Hugh, as above.[61]

In the first chapter of book 2 of the *Tripartite History*: "Also there shone bishop Paphnucius in the upper Thebaides and Spiridion in Cyprus":[62] there are other references also to these men.

Chapter 6:   On the Translation of the Bones of Saint John the Baptist

In the time of Julian the apostate, as if the reins had been loosened, the rage of the pagans burst out in all its savagery. From this, it happened that at Sebasten, a city in Palestine, fired by enraged minds and destructive hands, the pagans broke into the grave of blessed John the Baptist, dispersed his bones and then, after collecting them again, burnt them with fire, mixed the holy ashes with dirt and spread them through the fields and country-side. But, by the providence of God, it happened that some men arrived from Jerusalem, from the monastery of Philip, a man of God who had been forewarned in his prayers that they should come at that time. Who, when they saw such wickedness [fol. 334v] being done by human hands driven by savage minds and having more gracious habits than such wild excesses, they mixed carefully among those who were gathering the bones to burn and, as far as it was possible, they piously gathered these venerable relics in order to steal them away secretly from these drunken or insane creatures and to bring them to their holy father Philip. Having brought them to him, he venerated such a great treasure with appropriate vigils and then sent the relics of this immaculate victim to the archbishop of Alexandria, at that time Athanasius, by the hand of Julian his deacon, who became later bishop of a city of Palestine. Once Athanasius had received them and, after some consideration, they were enclosed in a reliquary embedded in a wall and so, moved by a prophetic impulse, he preserved them for future generations to come." Thus Rufinus in book 2 of his work, *The History of the Church*, chapter 28.[63]

At this time, the Carmelites multiplied in the Holy Land and in Egypt, many monasteries and hermitages being constructed and they spread beyond counting. And here they dwelt as solitaries, solicitously building up the cloister of the soul, striving vigilantly to serve God following the way of life which had been passed on to them. On whom, a certain person wrote something on the cloister of the soul.[64]

Chapter 7:   On the Cloister of the Soul

"Listen to me and do what I recommend and you will be perfect",[65] and if in everything and through everything they do only that which is good then they will be in the cloisters of holy thoughts. How can this be done, you ask? In yourself, I say, you create such a monastery, insofar as your peaceful heart is a monastery. In which, Jesus Christ is the father, discretion is the prior, gentleness the subprior, the Holy Spirit the student, patience the cellarer, all the brothers in the convent are the exercises of meditation, the porter is the fear of God, obedience the novice-master, the versicularian is silence, the chapter is truthfulness about sins, the housekeeper liberality, hatred becomes obeying discipline,[66] the refectory piety, prayer persuading enemies to live in peace, the grace of counsel, spiritual fervour is the priest hedomadarian, the church is unity together in the Lord, the choir is devotion, the altar charity, incense is love, religious modesty is the gatekeeper, the cantor gratitude, poverty the procurator, the accolytes are the angels. For all these administrators are, according to the Apostle, spirits sent to serve those who will be the heirs.[67] Knowledge of the truth is a cross. Thus Ecclesiasticus, chapter 6: "Who adds knowledge, accomplishes a good work",[68] and that in every faculty. Note that knowledge of the truth for the zealous is a cross as it is said by the Saviour, "An enemy on the way"[69] in which the man, hating his own flesh and other desires and wishes, comes to a knowledge of the truth, that is, as the gospel states: "Whoever wants to follow me, must forget himself and take up his cross, etc.[70] [fol. 335] In other words, he who lacks zeal commits betrayal, of whom the apostle says: "Betraying the word of God, etc."[71]

There follows the arms of Jesus Christ: "Zeal for the right is the lance, pangs of conscience are the three nails, which are for one's own and for others' sins, the crown of thorns is offences to God and violence to or oppression of one's neighbours, good practices are a solemn procession, gall is mixted with vinegar, remembrance of the dead is the cemetery, food is the word of God, mercy is the infirmary, spiritual sweetness is drink, temperance the dining room, the dormitory chastity, modesty the parlour, the cell simplicity, the table sobriety, the bed tranquillity of soul, the pillow a quiet mind, to have peace in oneself is to have a source always fresh, a peacemaker is like an orchard with all types of fruit. Always go over these principles diligently as to which of them or what or in how much you are lacking in them and, in your cell, carefully examine yourself daily on them. Then you will recover through prayer those lost feelings of remorse.

> Whenever a cell is rightly used, like a cleared space
> It may be well seen how the bad is separated from
>   the pure:
> The bad is put away and trust placed in heavenly
>   promises,
> Heaven gives the seed, other vanities come from
>   the earth.
> O cell, I bid farewell to you and, at the same time,
>   I bless you:
> It is you for a little while that brightens this sinful
>   world
> I praise you also, O friend, I unite to you in feeling:

You are for me a trial, comfort comes to me
   through your test.
But now, through you, I hope to mount the path
This to the hope, to which free from all concealment
This the Father, this the Spirit, this the Son have
   promised. Amen.

Chapter 8:   The Witness of Philip of Jerusalem

Abbot Philip of Jerusalem on the first chapter of John's
gospel:[72] "They sent," he writes, "priest and levites from Jerusalem to John the Baptist dwelling with his Carmelite brothers in
the hermitage near the river Jordan, and they asked him: 'Who are
you?'[73] And he confessed that he was not the Christ, which was
the belief that many of the public were discussing. Neither was he
Elijah nor a prophet.[74] For they were looking for Elijah and, in the
name of a prophet, for Elisha. Firstly, see how the idea of baptism
is prefigured in these two prophets. As secondly, because he lived
in the wilderness, John wore a garment woven from camel hair
just like Elijah. John girded a leather belt around his loins like
Elijah. Both also, that is John and Elijah, wore a garment around
their shoulders. These were tunics without sleeves, covering from
the neck down to the kidneys, open on both sides, [fol. 335v] with
the arms left bare and the rear part was joined over at the
shoulders.[75] John wore a white circular cloak which fell from the
shoulders to the ground, the front open but all the rest closed, just
like Elijah. Through this, Elijah taught his disciples, the Carmelites,
that they ought to wear a white cloak over everything, just as the
Lord had foreshown them dressed in white to Sabacha, the father
of Elijah, as before the birth of his son, Sabacha had seen in a
dream men dressed in white who saluted him. This white cloak,
Elijah the prophet and first member of the Carmelite religious
Order, left to Elisha when he departed from him and ascended
into the heavenly paradise.[76]

"These clothes together with a right finger and some bones of John the Baptist were recently presented to me by two monks from Mount Carmel. I have sent these garments and the bones by our beloved son, deacon Julian, to our venerable brother Athanasius, bishop of Alexandria."

O Order of Carmelites, how great you have become in the house of the Lord. For formerly you had your origin from the small fountain of Elijah, the prophet of God. And now behold you have grown into a great river. Formerly you were planted in a wilderness and now you have become a city full of people. You have as a founder one who is now living into paradise and the glorious Virgin Mary, queen of heaven, mistress of the world, as a unique patroness.

And a little after he adds: "Just as from him, formerly, there proceeded the patriarchs and the prophets, so now from him come the priests and levites, the doctors and evangelists, and those who are made the fathers and patrons of all the religious."[77] Thus this together with many other passages.

For this abbot Philip and his monks, see Rufinus, *History of the Church*, book 2, chapter 29: and the venerable Bede, *De temporibus (On the times)*: and Vincent refers to him in his *Speculum Historiale (Mirror of History)*, book 15, chapter 32.[78] And it is said that he was the 9th bishop of Jerusalem after saint James.

Chapter 9:   A Wonderful Miracle Worked by Saint Albert, Confessor

In the year of our Lord 1463, blessed Albert of the Order of the most highly exalted mother of God, Mary, of Mount Carmel, a friar in Agrigento, a city of no little fame in the kingdom of Sicily, worked many miracles. It was an accepted custom in that city, on the day on which this happy Albert bade farewell to our earthly darkness and entered heaven, that there should be a procession.

Aware of this, the venerable professor of sacred theology, Guglielmo di Guidone, a brother of the said Order and the prior in his house, went to the bishop asking to hold for a public celebration in his convent at which the bishop would be present so that the feastday of saint Albert, a member of his Order, should be most worthily commemorated. And so the bishop [fol. 336] came with the people in a procession and gathered in the convent of the said brothers, and the aforesaid doctor mounted into the pulpit and recounted the miracles which had been wrought by God because of the merits and intercession of this most saintly man. But there was more. A certain woman, among the innumerable people of both sexes in the crowds, was present at this sermon. This devoted woman, full of faith, hearing the words spoken about the beloved servant of God, Albert, was filled with a singular devotion. She had a young child who had been afflicted by an illness and who had passed away, in that same week as she heard the sermon from the said doctor on glorious Albert. Seeing that, the grieving mother sought divine aid and with a heartfelt plea to the greatest of all doctors, she spoke the following words: "O omnipotent God, who works many miracles through the most blessed Albert, I beg that through his recent merits, my son may be restored to life and safety." And God, wanting to glorify his saint once more, acted without delay; her son opened his eyes, regained the use of his limbs and straightaway was restored to life completely whole and sound. The excited mother, with her resuscitated son, went to the aforesaid convent, and gave her thanks before the picture of saint Albert for this amazing miracle. And then, with great joy, she related what had happened to the aforesaid prior, master Guglielmo, in the presence of the illustrious prince, lord Anthony, count of Calathamxerche, and the noble knight John of Landolin, both of whom had the previous Sunday been present during the sermon and taken part in the general procession with the said woman. This miracle the same doctor related at Ghent in 1468 at the time when Margaret, the sister of king Edward IV of England, wife of the most illustrious Duke Charles of Burgundy, was first received in Ghent.[79]

**Chapter 10:   Of Mount Carmel, from the Writings of Ludolph
von Suchem and Some Others**

Ludolph in his book *On the state and conditions of the Holy
Land and other lands beyond the seas* (which was dedicated to
Baldwin, bishop of Paderburn, in 1342 AD) says: "Near Acre, three
miles to the right, not far from the sea, is Mount Carmel. It is flat
and spacious and its summit is most beautiful, being covered with
many herbs and other delights. On this mountain, the prophet
Elijah dwelt and worked many miracles.[80] Also, on this mountain,
at his word, some groups of fifty soldiers sent by King Ahaziah of
Israel were consumed by fire from heaven. Also on this mountain
he prayed that it should not rain on the land and it did not rain
for three years and six months.[81] On this mountain can be seen
an exceedingly fine monastery which has been constructed in
honour of Saint Mary, [fol. 336v] and the brothers who had their
beginnings here are called Carmelites up to the present day. And
they are known to have had fifteen beautiful monasteries in the
Holy Land. On one side of the mountain there is a clear fountain
which runs away down to the sea, where the prophet Elijah drank
and it is still called the fountain of Elijah. At the other foot of the
mountain, it is known that there stood the most beautiful city of
the Templars, called Cayphas, but which is now totally destroyed.
Not far from this city is a small fountain which is the source of one
branch of the river Jordan. At the end of Mount Carmel a beautiful
city was sited, called Jesrahel, but this is now desert. There queen
Jezabel seized Naboth's vineyard and there she was thrown down,
as is related in the Book of Kings.[82] And near this city are the
camps of Mangadi where Joas, king of Juda, was killed.[83] Not far
from Mount Carmel and also sited on the mountain was formerly
the beautiful city of Sephora but this is now destroyed. There saint
Anne, mother of the Virgin Mary, was born."[84] This is written in
the aforesaid book by Louis of Sychem, along with other things.[85]

Also from the history of Wilbernus: "Between Acre and
Gaza, the Philistine city near Acco, four miles above the sea to the
right is Mount Carmel, not very high, oblong, flat on top, very

beautiful and fertile. Saint Elijah dwelt there and there the Order of Carmelites had its beginnings. That mountain contains many famous/holy churches and pleasing hermitages. At the foot of the mountain was the Christian city of Cayphas, now destroyed." Thus lord Wilbernus, lord of "Bendenscele Alcavus" in his *History of the Parts of the Holy Land*, which he compiled in 1336 AD at the request of his eminence Talleyrand, bishop of Perigord and cardinal priest of St. Peter in Chains.[86]

John Boccacio di Certaldo in his book *The Mountains* says: "Carmel is a mountain in Phoenicia, the home of the famous prophet Elijah, and noted for the olive trees, woods, and vineyards which surround it for about two days journey. At the foot of it is a lake called Candebora, from which a beautiful river flows, from which comes a sand which is used in making a crystal glass finer than all the others." Thus it is written.[87]

Chapter 11:   On François, Sister of the Order of Carmel

The most illustrious Françoise, widow of the dynamic Peter, duke of Brittany, at a time of life when her powers were at their height, in 1467 AD (according to the Gallic calendar)[88] on the Feast of the Annunciation of the glorious Virgin Mary, rejecting the king of France, the Duke of Brittany and other princes, conscious that they would impede her search for spiritual perfection, bidding farewell to the world, she received the holy habit of the same most blessed Mother of God, Mary of Mount Carmel, in the monastery of the sisters of the said Order outside the city of Nantes, near the convent of Bonidoni which she had founded, from our most reverend father, master Jean Soreth, prior general both of the Order of Brothers and–as often said–of Sisters and a most praiseworthy reformer. On the same day, one year later, to the same father, she made her profession of faith and her vow of perpetual celibacy, and she accepted Him as her spouse, whose mother was a virgin and whose father never knew a woman. She died on November 4, 1485. This account of her life was written by Mathieu de la Croix, her spiritual director and confessor.[89]

Chapter 12:   Of a Beautiful Miracle and Some Other Events

A certain brother of the Carmelite Order was tempted to leave the Order when he heard that brother Jordan had been drowned whilst travelling to Jerusalem. This master Jordan was the second prior general of the Order of Preachers and he was drowned in 1236 AD. The aforesaid Carmelite was more and more troubled, saying to himself: 'Either this man was not a good man for him to perish so, or God does not reward well those who serve him.' Having thus made up his mind to leave quickly, there appeared to him that same night a glorious figure surrounded by a very bright light. Shaking and nearly fainting, he prayed, saying: 'Lord Jesus Christ help, me and reveal to me what this is.' And immediately brother Jordan replied to him: 'Do not be disturbed, dear one, for I am brother Jordan about whom you are worrying. And I assure you that everyone will be saved who serves our Lord Jesus Christ until the end.' And this said, he disappeared, and so that brother had all his difficulties resolved and he persevered in his Order. This brother and the prior general of that Order, brother Simon Stock, a holy and trustworthy man, related this tale to our brothers of the Order of Preachers. This miracle is found in *The Lives of the Brothers of the Order of Preachers*, chapter 40, third part.[90]

In the same year, there lived Vincent who, on the approval of the Carmelite Order, wrote: "Pope Honorius III approved the rule of the hermit brothers living on Mount Carmel where, it is written, Elijah used to visit, and he awarded an indulgence to those who observed this rule which was written by the patriarch, the venerable Albert. After this, Honorius' successor, Gregory, confirmed the same rule. After this, in the year of our Lord 1238, because of the incursions of the pagans, they were compelled to leave their site on Carmel and were dispersed to the various regions of the world." This is in the *Speculum historiale*, book 31, chapter 23.[91]

Also, on the feast of the martyrs Primus and Felician[92] in the year of our Lord 1469, three brothers of the Order of Friars

Minor from the convent of Mount Sion in Jerusalem came to Ghent, seeking lodgings for a while in the convent of the Order of the most blessed Mary, Mother of God, of Mount Carmel. These had been sent by their guardian to the illustrious prince Charles of Burgundy, duke and count of Flanders, who at that time was staying in Ghent with his wife and daughter, in order to beg the duke to continue the subsidy which his father, the invincible Philip, had for a long time generously contributed. Whilst in the said Carmelite convent, these brothers related, amongst other things, that four or five Italian brothers from our Carmelite Order had, less than a year ago, gone to the Holy Land and petitioned the sultan in residence there that they might settle on Mount Carmel at the ancient site belonging to our fathers and that in the chapel of the holy Virgin Mary, which still remains to this day, they might fulfill their duty to their God. But that vile dog, an enemy of the cross of Christ, did not give any response to their earnest prayers. May our Lord Jesus Christ who has consecrated the whole of that land with his precious blood see fit to rescue it from the hands of the infidels and may the Order of Carmelite brothers once more peacefully dwell on Mount Carmel, the ancient possession of Elijah and Elisha. Amen.

The end of the brief chronicle of the Order of Carmel collected by brother Arnold Bostius of Ghent.

Endnotes

1. Eamon Carroll, "The Marian theology of Arnold Bostius, O.Carm. (1445-1499)," *Carmelus* 9 (1962), 197-236.

2. *Speculum Carmelitanum*, edited by Daniel a Virgine Maria, O.Carm. (Venice, 1680), I: 375-431.

3. The *De Patronatu* is found in (a) Cologne, Stadtarchiv, Ms. W 203, fos. 195-302 and (b) Brit. Libr., Ms. Selden supra 41, fos. 221-315 (copy made by John Bale c1524).

4. Arnold Bostius, *De viris illustribus*, in Christine Jackson-Holzberg, *Zwei Literaturgeschichten des Karmelitenordens; Untersuchungen und kritische Edition* (Erlangen: Verlag Palme und Enke, 1981), 122-169. Bostius' letters have been edited in Paul Demaerel, "Arnoldi Bostii, O.Carm. (1445-1499), vita et epistolae: Biografisch onderzoek en kritische, gekommenteerde uitgave van zijn korrespondie," 2 v. Licentiate thesis, Louvain, n.d. [1983]. However Demaerel was unaware of a further collection of letters by Bostius and his contemporaries which survives in Cambridge, Corpus Christi College, Ms. 152, fols. 93 ff. This collection contains 8 letters written by Bostius and 2 addressed to him. Two of these are not included in Demaerel's edition and a third contains poems which were not in the copy known to Demaerel. Among the other correspondents are the Carmelites John Oudewater (Paleonydorus) and John Hasart, the master general of the Trinitarians, Robert Gaguin, and the Benedictine abbot, John Trithemius. The Corpus Christi collection is in an unknown hand but it is reasonable to suppose that it was brought to England by Bale. Subsequently it passed into Archbishop Parker's library and on his death was bequeathed to Corpus Christi College.

5. "Breviloquium tripartitum de institutione, intitulatione ac confirmatione ordinis Deiparae Virginis Mariae de monte Carmelo", *Vinea Carmeli; seu historia Eliani Ordinis*

B.mae V. Mariae de Monte Carmeli, edited by Daniel a Virgine Maria, (Antwerp, 1662), 49-81.

6.   Purely textual notes have been omitted from this translation.

7.   Mathieu de la Croix was subprior at Ghent until 1467 when he was appointed prior of Liége by Jean Soreth. After a year, he moved to become the confessor to Bl Françoise d'Amboise and her nuns in Nantes where he remained for 17 years.

8.   The *Speculum historiale sectatorum sanctorum prophetarum Eliae et Elisei, de institutione et peculiaribus gestis ac viris illustribus sacri ordinis beatissimae Dei Genitricis Virginis Mariae de monte Carmelo* survives in Milan, Biblioteca Brera, Ms. A. E. XII, 22 (a copy made by John Gerbrand on December 11, 1491, at Leyden).

9.   For Beetz, see *Speculum*, p. 572 (Bostius has 1477 in error): for Van Riet, see p. 564: for Hunt, see p. 570.

10.   Oxford, Bodleian Library, Ms Bodley 73, fols. 118r-v.

11.   The *Speculum historiale* is normally dated to "before 1491", the date of the one surviving copy. However, little serious study has been made of its contents.

12.   Bale has not preserved a title for this chapter but it is composed of quotations from commentaries on the Song of Songs, on the text "Your head is like Carmel".

13.   Song 7:6.

14.   Jer 4:4.

15.   Acts 7:51.

16.   Bede, *In Cantica Canticorum*, edited by D. Hurst, CCSL 119B (1983), 325, lines 335-363.

17.   This commentary on the Song of Songs by the "abbot of Vercelli" has not been traced.

18.   A work unknown outside of Carmelite circles. This quotation, all that is ever cited, is first found in an early manuscript of John Baconthorpe's *Compendium* (copied in 1334). See Adrian Staring, O.Carm., *Medieval Carmelite Heritage* (Rome: Institutum Carmelitanum, 1989), 203.

The quote recurs in later Carmelite works and it was probably copied by Bostius from Felip Ribot's *De Institutione*, bk 3, chap. 3. See Paul Chandler, O.Carm., "The *Liber de institutione et peculiaribus gestis religiosorum carmelitarum in lege veteri exortorum et in nova perseverancium ad Caprasium monachum*" (Doctoral Dissertation, Toronto, 1991), p. 121.

19. Ps 68:16.

20. *Glosa ordinaria* (Strasbourg, 1480; facsimile reproduction, Turnhout, 1992), 4 vols. Not available for consultation.

21. Jer 4:4.

22. Is 35:2.

23. Robert Holcot is not known to have written a commentary on the Song of Songs. Cf. Richard Sharpe, *A Handlist of the Latin Writers of Great Britain and Ireland before 1540* (Brepols, 1997), pp. 553-558. The quotation here is so far untraced.

24. Is 35:2.

25. Bostius gives the title *Maiores et minores* but this gloss or commentary is so far untraced.

26. Jean Gerson, *Super Cantica Canticorum*, in *Oeuvres complètes* (Paris: Desclée & Cie, 1971) VII:630 (the two parts of the quotation come from lines 5-6 & 34-36). Bale has copied the date as 1429 in error.

27. John Cassian, *Conferences 14*, chapter 4, in *A Select Library of Nicene and Post-Nicene Fathers* (1894) Vol. XI; translation of Edgar C. S. Gibson, 436. Bale's text misreads "knowledge (*sciencia*)" in the title as "sect (*secta*)".

28. John Cassian, *Conferences 15*, chapter 3, in *op. cit.*, 447. (The translation has been modified slightly to fit Bostius' text. In the original, the first sentence refers to Abbot Macarius). Bale's text again misreads the title, having "On diverse (*diversa*) gifts" instead of "On divine (*divina*) gifts."

29. The title refers to the relaxation of the laws of fasting during the fifty days between Easter and Pentecost.

30. Hb 11:37-38: John Cassian, *Conferences 21*, chapter 4, in *op. cit.*, 504.

31. Cf. 1 Kgs 17:17-24.

32. Cf. 2 Kgs 2:1-13.

33. 2 Kgs 2:14-16.

34. 2 Kgs 2:19-22; 4:38-41; 4:8-37.

35. 2 Kgs 6:8-23.

36. Cf. 1 Kgs 22.

37. Jon 2:1-11.

38. *Recte* Hugh of St. Victor, *De vanitate mundi*, lib. 4 in PL 176:731C-D.

39. Song 8:6.

40. Num 25:6-8.

41. 1 Kgs 19:10.

42. Bede, *op.cit.*, lines 325-333.

43. Cf. 2 Kgs 4:38.

44. Thomas Aquinas, *Summa theologicae* (edited by Roland Potter, O.P., Oxford, 1970), 45:40.

45. Jn 1:17; the word "prophecy" is added by Bostius. Bede, *In Primam Partem Samvhelis Libri III*, in CCSL 119:232, lines 845-852.

46. Jean Belleus, *In Assumptione Virginis*, cap. 12. Not traced.

47. Juan Ballister (d. 1384), *De bello forti militantis ecclesiae & antichristo ipsam impugnante*. A copy of this work was sent to pope Gregory XI. The whole of this chapter was copied by Bale in *Bodley 73*, fol. 184v.

48. Jean Grossy (d. 1437), *Viridarium*, clavis prima (edited by Graziano a Santa Teresa, O.C.D., *Ephemerides carmeliticae* 7 (1956), 266.

49. Mt 11:7; Lk 7:24.

50. Ulrich of Wurzburg (fl. 1480), a Carthusian, addressed a formal letter to the Carmelites of Wurzburg accompanied by a poem commemorating Elijah, Elisha and the origins of the Carmelite Order. Parts of the poem survive in Bostius' *De Patronatu*.

51. Cf. Acts 11:26: Freculphus Lexovensis, *Chronica*, cap. 10, in PL 106:1125C-D.

52. Acts 11:27-30.

53. Cf. Eusebius, *Ecclesia historia*, lib. 2, cap. 3 in PG 20:143B. Bostius' quote is either from a different translation to Migne or he has adapted the text to suit his purposes.

54. F. Baptiste Mantuani, *Parthenice et Apologeticon* (Lyons, 1513), fol. 61v.

55. Acts 11:27-30.

56. Cf. Acts 11:27-30 in Eusebius, *Ecclesia historia*, lib. 2, cap. 8 in PG 20:155C. Bostius' quote again has significant differences. :

57. *Magna vita sancti Hugonis: The Life of St. Hugh of Lincoln* (Edited by Decima L. Douie and David Hugh Farmer; Oxford: Clarendon, 1985) II, 162-163.

58. *Vita Sancti Pachomii*, translated by Dionysius Exiguus, cap. 1: PL 73, 231A.

59. Athanasius (c.296-373), *Vita B. Antonii abbatis*, cap. 6 & 7, in *Sources chrétiennes* (Edited by G. J. M. Bartelink, 1994), V:400. 154-157; PL 73:131B.

60. Heb 11:37-38: John Cassian, *Conferences* 18, chapter 6, in *A Select Library of Nicene and Post-Nicene Fathers* (Translated by Edgar C. S. Gibson, 1894), XI:481.

61. *Recte* Hugh of St. Victor, *De vanitate mundi*, lib. 4 in PL 176:738D-739A.

62. Cassiodorus-Epiphanius, *Historia ecclesiastica tripartitaita*, lib 1, cap 2, in CSEL (Edited by R. Hanslik, 1952) , 85, lines 75-76.

63. Bostius has chapter 29 by mistake: Rufinus, *Historia ecclesiastica*, bk 2, ch. 28 in PL 21:536A-B.

64. No source for this reference and the text of the following chapter has been traced. Similar passages occur in chapter 2 of Bostius' *De Patronatu*.

65. Eccl 6:34.

66. *Lit* "odium parens disciplinam": probably a transcription error.

67.   Heb 1:14.

68.   Eccl 1:18.

69.   Mt 5:25.

70.   Mt 16:24 etc.

71.   2 Cor 2:17.

72.   *Recte* Jerome, *In evangelio Johannis:* PL 29:653D. This is not an exact quote as Bostius has added his own explanations and additions.

73.   Cf. Jn 1:19.

74.   Cf. *De Institutione*, bk 5 chap 2.

75.   Cf. *De institutione*, bk 7, chap. 4: Chandler, *op. cit.*, p. 257.

76.   Cf. *De institutione*, bk 7, chap. 5: Chandler, *op. cit.*, p. 259.

77.   Not found in Jerome or Ribot.

78.   *Recte* Rufinus, *Historia Ecclesiastic*, bk 2, chap. 28 in PL 21:536B: Bedae, *Opera de Temporibus* (Edited by Charles W. Jones; Cambridge, Mass.: Mediaeval Academy of America, 1943), p. 185 (line 38), and p. 234 (line 60), and p. 334 (note): *recte* Vincent of Beauvais, *Speculum Historiale* (1494) bk 14, chap 32.

79.   Bostius related the same story in his *De viris illustribus* where he dates the miracle to 1465.

80.   Cf. 2 Kgs 1:9-16.

81.   1 Kgs 17-18.

82.   2 Kgs 9:30-37.

83.   2 Kgs 12:19-22.

84.   Cf. the apocryphal gospel of James.

85.   Ludolph von Suchem, *Description of the Holy Land* (1350), in *Library of Palestine Pilgrim's Text Society* 12 (London), 64.

86.   Wilbernus, *Historia parcium Terre Sancte* (1336), not so far traced. Cardinal Elie Talleyrand of Perigord (1301-1364), legate of France and a noted benefactor of St. Peter Thomas.

87.   Giovanni Boccaccio di Certaldo, *De montibus, silvis, fontibus, lacubus, fluminibus, stagnis seu paludibus, et de nominis maris* (1355-1374), in *Opere latine minori* (Edited

by A. F. Massere; Bari, 1928). Volume not available. Note: this Boccaccio is the celebrated author of the *Decameron.*

88. The Gallic calendar did not begin the new year until March 25.

89. This work appears not to have survived.

90. Gerardus de Frachetto, O.P., *Lives of the Brethren of the Order of Preachers* (Translated by Placid Conway, O.P.; edited by Bede Jarret, O.P.; London, 1924), 116.

91. Vincent of Beauvais, *Speculum historiale* (c.1254), lib. 30, cap. 123. [(Douai, 1624) IV:1274-1275.] Note: As is common among early Carmelite historians, Bostius cites book 31 in error for book 30.

92. June 7.

Chants, Feasts and Traditions:
The Liturgical Celebration
of the Virgin Mary
in the Carmelite Rite

As members of a religious order founded in the Holy Land the Carmelites enjoyed a unique vantage point for appreciating the importance of celebrating the Virgin Mary liturgically, especially since so many Marian feasts originated in the east.[1] Once established in the west, what had been customary as a Holy Land celebration now became distinctive, making the Carmelite rite unique among western liturgical traditions; this uniqueness was especially felt in the Divine Office, since much latitude prevailed in its organization in the middle ages. This essay will discuss these Marian Carmelite offices and their chants and explore the textual and musical relationships among the chants of Marian feasts and closely related ones in the Carmelite rite.

While the origins of the Carmelites in the Latin Kingdom date to the rule[2] given to them by Albert, Patriarch of Jerusalem, some time during the years of his term in office, 1206-1214,[3] a distinctive and universally celebrated Carmelite rite was established only with the promulgation by the General Chapter of London in 1312 of an ordinal[4] compiled by the German Carmelite Sibert de Beka.[5]

Sibert de Beka's ordinal prescribed all the text incipits, or beginning words, for each antiphon, responsory, psalm, prayer and reading for the Divine Office as well as all the chants and prayers to be used for the celebration of Mass for every day of the year. This Carmelite ordinal was much simpler than the Dominican counterpart compiled by the Master General, Humbert of Romans, which included a complete set of liturgical service books, containing every detail of music and text for all the chants and prayers, as well as a portable copy for him to use for correcting the service books in each convent he visited.[6]

By the time Sibert's ordinal was issued the Carmelites had migrated from the Holy Land to western Europe, where they numbered ten provinces by 1281,[7] and had changed their lifestyle from an eremitical one to become a mendicant order in the tradition of the newly-formed Franciscans and Dominicans.[8] Thus their size as a religious order, coupled with their status as mendicants obliging them to chant the office, required such a standardized ordinal for their liturgy. In 1291 the last Carmelites were forced to flee Mount Carmel itself,[9] so that by the time Sibert's ordinal was promulgated the Carmelites were no longer hermits living in the Latin Kingdom but mendicants living throughout western Europe.

Tradition maintains that the first chapel on Mount Carmel was dedicated in honor of the Virgin Mary, and as early as 1252 the Carmelites were known by the title "Brothers of Our Lady of Mount Carmel".[10] Devotion of a religious group to the Virgin Mary was hardly unusual, however: the Cistercians, for instance, also had a long-standing and fervent devotion to the Virgin Mary.[11]

Liturgically the Carmelites on Mount Carmel observed the local rite of the Holy Sepulchre,[12] that is, the standardized usage of the Latin Kingdom of Jerusalem established as a result of the Crusader movement. This rite was essentially French, with considerable Augustinian influence, since the canons staffing the major shrines of the Holy Land followed the Augustinian rule. Thus the rhymed office for St. Augustine, common to the rite of Paris and other French usages, figured prominently in the rite of the Holy Sepulchre as well.[13] While the original Carmelite rule given by St. Albert of Jerusalem enjoined the hermits to assemble daily in their chapel for Mass,[14] the recitation of the liturgy of the hours was done privately by each hermit in his cell,[15] since the rule stipulates no common liturgical observance apart from daily Mass. Only with the revision of the rule in 1247[16] did the Carmelites adopt the choral recitation of the office and, presumably with it, the office tradition of the Holy Sepulchre usage.

Surviving liturgical manuscripts provide the only detailed information available enabling us to understand the details of the medieval Carmelite liturgy. Only four sets of manuscripts for the Divine Office have survived to modern times: two antiphonals from Pisa, now housed in the *Carmine* there, date from the first half of the 14th century, approximately 1312-1342;[17] a set of manuscripts from Florence, now housed in the San Marco Library and the *Carmine*, date from the 1390's;[18] two antiphonals of Krakow were written in 1397; and five antiphonals from Mainz, dated to the 1430's, are now in the Dom- und Diözesanmuseum of that city.[19] A comparison of the organization of office chants within the manuscripts shows that these codices, and hence the actual lived practice, followed the prescriptions of Sibert's ordinal with scrupulous fidelity. As a result, we can be reasonably certain that the medieval Carmelite rite was highly distinctive.

While these antiphonals demonstrate that the Carmelites actually followed the prescriptions of Sibert's ordinal, they do not indicate the relationship of this office custom to the rite of the Holy Sepulchre from the Latin Kingdom. A notated breviary from the Latin Kingdom area greatly illumines our understanding of the connection between the rite of the Holy Sepulchre and the Carmelite rite. This mid-thirteenth-century breviary from the Holy Land eventually made its way westward to the Carmelite convent of Piacenza in northern Italy; from there it entered the Bibliothèque Nationale de France around the time of the French revolution and now bears the signature 'ms. fonds latin 10478.' Although it lacks the opening folio, which would clearly indicate its provenance, and while it lacks any decoration linking it specifically to the Carmelites, liturgically it clearly comes from the Holy Sepulchre usage. Furthermore this breviary contains complete musical notation for all the office chants as well as the complete texts for all the readings, including the nine lessons for the office of Matins each day. It thus proves an invaluable resource for understanding liturgical practice in at least one church from the Latin Kingdom. Moreover, a detailed comparison of its liturgical contents indicates that it exercised considerable influence upon the ordinal of Sibert de Beka. In addition, a comparison of several examples of its music, indicates that even in musical detail it anticipated the Carmelite usage.[20]

The original Marian feasts contained in Sibert's ordinal all derived from the use of the Holy Sepulchre, but were celebrated universally as well: the Nativity (September 8), the Purification (February 2), the Annunciation (March 25), the Assumption (August 15), and the Saturday votive celebration for the Virgin Mary.

The feast of the Conception of the Virgin (December 8) was accepted into the Carmelite liturgy in 1306 by the General Chapter of Toulouse, thus entering the rite early enough to be included in Sibert's ordinal and thereby gain universal celebration throughout the Order. The Carmelite observance of this feast reflects the Order's participation in the medieval debate over the doctrine of the Immaculate Conception: the Dominicans, following the teaching of St. Thomas Aquinas, held that Mary had to have been sanctified while still in the womb rather that conceived immaculate, as the Franciscans maintained. The Carmelite celebration was a compromise between the two positions, so that Carmelite rubrics for the feast use both the terms "sanctification" and "conception"; nevertheless both Carmelite legislation and service books refer to the feast itself as the "conception," not the "sanctification" of the Virgin, perhaps suggesting a leaning more towards the Franciscan than the Dominican position on the question. This tendency towards the Franciscan viewpoint is confirmed in a printed breviary of 1495 which specifically refers to the feast as the Immaculate Conception and replaces the traditional Carmelite Conception office with one composed by Leonard Nogarolus.[21]

The hegemony of this Holy Land breviary upon the Carmelite rite is particularly evident in the five antiphons used for first Vespers for all these Marian feasts listed above, including the Conception of Mary: "*Hec est regina*," "*Te decus virgineum*," "*Sub tuum presidium*," "*Sancta Maria succurre*," and "*Beata Dei genitrix*," not only agree with this earlier breviary in textual detail but in musical detail as well.[22] This commonality of Marian first Vespers antiphons distinguished Carmelite usage from other western practices and maintained a Carmelite liturgical link with their ancestral rite of the Holy Sepulchre. This is especially the case with the Conception of the Virgin, where the Carmelites preferred continuity with their Holy Sepulchre tradition over other alternatives, including a rhymed office beginning with the text "*Gaude mater ecclesia*" for the first antiphon of first Vespers, which was used in France and elsewhere.[23]

While these standard Marian feasts drew upon a common fund of chants for their liturgical celebration, the selection and organization of these pieces differed from rite to rite. The entire liturgical contents of the five Mainz Carmelite office manuscripts have been published in electronic form through the CANTUS project, now at the University of Western Ontario in London, Ontario.[24] Listing all the textual incipits for every liturgical chant, they give us a ready appreciation of the ordering of chants for all feasts, including the Marian ones, for the entire Carmelite rite. These Mainz Carmelite codices scrupulously followed the prescriptions of Sibert's ordinal and thus can be considered standard for the Carmelites. Since there are currently more than thirty traditions already represented on the same electronic website, the ready availability of sources for comparison from one rite to another is astounding and is growing on a steady basis.

The medieval Divine Office liturgy consisted of antiphons which framed the psalms, and great responsories which were elaborate musical reflections upon the Scripture readings for the Matins and Vespers services.[25] The selection of antiphons and responsories varied from one tradition to another and therefore defined each liturgical tradition, including the Carmelite one.

Our Table shows the Matins chants used for three Marian feasts in the Carmelite rite: the Nativity, the Conception and the Annunciation of the Virgin Mary. A comparison of chants used for any of these feasts between Carmelite and other usages invariably highlights the unique organization of these Carmelite Marian chants. While the number of liturgical sources now readily available on the CANTUS website is astounding, what holds true for this small sampling of manuscripts is virtually guaranteed to be valid for a much larger number as well. The results, however, always show that while the Carmelites selected chants from a common fund of texts, their organization of these chants into an office celebration was unique, but consistent with the Holy Sepulchre organization of chants as represented by the noted breviary Paris, Bibliothèque Nationale de France, ms. latin 10478 mentioned above.

Each of these three Marian feasts has a series of chants for Matins and Lauds which is consistent within the Carmelite liturgy and different from the rites of other religious orders and dioceses. Thus a Carmelite celebration within any given medieval city was distinct from what was celebrated in its cathedral and parish churches, and distinct from the celebrations in other religious houses as well.

Each of these feasts featured the same series of first Vespers antiphons, beginning with "*Hec est regina*," which characterized the Carmelite and Holy Sepulchre usages and united these feasts thematically. The Matins chants were different in all three cases but consistent for each feast within all Carmelite manuscripts.

The three responsories concluding each nocturn for the feast of the Nativity of Mary, "*Solem iustitie*," "*Ad nutum Domini*" and "*Stirps Jesse*," were all written by Fulbert, Bishop of Chartres,[26] in the early eleventh century and featured prominently in the usage of Chartres cathedral and other French sites before becoming part of the Holy Sepulchre rite and from there entering the Carmelite liturgy. Significantly, the Carmelites used "*Stirps Jesse*" to celebrate the Conception of Mary as well, placing it here

TABLE

Matins Chants for Three Marian Feasts

Chant	*Nativity*	*Conception*	*Annunciation*
Inv	Corde et ore	In honore beatissime	Ave maria gratia
Na1	Hodie nata est	Ecce tu pulchra	Missus est angelus
a2	Beatissime	Sicut lilium inter	Ave maria gratia
a3	Quando nata	Favus distillans	Benedicta tu
R1	Hodie nata	Que est ista	Missus est gabriel
v	Beatissime	Et sicut dies	Dabit ei dominus
R2	Beatissime	Ista est speciosa	Ave maria gratia
v2	Cum jucunditate	Odor unguentorum	Quomodo fiet
R3	Solem iustitiae	Stirps Jesse virgam	Suscipe verbum
v	Cernere divinum	Virgo dei genitrix	Paries quidem
N2a1	Hodie nata est	Emissiones tue	Ne timeas Maria
a2	Dignum namque	Fons hortorum	Spiritus sanctus
a3	Benedicta et	Veniat dilectus	Dabit illi
R1	Gloriose virginis	Beatam me dicent	Ecce virgo
v	Hodie nata est	Et misericordia	Super solium
R2	Nativitas tua	Ornatam monilibus	Descendet dominus
v	Dignum namque	Astitit regina	Et adorabunt
R3	Ad nutum domini	Christi virgo	Ecce radix iesse
v	Ut vitium virtus	Quoniam peccatorum	Dabit ei dominus
N3a1	Nativitas est	Corde et animo	Ecce ancilla
a2	Ista est speciosa	Dignum namque est	Beata es maria
a3	Felix namque es	Dignare me laudare	Beatam me dicent
R1	Nativitas gloriose	Super salutem	Radix iesse qui
v	Nativitas est hodie	Valde eam nos	Super ipsum
R2	Corde et animo	Corde et animo	Nascetur nobis
v	Omnes in unum	Omnes in unum	Multiplicabitur
R3	Stirps Jesse virgam	Felix namque es	Christi virgo
v	Virgo Dei genitrix	Ora pro populo	Quoniam peccatorum
L a1	Nativitas gloriose	Pulchra es et	Prophete predicaverunt
a2	Nativitas est hodie	Sicut mirra electa	Angelus domini
a3	Regali ex progenie	In odore	Orietur sicut sol
a4	Corde et animo	Benedicta a filio	Ex quo facta est
a5	Cum jucunditate	Speciosa facta es	Maria autem

at the end of the first nocturn rather than of the third. Thus in the Carmelite rite the use of this responsory extended the work of Fulbert beyond his original intent, and also reinforced the unity among Marian feasts which the use of common first Vespers antiphons already had begun to accomplish.

While the ordinal of Sibert de Beka, first promulgated in 1312, standardized the liturgy for the Carmelites, new feasts, particularly Marian ones, continued to become part of western liturgical traditions in general and the Carmelite rite in particular during the fourteenth century. The first of these to be embraced by the Carmelites was the feast of the Three Marys; thus the acts of the General Chapter of Lyons in 1342 prescribed that on St. Urban's day (May 25th) there be added the feast of the sisters of blessed Mary, namely, Mary of James and Mary of Salome, as a duplex feast,[27] indicating that it was to be celebrated with great solemnity. The feast of the Three Marys is based on the medieval legend that St. Anne married Joachim and begot Mary, the mother of Jesus. After Joachim's death, Anne married Cleophas and begot another Mary, who in turn married Alphaeus and begot St. James the Lesser, St. Simon, St. Jude and St. Joseph the Just. After the death of Cleophas, Anne married Salomas and begot a third Mary, who became the mother of St. James the Great and St. John the Evangelist.[28] Carmelite enthusiasm for this feast had a literary counterpart as well, since the Carmelite chronicler Jean de Venette, who became prior of the Paris Carmel in 1339 and later provincial of France, wrote his celebrated *Histoire des Trois Maries* in 1357.[29] While the rubric identifies Mary Cleophas by her son James rather than by her husband, the same person is intended. The feast of the Three Marys features a rhymed office, that is, one with newly-composed texts for the antiphons and responsories, which have textual meter and rhyme and whose elaborate music is newly composed. This Provencal feast, once admitted into the Carmelite rite, became normative for at least most Carmelite houses, even those outside France. Although detailed rubrics were never added in later copies of Sibert's ordinal,[30] the ordering of chants for this feast in Florence and Mainz Carmelite usage is virtually the same.[31] Moreover, the inclusion of this feast in the Carmelite rite now extended beyond the Virgin Mary herself to include her sisters (at least by legend) as well.

Three additional Marian feasts were incorporated into the Carmelite rite by the General Chapter of Frankfurt of 1393, namely the Presentation, the Visitation, and Our Lady of the Snows. The Chapter Acts themselves prescribe the feast of Our

Lady of the Snows in general terms, indicating that the actual chants should be taken from the Saturday commemoration of the Virgin Mary.[32] Thus the Mainz Carmelites[33] organized standard Marian chants into a distinctively Carmelite format to celebrate the feast. They retained the "*Stirps Jesse*" responsory, originally composed by Fulbert of Chartres for the Nativity of Mary, as the final Matins responsory in this feast, thus establishing a connection with this older tradition in the newer feast. The Carmelites of Krakow, however, began the office with these five first Vespers antiphons but then chose a newly composed rhymed office for the Matins and Lauds chants rather than the Saturday commemoration chants prescribed by the Chapter Acts, an office which seems to be unique to this manuscript.[34] Since the Carmelite convent of Prague, where the Krakow manuscripts were produced in 1397, was named for Our Lady of the Snows,[35] the choice of an elaborate rhymed office to celebrate this feast is entirely understandable.

The feast of the Visitation for celebration on July 2 was promulgated by Pope Boniface IX in 1389 by his bull, "*Superni benignitas conditoris*," for the purpose of ending the western schism. Although the Dominican General of the Roman obedience, Blessed Raymond of Capua, composed a rhymed office, "*Collaetentur corda fidelium*," for use in the Dominican celebration, the Carmelites maintained the "*Exurgens Maria*" office as promulgated by Boniface IX. It occurs both in Mainz and in Krakow Carmelite usage.[36]

Several of the Mainz Carmelite Visitation chants are based directly on models from the Three Marys office. In other words, the Carmelites took the music of a chant in the Three Marys office and applied it to the new text for the Visitation feast. Thus the Visitation Vespers responsory "*Vox turturis*" is based on the Mainz Three Marys Matins responsory "*Gaudeamus hodie*"; the music of the Mainz Three Marys Invitatory antiphon "*Jubilemus*" was reused for the Visitation Invitatory antiphon "*In honore virginis*"; the responsory "*Miranda propagines*," common to both Mainz and Florence Carmelite celebrations for the Three Marys, was adapted to the new text "*En dilectus meus*," for the Visitation feast; the

Mainz Carmelite responsory "*Orto solis*" for the Three Marys became the basis of the Visitation responsory "*Ait autem Maria.*" This reuse of older music for a new office created a link between these two feasts in celebration of the Virgin Mary which had a precedent in the use of the same first Vespers chants in earlier Marian feasts, but now established a unique musical interrelationship between chants with different texts for two different Marian feasts.

The third feast promulgated in 1393 was the Presentation of Mary in the Temple, based on an account in the apocryphal Gospel of James. The feast was officially inaugurated in the west on November 21, 1372, with a celebration in the Franciscan church in Avignon in the presence of the papal court. The promoter of the office was Philippe de Mézières, chancellor of the duchy of Cyprus and friend of the Carmelite Peter Thomas, whose first biography he wrote.[37] Philippe maintained that he promoted the feast as he had experienced it on Cyprus, where much of the Latin Kingdom community, including the Carmelites, had taken refuge after being routed by the Saracens from the Holy Land. The chants and readings from this inaugural Avignon celebration are now preserved in a manuscript from the Bibliothèque Nationale de France, latin 17330 and its copy latin 14454 which have been the topic of some discussion.[38] The manuscripts contain an acrostic referring to a "Frater Rostagnus," sometimes identified with Philippe himself,[39] but now firmly identified as a Dominican friar.[40] While this office was occasionally adapted to Carmelite use,[41] the Carmelites of Mainz used a completely new and proper rhymed office, probably composed in that convent or adapted from a distinctly Carmelite exemplar elsewhere. The chant texts for this office essentially reflect on the Presentation event from a specifically Carmelite point of view. Moreover, almost all the chants of the new feast were adapted to these new texts[42] from other offices, primarily that of St. Thomas Becket. Two responsories came from offices other than St. Thomas Becket: Fulbert of Chartres' responsory "*Stirps Jesse*" for the Nativity of Mary was now set to a new text, "*Unam quam petii,*" while "*Hodie Marie*

Jacobi" from the Florentine Carmelite office of the Three Marys
was set to the new text "*Anna parens clausa*." Thus this distinctively new Carmelite creation nonetheless incorporated one chant
from each of two other Marian offices, placing the creation of
Fulbert of Chartres in a new textual setting and further reinforcing the musical network of relationships among chants in Marian
Carmelite feasts.

Carmelite devotion to St. Anne, mother of the Virgin Mary,
was a logical outgrowth of the Order's devotion to Mary herself.
The stories of St. Anne, like the Presentation account, derive from
the apocryphal Gospel of James. A French tradition maintains
that St. Lazarus brought her relics from Palestine to France,
where they were deposited in Apt towards the end of the fourth
century and discovered in 788.[43] While comparable in improbabil-
ity to the legend of St. Anne's three marriages, the account
nonetheless explains why the devotion to St. Anne emanated from
France. The Franciscans began observing her feast on July 26 in
1263; it was celebrated at Rome in 1307, granted to England in
1378, and extended to the universal Church in 1548.[44] The
presence of this feast in Sibert's ordinal at the rank of duplex is
a significant indication of the prestige St. Anne enjoyed within the
Carmelite rite as early as 1312. The rhymed office which occurs
in Mainz Carmelite usage[45] is a later incorporation into the liturgy,
since Sibert's ordinal prescribed the use of chants from the
common of a holy woman for this feast.[46] The Carmelite chapter
of Bonn (1411) prescribed a memorial of St. Anne to be said
throughout the year at Vespers and Matins,[47] suggesting an
increase in devotion to her, one which may have stimulated the
composition of the proper rhymed office for the Mainz Carmelites.
While almost all the chants for this office are proper to the feast,
it nonetheless still includes the responsory "*Stirps Jesse*" written
by Fulbert of Chartres for the feast of the Nativity of Mary, now in
honor of St. Anne, a unique phenomenon among western litur-
gies. Clearly the application of this Marian chant to St. Anne
linked the feast honoring the nativity of the Virgin Mary with that
of her mother.

The patronal feast of the Carmelite Order, known as the Solemn Commemoration of the Virgin or feast of Our Lady of Mount Carmel, entered the liturgy relatively late and was perhaps standardized through the printed breviaries such as that of 1495.[48] The rubric for the feast prescribed that everything be taken from the commemoration of the Virgin with one additional prayer.[49] Presumably the solemn commemoration, then, was based on the simple Saturday commemoration, indicating that no specific liturgical celebration for this feast had been developed by the end of the fifteenth century.

From the outset of their foundation as a religious community the Carmelites fostered a love for the Virgin Mary which they expressed liturgically in as complete a manner as they could. Their adoption of the choral office tradition through the revision of the rule in 1247 enabled them to celebrate the established Marian feasts of the Nativity, the Annunciation, the Conception, the Assumption, the Purification and the Saturday commemoration of Mary in a distinctive manner, reflecting their status as an Order whose liturgy originated in the Latin Kingdom's rite of the Holy Sepulchre. Their dedication to Mary and vivid consciousness of their unique origins enabled them to develop a distinctive liturgy in which the mother of God held a place of great prominence. Throughout the medieval period they participated in the widespread devotion to the Virgin Mary which in turn impelled them to incorporate the newly emerging feasts of the Presentation, the Visitation and Our Lady of the Snows into their own liturgy. At the same time their ever-expanding network of celebrations extended to the relatives of the Virgin, such as her mother, St. Anne, and step-sisters, Sts. Mary of Salomas and Mary Cleophas. As the Carmelites used the same five first Vespers antiphons for all Marian feasts in the earliest layer of their tradition, thereby both interrelating these feasts and reinforcing their liturgical and musical ties to the parent rite of the Holy Sepulchre, now in the process of assimilating new feasts into their tradition they adapted established chants to these new settings. Thus Fulbert of Chartres' responsory "*Stirps Jesse*," initially written for the Nativity of Mary and used also by the Carmelites for the feast of Mary's Conception, was now used for the feasts of Our Lady of the Snows and St. Anne, and then in turn adapted with a new text into the feast of the Presentation of Mary. In addition, the Carmelites applied the music for chants in the Three Marys office to the new texts of the Visitation and the Presentation offices. Their creativity in adapting and applying these chants into new liturgical situations thus further strengthened this already established Marian network of chant texts and music. At the same time, through their poetic, liturgical and musical creativity in establishing the offices for these new Marian feasts, the Carmelites not only celebrated their devotion and solidified their liturgical rite, but also made a permanent and invaluable contribution to the spiritual and cultural life of the Middle Ages.

James Boyce, O.Carm.

Endnotes

1. For a study of several of these Marian feasts and their western celebrations, cf. R. W. Pfaff, *New Liturgical Feasts in Later Medieval England* (Oxford: Clarendon Press, 1970).

2. The rule has been edited by Bede Edwards, O.C.D., and Hugh Clarke, O.Carm., *The Rule of Saint Albert*, (Vinea Carmeli I, Aylesford and Kensington: 1973), and also by Carlo Cicconnetti, O.Carm., *La Regola del Carmelo* (Roma: Institutum Carmelitanum, 1973).

3. Adrian Staring, "Alberto, patriarca di Gerusalemme, santo," *Biblioteca Sanctorum* I, cols. 686-90; V. L. Bullough, "Albert of Jerusalem, St," *New Catholic Encyclopedia* I: 258.

4. Benedictus Zimmerman, O.C.D., *Ordinaire de l'ordre de Notre-Dame du Mont-Carmel par Sibert de Beka (vers 1312) publié d'après le manuscrit original et collationné sur divers manuscrits et imprimés.* (Tôme Treizième, *Bibliothèque liturgique publiée par Ulysse Chevalier*. Paris: Alphonse Picard et fils, Libraires, 1910).

5. Born between 1260 and 1270, Sibert de Beka entered the Carmel of Cologne in 1280, eventually becoming prior of that house and later provincial of Lower Germany before being named master of students at Paris; he died probably on December 29, 1332, in Cologne and is buried in the Carmelite church there. Cf. Bartholomaeo Maria Xiberta, O.Carm., "De scriptoribus scholasticis saeculi XIV ex ordine Carmelitarum," *Bibliothèque de la Revue d'histoire ecclésiastique*, fasc. 6 (Louvain, 1931), pp. 142ff; Heinrich Denifle, "Quellen zur Gelehrtengeschichte des Carmelitenordens im 13. und 14. Jahrhundert," *Archiv für Literatur- und Kirchengeschichte des Mittelalters* V (1889), 371, f. 5.

6. This manuscript is preserved in the Dominican convent of Santa Sabina, Rome, Curia Generalizia dei Domenicani, ms. XIV, lit. 1; the portable copy used by the Master

General on visitation is now in London, British Library, Additional ms. 23935. The standard discussion of Dominican liturgy is William R. Bonniwell, O.P., *A History of the Dominican Liturgy, 1215-1945* (New York: Joseph F. Wagner, Inc., 1945).

7. The General Chapter of London of 1281 listed the ten Carmelite provinces in order of foundation as being the Holy Land, Sicily, England, Provence, Tuscany, Lombardy, France, Germany, Aquitaine and Spain respectively; cf. Ludovicus Saggi, O.Carm., "Constitutiones Capituli Londinensis Anni 1281," *Analecta Ordinis Carmelitarum* 15 (1950), 244.

8. The transformation of the Carmelites from hermits to mendicants has been discussed in my article, "From Rule to Rubric: The Impact of Carmelite Liturgical Legislation upon the Order's Office Tradition," *Ephemerides Liturgicae* 108 (1994), 262-298; this is now chapter 6 of my *Praising God in Carmel, Studies in Carmelite Liturgy* (Washington, D.C.: The Carmelite Institute, 1999), pp. 180-230.

9. Joachim Smet, O.Carm., *The Carmelites: A History of the Brothers of Our Lady of Mount Carmel* (Revised edition. Darien, Illinois: Carmelite Spiritual Center, 1988), I:25.

10. Smet, *The Carmelites* I:8 mentions that according to a French pilgrim's account of 1231 the oratory in the midst of the cells on Mount Carmel was dedicated to the Virgin Mary and that the title "Brothers of Our Lady of Mount Carmel" appears in papal documents as early as 1252.

11. For a discussion of the Cistercians, including their liturgy, cf. Louis J. Lekai, *The Cistercians, Ideals and Reality* (The Kent State University Press, 1977).

12. The rite of the Holy Sepulchre, and especially its calendar, are discussed by Francis Wormald in Hugo Buchtal, *Miniature Painting in the Latin Kingdom of Jerusalem* (Oxford: Clarendon Press, 1957).

13. For a discussion of the Augustinian, Jerusalem and French feasts in the Holy Sepulchre calendar, cf. Appen-

dix 1 of Buchtal, *Miniature Painting in the Latin Kingdom of Jerusalem*, pp. 107-109; this section was written by Francis Wormald.

14. In chapter eleven of the rule [Ed. note: now Rule, n.14]; cf. Edwards and Clarke, *The Rule of Saint Albert*, p. 85.

15. Chapter nine of the rule [Ed. note: now Rule, n.11] simply prescribes that those who can read are to say the psalms at the appropriate hours of the day, while those who cannot say a specified number of "Our Fathers" instead; cf. Edwards and Clarke, *The Rule of Saint Albert*, pp. 78-92 for the transcription of the rule and their discussion of it.

16. The mitigated rule was promulgated by Innocent IV on October 1, 1247, with his Apostolic Letter, "*Quae honorem conditoris*," which included the text of the revised rule; it is now preserved in the Vatican Archives, Reg. Vat. no. 21, folios 465v-466 and published in M.-H. Laurent, O.P. (ed.), "La lettre '*Quae honorem Conditoris*' (1er octobre, 1247): Note de diplomatique pontificale," *Ephemerides Carmeliticae* 2 (1948), 5-16.

17. These two antiphonals from the Carmine of Pisa, known as 'ms. D' and 'ms. sine signatura' respectively, have been studied in my article, "Two Antiphonals of Pisa: Their Place in the Carmelite Liturgy," *Manuscripta* 31 (1987), 147-165, and republished as chapter 5 of my *Praising God in Carmel*, pp. 151-179.

18. For a discussion of the Florentine Carmelite antiphonals, cf. Paschalis Kallenberg, O.Carm., *Fontes Liturgicae Carmelitanae, Investigatio in Decreta, Codices et Proprium Sanctorum* (Romae: Institutum Carmelitanum, 1962), pp. 247-256; and also my article, "The Carmelite Choirbooks of Florence and the Liturgical Tradition of the Carmelite Order," *Carmelus* 35 (1988), 67-93, reprinted as chapter 4 of *Praising God in Carmel*, pp. 115-150.

19. The five manuscripts are now: Mainz, Dom- und Diözesanmuseum, Codices A, B, C, D and E; cf. Kallenberg,

Fontes Liturgicae Carmelitanae, pp. 256-259; and James
Boyce, O.Carm., "Die Mainzer Karmeliterchorbücher und
die Liturgische Tradition des Karmeliterordens," *Archiv
für mittelrheinische Kirchengeschichte* 39 (1987), 267-
303, now reprinted as "The Carmelite Choirbooks of
Mainz and the Liturgical Tradition of the Carmelite Order," in *Praising God in Carmel*, pp. 71-114.

20.   This manuscript and its relationship to the rite of the Holy
Sepulchre and the liturgy of the Carmelites have been
discussed in my article, "The Search for the Early Carmelite
Liturgy: A Templar Manuscript Reassessed," *Revista de
Musicología* 16 (1993), 957-981, reprinted as chapter 9 of
Praising God in Carmel, pp. 299-327.

21.   The rubric for the feast on f. 370v reads as follows: *"Incipit
officium immaculate conceptionis virginis marie editum per
reverendum patrem dominum leonardum nogarolum
protonotarium apostolicum artium & sacrae theologie
doctorem famosissimum."* The office uses *"Sicut lilium inter
spinas"* as the first antiphon of first Vespers instead of the
traditional *"Hec est regina,"* used as the opening Vespers
chant for all Marian Carmelite feasts. Kallenberg discusses this breviary, printed in Venice by Andreas de
Toresanis de Asula on 1 February 1495 on p. 262 of *Fontes
Liturgicae Carmelitanae*. A copy of this incunable breviary
which was originally used in the Carmelite convent of
Bamberg is now in the library of Amherst College, with the
shelf-mark xRBR Incun 1495 B7.

22.   The significance of these first Vespers antiphons and their
careful transmission among Carmelite sources has been
illustrated in my "The Medieval Carmelite Office Tradition," *Acta Musicologica* 62 (1990), 119-151, reprinted as
chapter 7 of *Praising God in Carmel*, pp. 231-278.

23.   The *"Gaude mater ecclesia"* rhymed office for the Concep-
tion of the Virgin is found in Salamanca, Archivo de la
Catedral, ms. 7, beginning on f. 98. It also occurs in Paris,
Bibliothèque Nationale de France, ms. nouv. acq. 3003, a

fourteenth-century breviary from Syon; in Paris, Bibliothèque Nationale de France, ms. lat. 1266, Vol. I, a fifteenth-century breviary from Meaux; in Paris, Bibliothèque Mazarine, ms. 355, a thirteenth-century breviary from St. John's Hospital in Jerusalem; in Klosterneuburg, Augustiner-Chorherrenstift, ms. 1017; and in Vorau, Stiftsbibliothek, ms. 287 (29). Solange Corbin discusses this office in "L'office en vers `Gaude mater ecclesia' pour la Conception de la Vierge," *1° congresso internazionale di musica sacra* (Roma, 1950), pp. 284-286.

24.   The website is located at http://publish/uwo.ca/~cantus.

25.   In the Vespers and Lauds services used in the cathedral and mendicant traditions, including the Carmelite rite, after the opening invocation and singing of a hymn, five antiphons and psalms were sung, along with a reading, great responsory, prayers and petitions. The Matins service, often called the Night Office, began with the Invitatory antiphon introducing psalm 94 and was followed by a hymn and then by three nocturns, each of which consisted of three antiphons and psalms, three readings and great responsories, ending with the chanting of the *Te Deum.* For a detailed description of these services, cf. David Hiley, *Western Plainchant, A Handbook* (Oxford: Clarendon Press, 1993), especially pp. 25-30.

26.   Yves Delaporte, "Fulbert de Chartres et l'école chartraine de chant liturgique au XIe siècle," *Etudes Grégoriennes* 2, (1957), 51-81.

27.   "*Item in rubrica tertia de divino officio addatur quod de Sororibus beatae Mariae, scilicet Maria Jacobi et Maria Salome in die sancti Urbani fiat officium sicut in festo duplici est notatum.*" Cf. Benedict Zimmerman, *Monumenta Historica Carmelitana* (Lirinae: Ex Typis Abbatiae, 1907), I:141.

28.   Michael Terence Driscoll, O.Carm., "'L'histoire des Trois Maries': An Edition with Introduction" (M.A. thesis, Catholic University of America, 1973); and "'L'histoire des Trois

Maries' by Jean de Venette, O.Carm.," *Cahiers de Joséphologie* 23 (1975), 231-254.

29. Alfred Coville, "Jean de Venette, auteur de *l'Histoire des Trois Maries,*" *Histoire Littéraire de la France,* 38 (1949), 398.

30. For instance, the manuscript Dijon, Bibliothèque municipale, ms. 121, a French Carmelite ordinal of Sibert de Beka from the year 1468, includes the liturgical prescriptions of the chapter of Montpellier of 1369 (f. 55v) as part of its format; it reiterates the acceptance of the feast into the liturgy but does not discuss the details of the feast in the sanctoral section of the manuscript, although it is mentioned in the calendar. Cf. my "From Rule to Rubric," especially pp. 219-220, in *Praising God in Carmel.*

31. See my "The Office of the Three Marys in the Carmelite Liturgy," *Journal of the Plainsong & Mediaeval Music Society* 12 (1989), 1-38.

32. "*Quantum ad Ordinationes et Constitutiones. Primo ordinaverunt, quod fiat omni anno in die B.[eat]i Dominici de Mense Augusti totum Duplex Festum Sanctae Mariae de Nive et Festum Dominici transferatur in proximum diem vacantem et fiat Officium sicut consuevit fieri diebus Sabbathinis de Commemoratione Beatae Virginis; sed Lectiones sumantur de legenda, seu Miraculo praedicti Festi.*" Gabriel Wessels, O.Carm., *Acta Capitulorum Generalium Ordinis Fratrum B. V. Mariae de Monte Carmelo* (Romae: Apud Curiam Generalitiam, 1912), I:109.

33. The feast of Our Lady of the Snows occurs in Mainz, Dom- und Diözesanmuseum, Codex C, beginning on folio 259v.

34. The feast of Our Lady of the Snows begins on page 108 of Krakow, Carmelite Monastery, Codex 2; the page numbers rather than folio numbers probably were first used when the manuscript was revised and updated in 1743 under the direction of the provincial, Fr. Bonaventure Kielkowicz.

35. For a discussion of the foundation of the Carmelite convent of Krakow, cf. Tadeusz M. Trajdos, "Fundacja Klasztoru Karmelitów Trzewiczkowych na Piasku w

Krakowie" ("The Foundation of the Monastery of Carmelites Antiquae Observantiae in Crakov," *Nasza Przesztosc* 60 (1983), 91-127; for the Carmel of Prague and its dedication to Our Lady of the Snows, cf. Jan Muk and Olga Novosadová, "Byvaly kláster karmelitánu u Panny Marie Snezwné ve stredoveku" ("Das ehemalige karmeliterkloster an der Jungfrau Maria Schnee)," *Staletá Praha* 14 (1984), 103-110.

36.   The office of the Visitation occurs in Mainz, Dom- und Diözesanmuseum, Codex C, beginning on f. 196, and in Krakow, Carmelite Monastery, Codex 2, beginning on f. 77.

37.   The standard biography for Philippe de Mézières is Nicolas Iorga, *Philippe de Mézières 1327-1405 et la croisade au XIVe siècle* (Paris: 1896); for Philippe's biography of St. Peter Thomas, cf. Joachim Smet, O.Carm., *The Life of Saint Peter Thomas by Philippe de Mézières* (Rome: Institutum Carmelitanum, 1954). The complete texts for the office, Mass and drama, as well as supporting documents, all contained in the manuscript Paris, Bibliothèque Nationale de France, fonds latin 17330, have been edited by William L. Coleman, *Philippe de Mézières' Campaign for the Feast of Mary's Presentation* (Toronto: Pontifical Institute of Medieval Studies, 1981).

38.   I discussed the considerable differences in musical detail between chants in these two manuscripts in "Das Offizium der Darstellung Mariens von Philippe de Mézières, Die Handschriften und der Überlieferungsprozeß," *Kirchenmusikalisches Jahrbuch* 77 (1993), 17-38.

39.   For example, by Guido Maria Dreves and Clemens Blume in *Analecta Hymnica Medii Aevi* 52, pp. 44-45.

40.   Andrew Hughes, "*Fons hortorum*, The Office of the Presentation: origins and authorship," Walter Berschin and David Hiley (eds.), *Die Offizien des Mittelalters. Dichtung und Musik, (Regensburger Studien zur Musikgeschichte* I, Tutzing, 1999), pp. 153-177.

41. See my "The Office of the Presentation of Mary in the Carmelite Liturgy," *Land of Carmel, Essays in Honor of Joachim Smet O.Carm.*, ed. by Paul Chandler, O.Carm., and Keith J. Egan (Rome: Institutum Carmelitanum, 1991), pp. 231-245, and now reprinted as chapter 8 of *Praising God in Carmel, Studies in Carmelite Liturgy*, pp. 279-298.

42. The process of composition of the Mainz Carmelite office of the Presentation is discussed in my "The Carmelite Feast of the Presentation of the Virgin: A Study in Musical Adaptation," *The Divine Office in the Latin Middle Ages: Source Studies, Regional Developments, Hagiography, Written in Honor of Professor Ruth Steiner*, edited by Rebecca A. Baltzer and Margot E. Fassler, to be published by Oxford University Press.

43. F. G. Holweck, *A Biographical Dictionary of the Saints, with a General Introduction to Hagiology* (St Louis, Missouri: B. Herder Book Co., 1924), p. 79.

44. Holweck, *A Biographical Dictionary of the Saints*, p. 79.

45. Chants for St. Anne occur in Mainz, Dom- und Diözesanmuseum, Codex C, beginning on f. 226.

46. Sibert's text reads, "*Sanctae Annae matris gloriosae Virginis. Festum duplex. Ad matutinum lectiones de aliqua propria legenda vel de sermone. Cetera omnia sicut in commune unius matrone.*" Zimmerman, *Ordinaire*, p. 236.

47. "*Item ordinamus, quod de Beata Anna fiat per totam Ordinem memoria de B. Anna ad Vesperas et Matutinum.*" Wessels, *Acta Capitulorum Generalium* I:145.

48. The rubric for the feast occurs on f. 293 of the printed breviary of 1495. Joachim Smet, O.Carm., suggests, "Perhaps the new printed breviaries (Venice, 1481, 1490, 1495) and missals (Venice, 1504, 1509) contributed to this standardization," *The Carmelites*, (Private Printing, 1975), p. 136.

49.   The rubric reads: "*In commemoratione beatae Marie virginis totum duplex. Ad matut ad horas & c[etera]. ut in commemoratione eius.*"

Mary and the Saints
in Early Scottish Poetry

In the millennium before the birth of Christ, the Celts were, after the Greeks and Romans, probably the principal ethnic group in Europe. Unlike the Greeks and Romans, they never formed a single nation but were mainly tribal–barbarians in the eyes of the Mediterranean peoples. The Greeks called them *Keltoi*, a name similar to the modern term Celts, while the Romans called them Gauls. In those days they probably occupied the heartlands of Europe north of the Alps, and some surviving place-names give an indication of the wide extent of their settlements. Galatia, nowadays in Turkey, was a Celtic area in the far southeast, and we may suppose it was to Celts that Paul wrote his Letter to the Galatians. They eventually merged into the surrounding cosmopolitan Hellenistc population. Still in the east, but much further north, there is an area called Galicia, on the borders of Poland and the Ukraine. At the very other end of Europe, in the northwest corner of Spain, there is another Galicia, the name of which probably dates from the time when the Celts or Gauls were being driven ever further to the west by a kind of pincer movement, in which they were caught between the Roman Empire on the south and invading Germanic tribes on the north. Wales, also in the extreme west, is another example of the presence of the Gauls, for the names Wales and Welsh are variant forms of the terms Gaul and Gaulish–indeed, the French still refer to Wales as Pays de

Galles. France itself was known in ancient times as Gaul, and was in the main Celtic territory.

The earliest written reference to the Celts is probably one found in the writings of the Greek historian Herodotus. Writing about the middle of the fifth century BCE, he informs his readers that the River Danube rises in the land of the Celts. This seems good evidence that in his time the Celts were still living at the heart of Europe. About a century later, in his dialogue *The Laws*, Plato remarks that the Celts are much given to intoxication–a remark which, sadly, has still some truth in it. There were no Celtic historians in those days to record the history of their people, and we get glimpses of them only when they collided with the peoples of the south. In 390 BCE Celts from the north came down into Italy, where they captured and plundered the city of Rome itself. The violent events of that time are recorded by Livy, and for long afterwards the Romans remembered this barbarian visitation as one of the blackest days in their history. Just over a century later, in 279 BCE, another horde of Celts, this time from the Balkans, invaded Greece and raided the sacred precincts of Delphi.

Our particular interest is in that portion of the Celtic peoples called the Scots. Although nowadays we think of the Scots as the inhabitants of Scotland, the term was anciently used in a wider, more indefinite sense. The Scots were a Celtic people whose territory covered quite a large tract of land in both Scotland and Ireland. They all spoke the same Gaelic language, but were linguistically different from the Welsh, who also spoke a Celtic language but one which was markedly divergent from Gaelic, and closer to the Celtic languages of Cornwall and Brittany. All of the Celtic languages belong to the Indo-European family, their closest neighbor being Latin. But the Celtic languages have lost the sound represented by the letter *p*, while this has been retained in Welsh and Cornish. For example, the Latin word for 'father' is *pater*, and since the Celtic languages all belong to the Indo-European family, we would expect to find a word similar to *pater* being used for 'father' in Gaelic, but the Gaelic word is actually *athair,* "where the initial *p* has been completely lost, and even the *t* has been aspirated and in speech is reduced to an indistinct stop.

The fact that the people called Scots might be geographically from either Scotland or Ireland has sometimes been cause for confusion. Two great medieval theologians were both known as John the Scot (Ioannes Scotus). One was Ioannes Scotus Eriugena in the ninth century, the other Ioannes Duns Scotus in the fourteenth century. The former was obviously Irish, since the title Eriugena means "Irish-born," while the second was Scottish, taking the name Duns from his birthplace, a market-town in Berwickshire in the southeast of Scotland. But both might be called simply John the Scot. An amusing story about Scots and Scottishness is told concerning Eriugena. At one point in his life, he was teaching in the University of Paris and was invited to dine with the king, Charles the Bald. The two were sitting facing one another across the table when the king, in an attempt to be witty, propounded a question to the philosopher: "*Quid distat inter Scotum et sotum*" (What is the difference between a Scot and a sot)? Eriugena thought for a moment, and came back with the riposte, "Tabula tantum" (Only this table). The king, no doubt mellowed by wine, appears to have taken the reply in good part.

By the beginning of the Christian era, the Scots, Welsh and other Celtic peoples had been pushed to the very fringes of Europe, and occupied the inhospitable regions bordering on the Atlantic. There they gained a frugal living from farming and fishing. They continued to preserve their languages and these have survived to the present. Strangely, the Welsh, in spite of their proximity to England, have been most successful in keeping the old language alive as a tongue of everyday discourse. Attempts have been made in both Ireland and Scotland to revive the Gaelic but not much progress has been made, except among scholars and those who have an attachment to Gaelic literature. After all, nobody writes textbooks of nuclear physics or computer science in Gaelic.

Something must be said here about the ancient Celtic religion or religions, since some of the old attitudes and beliefs persisted into the Christian period. Like the religions of many early peoples, Celtic religion played a very large part in daily life. There were many gods and goddesses, of whom about four hundred names are known. Many of these were local deities and perhaps they would be better described as spirits, usually associated with some natural feature, a well or a rock or a hill. This should be remembered when we come to consider the role of the saints in Celtic Christianity, for many local saints took over the numinous traits of pre-Christian godlings. But there were also some high gods, notably Lugh, the master of all skills. His name is preserved in place names, such as Lyon (*Lugdunum*) in France and Legnica in Silesia (now in Poland but formerly in Germany when it was called Liegnitz). There were also powerful goddesses, of whom perhaps the best-known was Brigit. Although this religion was polytheistic, it was tending toward a kind of pantheism, understood to mean that although there was no single universally recognized supreme God, there was a deep sense of the immanence of the divine in all nature and also in all human activity.

A peculiarity of Celtic religion was that its devotees did not build temples for their gods. Caesar, who spent ten years of his life in Gaul, mentions this fact, and tells us that nevertheless the Celts set aside particular areas to serve as "holy places" (*loci consecrati*), "usually in the form of groves of oak trees. There are indeed some ancient pre-Christian structures in the former Celtic domains of Scotland (sometimes called the Gaelteachd), but it is quite likely that these are so ancient that they were already there when the Celts came to Scotland and had been erected by some still earlier and unknown people. For example, in the extreme northwest of Scotland, on the island of Lewis, at a place called Callanish, there is a circle of standing stones so impressive that, if it were not so remote, it might be a rival tourist attraction to Stonehenge. Some archaeologists believe that it is older than Stonehenge, and its stones may have been standing there for as long as 5000 years. It may have been associated with sun-worship but its precise nature is unknown. But although they did not build temples, the Celts did construct tombs for the departed, and many of these have been excavated and explored in various parts of Europe. Some of them have been found to contain artefacts, some of very high artistic quality, showing that these Celts were not quite the barbarians that the Greeks and Romans supposed them to be. If their exploits at the Battle of Alia and the raid on Delphi, to say nothing of their own internecine clan warfare, suggest that they were a warlike people, there was another side to their nature. They had a sense of beauty, a love of the still unspoiled world around them, a warmth of feeling for one another and even for their animals. These gentler aspects come into prominence after the coming of Christianity.

It is hard to believe, but it is the case, that when Christianity did come to these sturdy peoples, almost driven into the ocean but still clinging precariously to the barren Atlantic seaboard, they became a shining light to the rest of Europe. Exactly when the Christian faith first reached them is unknown. It was probably brought by Mediterranean traders or Roman soldiers, but it established itself and in the so-called "Dark Age" preceding the end of the first millennium, the Celtic realms preserved not only a considerable level of culture and learning but maintained a strong tradition of Christian piety when much of Europe was still pagan. The Ireland of that time has been called the "land of saints and scholars" and the description would apply equally to Scotland and Wales. Admittedly, that time is now long past, but it is not just a romantic figment of the imagination.

The transition from the old Celtic paganism to the Christian religion would seem to have been a smooth one. Just how smooth the transition was is strikingly symbolized at the old parish church of Govan, nowadays within the city boundary of Glasgow. The church there, which goes back to Celtic times and is dedicated to St. Constantine (no relation of the emperor!), possesses a unique collection of ancient carved stones. An interesting feature is that the churchyard is circular in shape, suggesting that it may preserve the shape of an ancient stone circle which, like the one at Callanish, may have been even pre-Celtic. The standing stones themselves have long ago disappeared from their places, but it is possible that some of them have survived in altered form among the carved stones.

I have mentioned above how a sense of the divine immanence was an important element in the Celtic religion, and this passed over into Celtic Christianity. God was conceived not so much as a distant power in the heavens as a circumambient and inescapable presence here on earth. I shall expand on this later, but here I would just mention that the sense of immanence can be traced even in modern Scottish theologians of Celtic background. A good example is John Baillie, a highly respected theologian of the Church of Scotland and one who was born and nurtured in the Highlands. In his book, *Our Knowledge of God*, he denies that such knowledge is primarily inferential and claims that "Distant though God may be in his transcendence, he may yet be nearer to me than my best friend"; and to emphasize the point, he quotes the famous lines of St. Patrick's Breastplate:

> Christ be with me, Christ within me,
> Christ behind me, Christ before me,
> Christ beside me, Christ to win me,
> Christ to comfort and restore me,
> Christ beneath me, Christ above me,
> Christ in quiet, Christ in danger,
> Christ in hearts of all that love me,
> Christ in mouth of friend and stranger.

A few years later he published his Gifford Lectures with the title, *The Sense of the Presence of God*, in which the immediate sense of the divine presence, as he had himself inherited it from his Celtic ancestry, was claimed to be the surest ground of our belief in the reality of God.

Baillie and the old Celtic Church before him did not, of course, deny the transcendence of God. They were not reverting to a pre-Christian pantheism, but they were seeking to balance the belief in transcendence with a due recognition of God's immanence in their midst. We remind ourselves of the imagery of the sun and its rays, much beloved of patristic theologians. The sun is not only "up there" at a vast remove from our earthly habitat, the life-giving warmth of the sun is among us day by day as we go about our activities. So those Celts had a tremendous sense of intimacy with God. He was present with them all the time, from getting up in the morning to lying down at night. "Christ within me, Christ behind me, Christ before me ...." For them, the universe is a holy place, for it is God's world. And when we reflect how we human beings have exploited and defaced and abused creation, including our fellow creatures, we realize the wisdom of such a reverential attitude toward the works of God. The sense of intimacy and closeness with God and with his Christ is expressed in brief poems and prayers which were used in the course of each day. There was not a time of day or a particular duty that did not have its appropriate prayer.

> This morning I will kindle the fire upon my hearth
> Before the holy angels who stand upon my path.
> No envy, hatred, malice, no fear upon my face,
> But the holy Son of God, the Guardian of the place.

Or in the evening:

> With God will I lie down this night,
>   And God will be lying with me.
> With Christ will I lie down this night,
>   And Christ will be lying with me.
> With Spirit will I lie down this night,
>   The Spirit will lie down with me.
> God and Christ and Spirit, Three,
>   Be they all down-lying with me.

The intimacy with God expressed in these lines, and the simplicity of the poetry itself, show the kind of society in which these people lived, a society in which genuine warm human relations and a genuine piety flourished. There is no irreverence in the intimacy with God which they expressed. Even when a number of clans recognized a "high king" over them, he was not so very high as to be out of touch with his people. The High King of Tara had his abode on the Hill of Tara, which is quite a low hill. Must not even God, sometimes called the "High King of Heaven," be likewise close to his people?

The stress on divine immanence, as I have mentioned, was already present in pre-Christian Celtic religion, and it received a new impetus and a fuller significance from the Christian belief in incarnation. It must too have been an influence in gaining for the saints the important place which they held in Celtic Christian spirituality. People for whom an utterly transcendent God or a highly exalted Christ were difficult ideas, and who had therefore come to think of God and Christ in ways which located them as closer to the earth and to the daily lives of men and women, saw their presence also in holy men and women who had exhibited in their lives the Christian virtues. Though the veneration accorded to the saints may reflect in part the polytheistic beliefs of earlier times, it was not understood in any idolatrous way. The saints were venerated only to the extent that they had been channels through which God had conveyed his grace. A French (Gaulish?) writer of the eighth century, Ermoldus Nigellus, expressed what the people of that time intended: "It is God whom we adore in his dear servants, whose prayers help us to reach heaven." We could say that the people whom he had in mind were firm believers in the communion of saints. The phrase "communion of saints" appears in the Apostles' Creed, though it was not a part of the creed in its earliest form. It is, however, not just a repetition of the preceding article, "the Holy Catholic Church." According to the current *Catechism of the Catholic Church*, reminding us of the use of the words "*Sancta sanctis*" (God's holy gifts for God's holy people!) in the Eastern liturgy, the term "communion of saints" has two closely linked meanings: communion in holy things (*sancta*) and communion among holy persons (*sancti*). At the fraction in the Anglican Eucharist, the priest says, "We break this bread to share in the Body of Christ," and the people reply, "Though we are many, we are all one Body, because we all share in the one Bread." Communion in the holy things signifies and effects a spiritual communion of the believers with Christ and with one another.

The Celtic Christian of the first millennium therefore thought of himself as a member of Christ's Church, but this did not mean simply the local congregation or even the worldwide Church. His Church extended through time as well as space. There was an unseen cloud of witnesses surrounding and supporting the Christians who were still on their earthly pilgrimage. At the head of this company was Mary, then the apostles and evangelists, then the teachers and missionaries of the Church, and soon some of the Celts themselves. In Scotland, Ireland and Wales the Celtic churches produced men and women of saintly stature from perhaps the fourth century onwards."[1] Some were shared among the three areas. Patrick became patron saint of Ireland and did his main work there, but he came originally from the British mainland, though whether from Wales or Scotland is a disputed–and even hotly disputed!–question. Columba, on the other hand, had his origin in Ireland, but moved over to Scotland to found his famous abbey on Iona and to labor among the people of Argyll and further afield. Kentigern is patron saint of Glasgow, but he had also close associations with Wales. One could mention also Ninian, Serf, Conval and many others, including many local saints who took over sacred sites from the old pagan deities. Among women saints, St. Brigid acquired a special reputation, and it seems probable that she inherited something of the aura that had attached to the old goddess Brigit. But these saints were as much alive in the feelings and affections of the people as were their still living neighbors. We could not even say that the saints were invisible, for visions seem to have been a common experience among the Celts. I have myself spoken to an islander from Lewis who claimed to have had a vision, and it certainly had been a reality, indeed quite a formative reality for his own life. The vividness with which these people experienced the saints may be illustrated from the following short poem:[2]

Who are these in my fishing-boat today?
Peter and Paul and John Baptist are they.
At my helm the Christ is sitting to steer,
The wind from the south making our way.
Who makes the voice of the wind to grow faint?
And who makes calm the kyle and the sea?
It is Jesus Christ, the Head of each saint.

The situation described in this poem makes it clear that for the Celts of that time, the "communion of saints" was not just an article in the creed but a daily lived experience.

Poems like the one just quoted have been transmitted for centuries in Scotland, but only in relatively recent times has the extent and the value of this treasure been appreciated. In the nineteenth century, Gaelic scholars toured round the Highlands and Islands collecting these poems from the mouths of the people, especially the older people. Many of these poems appear to have remained unchanged over long periods. It has been said that they are more durable than even the ancient stones, and they are imbued with a deeply religious feeling. Chief among the collectors was Dr. Alexander Carmichael, who published in 1900 two substantial volumes of poems, the *Carmina Gadelica*[3] supplying English translations as well as the Gaelic texts. He died in 1912, leaving behind him a large quantity of unpublished material, some of which has since seen the light of day.

Mary had her special place in that spirituality. One of the earliest hymns from those days is in fact a hymn to Mary.[4] It was composed by a monk of Iona Abbey and has been dated with a high degree of probability to about the year 700, little more than a century after the death of Columba. The monk had a name that sounds strangely to us. He was Cu Chuimne, which means in Gaelic "Hound of Memory". The hymn was written in Latin, as it was intended for use in church, whilst the popular hymns and poems were in Gaelic. The rhyming Latin of this hymn is very elegant and attests to the learning of the monastic author and explains the reputation of the Gaelteachd as a "land of saints and scholars." The hymn is a long one, thirteen stanzas, and the second stanza indicates that it was sung antiphonally. I shall quote only the first six stanzas, first in Latin, then in English:

> Cantemus in omni die
> concinentes varie
> conclamantes Deo dignum
> ymnum sanctae Mariae.
>
> Bis per chorum hinc et inde
> collaudemus Mariam
> et vox pulset omnem aurem
> per laudem victoriam.
>
> Maria de tribu Iudae
> summi Mater Domini
> opportunam dedit curam
> egrotanti homini.
>
> Gabriel advexit verbum
> sinu prius paterno
> quod conceptum et susceptum
> in utero materno.
>
> Haec est summa, haec est sancta
> Virgo venerabilis
> quae ex fide non recessit
> sed exstetit stabilis.
>
> Huic Matri nec inventa
> ante nec post similis
> nec de prole fuit plane
> humanae originis.
>
> Let us sing every day,
> Harmonizing in turn,
> Together proclaiming to God
> A hymn worthy of holy Mary.

In twofold chorus, from side to side,
let us praise Mary
so that the voice strikes every ear
with alternating praise.

Mary of the tribe of Judah,
Mother of the Most High Lord,
gave fitting care
to languishing mankind.

Gabriel first brought the word
from the Father's bosom
which was conceived and received
in the Mother's womb.

She is most high, she is holy,
the venerable Virgin
who by faith did not draw back
but stood forth firmly.

None has been found, before or since,
like this Mother,
not out of all the descendants
of the human race.

As I have said, this Latin poem is elegant and beautiful, a splendid tribute to Our Lady. Yet it is also ecclesiastical and therefore somewhat formal. The Gaelic poems from the people are, by contrast, warm, and, though not lacking in literary merit, they are relatively artless. But they make up for any literary shortcomings by their obvious sincerity. They are speaking of Mary out of the communion of saints. I remarked earlier that the veneration of the saints is justified because this veneration arose among simple peoples for whom the notions of God and even of Christ so far transcended their ordinary lives that they looked for the divine as it manifests itself in the grace-filled lives of human beings like themselves. So in these vernacular poems, Mary does not appear as she does in church, in a statue, let us say, or in a stained glass window. She is one of the community, sharing the home and the work-place, like those apostles whom we have already seen on the fishing-boat, not as passengers but as companions and helpmates. So Mary is in the kitchen, at the bedside of the sick, among the farm animals, comforting the dying. The mariology of the Celts has something to teach us. If veneration for Mary did indeed arise out of her being fully a fellow human being, then if we exalt her too much in the liturgy or in dogma, we push her to a distance and turn her into a demi-goddess. But the Celt spoke of her with an affectionate intimacy. Her care is for the family and even for the animals.

> Who keeps the night-watch now and over mine?
> Who but the Lord Christ of the poor is there,
> And the milk-white Bride, the Maiden of the kine,
> The milk-white Mary of the curling hair.[5]

This Mary is close to us in the communion of saints.

In the journal of Mundelein Seminary, I came across a piece by the American poet, Alice Tarnowski, which I think, sums up in a modern idiom the understanding of Mary found in the Celtic tradition. Addressing Mary, the poet says:

> O Lady of Guadalupe,
> Madonna of Czestochova,
> Queen of Patriarchs,
> Mystical Rose,
> Do you sometimes long to cry out
> [To devout Christians]
> Stop! Be silent, listen to me!
> I'm Miriam, the Jewish girl from Nazareth
> Who said Yes to life.

John Macquarrie

Endnotes

1. For the early Scottish saints, see Alan Macquarrie, *The Saints of Scotland* (Edinburgh: John Donald, 1997).
2. Two stanzas, conflated and slightly altered, from G. R. D. McLean, *Poems of the Western Highlanders* (London: SPCK, 1961).
3. The two original volumes were reprinted by the Scottish Academic Press, Edinburgh, in 1971. Further volumes have been published since then at various dates.
4. T. O. Clancy and G. Markus, O.P., *Iona: The Earliest Poetry of a Celtic Monastery* (Edinburgh: Edinburgh University Press, 1995).
5. McLean, *op. cit.*, p. 414.

The Honor of Our People:
Mary and the Lay Carmelites

Father Eamon Carroll has done more than any other modern Carmelite to encourage devotion to the Mother of God among Catholics in the United States. Both as a scholar and as a pastoral theologian, he has left his mark on bishops, fellow theologians, priests, religious, and the laity. The work to which Eamon has dedicated his life is far from complete, however. The Fathers of the Second Vatican Council gave a clear new focus to Mary's place in the Church, but there remain many ambiguities about her position in popular Catholic piety. Indeed, Mary is in many ways a potent symbol of the loss of consensus in the Church in the United States. Catholics across the theological spectrum appeal to the Blessed Virgin Mary to reinforce their divergent opinions.[1] At times there is even an impression that for some Mary is more a hostage of competing ideologies than an object of genuine devotion. This ambiguity presents both a challenge and an opportunity to Carmelites, religious and lay, as an Order dedicated to the Blessed Virgin Mary and traditionally associated with spreading devotion to the Mother of God. The challenge is to prevent Marian devotion from being manipulated by factions in the Church for their own agendas. The opportunity is to draw on the universal popularity of Mary among Catholics to forge a Marian devotion that can be both a healing and a reconciling common ground for all in the Church.

173

This article consists of three parts. One is the current experience of Lay Carmelites in their devotion to the Virgin Mary; the second, a very brief outline of Mary's place in the Carmelite Tradition; and finally, the challenges and opportunities that Mary presents for the Lay Carmelite movement today.

The Current Experience of Mary among Lay Carmelites

In order to get a sense of what Marian devotion means to Lay Carmelites, I asked approximately eight regional coordinators or directors of lay Carmelite communities to gather written testimonies from their membership commenting on their devotion to Our Lady. It was not my intent to gather a scientific sampling; I was interested simply in gathering responses that would tell me about the devotion of individuals and in seeing whether there are some common themes that emerged. The more than three hundred responses gathered cover a wide spectrum of reasons why Lay Carmelites are devoted to the Blessed Virgin as well as of ways in which that devotion is expressed. The responses also reflect a myriad of theological stances concerning not only the Blessed Virgin Mary, but such other topics as Christology, ecclesiology, soteriology and Christian anthropology. This initial sampling makes me wish for a larger and more scientific study, one that I suspect would produce fascinating insights into several of the subcultures lying beneath the surface of American Catholicism. An interdisciplinary study of the place of the Blessed Virgin Mary among American Catholics from theological, sociological, anthropological, and historical perspectives could provide a valuable tool for better understanding the Catholic Church in the United States.

Many of the replies from Lay Carmelites, indeed the vast majority, while obviously sincere, were rather bland and even vague. However, they leave no doubt that the Blessed Virgin Mary is very important to every Lay Carmelite who responded. A few of the responses showed some profundity and sophistication, while others implied an inadequate appreciation for key doctrines of the faith. Not a few indicated a commitment to theological and political ideologies that Mary seems in some way to represent to them.

For a considerable number, though by no means an overwhelming majority, Mary is primarily a model of discipleship. Mary is seen as the woman of faith whose trusting *fiat* to the Will of God is the paradigm for all who follow her Son. Several Lay Carmelites wrote how Mary's courage helped them face various events of their lives: an unexpected and perilous pregnancy, a son who broke an engagement and quit a job to go and work in the Peace Corps in Africa, watching an adult child die of AIDS. The influence of Mary as a model was expressed by one Lay Carmelite who wrote: "Her 'yes' ... is powerful to me as a human constantly struggling to do God's will."

The response of many Lay Carmelites indicates they understand that discipleship involves faithfulness in the various dark nights that have troubled their souls and that they experience in Mary's discipleship a comfort for their troubled hearts. They understand Mary and have a confidence that their Blessed Mother understands them, for life has left them with hearts run through, like hers, with sorrow. Exceptionally touching and candid responses spoke of how it was Mary to whom women could turn for comfort during episodes of sexual abuse, physical assault, early widowhood, and the loss of a child. Some of the women wrote that they had come to Carmel precisely because Mary had helped them through trauma, and in gratitude they wanted to live a life of devotion to her. She has continued to sustain them in the abiding pain that trauma has left in their lives.

The titles of Mediatrix and co-Redemptrix were often used in the responses. As long as these titles are understood within their historic usage in the Church they should not be seen as problematic. Karl Rahner wrote–with some exuberance–of Mary as Mediatrix of Grace, declaring that "we proclaim Mary our mediatrix, spontaneously, gladly, joyfully, by our prayers, and the honour and trust we show her."[2] He made it very clear, however, that "the word must therefore have quite a different sense from what it has when, with Holy Scripture, we recognize our Lord as our sole mediator."[3] While more than a few Lay Carmelites expressed a strong sense of Mary's mediation, every reference to Mary as mediatrix was in relation to her Son. Mary is seen as a powerful intercessor with her Son, and not a single response indicated replacing the unique mediation of Christ with that of his mother. Most often Lay Carmelites talked about this mediation which Mary has with her Son as an expression of confidence in the love that a son has for a mother. Several responses, however, portrayed Mary holding back the wrath of a Christ who is anxious to punish the world for its serious sins.

Many people who responded to my questions find their devotion to the Blessed Virgin rooted in their positive relationship with their own mothers. One woman wrote that she was devoted to Mary "for the same reason I am devoted to my earthly mother who constantly directed me to Jesus and His father and their Holy Spirit. Both mothers have a divine-like love for me and I return that love to them and to God." Another woman wrote from a different perspective: "Because I lost my own mother at an early age and for years thought I was without one until it dawned on me that I had the greatest 'Mom' of all–Our Lady." Another Lay Carmelite was very honest and wrote: "I had a wonderful mother and a not too wonderful father. I associated God as like my Father, so fear and accountability was [sic] associated with God. And love and caring with Mary." This person's spiritual development, fortunately, was not frozen. She continued to write: "As an adult, I learned to forgive my father. I found a loving Father God, Jesus, and the Holy Spirit. Because of Mary I found Jesus. 'To Jesus through Mary'."

This last response echoes a theme found in many responses. Many Lay Carmelites have come to Jesus and a Christocentric faith experience through Mary. Mary has been for them an essential step on the journey to Christ, but in the end the journey has been a journey to Christ. One Lay Carmelite answered the question about the reason for his devotion to Mary by writing: "Because she brings me to Jesus. I live my life for Jesus."

Not all the news is good, however. Many of the responses stressed Mary's humanity as if to imply that the humanity of Christ was in some way defective and left us in need of a mediatrix with the Mediator. Several Lay Carmelites wrote that Mary's humanity opens her to a tenderness, a compassion, an understanding of our human situation so that she can serve as a mediator with her divine Son. Mary's tenderness, compassion, and understanding of our human situation is part of the tradition of the Church, but it cannot imply an inadequacy in the tenderness, compassion and understanding of the One who is the very incarnation of God's Mercy. Several Lay Carmelites, as pointed out above, wrote of Mary's tenderness needing to hold back Jesus' anger and wanting to destroy a world lost in sin.

For some Lay Carmelites Mary takes the central role in their piety. They ascribe images and roles to her that most properly belong to Jesus. One Lay Carmelite wrote: "I love Her. She is my rock. I know that when everyone has let me down I can always rely on Her help and comfort." Another wrote ascribing to Mary the unique union Jesus has with his Father: "She is always in union with God, their [sic] Triune God." These are not deliberate or conscious displacements of Jesus with his mother, but there is no doubt that Mary is a more accessible figure to some than is Jesus.

Sometimes the responses echoed a defensiveness of Mary against those who are perceived as lessening her position in the Church or the Order. There has been a dramatic refocusing of Marian piety in the forty years since Vatican II. Andrew Greeley claims that a false sense of ecumenism led some Catholic pastors and theologians to de-emphasize many of the images in our Catholic tradition that most capture the Catholic way of seeing God present in the world, and the chief victim of this purge has been the Blessed Virgin.[4] While Greeley may have a point, it is only part of the story. René Laurentin, a conservative Marian theologian, describes the natural cycle of historical movements within the Church; and he declares that when movements attain their goals, they disappear. Laurentin says that Catholic life for the past three centuries has been characterized by the "Marian

Movement," but that movement reached its major objective with the 1854 declaration of the dogma of the Immaculate Conception and was waning long before Vatican II.[5] As natural as Laurentin believes this ebb may be, it has caused anger and fear among many who are devoted to Mary and are suspicious that liberal forces in the Church are in fact squashing Marian devotion. Indeed, an extreme Marian devotionalism is often the standard under which those who are trying to overturn the Council gather.

Some Lay Carmelites are among those who have the greatest difficulty in accepting the changes in Catholic life that have come about as a result of the Council and who flee *sub tuum praesidium* for safety from change. They cling ardently to forms of piety unaffected by Vatican II. Many Lay Carmelite groups have refused to accept the Liturgy of the Hours, for example, in favor of clinging to the Little Office or substituting the rosary in its place. The Order's attempts to develop a more sound catechesis on the brown scapular have evoked a strong negative reaction among many. The Our Lady of Aylesford Lay Carmelite Community received a written questionnaire asking: "Please answer this question in your own words: why are you devoted to our Blessed Mother?" That particular community has had a tense relationship with the friars for many years and has been particularly agitated over the scapular catechesis. Most of the responses were quite helpful in understanding their devotion to Mary, but several remarks showed a high level of distrust of the larger Order. One Lay Carmelite responded: "I am a daughter of the Church. I have always listened to the Church, popes, saints, (including Carmelite saints) ... they all had devotion to the Mother of God, why shouldn't I?" But then the respondent added, "What are you fishing for? Your intentions are suspect." Another member of the same community wrote: "I had a love for his mother and that was my favorite movie when I was a child. Our Lady of Fatima movie. I was away from the Catholic Church from age 14 to age 32. I attributed Our Blessed Mother in bringing me back. And the Holy Spirit of course. By the way I still believe in the sabbatine privilege for the scapular and I will believe in it till the day I die and I will pray for you and all the other mixed up priests ... and hope Someday you will know the truth."

Suspicion of the friars or the clergy in general surfaced rarely in the responses given to my questions, but it often surfaces as the Lay Carmelite leadership team visits communities throughout the country. One particularly neuralgic point has been the shift of emphasis on the brown scapular from the promises traditionally associated with it to an affiliation with the Order. This has profoundly angered some Lay Carmelites for whom the scapular is first and foremost an assurance of salvation and deliverance from purgatory. Other neuralgic points concern issues of religious garb, liturgical practices, and the perceived liberalism of the Order. The people who are angry with the Order, however, are almost invariably angry with the institutional Church as it is represented by the local bishop and parish clergy. The Blessed Virgin Mary can be a particularly potent symbol for the disaffected in the Church. Mary provides for some alternative authority to the hierarchical Church in which these disillusioned people have lost confidence. Marian apparitions are very appealing to those who perceive themselves disenfranchised in the Church because the visions bypass–and thereby discredit–the normal channels of religious authority. According to Sally Cunneen, anthropologists Victor and Edie Turner understood that visions point to the "hidden, nonhierarchical domain of the church and stress the power of the weak, the community, the rare and the unprecedented, as against the regular, ordained, and normative."[6] As one Lay Carmelite put it, "In this age when you don't know whether to trust your priest or even the bishop, you know that the Blessed Mother won't lead you astray. We need to trust in her promises at Fatima and Garabandal."

Popular Marian devotion among American Catholics in the middle decades of the twentieth century–and particularly the cult of Our Lady of Fatima–was strongly linked to Cold War ideology.[7] Mary's message was clear: only penance and prayer, particularly the rosary, could defeat atheistic Communism. This link between Marian apparitions and deliverance from an Armageddon created a uniquely Catholic version of the apocalypticism that has been part of the American Christian scene since the nineteenth century.[8] While Communism has been defeated–and due no doubt in great part to prayer and penance–apocalypticism is not so easily banished. Thus, there continues to be for some Catholics a certain fascination with extraordinary phenomena and private revelations, particularly those that stress an impending divine punishment. This predilection was reflected in several responses to the questionnaires. Various visions, approved, pending, suspect, and condemned, were cited for support of particular opinions or devotions. Over a dozen Lay Carmelites wrote of experiencing visions or other supernatural phenomena themselves. One person wrote me that the Blessed Virgin has appeared to her several times. This same woman also experienced other extraordinary phenomena, in particular that "the wounds of Christ ache on my hands." Another Lay Carmelite wrote "often I am blessed with the scent of Roses at specific times, signifying her [Mary's] approval of my thoughts. She nudges me to certain words, to select in saying prayers 'her' way."

It is beyond the scope of this article to look at the Christological, ecclesiological, and soteriological ramifications of many of the responses received. Suffice it to say that sound opinions on Mary tend to reflect general appreciation of Catholic doctrine; doctrinal deviations on Mary tend to reflect deviations in other areas of theology as well.

A History of Marian Devotion

There is a strong theme in Carmelite history and spirituality that assures us of Mary's patronal protection. When Catholics today speak of Marian spirituality they usually mean a spirituality that focuses around Mary as its organizing principle. The writings of Louis Grignon de Montfort are often interpreted, at least on a popular level, to provide this approach. Carmelite spirituality, on the other hand, is Christocentric. Its goal is a life of discipleship of Jesus Christ.[9] The Carmelite traditionally finds a path of direct access to Jesus, an access through his humanity. Mary, as the one through whom this humanity enters history, and as the first disciple of her Son, occupies a pivotal place in Carmelite spirituality, but one cannot say that she is its organizing principle.

While the Blessed Virgin Mary is mentioned in neither of the Order's two great 13th century foundational documents: the *Rule* and the *Fiery Arrow*, she was profoundly important to the hermits. The chapel on Mount Carmel was dedicated to her; she was the Lady of the Place, to whom the hermits had a particular loyalty. The hermits were known as *her* hermits, *her* brothers. When they began migrating back to Europe in the middle of the thirteenth century, this devotion came with them and already at that time many of their churches were known to be centers of the Marian cult.

From their first days on Mount Carmel the Carmelites saw Mary as their protector. Their church, on the frontier of the Saracen world, on the very front line of the Crusades, was not put under the patronage of the warrior saints who could defend it with arms, saints such as Michael or George. The hermits chose to entrust themselves and their foundation to Mary. But the most important defense of the Carmelite Order that its heavenly patroness would have to mount was not against the Saracens, but against the hierarchy. At the Second Council of Lyons in 1274 the Carmelites and the Augustinians were threatened with suppression by the assembled cardinals, bishops, and abbots. The monks and the diocesan clergy did not like the mendicants who were very popular with the common people. Vocations and financial support were going to these new orders rather than the traditional Church institutions. The Dominicans and Franciscans were too big and too close to the papacy for their enemies to eliminate, but the Carmelites and Augustinians were seen as easy pickings. The strategy was simple. Lateran IV had decreed in 1215 that there should be no new religious orders. The Augustinians were clearly instituted after this date having been formed by the Great Union of 1256 uniting a number of Italian hermit communities under the Rule of Augustine. The Carmelites, for their part, claimed to predate the ban, but had no papal approbation before 1226. The two small mendicant orders would simply be abolished as having been founded contrary to the canons of Lateran IV.

The Augustinians had a Cardinal friend, Riccardo Annibaldi, who worked hard on their behalf, but the Carmelites were more or less on their own. Their only help could come from their heavenly patroness. The date was set for the canon suppressing the orders to be presented to the Council: July 17th. It would take a miracle.

The miracle came through, though it is not clear exactly how. Perhaps it was the confusion in the council caused by the death of one of the leading members of the papal household and council fathers, the Franciscan Cardinal (Saint) Bonaventure of Bagnoreggio, during the night of July 15th. Whatever the cause, the council's course of action changed substantially and the Order was given a deferment from suppression. Although that reprieve was not made permanent until 1298, the Order's closest brush with extinction (though not its last) had been overcome.[10] The Carmelites had had a close call, and they remembered the deliverance that Mary's protection had won them. Cicconetti claims that after 1274 the Carmelites associated July 17th with deep gratitude to our Blessed Lady for her protection.[11] This deliverance could not be celebrated on July 17th, the feast of the then very popular Saint Alexis, so it came to be celebrated on July 16th. It was only in the late 14th century that this date replaced August 15th as the preeminent feast in honor of the Virgin for Carmelites.[12]

Carmelite devotion to Mary was not merely turning to her protection, however. The Carmelites looked at Mary as a model of the relationship which they sought with her Son. At the end of the 14th century, the Order's third and final great foundational document, *The Institute of the First Monks*, presented a very thorough treatment of the Blessed Virgin in Carmelite heritage. In *The Institute of the First Monks* Mary is seen primarily as a model for Carmelites to imitate in their life of discipleship.

Protection and discipleship combine in the spread of the Brown Scapular of Our Lady of Mount Carmel. The idea of Mary bestowing a habit on a religious community that pleased her was not a new one. The Dominicans had long circulated stories about Mary giving their habit to Blessed Reginald in a dream. Similarly, stories had long circulated about religious habits having the power to save their wearer's from both spiritual and physical dangers. Franciscan preachers claimed that Francis of Assisi came to purgatory once a year and rescued all the Franciscans there. While these stories often led to abuses, their purpose was not to mislead the faithful but to illustrate God's bestowal of saving grace on those who persevered in their commitment of discipleship.

In a debate with the Dominican, John Stokes, Carmelite John Hornby, testified to the Dominican custom of presenting, in each of that order's churches, an image of the Blessed Virgin bestowing the Dominican habit.[13] Carmelites also kept an image of the Blessed Virgin Mary in their churches. In the thirteenth and fourteenth centuries these images, while not portraying the scapular being given to Simon Stock, often provided a center for the popular cult of the Blessed Virgin Mary. Notable among these images are *La Bruna* from the *Carmine Maggiore* of Naples, the *Madonna del Popolo* of the *Carmine* basilica in Florence, and the marble image of the Madonna at Trapani in Sicily. These images are all connected, not to a specifically Carmelite devotion such as the scapular, but to a popular Marian cult in their respective Carmelite churches. The faithful came to these churches to encounter Mary and her protection. These images functioned as icons of the Madonna to whom the people of Naples, Trapani, and Florence had recourse in their needs. They were images that the Carmelites made available to the people for the people's needs and did not stress any particular patronage of the Blessed Virgin over the Carmelites themselves.

Mary's protection over the Carmelites themselves is displayed in a fascinating icon of the Blessed Virgin Mary currently located in a museum on Cyprus. It is hard to date, and it would be tempting to think that this picture might be from Mount

Carmel. However, as the Carmelites gathered under Mary's mantle are wearing white cloaks, not barred mantles, the painting must be dated after 1287-1290, and therefore most likely comes after the final exodus from the Holy Land in 1291. This painting expresses the patronage of the Blessed Virgin over the Carmelites not by means of the scapular but by depicting Carmelites huddled under Mary's mantle. This visual device originated with the Cistercians and was subsequently used by many religious orders to portray Mary's protection.

The first images of Mary actually bestowing the scapular upon the Carmelites date only from the fifteenth century. Stories of Mary appearing to Simon Stock and giving him the scapular began to circulate in the final quarter of the fourteenth century, and the scapular devotion had a relatively slow beginning.[14] In the late fifteenth century Carmelite preachers began to circulate stories of Mary's promising Pope John XXII in 1322 that she would deliver the souls of those who died in the scapular from purgatory on the first Saturday after death. The "Sabbatine Bull" of John XXII confirming this promise has been judged by historians to be a fifteenth century forgery from Agrigento in Sicily.[15]

Carmelites in the Middle Ages were allied with the Franciscans in proposing the doctrine of Mary's Immaculate Conception. This doctrine was a major area of theological debate in the Middle Ages because Dominican theologians, following Saint Thomas, found the doctrine theologically unacceptable. Carmelites vigorously defended the doctrine, both in speech and in ink, against their Dominican confreres. Carmelite theologians in the Middle Ages and early Renaissance wrote extensively on Marian themes, particularly the Immaculate Conception. John Baconthorpe (d. 1348) may be considered the first of the Order's Marian authors.[16] A long line of Carmelite theologians followed him in writing about the Blessed Virgin Mary and the tradition reached its zenith with Arnold Bostius (1445-1499) who in 1479 wrote *De patronatu et patrocinio B(eatae) V(irginis) M(ariae) in dicatum sibi Carmeli ordinem*. According to Smet, Bostius recommended his readers to offer all to God through the hands of the

Blessed Virgin Mary, thus proposing a true Marian spirituality.[17] Bostius was a contemporary of Jeanne de Valois (1464-1505) and reflected the same new Marian trend in spirituality that led eventually to Michael of Saint Augustine and Louis Grignon de Montfort. This trend did not, however, leave a significant imprint on the mainline of Carmelite spirituality, which would veer off in another direction under the Spanish mystics.

When the Carmelite tradition reached its apex with the two doctors of the Church, Teresa of Avila and John of the Cross, Mary continued to remain a steady but subtle presence in Carmelite spirituality. Both Teresa and John had a strong devotion to the Mother of God, but neither ever takes their focus off the humanity of Jesus as the center of their spirituality. Mary receives no more than passing mentions in the great classic works of these Carmelite authors. There is a deep appreciation for her role in salvation and a confidence in her as mother and sister, but the soul of each yearns only for union with Jesus. Of course, if we accept Laurentin's thesis that the "Marian Movement" has been with the Church for only three centuries, these great Carmelite mystics reflect an older spiritual tradition that predates the Marian emphasis that rose in the 17th century.

An exception to this general trend in the Carmelite Spiritual tradition is the Belgian friar of the Touraine reform, Michael of Saint Augustine. Michael wrote extensively on Carmelite spirituality and never lost a Christocentric focus. His most popular book, however, is his treatise, *The Mary-form and Marian Life in Mary*.[18] Michael anticipated many of the themes that Louis Grignon de Montfort would eventually make popular in his works. In his strong Marian emphasis, Michael of Saint Augustine reflects seventeenth century French spirituality–and the origins of what Laurentin calls "The Marian Movement"–as much as, or even more than he reflects the older Carmelite tradition. On the other hand, the clear emphasis in his treatise, usually referred to simply as "*The Mariform Life*," is Mary as the model of discipleship.

As the Order recovered from the trauma dealt it by the French Revolution and subsequent secularist regimes and began producing saints again in the late nineteenth and twentieth centuries, its saints took the paths outlined by Teresa and John. For Edith Stein, Elizabeth of the Trinity and others, Mary occupies a place of love and respect, but the soul always is looking beyond her to Jesus. Thérèse of Lisieux, the latest Carmelite to be named Doctor of the Church, had a strong personal devotion to Mary, perhaps all the stronger for her having lost her mother so young, but even in her writings Jesus always remains the central organizing feature. The sobriety of the Marian dimension of these Carmelites' spiritualities is in marked contrast to much of the spiritual literature of the time that was shaped by the "Marian Movement."

The Task of Shaping Marian Devotion
for Lay Carmelites Today

Laurentin's insight is valuable. While Marian devotion continues in the Church, the "Marian Movement" has come to its peak and is in a state of natural decline. It was prolonged, Laurentin wrote, for a century beyond its 1854 success, but only with a certain measure of artifice.[19] With the declaration of the second Marian dogma, the Assumption, in 1950, the energy required to maintain the movement at the center of the Church's life had been sapped. The role of the Fatima visions in Catholic popular imagination concealed a shift in the theological and hierarchical levels of the Church. That change was clearly signaled at Vatican II when the Council Fathers decided to include Mary in the Document on the Church and not prepare a specific document concerning her. This decision was not a denigration of the Blessed Virgin Mary, but a clear statement that she had a new place in the Catholic cosmos. She no longer stood above the community of the faithful, between it and her Divine Son, but she stands within the community of the faithful as its first and most glorious member. The impetus today for further Marian dogmas seems to be unable to gather hierarchical support, even from John Paul II, this most Marian of popes. Mary is in a different place in Catholic understanding than she was sixty years ago, and there are no signs that that history is to be reversed. That new position is not the work of sinister and dissident forces within the Church, but of the magisterium itself.

Mary's being in a different place than she had held for the previous three centuries does not mean, however, that she is eclipsed in any way. Greeley claims that Mary remains a pivotal symbol of our Christian faith not only for older Catholics, but for younger ones, and for younger non-Catholic Christians as well.[20] If Mary is so central to popular Christianity, we Carmelites need to realize that we hold a valuable card in our rich Marian tradition. The trick is to bring that tradition forward in a way that is harmonious with the direction the hierarchical Church is taking and that has credibility among the faithful. Such a change in direction, however, will confuse and anger the small minority of Catholics who have not accepted the theological shifts of the Second Vatican Council. An example of this conflict of paradigms can be found in the attempts to update the catechesis on the Brown Scapular. The Congregation for Divine Worship wrote in their introduction to the current rites for blessing and enrolling the faithful:

> More recently, thanks to a deeper understanding of our tradition and the fruit of research and of the process of renewal in the whole Church, the approach to popular devotions and, therefore, to the scapular, has changed.[21]

No task in our Lay Carmelite ministry has been more difficult than to convince many devotees of the scapular that there indeed has been a change in the Church's approach to the Brown Scapular. Every citation from the Congregation's doctrinal statement is challenged by quotes from Howard Rafferty, Kilian Lynch, St. Alphonsus Ligouri, any number of popes, and Our Lady herself at Fatima. The problem, of course, is not the Brown Scapular, or even Marian Devotion. The Scapular is simply the occasion in which the hostility, anger and fear of some come to the surface. The problem is the resistance to the development of doctrine that happened at the Second Vatican Council. The scapular is a particularly potent symbol of that shift. Those who wish to see Mary in her old position as above the Church, mediating between it and her Divine Son, see the scapular as a symbol of the mediatrix's tender promise to rescue them from the fires of hell and purgatory. Those who embrace the Council's theology of Mary as the first disciple understand the scapular as a sign of affiliation to the Order that walks with its patroness *in obsequio Jesu Christi.*

Rejection of the Second Vatican Council is not limited to those who cling to a preconciliar understanding of the scapular. There are those, both on the left and the right, who try to steer the Church in ideological directions contrary to the direction set by the Council and maintained by the post-Conciliar papacies. Various groups that label themselves as *The Reform of the Reform* or the *Reform of the Renewal* profess loyalty to the Church and even cite conciliar and papal authority for agendas that are in marked contrast to the Council and to authentic papal teaching. They create an illusion of faithfulness and orthodoxy by an exaggerated adherence to superficial traditions. Their energies seem to be primarily directed to restoring a pre-conciliar ecclesiology, liturgy, and consecrated life. Some Lay Carmelites have been drawn to these groups thinking that they represent an authentic Catholicism over and against the Church led by their bishops and pastors. In a few places Lay Carmelites have become divisive in their dioceses or parishes, challenging the orthodoxy of the pastors who do not adhere to the emerging shadow magisterium found both on airwaves and in print. Lay Carmelites who believe that their bishops are leading them into error cannot have much confidence in the Order either. We must reconcile ourselves to the inevitable loss of those members who favor a restorationist Catholicism. Fortunately, it is a small percentage of the Lay Carmelite movement. While most Lay Carmelites are by no means enthusiastic liberals, the majority have embraced the Council, are happy with the current Liturgy, and trust their bishops.

Since Father Al Sieracki's time as Provincial Director of the Lay Carmelites, we have recognized the strong need to develop suitable formation materials for our Lay Carmelites. Tom Zeitvogel, T.O.Carm., has been an invaluable asset in this task. But the task is far from complete. An urgent need is a total reediting of *Carmel's Call*, the handbook and devotional resource book for Lay Carmelites. Devotional life in the Lay Carmelite communities must be made consistent with the life of the larger Church and Order. Formation materials are only one component in the need to thoroughly catechize our Lay Carmelites so that they may be empowered to take on the role to which Vatican II has called the laity, to be the agents of the Church in the world. In particular the Lay Carmelites must be empowered to help vivify the larger Church with the rich traditions of spirituality which is Carmel's unique heritage and mission.

This catechesis must be a comprehensive restatement of the faith of the Church as it is expressed in our spiritual tradition. The responses of Lay Carmelites to the questionnaire surfaced some troubling issues regarding the humanity of Christ, the theology of grace, the relationship of the Eucharist to the Church, the nature of the Church, the desire of God for the salvation of all persons, the nature of revelation, and other theological topics. Because the humanity of Christ is fundamental to our Carmelite spiritual tradition, catechetical materials for Lay Carmelites particularly need to emphasize the role of Christ's human nature in our redemption. The *monita* of John of the Cross towards private revelation and extraordinary phenomena must also receive a much stronger emphasis, as must a clear explanation of the role and authority of the visible Church, particularly the Ecclesiology of the Second Vatican Council. These topics are not peripheral to our Carmelite vocation. We cannot establish a healthy spirituality on a faulty interpretation of our faith. The task of educating and forming our Lay Carmelites is an ongoing one, even as it needs to be for the friars.

This, of course, introduces the need for ongoing education and formation of our own Carmelite religious in Carmelite spirituality, and indeed in the wider field of theology. We need to build stronger ties between the Lay Carmelites and the Carmelite religious. Many of our religious are reluctant to work with our Lay Carmelites because they, the religious, do not feel confident in their appreciation of our tradition. Not only for the sake of our Lay Carmelites, but for the sake of the larger Church, we must do everything we can to help Carmelite friars, nuns, and religious sisters to become more familiar with the riches of our tradition so that they can be resourceful to the many members of the Church who are searching for spirituality and turning to Carmel in hopes of finding it.

An important part of the catechesis we must provide for Carmelite laity will be how best to articulate the place of Mary in Carmelite life and spirituality. No small work has been done already on this topic. The 1998 conference on the Blessed Virgin Mary sponsored by the Carmelite Institute in Reno, Nevada, produced a series of fine papers on this topic. This *Festschrift* too will produce a number of articles that hopefully will contribute further to the subject of Mary and Carmel. The task remains, however, how best to get the work of scholars into the hands and more importantly into the hearts of Lay Carmelites.

The scapular will remain the primary visible sign of our dedication as Carmelites to Mary. We must continue to develop a scapular catechesis that will not deny the protective element of Mary's solicitude, but contextualize it within a commitment to follow Mary's example of discipleship. The scapular must consistently be presented as a sign of affiliation to the Carmelite Order and a commitment to participate in its following of Jesus Christ. The connection between the scapular and the Order, and through the Order to Mary's protection, needs to be reestablished in popular Catholic understanding.

The task ahead of us, this task of helping our Lay Carmelites, and indeed helping the larger Church, better to appreciate the role of the Blessed Virgin Mary in our redemption and better to appropriate a relationship with her in Christ Jesus, is a task to which the life and ministry of Eamon Carroll has long been committed. It is a privilege to continue this work, even in our small ways, and to work alongside Eamon in this wonderful mission.

Patrick Thomas McMahon, O.Carm.

Endnotes

1. Andrew Greeley, *The Catholic Myth: The Behavior and Beliefs of American Catholics* (New York: Touchstone, 1990). In chapter 13, "Mary and the Womanliness of God," Greeley makes an effective argument that the Blessed Virgin is such a powerful symbol for American Catholics that she transcends commitment to any one doctrinal position, even orthodoxy. See p. 246.

2. Karl Rahner, *Mary Mother of the Lord: Theological Meditations* (New York: Herder and Herder, 1963), p. 95.

3. Rahner, *Mary Mother of the Lord*, p. 95.

4. Greeley, *The Catholic Myth*, pp. 61-62.

5. René Laurentin, *A Short Treatise on the Virgin Mary* (Translated by Charles Neumann, S.M., Washington, New Jersey: AMI Press, 1991), p 144.

6. Sally Cunneen, *In Search of Mary: The Woman and The Symbol* (New York: Ballantine, 1996), p. 234. The Turners, incidentally, were converts to Catholicism through the ministry of Father Malachy Lynch, O.Carm., of Aylesford in England.

7. Charles R. Morris, *American Catholic: The Saints and Sinners Who Built America's Most Powerful Church* (New York: Vintage Books, 1997). pp. 228-229.

8. For the origins of Millennialism and the role of chiliastic prophecy in American Protestantism, see Sydney E. Ahlstrom, *A Religious History of the American People* (New Haven: Yale University Press, 1972), pp. 478-481.

9. George Tavard, *The Thousand Faces of the Virgin Mary* (Collegeville, Minnesota: The Liturgical Press, 1996), p. 175. Tavard dates the oldest Marian Spirituality to St. Jeanne de Valois, a French princess who had visions at the end of the 15th century. When one sees the writings of other authors of this period, notably the Carmelite Arnold Bostius, one would be hesitant to attribute this

new spirituality to the French Princess, but rather see her spirituality as embodying, and publicizing, a Mary-centered spirituality that existed somewhat independently of her. Nevertheless her influence was to stamp much of French spirituality, especially in the 17th and 18th centuries. The Carmelite Michael of St. Augustine and later St. Louis Grignon de Montfort will be the high water marks of this type of spirituality. Montfort certainly did not propose a Marian spirituality as differentiated from a Christocentric spirituality but, very much in the spirit of the late seventeenth and eighteenth centuries, French spirituality saw Mary as the path towards Christ. Unfortunately, many devotees of Montfort's writings have so immersed themselves in the Marian characteristics of his spirituality that they do not have the focus on Christ that he proposes.

10. For a more detailed account of these events, see Carlo Cicconetti, O.Carm., *La Regola del Carmelo: origine, natura, significato* (Roma: Institutum Carmelitanum, 1973), pp. 331-353.

11. Cicconetti, *La Regola del Carmelo*, p. 347.

12. As the scapular stories emerged, the date was associated not only with Mary's protection over the Order, but explicitly with the conferral of the sign of that protection, the scapular, to Saint Simon Stock. I gave a more extensive treatment of this subject in a talk in Darien, Illinois, celebrating the 40th anniversary of Aylesford. This talk will be published in the 2000 edition of *The Sword*.

13. Richard Copsey, O.Carm., "Simon Stock and the Scapular Vision," *Journal of Ecclesiastical History* 50:4 (October, 1999), p. 666.

14. For an extensive treatment of the emergence of the scapular stories, see Copsey, "Simon Stock and the Scapular Vision," pp. 652-683.

15.   Joachim Smet, O.Carm., *The Carmelites: A History of the Brothers of Our Lady of Mount Carmel* (Darien, Illinois: Carmelite Spiritual Center, 1988), I:118.

16.   Smet, *The Carmelites*, I:55.

17.   Smet, *The Carmelites*, I:117.

18.   Smet, *The Carmelites*, III:445.

19.   Laurentin, *A Short Treatise on the Virgin Mary*, p. 144.

20.   Greeley, *The Catholic Myth*, p. 244.

21.   Congregation for Divine Worship and for the Discipline of the Sacraments, *"Rite of Blessing and Enrollment in the Scapular of the Blessed Virgin Mary of Mount Carmel,"* November 29, 1996. Prot. 2243/96/L.

A Changed Context
for Marian Doctrine

Eamon Carroll's career as Mariologist spans a period of more than fifty years. He became a member of the Mariological Society of America in the early 1950s and has attended virtually all of that organization's annual meetings. Since 1967, he has presented a "Survey of Mariology" at the annual meetings, which later appeared as an article in *Marian Studies* (the proceedings of the annual meetings of the Mariological Society of America). His "Survey," consisting of reviews and comments on the significant Marian literature published during the previous year, usually opened with the "three highlights of the year," and then proceeded to review the documents of the magisterium, articles in scholarly European journals, significant publications in Scripture, doctrine, liturgy, "devotion and devotions," ecumenism. It frequently concluded with a few lines of poetry.

Any overview of the topics discussed by Mariologists in the last fifty years (as, for example, those found in the fifty issues of *Marian Studies*) will reveal that the Second Vatican Council was the great watershed or dividing point which changed both the focus and organization of Mariology and the expressions of Marian devotion. A cursory comparison of Marian documents from the preconciliar and postconciliar periods will indicate some of the transformations brought about by the various scholarly movements which influenced the deliberations of Vatican II. The biblical movement, the resurgence in patristic studies, the liturgical movement–all deeply influenced and enriched Vatican II's text on the Virgin Mary. Consequently, postconciliar Marian texts clearly demonstrate a more biblical, patristic, and liturgical orientation than those written before the council. One need only compare John Paul II's *Redemptoris mater* (1987) with Pius XII's *Fulgens corona* (1953) to note the changes which have occurred.

But there is another significant type of change which has occurred, one related to the way individual doctrines are presented and to how a treatise on the Virgin Mary is organized. This change is a bit more difficult to identify, since it deals with the way or the context within which the Marian doctrines are situated. This essay attempts to compare the contours of preconciliar Mariology and its context for expressing the Marian dogmas, with the contours and context of the Marian dogmas which appear in the conciliar and postconciliar Marian texts, especially postconciliar Marian liturgical texts. It will also analyze a few basic concepts from Vatican II, evident in the documents on liturgy and the Church, which resulted in the changed context for Marian doctrines.

I. Doctrine in Preconciliar Mariology and Devotion

Until the beginning of Vatican II, almost all theology was dominated by dogma, and Mariology, in the opinion of a knowledgeable scholar, "was unquestionably the most active area in dogmatic theology."[1] The preconciliar Mariological movement originated in the mid-nineteenth century; Juniper Carol wrote that it "owes it origin and inspiration to the dogmatic definition of the Immaculate Conception in the year 1854."

> It is now generally conceded that the scientific treatment of Mariology, as we know it today, is the logical outgrowth of that epoch-making papal pronouncement. It was the impetus given in this direction first by Pius IX, and later by Leo XIII

through his immortal Marian encyclicals, that
stimulated Catholic theologians to devote great
attention to this noble branch of the sacred sciences.[2]

The definition of the Assumption (1950) and the proclamation of
the Marian Year (1954) marked the apex of the movement. The
rise of the Mariological movement also coincided with the revival
and the dominance of neoscholasticism as the accepted framework for the expression of doctrine. The modern Mariological
movement, from its nineteenth century origins, was imprinted
with three characteristics: 1) a highly, almost exclusively, dogmatic orientation; 2) a reliance on papal pronouncements; and 3)
a dependence on neo-scholastic philosophy and terminology.

The great Mariological treatises and manuals of the
preconciliar period–from those of Cardinal Lepicier, Emilio
Campana, Gabriel Roschini to Emil Neubert and Juniper Carol–
all reveal the great influence which doctrine had on the organization of Marian treatises.[3] The opening sections of these works
usually dwelt on the implications of the Divine Maternity, and
then proceeded to Mary's participation in the redemptive work of
Christ (the New Eve, co-redemption, mediation). Next came
sections on the Immaculate Conception, the Assumption, and
Mary's spiritual or universal motherhood. The deductive method,
common to manual theology, was employed: the thesis was stated
and then proven by reference to the sources, with highest place
given to the statements of the magisterium. Doctrines were clearly
and coherently expressed, in concepts corresponding to their
perennial character. Since Mariology was a science in the
neoscholastic sense, it required a "primary principle" or "a
fundamental truth which furnishes the ultimate reason for the
various theses of a given science ... a basic proposition, accepted
by all, which alone gives organic coherence and logical nexus to
the whole treatise."[4] The divine maternity was usually offered as
the basic principle, but other proposals included Mary's role as

co-redemptrix, the plenitude of grace (Alois Mueller), and the bridal maternity of Mary (M. J. Scheeben).

The high place given to statements of the magisterium by the modern Mariological movement was very much part of the heritage of Vatican I (1870), which spoke of papal primacy and infallibility, and of the Church's responsibility to "jealously guard and faithfully explain the revelation or deposit of faith that was handed down through the apostles."[5] Because of its origins in the papal definition of the Immaculate Conception, modern Mariology, perhaps more than any other area of theology, devoted much effort to the explanation of statements of the magisterium and advocated additional doctrinal definitions.[6] In the 1950s, Monsignor George Shea assessed this trend:

> If we may high-light some of the more important features of contemporary Mariology, the first to be noted is the growing preoccupation with the declarations of the ecclesiastical magisterium, the ordinary as well as the extraordinary. This is a most fruitful development. For one thing, such declarations furnish the supreme argument in theology and are an indispensable safeguard in interpreting the data of Sacred Scripture and Tradition.[7]

This great concern with dogma influenced the Mariologist's approach to history and liturgy. Studies in Church history and liturgy were frequently ways of assessing the consent of previous generations to the major Marian doctrines as defined in the nineteenth and twentieth centuries. In Juniper Carol's *Mariology*, studies on Mary in the early Church and in liturgy reveal the underlying concern for the Marian dogmas which guided them. Walter Burghardt's article, "Mary in Western Patristic Thought," was an investigation of the writers of "the first seven centuries on the five prerogatives linked inseparably to Our Lady in contemporary Catholic theology."[8] In another article, on Mary in the liturgy, Simeon Daly, O.S.B., stated that the purpose of surveying the references to Mary in the liturgy was "to find reflected in the Western liturgy evidence of the dogmatic truths we profess concerning our Lady."[9]

This dominance of doctrine was reflected in the early twentieth-century Mariological congresses and societies. The Flemish Mariological Society, founded in 1933, was an extension of the movement for doctrinal definition of Mary as Mediatrix of All Graces. Similarly, the early years of the French Mariological Society showed a preoccupation with dogma, especially Mary's relation to the work of redemption. The Mariological Society of America, founded in 1949, stated as its purpose: "the study and dissemination of doctrine relating to the Blessed Virgin Mary."[10] In the first decade, the 1950s, the Mariological Society of America, as reflected in the issues of *Marian Studies*, dealt almost exclusively with doctrinal topics. Only in its second decade, which corresponded to Vatican II, did studies on Scripture, ecumenism, and new approaches to Marian doctrines appear.

In the preconciliar period, the Marian dogmas were viewed in the same context as the other great doctrines. Classical treatises on dogma rarely related directly to the lives of believers (the exception being the occasional *corrolaria pietatis*). After the condemnation of the errors of the Modernists (1907), there was even a greater hesitancy to relate doctrine to life. Doctrines were classically expressed in ahistorical and impersonal terms. Doctrines were to regulate life–not the reverse. Seeking confirmation for doctrine within personal experience could lead to the position that experience in some way validated or invalidated doctrine.

Though acknowledged as the cornerstones of faith, the great dogmas–the Trinity, the Incarnation, the Redemption–did not directly configure or influence moral conduct. They provided assurance and certitude to the individual, but they were not proposed as providing patterns or models for daily living.[11] This attitude is conveyed in the "old" (1909) *Catholic Encyclopedia*'s explanation of the way in which doctrine influenced the life of the believer:

> Dogmatic belief is not the be-all and end-all of
> Catholic life; but the Catholic serves God, honors
> the Trinity, loves Christ, obeys the Church, fre-
> quents the sacraments, assists at Mass, observes
> the Commandments because he believes mentally
> in God, in the Trinity, in the Divinity of Christ, in
> the Church, in the sacraments and the Sacrifice of
> the Mass, in the duty of keeping the Command-
> ments, and he believes in them as objective,
> immutable truths.[12]

Because of their concentration on dogma, Mariological treatises and societies excluded popular Marian devotions from their consideration.[13] Consequently, popular Marian devotions were frequently bereft of much dogmatic content. The prayers and hymns used at the novena services presented Mary as a loving and powerful mother who, though dwelling in lofty heights, had a personal, motherly concern for every individual. Her privileges increased her intercessory role; yet the features of her doctrinal physiognomy—the Divine Maternity, Co-redemptrix, Immaculate Conception, Assumption—were not directly related to individuals. The "imitation of Mary" was a frequent theme in popular piety, but it was not the doctrinal truths about Mary which were presented for imitation, but rather her example of obedience, humility, purity.[14] (Among Marian dogmas, Mary's virginity was the one most frequently proposed for direct imitation.) With few exceptions, the Marian collects of the Roman Missal (1962) rarely developed the implications of doctrinal affirmations. The doctrinal "thinness" of preconciliar Marian liturgical texts can be seen in the Commons of the Blessed Virgin: the opening prayer of the votive Mass for Saturday of the Blessed Virgin asks "to enjoy health of mind and body" and "to be freed from the sorrows of this life so as to have future joy" through the intercession of the Blessed Virgin Mary.

The lofty atmosphere of Mariological treatises and societies mirror the pronouncements of the magisterium on the Virgin

Mary. It would almost appear that papal pronouncements wished to show the great distance–the enormous chasm–which separated Mary from humanity. Pius IX's *Ineffabilis Deus* (1854) spoke of Mary as the one

> most pure in soul and body, who transcends all integrity and virginity, who alone and in her entirety has become the dwelling place of all the graces of the Holy Spirit, and who, God alone excepted, is superior to all, and by nature more fair, more beautiful, and more holy than the very Cherubim and Seraphim and the entire angelic host; she whom all the tongues of heaven and earth cannot sufficiently extol.

Pius XII's definition of the Assumption in *Munificentissimus Deus* (1950) spoke of

> the privileges which an all-provident God had lavished on this beloved associate of our Redeemer; privileges which reached so lofty a peak that, apart from the human nature of Jesus Christ, no creature other than she has ever attained them.

In *Fulgens corona* (1953), this latter Pontiff referred to the Immaculate Conception and the Assumption as

> two very singular privileges, bestowed upon the Virgin Mother of God, [which] stand out in most splendid light as the beginning and as the end of her earthly journey, for the greatest possible glorification of her virginal body is the complement, at once appropriate and marvelous, of the absolute innocence of her soul, which was free from stain.

These documents gave no indication of how the great Marian privileges related to the Church or influenced Christian life.

II. Dogma at Vatican II

In preparation for Vatican II (1962-1965) a set of documents, written by the Preparatory Theological Commission, was presented to the body of bishops as the basis for their deliberations. These documents were rejected, because they were couched in terms which lacked the pastoral approach that John XXIII had indicated for the council; they did not speak a language comprehensible to contemporary society.[15] Those who criticized the preparatory drafts were encouraged by Pope John XXIII's opening speech, *Gaudet Mater Ecclesia*, which noted that the purpose of the council was not to proclaim doctrine but rather to present that which had already been defined in a way comprehensible to contemporary humanity. The pope's address continued with a statement allowing, in some instances even encouraging, a reformulation of doctrinal statements.

> The substance of the ancient doctrine of the deposit of faith is one thing, and the way in which it is presented is another, and it is the latter that must be taken into great consideration with patience if necessary, everything being measured in the forms and proportions of a magisterium which is predominantly pastoral in character.[16]

The council's discussion on the nature of revelation would influence the manner in which doctrine was presented. *Dei Verbum*, the dogmatic consitution on divine revelation, stated that the center is God's self-revelation, communicaed by "deeds and words having an inner unity." Divine revelation was not expressed in abstract, essentialist concepts, but rather in words, signs, and symbols, formulated in the language and culture of the people. The council's discussion on revelation also gave evidence of an "historical consciousness," that is, an awareness that revelation is communicated in and through history. At the council, thought patterns and philosophies appeared which were centered upon the individual living in time, and which were in sharp contrast to the approach of neoscholasticism. This new manner of thinking—generally characterized as existentialist— had influenced Catholic theology in Europe after 1930. This great shift within Catholicism from neoscholasticism to existentialism is usually associated with Karl Rahner, Otto Semmelroth and Edward Schillebeeck.[17] "In the last century there was an attitudinal shift from the Enlightenment to Romanticism, so also in our century there was a cultural shift from Reason to Living, and this intellectual trend also had an impact on Catholic thought."[18]

One way of outlining the factors which influenced the context for presenting doctrine, and which influenced the expressions of Marian doctrines, can be seen in the deliberations on the first topics considered at the council–namely, the liturgy and the Church. The older definitions were not rejected, but rather expanded and placed in a larger context. Here, under three headings—1) mystery, 2) symbol, and 3) participation—we will summarize some of the changes in liturgy and ecclesiology which occurred early in the council and which influenced the Marian statement found in chapter eight of *Lumen gentium.*

1) Mystery

Vatican II avoided scholastic definitions to describe the liturgy and the Church. Instead, it used the Scriptural and patristic concept of *mystery.* The Constitution on the Liturgy contains at least twenty-three references to the mystery celebrated in liturgy (e.g., the mystery of Christ, the mystery of redemption, the mystery of salvation, the paschal mystery). "The Mystery of the Church" is the title of the first chapter of *Lumen Gentium.* The mystery of Christ and the Church were proposed as fundamental or pivotal concepts around which other truths, for example, those related to the Virgin Mary, would be formulated.

As mystery, the Church is the sacrament of the encounter of God with humanity. Mystery is a comprehensive and inclusive term: a mystery, in the words of Gabriel Marcel, "can only be thought of as a sphere where the distinction between what is in me and what is before me loses its meaning, its initial validity."[19] Quite compatible with modern philosophy, the notion of mystery is derived from the patristic concept; it is a term of union, one that includes both Christ and the Christian. In the words of St Leo the Great, "'What was visible in the Lord has passed over into the mysteries."[20] *Mystery* appears in the title of Vatican II's statement on the Virgin Mary: "The Blessed Virgin Mary in the Mystery of Christ and the Church" (LG, ch. 8).

2) Symbol

A second context for describing doctrine was the symbolic. A symbol is a way of denoting a similarity or likeness between two objects. Patristic biblical commentary spoke frequently of antitypes which in some way anticipated what would be contained in the type (this style of comparison was revived in the preconciliar period, especially in the works of Jean Danielou). In Greek thought, *symbol* exerts an inner attraction over the subject, drawing it to itself. In the conciliar documents, symbol is used principally to express the relationship between Mary and the Church, and then between Mary and all believers.[21] This symbolic relation of Mary to the Church and to individual Christians is expressed in different terms: *imago, typus, forma, exemplar*. The symbolic image of Mary has at least three functions:

a) *Formation* – The Virgin Mary is first of all the "type" of the Church; she exercises a formative influence over the Church. "The Church continues its earthly journey, continually *conforming* itself to its type in faith, hope, and charity" (LG, 65).

b) *Identity and Completion* – The council's first document, *Sacrosanctum concilium*, the constitution on the liturgy, well anticipated what would later be said in *Lumen gentium* on the way the Church sees herself in Mary and looks to her for completion. "In her [Mary], the Church holds up and admires the most excellent fruit of the redemption, and joyfully contemplates, as in a faultless *model* (*imago*) that which she herself wholly desires and hopes to be" (SC, 103).

c) *Exemplar* – Mary stands before the Church as the exemplar of virtue (LG, 65). Later, in *Marialis cultus*, Paul VI developed the notion of Mary's exemplarity by proposing Mary as "the model of the Church for worship." Mary's exemplarity is based on the fact that she illustrates in her person what the Church at worship is in its deepest level, on "the absolute union with Christ" which is the heart of worship and, for that reason, she is the exemplar or "model of the spiritual attitude with which the church celebrates and lives the divine mysteries" (MC, 16). Mary is "above all the example of that worship that consists in making one's life an offering to God" (MC, 21).

3) Participation

A third aspect of Vatican II's approach to ecclesiology and liturgy, which influenced its approach to Marian dogma, was the participative dimension of the mystery of Christ and the Church. *Sacrosanctum concilium* called for the "full, conscious, and active participation" (SC, 14) of those who participated at liturgy. *The Catechism of the Catholic Church* defines liturgy as "the participation of the People of God in the 'work of God'" (CCC, 1069-1072). But this "active participation" is based on an interior incorporation in the mystery of Christ and the Church, and it is not limited to the liturgical celebration. Participation also includes the mystagogical dimension of "living the mystery."

> The liturgy ... is the outstanding means whereby the faithful may express in their lives, and manifest to others, the mystery of Christ and the real nature of the Church (*SC*, 2). In the liturgy, the

Church prays that "they [the faithful] may hold
fast in their lives to what they have grasped by
their faith" (SC, 10); priests are urged "to live the
liturgical life" (SC, 18).

Terms of participation influenced the formulation of Marian
doctrine and the approach to Marian devotion. Instead of using
the doctrinal language of mediation and co-redemption in reference to Mary, Vatican II spoke of Mary's participation, association, and sharing in the Christ's redemptive work. No longer could
Marian devotion be described as solely an act of the virtue of
religion, as, for example, "an act of honor and respect . . . gratitude
. . . loyalty and obedience."[22] Rather, devotion was to be based on
interior union and expressed in commitment of life. "Genuine
devotion to the Mother of the Redeemer cannot limit itself to a
series of sporadic devotional exercises; it must be reflected with
daily life."[23]

III. Marian Doctrine in Postconciliar Liturgical Texts

Here we intend to show how Vatican II's sacramental,
symbolic, and participative language related to dogma has begun
to influence expressions of Marian doctrine, as found especially
in the Marian liturgical texts which have appeared since Vatican
II. By contrast with the preconciliar approach, the Mariology of
Vatican II is, from its starting point, relational. The title of the
eighth chapter of Lumen gentium clearly indicates the relational
and integrative dimension: "The Blessed Virgin Mary, God-Bearer,
in the Mystery of Christ and the Church." The chapter begins with
a preface, continues with the description of the role of the Blessed
Virgin, first, in the Economy of Salvation, and then in the Church.
The final section deals with "devotion to Mary within the Church."
An epilogue, entitled "Mary, Sign of Sure Hope and Comfort for
God's Pilgrim People," serves as the conclusion for the entire
document. Note that the Marian doctrines are no longer the

organizing focus for the treatise on Mariology;[24] but have been integrated into a larger context.

Within *Lumen gentium*, the Marian doctrines–Mary's motherhood and virginity– stand not in isolation but are related to and find their completion in the Church: "For in the mystery of the Church, herself rightly called mother and virgin, the Blessed Virgin Mary stands out, presenting in a preeminent and singular way the model of both virgin and mother"(LG, 63). The maternity of Mary reinforces the motherhood of the Church: "By contemplating its model, the motherhood of the Church is strengthened– she herself becomes mother by faithfully receiving the word of God" (LG, 64). The comparison between the motherhood and virginity of Mary and of the Church is developed in the *Catechism of the Catholic Church:*

> At once virgin and mother, Mary is the symbol and the most perfect realization of the church: the church by receiving the word of God in faith becomes herself a mother. By preaching and Baptism she brings forth sons, who are conceived by the Holy Spirit and born of God, to a new and immortal life, she herself is a virgin, who keeps in its entirety and purity the faith she pledged to her spouse.[25]

The new liturgical texts which appeared after Vatican II show how the context for viewing the Immaculate Conception and the Assumption had changed. For the Feast of the Immaculate Conception, the 1969 Lectionary indicated as a reading Ephesians 1:3-6, 11-12 which, in this liturgical context, would appear to place the Immaculate Conception among God's "universal blessings," with the exhortation that all should strive to be "holy and blameless before God." The post-Vatican II Preface of the Immaculate Conception speaks of Mary's sinlessness as God's "sign of favor to the Church at its beginning, and the promise of its perfection as the bride of Christ, radiant in beauty." In her

Immaculate Conception, Mary is proposed both as "our advocate" and as "our pattern of holiness."

The new Lectionary's reading for the Solemnity of the Assumption places Mary's Assumption within the context of the general resurrection. The "first fruits" of the redemption are seen in Christ's resurrection, which, one day, all will enjoy, "each in his own order" (I Cor 15:20-27). The newly-composed preface for the Mass speaks of Mary's Assumption as "the beginning and the pattern of the Church in its perfection, and a sign of hope and comfort for your people on their pilgrim way."[26]

The first Marian Mass text which appeared after the council, "Mary, Image and Mother of the Church,"[27] composed for the Holy Year 1975, contains a preface that makes a connection between the gifts bestowed on Mary and the life of the Church:

1) In conceiving and nourishing Christ, Mary nurtured the Church at its beginnings;
2) At the cross, receiving God's parting gift of love, she became the mother of all brought to life by the death of her Son;
3) With the apostles in prayer, she became the "perfect pattern of the Church at prayer."
4) Through her Assumption, she cares for the pilgrim Church "with a mother's love."

The Collection of Masses of the Blessed Virgin Mary continued the development of Mary's relationship to the Church and to the individual. In relation to the Church, Mary is "model of the Church, our Mother" (16); at the cross, she stands as "model of the Church, Bride of Christ" (11). In giving birth to Christ, she is "model of the Church bringing to new birth . . . a people of faith" (16). The image of Mary joined in prayer awaiting the Holy Spirit is "the perfect pattern of the Church at prayer" (25). She is the "perfect image" of the Church as mother of "its future glory" (27). Mary offers an example of Christian virtue to the members of the Church: she is "the example of the faithful disciple" (10), "model of sublime love and profound humility" (26), "model of divine hope" (47), "model of perfect acceptance of your will and whole-hearted conformity to Christ" (44), "model of all who live by the spirit of the Gospel" (32).

The *Collection* also well illustrates the notion of participation–the Virgin Mary's participation in the work of Christ and our own participation in the mystery of Christ celebrated in the liturgy. (Participation is frequently expressed through the patristic title of *socia* and related words: *sociare, associare,* and a word of more recent origin, *particeps*). God "has associated the compassionate Mary with her Son's suffering" (12), "associated her in the sacrifice of the altar" (12). She is "associated in the mystery of human redemption" (30), "intimately does she share in the mystery of Christ" (32).

Together with Mary, the members of the Church also participate in Christ's saving work. "We have shared in your mysteries" (33); "we share in the eternal banquet" (29); "we come to share with her [Mary] in your own divine love" (37). We ask that we may be joined "more closely with her [Mary] in sharing the redeeming work of her Son (25), that by "carrying our cross each day we may come to share in his resurrection" (12, 44). We also pray that "the sacred mystery in which we have shared ... may make us always share in the divinity of her Son" (47); we come together "to partake of this spiritual food and drink" (22); "we may come to share with her [Mary] in your own divine love" (37).

In the last half century, there has been a significant development in the way the great truths the Church professes concerning the Virgin Mary are presented. The former approach required that doctrine be clearly and precisely stated, with little or no relation either to the Church or to the life of the believer. Vatican II's discussion on revelation as primarily God's self-communication and its turn toward a more personalist philosophy was reflected in its view that doctrine also be related to Christ, to the Church, and to the life of the believer. At the Council, the relational concepts–mystery, symbol, and participation–which surfaced in the deliberation on the nature of the Church and of the liturgy, would also influence the formulation of Marian doctrine. This evolution in the approach to the Marian doctrines well illustrates the *Catechism of the Catholic Church*'s position on the "organic notion of doctrine," which relates the individual dogmas to each other and to daily living.

> There is an organic connection between our spiritual life and dogmas. Dogmas are lights along the path of faith; they illuminate it and make it secure .... Conversely, if our life is upright, our intellect and heart will be open to welcome the light shed by the dogmas of faith.[28]

Thomas A. Thompson, S.M

Endnotes

1. Alois Muller, "Contemporary Mariology," *Theology Today* (Milwaukee: Bruce Publishing Co., 1965), p. 109.
2. Juniper Carol, O.F.M., *Fundamentals of Mariology* (New York: Benziger Brothers, 1956), p. 10.
3. In 1949, on the occasion of the sixtieth anniversary of the *American Ecclesiastical Review*, Lawrence P. Everett, C.Ss.R., wrote that "every phase" of Mariology ... had been covered in the pages of the that journal under the following six headings: "the Immaculate Conception, the Assumption, the Divine Maternity, the Virgin birth, Mary's grace and Mary's knowledge; "Our Lady in the American Ecclesiastical Review," (October, 1949), 286-300.
4. Carol, *op. cit.*, pp. 7-9.
5. PA, 4.
6. Piet F. Franzen, *Hermeneutics of the Councils to Other Studies* (Leuven University Press, 1985), p. 271, refers to the trend initiated after Vatican I in Catholic theology which held that "the highest dignity a revealed truth could attain was to be defined by the pope or an ecumenical council." There was much evidence of this trend in Mariology.
7. George W. Shea, "Outline History of Mariology in the Middle Ages and Modern Times," *Mariology*, edited by Juniper B. Carol, O.F.M. (Milwuakee: Bruce, 1955) I:322.
8. Walter J. Burghardt, "Mary in Western Patristic Thought," *Mariology* I:110.
9. Simeon Daly, "Mary in the Western Liturgy," *Mariology* I:245.
10. Bylaws of the Mariological Society of America.
11. St. Thérèse of Lisieux complained of sermons on Mary which failed to make a relation to daily living. "They [sermons] show her to us as unapproachable, but they should present her as imitable, bring out her virtues, saying that she lived by faith just like ourselves . . . . It's good to speak of her privileges, but it's necessary above all

that we can imitate her." (*Derniers Entretiens* 23.8.6; 23.8.7).

12. Robert Appleton, "Dogma," *The Catholic Encyclopedia* (1909), V:91.

13. Popular Marian devotion was not of "direct concern" to Mariologists. Cf. Carol, *Fundamentals*, p. 10.

14. John F. Murphy, "The Origin and Nature of the Marian Cult," Carol, *Mariology* III:20. "In the realm of morals, Mary's example of virginity, dedication to vocation, and loyalty to Christ has been the inspiration of religious groups down through the centuries."

15. Klaus Wittstadt, "On the Eve of the Second Vatican Council," *History of Vatican II*, edited by Guiseppe Alberigo and Joseph A. Komonchak (Maryknoll, New York: Orbis, 1995), I:419-428.

16. John XXIII, "Gaudet Mater Ecclesia,"*Acta Synodalia Sacrosancti Concilii Oecumenici Vatican II*, vol. 1, pt. 1, 172.

17. One example of the influence these individuals had on ecclesiology can be found in Bernard Przewozny, O.F.M.Conv., *The Church as the Sacrament of the Unity of All Mankind in 'Lumen gentium' and 'Gaudium et spes' in Semmelroth, Schillebeeckx and Rahner* (*Miscellanea Francescana*, Rome, 1979).

18. John F. Kobler, "Toward a History of Vatican II," *Chicago Studies* 38 (Summer-Fall, 1999), 181.

19. Cited in George Tavard, *The Pilgrim Church* (New York: Herder and Herder, 1967), p. 42.

20. For more references to the Church as mystery, see Dom Odo Casel, *The Mystery of Christian Worship and Other Writings*, edited by B. Neunheuser (Westminster, Maryland: Newman, 1962), p. 12.

21. HCCC, 507, speaks of Mary as "the symbol and most perfect realization of the Church."

22. Murphy, *op. cit.*, p. 14.

23. *"Consilium Primarium Anno Mariali Celebrando, 'Terza Lettera Circolare ai Vescovi, 21 November 1987,'"Marianum*

49 (1987), 24-31.

24. Chapter eight makes only one reference to the Immaculate Conception: "the immaculate virgin, preserved free from the original fault" (59). The word *assumpta* does not appear in the document, although Mary is called "the first fruits of redemption."

25. CCC, 507; LG, 64, cf. 63.

26. In *Marialis cultus,* Paul VI noted "We have the theme of Mary and the Church, which has been inserted into the texts of the Missal in a variety of aspects, a variety that matches the many and varied relations that exist between the Mother of Christ and the Church. For example, in the celebration of the Immaculate Conception such texts recognize the beginning of the Church, the spotless Bride of Christ" (11).

27. Now in *The Collection of Masses of the Blessed Virgin Mary* (New York: Catholic Book Publishing Co., 1992), 207.

28. CCC, 88-89.

Blessed Among Women

This is a very simple article. It shares the result of work done by our communities. It reflects the efforts of a group of Carmelites called the Brazilian Carmelites' Reflection Network (INTERCAB) or the Brazilian Carmelite Dialogue; this is a group of brothers and sisters that draws together Carmelites from a variety of orders and congregations; it proposes to attempt a joint re-reading of the Carmelite charism in the light of the current situation of the Church and of the Brazilian people.

INTERCAB was born in 1987. Among its other activities it has been sponsoring each year eight-day gatherings, called "Carmel-Bible"; this is a time when its participants investigate, in the light of Scripture, a particular question of Carmelite Spirituality within the context of Brazilian reality. Thus, in January, 1997, the topic was Mary; the group met for a week to deepen our understanding of Mary's meaning, both in the Bible and in our individual lives.

During the first two days, before beginning our biblical study of Mary, the participants introduced themselves to one another at length–all members of the Carmelite family, though with different histories and activities. We then did an analysis of the plight of Brazilian women today, as well as of the devotion to Mary found among the Brazilian people. This is why our reflection contextualizing women's situation in the Old and New Testament takes up such a large part of this article. Those reflections form an integral part of our study. The title, "Blessed Among Women," reflects the group's objective: to locate Mary, as a woman among many women, both in the Bible and for today. This context-study had a two-fold objective: first, to help us perceive the environment from which biblical texts concerning Mary, the Mother of Jesus, had come down to us and how they should be interpreted; secondly to help us perceive the call of God which springs from the plight of today's women, marginalized by both Church and society.

Our study of the Marian biblical texts was not exhaustive from an exegetical point of view. Indeed this was not our purpose. Yet it had sufficient depth to shed light upon the questions arising from the lived reality of the participants.

Old Testament Context

In its account of Divine Wisdom's manifestations in the history of God's People (Sir 44-50), Sacred Scripture does not mention women. It records only the names of men. When the Book of Sirach mentions women, a certain contempt can be perceived (Sir 25:13). When ben Sirach does speak well of women, it is only from a male point of view (Sir 26:1-2; 13; 36:21-27). On the other hand, when the text speaks of Divine Wisdom, Wisdom is personified and praised by using the image of a woman (Sir 4:11-19; 14:20-15:10; 24:1-29). These two tendencies, the marginating of and the valuing of women, appear throughout the Old Testament, and in a progressive way. As the marginating increases so, too, does the resistance against it and the sense of women's value.

Increasing Margination of Women

A comparison of women's status during the post-exilic period with their status before the exile reveals a loss of ground in their position. From Ezra to Nehemias, the official tendency was to exclude women from every public activity; they are considered incapable of any participation in society, any role other than that of mother and domestic worker, one who educates the children.

What most contributed to women's margination was the law on purity. Women were declared impure as mothers, as wives, as daughters, as women. As mothers: by the act of giving birth, women became impure (Lv 12:1-5); as daughters: a newborn boy meant 40 days of impurity for the mother (Lv 12:2-4), but if the newborn were a girl, that meant 80 days (Lv 12:5); as wives: sexual relations made a woman impure for one day (Lv 15:18); as women: menstruation made a woman impure for seven days, and also caused impurity in others (whoever touched a menstruating woman had to be purified (Lv 15:19-30). Over and above these laws, there were others, forbidding contact, for example, with animals (Lv 11:1-47), with those who had skin diseases (Lv 13:1-59), with human impurities (Lv 5:3), with the deceased (Nm 19:11-16). And there was no way whereby a woman might keep her impurity secret, since the law required others to report her (Lv 5:1-6).

This legislation made daily living together unbearable since it gave rise to a mentality which saw women as inferior to men. Some proverbs reveal this discrimination (Sir 42:9-11; 22:3). The margination went so far as to consider women a danger, and the cause of every evil (Sir 42:13-14; 25:13; 25:24).

The factors contributing to this unbelievable scorn toward women are various: the male will to maintain dominance, the system's interest in increasing reproduction in order to have a greater number of people available for productive work; the Temple's interest in guaranteeing the offerings from the purification rites; cultural taboos linked to life, death and blood; women as objects of pleasure for men.

Some people become frightened when they discover these things in the Bible. This is nothing to be scared of at all! Give thanks to God! The Bible records *unerringly* the errors of the past. It *pictures without* lying the deceitful society just as it was, with all of its failures and struggles. St. Paul says that all these things, both the good and the evil, were written to serve as instruction for those of us who live in these end times, that we may not err where they erred (I Cor 10:6-11). All of this shows how God helps His people grow. It shows, above all, the joy of the Good News of Jesus for the people of that time and for us down to this day!

A Growing Appreciation for and Resistance by Women

In the context of that time, the plight of women among the biblical people was neither better nor worse than their plight among other peoples. It was part of the general culture. Even today this same mentality continues to exist among many peoples. But just as today, so in ancient times, there were opinions opposed to the marginating of women from the very beginning of the Bible's people: Hagar, rejected by Sarah and Abraham, was accepted by God and had a divine vision (Gn 16:1-15; 21:1-20); Shiphrah and Puah, two midwives, were present at the beginning of the liberation from Egypt (Ex 1:15-22); Miriam, Moses' sister, called the women to sing together, to encourage the people on their journey (Ex 15:19-21); Deborah leads the army to free the people from oppression (Jgs 4:1-16; 5:1-31); Jael, the Kenite woman, conquers and kills Sisera, the general of Jabin, king of Canaan (Jgs 4: 17-24). The memory of these acts of resistance was like a seed of resistance. In these actions a dissatisfaction with the marginating and excluding of women comes shining through. The same kind of seed of resistance is evident in the Bible's opening pages, where the equality of men and women as image of God is affirmed (Gn1:27).

These seeds begin bearing fruit especially after the exile, when Jewish women were marginated as impure (see Lv 15:19-30; 12:1-8), and foreign women were expelled as dangerous (see Ezr 9:1-12; 10:1-3). In other words, the resistance of and appreciation for women grew during the period in which their plight of margination was at its worst. Several books in the wisdom literature record this voice of opposition:

1. *The Song of Songs.* Woman appears as an indepen-
    dent person who, in order to find her beloved,

stands up to the city guards (Sg 3:1-4; 5:2-8), to the rival who is chasing her (Sg 8:11-12), and to the siblings who want to protect her (Sg 8:8-10). The Song of Songs reaffirms women's dignity, speaking of them as women and not as mothers.

2. *The Book of Ruth.* Two poor women, both of them widows, one of them a foreigner, are present at the origins of the people's reconstruction. It is they who take initiatives to recover the rights lost and to see that the law on ransom is honored. An ancestor of the Messiah is born of a foreign woman (Ru 4:17-22).

3. *The Books of Judith and Esther.* Judith, a woman from a large imaginary Samaritan town, challenges the decision taken by the priests and elders. Singlehandedly, she faces up to the enemy army and manages to overcome General Holofernes, cutting off his head. Esther is a woman committing herself in the struggle for her people's survival.

In these books, women appear not as mothers or wives, but rather as women who know how to use their beauty and femininity to struggle for the rights of the poor, defending the people's covenant in this way. And women struggle not for the sake of the Temple, nor for the sake of abstract laws, but rather to defend life for the people's sake.

New Testament Context

Jesus and Women

In the New Testament era, women suffered margination. They did not participate in the synagogue, nor could they be witnesses in public life. Nevertheless, many women did stand up against this exclusion. From the time of Ezra on, women's resistance continued to grow, as we saw in the stories of Judith, Esther, Naomi, Susanna, the Sulamite woman, and others. This resistance found an echo and a welcome in Jesus. Here are some episodes in which women's daily dissatisfaction and resistance show through, as does Jesus' openness toward women:

   • The young woman *prostitute* has courage in challenging the norms of society and religion. She enters the home of a pharisee to meet Jesus, and she does things which reflect independence, such as, for example, letting her hair down in public, which was not permitted to women. Reproached by the pharisee, she is not reproached by Jesus for having broken norms. On the contrary, in Jesus the woman finds love and forgiveness. Jesus welcomes and defends her against the Pharisee (Lk 7:36-50).

   • The *bent-over* woman is not troubled by the shouts of the synagogue leader. She seeks healing, even on the Sabbath. When life is up for grabs, people can see the laws as relative. The bent-over woman is welcomed by Jesus as a *daughter of Abraham*, that is, as a full member of God's people, and she is defended by him against the synagogue leader (Lk 13:10-17).

   • The woman considered *impure* because of her hemorrhage has the courage to go into the midst of the multitude and the spirit to think the exact opposite of the official line. The doctrine says: "If I touch him, he will become impure!" But she says: "If I touch him, I will be cured!" (Mk 5:28). This woman is welcomed without censure and is cured. Jesus declares that her cure is a fruit of her faith (Mk 5:25-34). That is, it springs from the woman's initiative and her trust in Jesus, a trust awakened in her by Jesus' way of acting.

   • The Samaritan woman, despised as a *heretic*, has the courage to question Jesus, changing the subject of a conversation initiated by him (Jn 4:19-25). Jesus seeks to communicate with her at the level of work (water) and family (husband). But she pushes the matter to religion ("Where are we to worship God?").

She is the first person to receive the secret that Jesus is the Messiah (Jn 4:26).

• At the border of Tyre and Sidon, the woman who is a *foreigner* in Tyre and Sidon refuses to accept her exclusion, arguing to the point of getting Jesus to change his mind and respond to her need (Mk 7:24-30). This episode shows that Jesus was discovering the Father's will through his continuing sensitivity to the reactions of people.

• Jesus *does away with male privilege vis-à-vis women*, suggesting a new kind of relationship between the two. On the one hand, he won't allow for a marriage in which the man has a right to send the woman away. On the other, he doesn't permit the celibacy of a person who refuses marriage because he won't live in a situation of equality with women (Mt 19:3-12).

• *Mothers with small children* confront the disciples, then are welcomed and blessed by Jesus (Mt 19:13-15; Mk 10:13-16). The disciples' resistance comes, most likely, from the fact that women with tiny youngsters are considered as living in a permanent state of ritual impurity. Love of life and of children leads the women to go against the norms of purity. And Jesus gathers them up and responds to them, touching, embracing and blessing the children.

• The women who challenged power, remaining by the cross of Jesus (Mt 27:55-56, 61), were the first to experience the presence of the risen Jesus (Mt28:9-10). Later tradition forgets this fact, eliminating women from its list of official resurrection witnesses (cf. I Cor15:2-8). Mary Magdalene, considered *a woman possessed* though cured by Jesus (Lk 8:2), received the *order* to share the Good News of the resurrection with the disciples (Jn 20:16-18). Thus, ancient tradition gives her the title *Apostle to the Apostles*, a title also forgotten by later tradition.

Women Follow Jesus as Disciples

Jesus allowed a group of women to "follow" him (Lk 8:2-3; 23:49; Mk 15:41). The expression *to follow Jesus* has here the same meaning as when it is applied to the men who follow Jesus. These women were *disciples* of Jesus. Subsequent ecclesiastical tradition failed to give the women's following of Jesus the same weight given to that of the men.

The Gospels preserve several lists of names, not always the same, of the twelve disciples who *were following* Jesus (Mk 3:16-19; Mt 10:2-5; Lk 6:14-16). There were also women who *were following* Jesus, from Galilee to Jerusalem. The Gospel of Mark defines the attitude of these women in three expressions: *following, serving, going up* to Jerusalem (Mk 15:41). The first Christians did not manage to put together a list of the names of these women disciples who had followed Jesus as had the men, or had followed Jesus with the men. But the names of seven of these women are scattered through the pages of the Gospels: Mary Magdalene, Joanna, mother of Chuza, Susanna (Lk 8:3), Salome and Mary, the mother of James (Mk 15:40), Mary, the wife of Clopas, and Mary, the mother of Jesus (Jn 19:25). A beginning list is already envisioned in Luke 8:2-3.

It is St. Luke's Gospel that offers the largest number of episodes highlighting Jesus' relationship with women. But the novelty, the Good News of God for women, lies not in the abundance of references to women's presence around Jesus. The really good news has to do with Jesus' attitude toward women. Jesus touches them or allows himself to be touched by them, without fear of falling into ritual impurity (Lk 7:39; 8:44-45, 54). In contrast to the teachers of that period, Jesus accepts women as followers and as disciples (Lk 8:2-3; 10:39). God's liberating force, functioning in Jesus, lets women rise up and take on their dignity (Lk 13:13). Jesus is sensitive to the widow's suffering and shows solidarity with her pain (Lk 7:13). Women's work of preparing food is seen by Jesus as a sign of the Kingdom (Lk 13:20-21). The persistent widow who struggles for her rights is given as a model for prayer (Lk 18:1-8), and the poor widow who shares the little she has with others is set as a model for commitment and giving (Lk 21:1-4). At a time when the testimony of women was not considered valid, Jesus chose women as witnesses of his death (Lk 23:49), burial (Lk 23:55-56) and resurrection (Lk 24:1-11, 22-24).

Women's Participation in the First Communities

The last chapter of the letter to the Romans is permeated by a sense of women's place in the life of the communities founded by Paul. *Phebe* is called "our sister, deaconess of the Cenchrea community" (Rom 16:1). *Priscilla* and *Aquila* are called "my collaborators" (Rom 16:3). Andronicus and *Junia* are called "my relatives, companions in prison, important apostles" (Rom 16:7). Paul speaks of women with complete naturalness as *deaconesses, collaborators* in Jesus Christ, or *apostles.* These are central titles or functions in the life and organization of the communities.

In the culture of that time, a woman could not participate in public life, where no space was allowed her. Women's function was to be within the home, in the life of her family. And in the home, women did, in fact, coordinate things; a woman was the lady of the house. Similarly, in the Church women could have a place and a participation only when the Church functioned in a home-setting.

Nevertheless, the communities founded by Paul did meet in people's houses. Therefore these have been called "Domestic Churches" or "House Churches." In almost all the domestic churches mentioned in Paul's letters a woman's name appears, the woman in whose home the communities gathered: in the home of the immigrant couple, *Priscilla* and *Aquila,* both in Rome (Rom 16:5) and in Corinth (I Cor 16:19); in the home of Philemon and *Apphia* (Phil 2); in the home of *Lydia* in Philippi (Acts 16:15); in the home of *Nymphas* in Laodicea, who herself received a letter from Paul, a letter no longer in existence (Col 4:15); in the home of Philologus and *Julia,* Nereus and *his sister,* and *Olimpas* (Rom 16:15). And so, through the creation of domestic churches, Paul opened up a space for women, that they might exercise the function of coordinators in the communities.

In evaluating the reach and the novelty of this Pauline initiative, it is wise to remember the following: in that time Jews were not allowed to set up communities or synagogues for women alone. It was required that there be *ten men*, at least, in order that a community might be formed. Due to this requisite, there was no synagogue in Philippi, where there was only a group of women. These women used to gather outside the city to pray (Acts 16:13). Paul had the courage to go against his own people's custom, allowing the group of women in Philippi to form a community (Acts 16:13-15).

In the context of their times, these communities took initiatives which contrasted with the reigning culture. For example, Paul had the courage to recommend that young women not marry, devoting themselves to the Lord (I Cor.7:27-28; 33-34). This meant a step of independence on women's part, since the custom was to marry and never to remain single.

Some Gospel Texts on Mary, the Mother of Jesus

This information on the status of women in the Old and New Testaments is the background for what is affirmed and reported in the Gospels on Mary, the Mother of Jesus. We did not study all the texts, but simply a few, according to the time available to us.

A text is born of a dialogue between author and readers. The choice of words depends upon two factors: upon the matter which the author wishes to communicate, and upon the person for whom the author is writing. The Gospel authors thought about the communities for which they were writing. The situation faced by these communities had an influence on the choice of words which now appear in the text. Thus, not everything affirmed of Mary in Gospel texts on the infancy comes from the real facts which occurred during Jesus' infancy. Many elements in these texts reflect more the situation of communities in the years 80 to 100 than the historic reality at the time of Jesus' infancy. It is very difficult to discern and separate one aspect from the other.

Matthew's Gospel

The Gospel of Matthew speaks to the communities of Syria and Palestine, communities which, in their majority, were composed of converts from Judaism. The communities were also trying to be open to the people of other races. In the years between 80 and 90, these very small communities, sometimes composed of two or three families (Mt 18:20), experienced profound conflicts, both external and internal. The external conflicts were with fellow Jews who accused them of infidelity to the Scriptures because of their having accepted Jesus as the Messiah. Many Christians were even expelled from the synagogues in which they had always participated (Mt 10:17-20). Given their faith in Jesus, many families experienced a life of tragic division (Mt 10:21). The internal conflicts arose from various tendencies among the Christians themselves. One group, linked to the Pharisees, thought that the law should be observed with all the vigor of the past (Mt 5:17-20). Such demands scandalized and distanced the little ones, those least trained in the minutiae of the law (Mt 18:6-7), impeding the entry into the community of people from other races.

These problems led the author of St. Matthew's Gospel to choose the words and actions of Jesus which best responded to the communities' issues. The writer's purpose was to help them overcome the trauma of exclusion, confirming them in their faith that Jesus really was the Messiah (Mt 1:1-22; 2:5; etc). But the evangelist also writes to inspire reconciliation and to prevent scandal among the little ones. He criticizes those whose pharisaical mind set insists on rigorous observance of the law (Mt 5:20).

The opening passage of Matthew's Gospel and of the entire New Testament is a long list of names (Mt 1:1-17). Throughout his account the author of St. Matthew's Gospel shows who Jesus is and how God has acted surprisingly to fulfill His promises. In the patriarchal society of the Jews, genealogies, which served to prove the purity of their race, traced only the names of males. Because of this, the fact that Matthew places the names of five women among Jesus' ancestors is surprising. These five women are: Tamar (1:3); Rahab (1:5); Ruth (1:5); Bathsheba, the wife of Uriah (1:6); and Mary (1:16). If the evangelist included only these five women together with over forty men, it is worthwhile posing the question: "Why did he choose precisely these women and not others, who were much better known in the biblical tradition? What do these five women have in common?"

At the beginning and end of the genealogy, Matthew makes clear what the identity of Jesus is: He is the Messiah, son of David and child of Abraham (Mt 1:1, 17). As a descendent of Abraham, Jesus is a fountain of blessing and hope for all the nations of the world (Gn12:13). Thus, both the Jews and the pagans, who were part of the communities in Syria and Palestine, could see their hopes realized in Jesus.

In composing the long list of Jesus' ancestors, Matthew developed a schema of 3 x 14 (14 = 2x7) generations (Mt 1:17). The number 3 is the number for divinity. The number 7 is the number for perfection. At that time it was common to interpret or calculate God's action in life through a particular number of dates or times. Through these symbolic calculations, Matthew shows God's presence throughout the history of the generations. Matthew expresses the communities' conviction that Jesus appeared in the time set by God. With Jesus' arrival, history had come into its fulness.

Jesus is God's answer to the expectations of both the Jews and the pagans, but He is so in a surprising way. The five women cited in the genealogy are outside the normal patterns of behavior for that time. These women did not satisfy the demands of the laws on purity.

1. *Tamar*, a Canaanite, a foreigner, and a widow, passes for a prostitute in order to oblige Judah to give her a son. She was more faithful to the Law than was the patriarch Judah, her father-in-law (Gn 38:1-30).

2. *Rahab*, a Canaanite, a foreigner, and a prostitute, was able to perceive Yaweh's coming and made an alliance with the Israelites. She helped them enter into the Promised Land, professing her faith in the liberating God of the Exodus (Jos 2:1-21).

3. *Bathseba* was a Hittite, a foreigner, and the wife of Uriah, victim of King David's desire. She was seduced, subjected to violence, and made pregnant by King David, who, on top of it all, had Bathsheba's husband killed (2 Sm 11:1-27).

4. *Ruth*, a Moabite, a foreigner, and a poor widow, opted to remain at Naomi's side, opening up, by this, a new way of entry into the people of God (Ru 1:16-18). Counseled by Naomi, Ruth imitated Tamar, spending the night on the threshing-floor near Boaz, forcing him to comply with the law and give her a child. From the relationship between these two, Obed, the grandfather of King David, is born (Ru 3:1-15; 4:13-17).

5. *Mary*, a poor woman of Nazareth, was found with child before living with Joseph, her husband, which at that time would have merited her public denunciation, with the danger of her being stoned (Mt 1:18-19).

These five women do not fit the required behavior called for by the behavior patterns which patriarchal society imposed. These women are outside the traditional domestic schema. Even so, their scarcely conventional initiatives provide continuity for Jesus' lineage, bringing God's salvation to the whole people. It is through these women that God carries out the divine plan, sending the promised Messiah.

Thus, Matthew's Gospel criticizes the attitude of those who, in the years 90-100, insisted on rigorous observance of the laws and norms on purity. And, as would have been said to them: "Be careful! Do not expel those not within the norms of the law! Had God observed the norms as you demand, Jesus would never have been born!" In the genealogy found in Matthew's Gospel, Jesus, the Messiah, son of Abraham and son of David, appears as the son and descendent of a single mother, a prostitute, a foreigner, and a woman subjected to violence. To Matthew, these women, despite their being found outside the schema of ritual purity, were found within the demands of a new justice, a greater justice than that of the pharisees (Mt 5:20). Joseph, the husband of Mary, was just, and therefore he did not denounce her publically (Mt 1:19). Had Joseph been just according to the justice demanded by Christians of a pharisaical stripe, he would have had to denounce Mary, and she would have had to be stoned; and Jesus would never have been born! What was for some outside the law was, in fact, the work of the Holy Spirit! Here is an important note for our churches and communities, where we have many laws that exclude so many people in God's name: people who are divorced, single mothers, those who suffer from AIDS, prostitutes!...

Luke's Gospel

Of the four Gospels, Luke's is the one which most informs us about Mary in its two chapters on the infancy. When Luke speaks of Mary, he thinks of the communities. In her way of relating to God's Word, Luke sees the most correct way for the community to relate to God's Word: welcoming the Word, incarnating it, living it, delving into it, pondering it, giving it birth and helping it to grow, allowing itself to be molded by it, even when not understanding it, or when it causes us to suffer. This is how we reach the ideal, described in the Acts of the Apostles: everyone in unanimity, around Mary, at prayer before God (Acts 1:12-14): "Happy is the one who hears the Word and puts it into practice" (Lk 11:27-28). With these reading keys, provided by Luke's Gospel, our gathering's participants used the following seven texts for our daily *Lectio divina* (or prayerful reading of Scripture) in several groups.

1. Luke 1:26-38, the Annunciation: "Be it done unto me according to your word!" Knowing how to open ourselves, in order to receive God's Word.

2. Luke 1:39-45, the Visitation: "Blessed is the one who believed!" Knowing how to recognize God's Word in the details of life.

3. Luke 1:46-56, the Magnificat: "The Lord does marvels in me!" A subversive song of resistance and hope.

4. Luke 2: 1-20, the Birth: "She held all these things in her heart." The marginated ones welcome the Word.

5. Luke 2:21-32, the Presentation: "My eyes have seen your salvation!" Many years of life can purify our vision.

6. Luke 2:33-38, Simeon and Ana: "A sword shall pierce your heart" Being a Christian is a sign of contradiction.

7. Luke 2:39-52, At the age of twelve: "Didn't you know that I must be about my Father's work?" They did not understand the Words that He said to them!

John's Gospel

Jesus' mother appears twice in the Gospel of John: in the beginning, at the wedding of Cana (Jn 2:1-5), and in the end, as she stands by the Cross (Jn 19:25-27). These two episodes, mentioned in John's Gospel alone, have very deep symbolic value. In both cases Mary represents the Old Testament which awaits the arrival of the New; and, in both cases she helps the New to come. Mary is the connecting thread between what went before and what will come after. At Cana it is she, the Mother of Jesus, symbol of the Old Testament, who perceives the limits of the Old and takes steps that the New may arrive. At the hour of death, once again it is Mary, the Mother of Jesus, who receives the "Beloved Disciple." The Beloved Disciple and the community which grew up around Jesus is the child born of the Old Testament. At Jesus' request, this child, the New Testament, receives Mary, the Old Testament, into his home. Jesus' mother also represents Eve, mother of all the living. The Beloved Disciple represents the new humanity as well, the humanity formed by Gospel living. The two must journey forward together. For the New cannot be understood without the Old: it would be a house with no foundation. And the Old without the New would be incomplete: It would be a tree without fruit.

Conclusion

This reflection is the result of our study at the INTERCAB gathering. Generally the study was done as a group, preceded by personal reading, which was guided by several questions. At the same time, this study was nurtured and accompanied by much prayer and song and by the joy of our shared experience.

Carlos Mesters, O.Carm.

Overshadowed by the Holy Spirit

Not long ago I was privileged to be a participant in an open discussion with Christians of various denominations. In confirming a point made by an evangelical lady who had mentioned Peter's walking on the water, I had referred to him as 'Saint' Peter, and somewhat later, treating an entirely different topic, I had spoken of a text from 'Saint' Paul. A member of a non-denominational church remarked that he presumed I was Roman Catholic, since I had used this title for the two apostles.

The conversation continued in good form until, in a weak attempt at humor, I asked if I might use the title 'Mother' (I had intended to bring in the example of Mother Teresa of Calcutta); at once the same gentlemen, thinking I was about to refer to Mary the Mother of Jesus, interjected that he would have no objection so long as I didn't attempt to refer to her as a divinity!

That exchange reminded me of another occasion. In 1979 I had been invited to give a paper to the Ninth Annual Convention of the Society for Pentecostal Studies in Vancouver, British Columbia. My topic was the place of Mary in Salvation History. I have to admit that I was more than a little nervous about facing Pentecostal and evangelical theologians with the presentation of a topic so out of step with their fundamental beliefs. As it turned out, shortly before I was scheduled to speak, that wonderful South African Pentecostal minister, the late Reverend David du Plessis–known around the world as "Mr. Pentecost"–had made a

231

major presentation to the World Pentecostal Conference that had been celebrated in Vancouver that same week. He had called the Pentecostal world to task because, as he put it, although Pentecostals consider themselves to be Bible Christians, there are certain passages, even of the New Testament, which they have chosen to ignore: specifically those passages that speak of Mary the Mother of Jesus. I could not have asked for a more encouraging introduction to my talk.

To my delight the Society demonstrated sincere interest in the topic, and my presentation was followed by a longer than usual session for questions and discussion. The thing that most impressed me, however, was first the degree of misinformation uncovered in our exchange, and second their surprise–and pleasure–that they were being provided with specific references to the authentic position of the Catholic Church, especially as found in the closing chapter of *Lumen Gentium.*

Mary continues to be a frequent topic of conversation among Christians, whether it focuses on evangelicals' accusations that Mary is being divinized by both Catholics and Orthodox Christians, on reports from various parts of the world about recent apparitions under nearly incredible circumstances, or on scholarly attempts to increase understanding of the place of the *Theotokos* within the economy of salvation.

The man in whose honor the essays in this volume have been written has lived 'on the cutting edge' of inter-denominational dialogue on Our Lady. Father Eamon R. Carroll, my brother in Carmel, is a seeker after truth. Throughout his long and distinguished career, a focal point of his Mariological studies has been Mary of the Scriptures and the significance of the Holy Spirit on her life and calling.

Those acquainted with his work are aware of the depth and breadth of his research. Not only has he studied the biblical texts themselves, but he has sought to master the wisdom and insights of the early Fathers and the great Doctors of the Church, as well as the statements of Popes and Councils. Moreover, as is demonstrated elsewhere in these essays, he keeps abreast of current discussions among his peers, non-Catholic and Catholic alike.[1] Carefully attentive to the ideas and arguments of others, across the more than fifty years of his professional career, he is ever a gracious interlocutor who responds not so much with rebuttals as with explanations of the position of the Catholic Church, explanations that are both thorough and patient. All these factors have made him a sought-after participant in inter-denominational dialogues both at home and abroad. As he himself has stated, his has been "the privilege and joy of the changing scene" of Mariology.[2]

Key to his successful dialogues with non-Catholics is his emphasis on data about Mary found in Sacred Scripture. There is a vital point of contact here. Once Catholics are able to convince Protestants that the Church's doctrine with regard to Mary is grounded in the Bible, a major obstacle to understanding is removed. This is not an easy task, but it is not an impossible one.

Acknowledging Jesus' promise to remain with his follow-ers always, Christians–Protestants and Catholics alike–generally agree that he intended the Gospel to be proclaimed to all peoples of all times. He therefore provided that the self-revelation of his Father be preserved intact through his handing over the deposit of the faith to his Church through the hands of his apostles under the leadership of Peter, and through their successors. To this end he sent the Holy Spirit from the Father and promised that this same Spirit would be present in the Church until the end of time.

For Christians, the New Testament provides an inspired account of the early Christian communities; it documents how, step by step, these proto-Christians came to understand the reality of the Incarnation and the significance of the Good News proclaimed by Jesus the Messiah. Moreover, it attests to the fact that–as Jesus had promised–the Holy Spirit continually assists Jesus' followers to an ever increasing comprehension of all he had said and done. This Advocate, Jesus had declared, is to remind his disciples of all his words and deeds; this Spirit of Truth, without adding to what Jesus has revealed, is to guide his followers into an increasingly profound understanding both of the revelation itself and of its application to the changing circumstances they will encounter down through the ages.

The New Testament itself provides instances of this process. For example, even though many of the early Christian community in Jerusalem had been present when Jesus ascended into heaven, and they had themselves heard his final command "to be [his] witnesses in Jerusalem, throughout Judea and Samaria, yes, even to the ends of the earth" (Acts 1:8), they did not fully comprehend its import until–following the martyrdom of Stephen– "a great persecution" forced them to flee Jerusalem and to scatter "throughout the countryside of Judea and Samaria." It was only then that the Good News was first proclaimed to non-Jews by Philip the Deacon (Acts 8:1-8, 26-40). It was later still, following two visions and a sovereign act of God, before Peter acknowledged that his commission included making the Good News known to God-fearing gentiles (Acts 10-11:18), and eventually even to pagans (Acts 11:19-26). Thus under the influence of the Holy Spirit first generation Christians finally became convinced that, when Jesus had said "to the ends of the earth", he really did intend to include "all the nations" among his followers (cf. Lk 10:1-11; 18; Mt 28:19). Step by step the Holy Spirit had made it clear that the Gospel of salvation was intended not merely for Jews, not merely for other related peoples (e.g., the Samaritans), not merely for those who were in the process of conversion to Judaism (i.e., God-fearers), but for all mankind.

Nineteen centuries later, continuously stimulated by the Holy Spirit, we Christians are still engaged in a process of 'unwrapping' the full significance of the revelation entrusted by Jesus to his Body through the hands of the Apostles, and of discerning its consequences for our own time and place. Consequently–if indeed we have not been completely blind, if we have opened our ears however slightly–by God's grace Christians today do understand far more about these unfathomable mysteries than did our fathers; and we may joyfully anticipate that the next generation will have a better comprehension still.

Among the many mysterious doctrines not clarified explicitly in the Bible are those that refer to Mary the mother of
Jesus, and in particular to her position within the economy of
salvation. While Catholics may have tended to exaggerate their
significance, Protestants have often ignored them altogether.
Today as we Catholics, thanks to increased dialogue with our
'separated brethren,' are placing far greater stress on the biblical
aspects of Mary's ministry, there is increasing evidence that there
is developing a corresponding willingness among many Protestants to restore the honor due to the Mother of the Savior.[3] While
most Protestants do not accept the primitive Christian community's
recognition of Mary's role "in the upstairs room," described in the
Acts of the Apostles, as a paradigm of her God-given function
within the Body of Christ, nevertheless in their ongoing study of
the Bible, in their sincere search for a deeper understanding of the
church, some of them, especially among evangelicals, are coming
to understand and to appreciate Mary's role in the economy of
salvation. They are re-discovering as well the witness of Christian
men and women during the first fifteen centuries of Christian
history: a piety expressed in architecture and art, in poetry and
prose, in music and theater, as well as in liturgy and in daily
personal devotion.

Moreover, numerous recent studies have pointed out that
the marginalization of Mary from Protestant piety and worship did
not begin until long after the time of the reformers themselves.
"Whatever may be true in Protestant churches today," writes Dr.
Ross Mackenzie,

> none of the Reformers or their immediate succes-
> sors questioned the biblical foundation of the two
> phrases of the ancient creeds, that Christ was
> 'conceived by the Holy Spirit, born of the Virgin
> Mary.' Calvin, like Luther and Zwingli, taught the
> perpetual virginity of Mary. The early reformers
> even applied, though with some reticence, the title
> Theotokos to Mary, because 'she bore him who is

also God.' Lutherans and Calvinists were in agreement that Mary's prophecy–'all generations will
call me blessed'–was constantly being fulfilled in
the Church. Calvin called on his followers to
venerate and praise her as the teacher who instructs them in her Son's commands.[4]

It is Assemblies of God theologian Jerry Sandige who has stated
that Protestant objections to Marian devotion are more emotional
than theological, and they are due primarily to ignorance of
authentic Roman Catholic doctrine about Mary and to a tendency
to emphasize the abuses—which are equally deplored by orthodox Catholics.[5]

No one, Catholic or Protestant, will question that there
have been excesses in popular devotion among some Catholics;
however, Protestants' neglect of Mary's role *as revealed in Scripture* is coming to be seen as an even greater abuse. If the "full
gospel" is to be proclaimed, there can be no "zones of silence"
imposed on biblical texts that mention the Mother of the Lord.
Catholics and Protestants alike would do well to reflect on the
principle underlying the Marian devotion of the most recently
declared Doctor of the Catholic Church, St. Thérèse of Lisieux,
who encouraged us to leave aside the creations of pious imaginations and focus on the facts about Mary given in the Bible.[6]

It would be superfluous to do more than recall here what
Fr. Eamon has dealt with so thoroughly in his own studies.[7] He
has argued that from the very earliest episode of Mary's life
provided us in the New Testament to her final appearance in the
sacred text, she is always identified as the mother of Jesus and
she is invariably described as living in the presence and under the
influence of the Holy Spirit.

One need only recall his treatment of the 'hard sayings'–
the account of the enthusiastic woman (Lk 11:27-28) and of the
true kinsman (Lk 8:19-21 and parallels)–where he demonstrates
that, far from expressing a negative evaluation of Mary's place in
the ministry of her Son, in these very texts Jesus himself praises

Mary's response to the Holy Spirit as a model for all his followers: through hearing the word and pondering it in her heart, Mary allows it to bear fruit. As St. Augustine proclaimed: "Mary heard God's word and kept it, and so she is blessed. She kept God's truth in her mind, a nobler thing than carrying his body in her womb."[8]

Fr. Eamon likewise recalls Matthew's use of genealogy to describe the Incarnation as the New Creation; the relationship between the woman of Genesis 3:15 and Mary as New Eve whose offspring will crush the serpent's head; the many points of similarity between Cana and Pentecost, recognized already in the late fourth or early fifth centuries by St. Gaudentius of Brescia.

He has taken full advantage of the advances made in biblical scholarship, pointing out for example the parallels that exist between Luke's account of Jesus' infancy (Lk 1-2) and the history of the birth of the Church in the Book of Acts (Acts 1-2). Mary is present in both, and in both she is filled with the Holy Spirit: "The Holy Spirit will come upon you and the power of the Most High will overshadow you" and "Tongues as of fire appeared ... and came to rest on each of them. All were filled with the Holy Spirit...." Moreover both accounts stress a prophetic community. In the Gospel Mary utters a prophetic word, magnifying the Lord in the inspired words of the *Magnificat*; Elizabeth "cries out in a loud voice" in praise of the work of God in her cousin; and Zachariah, "filled with the Holy Spirit," blesses the Lord. In Acts, under the leadership of the Apostles, the entire community, gathered in the Upper Room with Mary–identified explicitly as Jesus' mother–in its midst, "filled with the Holy Spirit ... began to express themselves in foreign tongues and make a bold proclamation as the Spirit prompted them." Thus the Lukan narratives provide a description of Mary's life and ministry: the action of the Holy Spirit is the 'dynamo' not only for the events leading up to the birth of Jesus, but also for those leading to the birth of the Church on Pentecost.

The Gospel according to John also makes it clear that, due to the influence of the Holy Spirit, the mother of Jesus is mother of the Church as well. The beloved disciple presents Mary both at the beginning and at the end of Jesus' public life: at Cana (Jn 2) and on Calvary (Jn 19). Cana is the sign, Calvary the fulfillment. Scripture scholars point out several threads uniting the two events: e.g., both are described as theophanies, with references to the theophany of Sinai (Ex 19): it was "on the morning of the third day" when Moses led the people out of the camp, and "on the third day" that the events at Cana took place; at the foot of the mountain the People of God pledge that "Everything the Lord has said we will do", while at Cana Mary instructs the waiters, "Do whatever he tells you."

Again, although at Cana Jesus' "hour" has not yet arrived, at Calvary that "hour" is upon him–the moment of his glory, his Death-Resurrection–and he is 'lifted up' (Jn 3:14-15) so as to draw fallen humanity to himself. At the marriage feast Jesus changes water into wine, symbolic of that "new wine," frequently mentioned in the Old Testament as a sign of the coming of the Spirit in the messianic age; on Calvary Jesus tastes the "common wine," symbolic of the Old Law, and says, "'Now it is finished.' Then he bowed his head, and delivered over his spirit." At Cana the wine is described as rich and abundant, symbolic of the Age of the Spirit; at Calvary the sign is richly and abundantly fulfilled with the reality of the new wine of the nuptials between Christ and his Church.

At both Cana and Calvary Jesus addresses Mary as "woman"–for John clearly a reference both to Genesis and to Revelation–a term frequently used in the Old Testament to indicate Israel but now applied to Mary, symbol of the new Israel. At Cana Mary, addressed as 'Woman', is seen ministering to the needs of the wedding party when she requests Jesus to work the sign that "revealed his glory, and his disciples believed in him"; on Calvary, as her son is lifted up, Mary is given a maternal ministry to his disciples, to the Church being born from her son's pierced side: "Woman, there is your son." As she once cared for and nurtured the child born to her by the power of the Spirit, so now she is commissioned by her son to continue her ministry to his Body, to her new children (cf. Rom 8:29, Rev 12:17). Along with the disciple whom Jesus loved, all Christians are invited to receive from Jesus the gift of Mary.[9]

According to the Scriptures, then, it is the motherhood of Mary that is the basis for her position within the divine plan for redemption, and that is the foundation of her ministry to her Son, both head and members. It is because she is Mother of Jesus, God-bearer, that she is "highly favored daughter ... blessed ... among women" (Lk 1:28) as well as the "woman clothed with the sun, with the moon under her feet and on her head a crown of twelve stars" (Rev 12:1). It is the divine maternity that underlies all her privileges, whether these be perceived in the restricted sense common to most Protestants or in the fuller sense generally accepted by both Orthodox and Roman Catholics.

A crucial ecumenical problem arises, however, when we come to a consideration of Mary as intercessor. In general Protestants, focusing on the New Testament text describing Jesus as the sole mediator between God and man (1 Tim 2:5; cf. Heb 10:15), reject the Catholic doctrine of the intercessory ministry of the saints in general and of Mary in particular as unfounded in Scripture.

Yet we may ask whether the Protestant and Catholic positions on intercession are necessarily as far apart as it may at first glance appear. Dr. Ross Mackenzie appears to have been able to bridge the gap: he writes

> To intercede means to pray for others. Literally, it means to go between, to mediate, to intervene between contending parties with a view to reconciling them. Intercession is based on a loving concern for one another. To ask someone to intercede for us is to ask to be taken to that person's heart in a special way. ... To ask someone to intercede for us is the very opposite of manipulating God. It is to ask that God will visit us with grace and blessing, to ask that God will act upon us.[10]

Protestants and Catholics alike have no hesitation about seeking the prayers of relatives, friends, even unknown persons, for themselves or for others in time of need: e.g., for the sick, for troubled marriages, for improved circumstances, etc. Often enough such requests are made publicly during the course of religious services or prayer meetings. This common and well-established practice is neither more nor less than intercession, requesting these individuals or groups to pray to God for us. But is there any foundation for it in the Bible?

In several Old Testament accounts concerning the royal family of the Kingdom of Judah there is found a seldom commented on title, a title that may quite possibly point toward a biblical foundation for the intercessory position Catholic tradition has assigned to Mary in the economy of salvation. The title is that of the mother of the king: $g^e b\bar{i}rah$, usually translated as "great lady."

Fr. George Montague[11] dealt with this topic some years ago; more recently two of my brother Carmelites, Fr. Craig Morrison, who teaches at the Pontifical Biblical Institute in Rome, and Fr. Alexander Vella, whose doctoral studies were interrupted and who is now serving on the General Council of the Order, have provided me with supporting data.

It is well known that during the period covered by the Kingdoms of Israel and Judah, the kings had many wives, often for reasons of politics, and among the ladies of the harem there was frequently a favorite (e.g., Bathsheba for David, Jezebel for Ahab, Athaliah for Joram, Maakah for Jeroboam). Unlike the Kingdom of Israel and other countries of the region where the favorite was given a title corresponding to 'queen' (e.g., the Queen of Sheba, the Queen of Persia), in the Kingdom of Judah these favorites did not receive that official title.[12]

On the other hand, in the sketches of individual reigns in the Kingdom of Judah, the Books of Kings nearly always mention the name of the king's mother, designated as the $g^e b\bar{i}rah$; for the Kingdom of Israel. However, in similar introductions to the reigns of their kings, the sacred texts do not mention their mothers.

Apparently in the Kingdom of Israel there was little or no concern with dynastic descent from King David. In the Kingdom of Judah, on the other hand, belonging to the Davidic lineage was extremely important. In all probability this was due to the prophecy of Nathan (2 Sm 7:11-16) that David's kingdom is to be everlasting. But it is the king's mother, not his own wife–who would not normally have been of David's line–who is witness and guarantor of the king's descent from David.

For this reason, even when a particular king proved to be an utter failure, the fulfillment of Nathan's prophecy is nevertheless to be realized in a subsequent king and descendant of David. One example may be found in the birth of Immanuel foretold in Isaiah 7:13 (cf. Mi 5:1-4).

In the Davidic succession, consequently, official rank is accorded the *g^ebîrah*,[13] the Great Lady, a title reserved for the mother (and at least in one case for the grandmother) of the reigning king. The *g^ebîrah*'s rank is recognized upon her son's accession to the throne, or possibly as soon as he is designated heir (cf. 2 Ch 11:21-22). Though she is clearly subject to the king himself, her title is not merely honorific proceeding from the fact of her relationship to the king as his mother: the *g^ebîrah*'s position is one of prestige and even of influence. King Solomon, for example, received his mother, Bathsheba, with great honor and has her sit on a royal throne at his right hand (1 Kgs 2:19; cf. Jer 13:18). Her position, moreover, enabled her to influence policy; it was, after all, because of her misuse of authority that King Asa deposed the *g^ebîrah*, his grandmother–she had abused her position by favoring the idolatrous cult of Asherah (cf. 1 Kgs 15:13, 2 Ch 15:16). At times the *g^ebîrah* was considered as a senior counselor and on at least one occasions served as regent (cf. 1 Kgs 11:1-3).[14]

Moving forward to the New Testament, Luke takes care to note that Joseph took Mary and her unborn Son to Bethlehem because he was "descended from the house and lineage of David" (Lk 2:4), and there Jesus was born, "the ruler in Israel; whose origin is from of old, from ancient times" (Mi 5:2). Already in the

Annunciation narrative (Lk 1:31-33), there had been a reference to these prophecies (i.e., Is 7:13-14 and Mi 5:2).

On Calvary too the Davidic theme is evident: it is in Jerusalem, the capital of David's kingdom, that Jesus is enthroned, lifted up; it is there that Mary, mother of the Davidic king, takes on the characteristics of the *gᵉbîrah*, the Great Lady.

Following the Ascension of Jesus, the straggling followers of the Crucified gathered in the Upper Room around her, the mother of the Messianic King who had been 'lifted up' on Golgotha. With her they prayed for the promised coming of the Holy Spirit who would remain with them until the end of time.

While it may be argued that the Old Testament references to the *gᵉbîrah* do not lend themselves to literal application to the Mother of Jesus, surely as Mother of the Davidic King she holds title to it at least in the allegorical or accommodated sense so beloved of early Christian writers. As Father George Montague concludes: Mary "is honored by her son, is a recognized power at court, often intercedes with the King, and has a throne (not as queen-consort but as queen-mother) next to his.[15]

With her *Fiat* Mary had embraced the totality of the Father's plan for her Son and for herself, thereby opening the way to the coming of the messianic age. Her role in the birth of Jesus is therefore not confined to that event alone: for as she nurtured him, cared for him, followed him even to Calvary, so–carrying out her maternal mission to "the rest of her offspring" (cf. Jn 19:26-27; Rev 12:17; Rom 8:29)–she continues to minister to him in his brothers and sisters brought forth from his pierced body. Both at Cana and in the Upper Room Mary exercises this 'maternal intercession.'[16]

Jesus to be sure is the unique mediator between God and man. Nevertheless his mediatorship is inclusive rather than exclusive: it is fundamentally communitarian and involves every Christian, Mary not excepted. While Mary is unique, all Christians are called to participate in the mission of intercession, each according to the divine plan.

It is not surprising that Mary's share in the mission of her son is altogether special and extraordinary, yet understood as always and essentially a subordinate one. It is of course an extraordinary role because her relationship to Jesus is unique: she alone is his mother, both biologically and in the order of faith.

Mary is consequently the supreme collaborator with her Son's ongoing ministry to his Body. Her role, however, remains an essentially 'maternal participation' rather than an apostolic one: today, as in the Upper Room, she ministers to the members of his Body through watching and praying for the coming of the Spirit upon them. As Jesus himself has not left the Church an orphan but continues his mission within her through the presence and the power of the Holy Spirit he has given her, so Mary continues her part through her constant intercession for those called to be members of his Body.[17]

Following the lead of Vatican II,[18] in the Encyclical Letter *Redemptoris Mater* Pope John Paul II describes Mary's mission, her intercessory role, as that of "mediatrix."[19] The encyclical is careful to make clear, however, that his use of this term in no way diminishes the role of Jesus as the one mediator:[20] Mary's mediation, like that of the Church, is a "participated," "shared," "subordinate," and even a "maternal" mediation. It is Jesus' own mediation expressed through her maternal relationship to the whole Christ, head and members.[21]

Hence Mary's mission to bring the Savior into the world is destined to be prolonged within the communion of saints. She continues to pray for the unity of God's family, and she–who "'precedes' us all at the head of the long line of witnesses of faith in the one Lord, the Son of God, who was conceived in her virginal womb by the power of the Holy Spirit"[22]–may one day, please God, be recognized as our common mother. As Protestant theologian Ross Mackenzie has written: "We ask the saints to pray for our sake, but they are praying for Christ's sake. ... Their prayer flows from the Holy Spirit. And if that is true of them, it is supremely true of Mary. She is the intercessor *par excellance*, meaning, in the excellence of her humility."[23]

Indeed, like the mission of Jesus himself, the horizons of *Redemptoris Mater* are not limited but extend outward to include all of humanity.[24] For us, as disciples of Jesus, we are invited to imitate the response of the beloved disciple and to receive the gift of Mary from the Son of David: by receiving this gift we receive him in a deeper way.

Bishop Alan Clark has written: "Mary is not the centre of Christian living and dying but she is *found* at the centre and leads us *to* the centre. It is the Holy Spirit who transforms us into the body of Christ, but she is integral to that body."[25]

Louis P. Rogge, O.Carm.

Endnotes

1. See the Bibliography at the end of this volume; more briefly see Eamon R. Carroll, O.Carm., *Understanding the Mother of Jesus* (Wilmington, Delaware: Michael Glazier, Inc., 1979).

2. Eamon R. Carroll, O.Carm, "Revolution in Mariology 1949-1989" in *The Land of Carmel: Essays in Honor of Jochim Smet, O.Carm.*, edited by Paul Chandler, O.Carm., and Keith J. Egan (Roma: Institutum Carmelitanum, 1991), pp. 464-465.

3. Cf. *Redemptoris Mater*, 29-30. Henceforth cited as RM.

4. Ross Mackenzie, "Mary As an Ecumenical Problem" (Paper given on April 29, 1976, to the Ecumenical Society of the Blessed Virgin Mary, Washington, D.C. London: The Ecumenical Society of the Blessed Virgin Mary, 1976), p. 2.

5. Jerry Sandige, "A Pentecostal Response to Roman Catholic Teaching on Mary," *Pneuma* 4:2 (1982), 33-42.

6. Thérèse of the Child Jesus and of the Holy Face, O.C.D., *The Poetry of Saint Thérèse of Lisieux* (Critical Edition: Texts and Introductions. Translated by Donald Kinney, O.C.D.) *Critical Edition of the Complete Works.* (Washington, D.C.: ICS Publications, 1996), PN 54. See too Kilian J. Healy, O.Carm., "Three Devotions of St. Thérèse," *Carmel In the World* 36 (1997), 168-171; also Bartholomew M. Xiberta, O.Carm., *Charlas a las contemplativas* (Barcelona, 1967), p. 27, cited in Redemptus Maria Valabek, O.Carm., *Mary, Mother of Carmel: Our Lady and the Saints of Carmel* (Roma: Edizioni Carmelitane. n.d.), II:188-189.

7. E. g., see Carroll, *Understanding the Mother of Jesus.*

8. Augustine, *Sermo 25*, 7-8, cited in *Liturgy of the Hours* IV:1573.

9. Cf. George T. Montague, S.M., *Our Father, Our Mother: Mary and the Faces of God: Biblical and Pastoral Reflec-*

tions (Steubenville, Ohio: Franciscan University Press, 1990) 113-131.

10. J. A. Ross Mackenzie, "'The Virgin for a Good Understanding': Reflections on Intercessors," in *Mary and the Churches* Papers of the Chichester Congress, 1986, of the Ecumenical Society of the Blessed Virgin Mary (Edited by Alberic Stacpoole, O.S.B. Blackrock, County Dublin: The Columbia Press, 1987), pp. 26-27.

11. Montague, *Our Father, Our Mother*, pp. 89-99.

12. Roland DeVaux, *Ancient Israel: Its Life and Institutions* (London: Darton, Longmann & Todd, 1980), p. 117.

13. *Ibid*, 117-119.

14. *Ibid.*; see too Montague, *Our Father, Our Mother*, pp. 89-99.

15. Montague, *Our Father, Our Mother*, pp. 89-99.

16. See Christopher O'Donnell, O.Carm. *At Worship with Mary: A Pastoral and Theological Study* (Wilmington, Delaware: Michael Glazier, 1988), pp. 41-46. This excellent treatment of Mary's ministry of intercession is further developed in *Milltown Studies* No. 22 (1988), pp. 95-110.

17. RM 28, 40; cf. *Lumen Gentium* 62. Henceforth cited as LG. See too Carroll, *Understanding the Mother of Jesus*, p. 25.

18. LG 60, 62.

19. RM 21.

20. RM 4, 38; cf. LG 60, 62.

21. RM 43; cf. Gal 4:19, and Cardinal Ratzinger's comments in *L'Osservatore Romano*, March 27, 1987. See too Pablo María Garrido, O.Carm., *La Virgen de la Fe: Doctrina y piedad marianas entre los Carmelitas españoles de los siglos xvi y xvii* (Roma: Edizioni Carmelitane, 1999). p. 172.

22. RM 30.

23. Mackenzie, "'The Virgin for a Good Understanding': Reflections on Intercessors," p. 28; see too Carroll, *Understanding the Mother of Jesus*, p. 95.

24. RM 49-50.

25. Alan Clark, "The Holy Spirit and Mary" (London: The Ecumenical Society of the Blessed Virgin Mary, 1976), p. 4.

The Ordination of Women: Gender Symbolism and the Blessed Virgin Mary[1]

We are all well aware what decisions the various Christian churches have taken concerning the ordination of women to the priesthood. In this paper I have no intention of calling any of those decisions in question. My purpose is rather to consider one factor which is invoked by both sides of the debate, namely the symbolic power of gender: other scriptural, historical and theological considerations lie outside my self-assigned brief. However, even if everything I write wins the reader's assent, I will not have resolved all the differences between the churches and between their members.

Let us examine an example of this appeal to gender-symbolism, namely the *Declaration on the Question of the Admission of Women to the Ministerial Priesthood*, promulgated by the Congregation of the Doctrine of the Faith in 1976 while Cardinal Seper was still its Prefect.[2]

The Declaration does not begin with the symbolic force of gender. It first sets out three other factors under distinct headings: 1) The Church's constant tradition; 2) The attitude of Christ; 3) The practice of the Apostles. A fourth section then maintains 'The permanent value of the attitude of Jesus and the Apostles, concluding that the practice of the Church has a normative character; in the final analysis it is the Church, through the voice of her Magisterium, that ... decides what can change and what must remain immutable."[3]

It is only then that the declaration proceeds to propose further considerations. It is made crystal clear that the aim is not to bring forward a 'demonstrative argument;' the aim is to 'clarify[ing]' the teaching, not to prove it, to 'illustrate' the norm by showing its 'profound fittingness.' The appeal is to the 'analogy of faith':[4] that is to say, considerations drawn from one area of theology, such as Christian anthropology, are expected to cast light on other areas, such as the theology of priesthood, because Christian truth is a harmonious whole.

The Congregation's fundamental notion is that the bishop or the priest, in the exercise of his ministry, especially at the Eucharist, "does not act in his own name, *in persona propria.*" He acts through the *power* conferred on him by Christ, and also in the *person* of Christ, "taking the role of Christ, to the point of being his very image, when he pronounces the words of consecration."[5] The Declaration confirms this view by quoting several passages from Vatican II. It also appeals to the teaching of St. Thomas. For Aquinas, just as the celebration of the Mass is the 'representative image' of Christ's cross, so too the priest "enacts the image of Christ, in whose person and by whose power he pronounces the words of consecration."[6] It is a fundamental principle of sacramental theology that sacraments are not only causes but also signs of grace; as such, they not only signify the grace they effect, but effect it precisely as signs, effecting it through signifying it. Moreover such signs are not arbitrary symbols, like an asterisk used in a time-table to denote a change of trains. In the words of St. Thomas, "sacramental signs represent what they signify by natural resemblance."[7] This resemblance, the CDF concludes, would not exist if the priest were not male, for "Christ himself was and remains a man."[8]

The CDF acknowledges that Christ is the firstborn of *all* humanity, female as well as male; nevertheless it was in the male sex that the Word became flesh. This fact is not accidental to God's plan; it is "in harmony with the entirety of God's plan as God himself has revealed it, and of which the mystery of the Covenant is the nucleus."[9] To develop the CDF's argument, there are some facts about our Lord's humanity which are not essential to his saving work, such as his social class or the color of his eyes; but other features are essential, above all the fact that he was male. Consequently, if the priest is to bear the natural resemblance to Christ of which the Declaration has been speaking, he need not be a dark-eyed member of a country artisan's family, but he *will* need to be male. (But what of his Jewishness, which was also essential to God's plan?)

The prophets explained the covenant between God and his chosen people in nuptial imagery, in which he is the Bridegroom, and his people are his 'ardently loved spouse;' the CDF refers to Hosea 1-3 and Jeremiah 2. The New Testament develops the same imagery to describe the New Covenant, only now the Bridegroom is Jesus Christ, and the Bride the Church. St. Paul expresses these ideas in 2 Corinthians 11:2 and Ephesians 5:22-23; in the Johannine writings they occur in John 3:29 and Revelation 19:7,9. In the Synoptic Gospels too our Lord speaks of himself as the Bridegroom (Mk 2.19). "And therefore," the Declaration infers,

> unless one is to disregard the importance of this symbolism for the economy of Revelation, it must be admitted that, in actions which demand the character of ordination and in which Christ himself, the author of the Covenant, the Bridegroom and Head of the Church, is represented, exercising his ministry of salvation—which is in the highest degree the case of the Eucharist—his role (this is the original sense of the word *persona*) must be taken by a man. This does not stem from any personal superiority of the latter in the order of values, but only from a difference of fact on the level of functions and service.[10]

Of course it has long been acknowledged that the priest acts also in *persona Ecclesiae*, representing the whole Church made up of women as well as men. It consequently can be argued with good reason that a woman priest could be an appropriate symbol of the *Bride*. The Congregation's response to this counterargument is to indicate that the priest represents the Church, the Body of Christ "precisely because he first represents Christ himself, who is the Head and Shepherd of the Church."[11]

When Pope John Paul II reaffirmed the teaching of *Inter insigniores* in his 1994 statement *Ordinatio Sacerdotalis*, his brief summary of the reasons for the Church's decision made no mention of gender symbolism.[12] Nevertheless, since the symbolic function of gender played an important, though not a decisive, part in the Declaration of 1976, and has continued to feature largely in discussions of the subject, it seems worth while to explore this symbolism further. This is the aim of my paper.

It is implied in the argument above that this symbolism is living and effective; the resemblance between Christ and the priest must be 'natural' and not merely theoretical. I ask my readers accordingly to reflect without prejudice on their own experience, to see to what extent this is indeed so. In simplest terms, when we take part in the Eucharist, what difference does the gender of the priest make to the way in which he or she represents Christ the Bridegroom and the Head of the Church to our minds and our hearts? I am inviting readers therefore to an exercise of imaginative introspection. It may help if I offer certain observations.

The Importance of Gender Symbolism

I would like to reflect a little more deeply on the symbolic importance of gender in many areas of life, not only in the liturgy. But let us first consider briefly some of the problems.

First, there is today a general recognition of the inaccuracy of stereotypes based on gender. So keen are we sometimes to avoid these stereotypes that in one North American University in which I have taught, certain procedures are proposed to faculty members. One procedure consists of a form of reverse discrimination: if you wish to write about an active, adventurous child, make it a girl: "Jane climbed boldly to the top of the tree"; if about a sensitive child, make it a boy: "Tom cradled the kitten carefully in his hands." Some women are stronger, or taller, or more aggressive, or deeper-voiced than some men. Again, there are almost always present in men in a diminished degree some of the qualities which we regard as typically feminine, such as compassionate insight; and in women some of the qualities which we regard as typically male, such as competitive energy.

Secondly, gender symbolism does not sit comfortably with the egalitarian ethos of modern Western society. Even in his day St. Thomas Aquinas judged it necessary to indicate that his appeal to the 'subjection' of women was independent of whatever status they held in society. After arguing that a woman could not be a priest because she could not represent Christ the Head, he continued that this remained true even if temporal power might be open to her (*temporaliter dominari*).[13] Unfortunately, in this passage at least, Aquinas does not explain the considerations whether of anatomy or biology or psychology which lead him to this conclusion.

How can such attacks on gender-symbolism be answered? I suggest the basic answer may be that the fact that a symbol depends on a stereotype does not rob it of validity. A symbol depends on what is *perceived*. A Rolls Royce is a symbol of opulence, even though there exist Rolls Royces with broken springs and slashed upholstery. Even in modern society a woman is a symbol of something which a man is not, and vice versa. Of course, if it became the norm for women to be hard-nosed, thrusting, childless executives, and for men to be ineffectual wimps, then the symbolism would cease to work; but, please God, we have not reached that state yet.

Or am I conceding too much here? Should not one rather say that gender-symbolism is based on permanent differences between the sexes which are too deep to depend upon the changing conditions of a particular society? The sexes are related in such a way that, except in the most freakish circumstances, the man is necessarily the initiator of sexual activity, and the woman the recipient, and the main carrier of the consequences. To put it bluntly, women cannot commit rape, and men cannot have babies. I am not of course suggesting that the reason why the male priest can represent Christ at the altar is that he is a potential rapist; my point is that the violent sexual initiative of the deviant is the corruption of the initiative which is present in healthy form in normal sexual activity. I know no reason to believe that these different sexual roles are restricted to the physiological level, and have no echoes in psychology. Gender differences are inescapable, and provide a basis for gender symbolism.

It would be useful to take into account whatever empirical studies psychologists have made concerning the differences in the behavior of boys and girls at play. I have not had time, and have no competence, to do this. Nevertheless the evidence of one's eyes suggests that in the playground of a primary school you will find the boys playing different types of games than the girls; and if you were to listen, I believe you would find them talking of different things.

Anecdotal evidence suggests that men and women undergraduates work in characteristically different patterns: the men often show more self-confidence than the women, even though their ability and knowledge may not warrant it; while the women often manifest greater concern with producing the kind of work which they judge is required of them. Moreover, while the achievements of women in some intellectual and cultural fields often equal or surpass those of men, there are some surprising areas in which men seem to outperform women. In the English language, women novelists have a record at least as good as that of men; it is surprising therefore that it is not easy to name two world-class women dramatists. What could be the reason why there have been so few great women painters or composers? Why are there so few first-class women chess-players, so that the Polgar sisters seemed to burst from a clear sky? Since it is hard to find adequate sociological explanations for these admittedly loosely observed facts, one is left with the conclusion that there are characteristic differences between the male psyche and the female, which help to provide an objective basis for the different symbolic power of each of the genders.

Again, speaking unscientifically–which is, to repeat, the level at which symbols operate–although the external, homemaking roles of the father and the mother may no longer be as easily distinguishable as they used to be, there is something lacking to the child cared for by a single parent or by two partners of the same gender; at least they lack a role-model for forming a responsible relationship with the opposite sex.

Pope John Paul II on Gender Symbolism

I have so far tried to justify the belief that the symbolic significance of male and female remains different even in contemporary Western society. I shall now turn to Pope John Paul II's more philosophical exposition of the same point, which he proposed in his Encyclical *Mulieris dignitatem*, written for the Marian Year of 1988.[14]

The Pope takes as his starting-point a statement in the documents of Vatican II to the effect that human beings find themselves only in the gift of self.[15] This principle *"gives an essential indication of what it means to be human."* In the Genesis account of creation the image and likeness of God is linked with the relationship between men and women: "in his own image God created them, male and female he created them" (Gn 1.27). This relationship, the Pope explains, finds its fullest expression in the mutual self-giving of marriage, which "opens to the gift of a new life."[16] (It is not our purpose to consider the Pope's other way of self-giving, which is "Virginity for the sake of the Kingdom."[17])

Within this relationship, Pope John Paul believes that the different 'parts' of man and woman can be identified. The woman's part is 'motherhood', which

> implies from the beginning a special openness to
> the new person .... In this openness, in conceiving
> and giving birth to a child, the woman "discovers
> herself through a sincere gift of self."

This contact with the new life which the mother carries in her
womb gives rise to an attitude to *all* human life which "profoundly
marks the woman's personality." (We can see here some of the
reasons why the Pope is so implacably opposed to abortion and
contraception.) "It is commonly thought that *women* are more
capable than men of paying attention *to another person*." Because
the man remains outside the process of pregnancy and birth, "he
has to *learn* his own *'fatherhood'* from the mother."[18]

Gender Symbolism in Scripture

Let us now consider some of the many ways in which the
Bible applies gender-imagery to the relationship between Yahweh
and his people in the Old Covenant, and between Christ and his
Church in the New. We have already given a little thought to the
use of nuptial imagery by the prophets and St. Paul in the course
of our examination of *Inter insigniores*. To this we can add the use
of symbols derived from fatherhood and motherhood. Yahweh is
the Father of his people: "Is he not thy Father who has bought
thee? Has he not made thee and established thee?" (Dt 32:6). More
surprisingly, in the prophetic writings Yahweh becomes also the
mother: "Can a woman forget her sucking child, that she should
have no compassion on the son of her womb? Even these may
forget, yet I will not forget you" (Is 49:15). "As one whom his
mother comforts, so I will comfort you" (Is 66:13). Our Lord also
applied a maternal image to himself: "O Jerusalem, Jerusalem,
killing the prophets and stoning those who are sent to you! How
often would I have gathered your children together as a hen
gathers her brood under her wings, and you would not" (Mt

23:37). Later Paul also compared himself to a mother "in travail" giving birth to his spiritual children (Gal 4:19).

The same maternal imagery is applied to the Church, especially under the form of the new Jerusalem. Under the old covenant Isaiah had invited the people to "Rejoice with Jerusalem ... that you may suck and be satisfied with her consoling breasts" (Is 66:10). Paul directs his readers' attention from the "present Jerusalem" to the "Jerusalem above," who is "our mother" (Gal 4:26). (Revelation on the other hand envisages the new Jerusalem as the Bride coming down from heaven for her wedding with the Lamb (Rv 21:2,9). Early in the second century the *Shepherd of Hermas* recounts a vision of the Church in the form of an old woman. Since then it has become almost a cliché to speak about 'holy Mother Church.'

Gender Symbolism and the Blessed Virgin Mary

Images, when applied to divine mysteries, cannot always be used consistently. Thus, while the Church is called our Mother, we also address Mary as our Mother and as the Mother of the Church. This last title can be traced back to John 19:26-27, where Mary is entrusted with maternal responsibility for the whole Church in the person of the beloved disciple. Although there is no passage in the New Testament which speaks of Mary explicitly as the Mother of the Church, the title is close enough to scripture for Pope Paul VI to have made its promulgation a matter of first importance during the Second Vatican Council.

The title Mother of the Church needs to be understood in two ways. First, Mary is the mother *within* the Church, while herself being a member of it. While each member has a special endowment given by the Holy Spirit to equip him or her for personal service of the whole Church–some are apostles, some teachers etc. for the building up of Christ's Body (Eph 4:11-12)–Mary's special charism is to be the member of the Church who serves as Mother. Those familiar with the English scene may recall the analogy of the 'father (or mother) of the House of Commons,' the senior Member of Parliament, who is a father- or mother-figure among fellow members.

Mary is not only the one *within the Church* who has the responsibilities of a mother; she is also Mother of the Church in the sense that *her relationship to the Church* is that of a mother to her offspring. This follows immediately from her relationship to her Son: she is the Mother of the one whose body is the Church. The title does not simply commemorate a relationship which has ceased, now that her physical mothering of Jesus has been completed. It expresses an enduring relationship with practical consequences: Mary, who took the beloved disciple as her son at the foot of the cross, continues to support the Church with her prayers. Gerard Manley Hopkins expressed Mary's continuing motherly action in the well-known passage from his poem 'The Blessed Virgin Mary compared with the air we breathe.'

> Of her flesh he took flesh:
> He does take fresh and fresh,
> Though much the mystery how,
> Not flesh but spirit now
> And makes, O marvelous!
> New Nazareths in us,
> Where she shall yet conceive
> Him, morning, noon and eve;
> New Bethlems, and he born
> There, evening, noon and morn...

Mary's role as the Mother of the Church is not separate from her role as type or model of the Church, which received such clear emphasis at Vatican II. In the contemplative faith and obedience, which the Third Gospel picks out as her characteristics (Lk 1:45; 2:19; 2:51; 8:21; 11:28), she provides an example of what it is to be her Son's disciple. She demonstrates uniquely in her own person the working of God's grace in us all. This is especially true of the two most recently defined Marian dogmas.

Mary's fullness of grace and preservation from original sin through her Immaculate Conception, and her reception, body and soul, into heaven at the Assumption, are divine actions *already* accomplished in her, pointing to a similar destiny to which we are all *called* in eternity.

Hans Urs von Balthasar developed the understanding of Mary's maternal relationship to the Church in a new way, which Pope John Paul II has taken into his own thought, paying him the very rare honor of citing him by name in a footnote to an encyclical;[19] for by custom it is only the deceased who are quoted as authorities. For von Balthasar, there are two fundamental symbols of the Church, namely Mary and Peter. The Church is Marian in its 'active receptivity,' after the model of the one who heard the word of God and kept it. This Marian, and therefore feminine, dimension corresponds to the priesthood of all the baptized, who through the sacrament become a 'royal priesthood' (1 Pt 2:5,9). But within this general priesthood, the Church is also endowed with the hierarchical or ministerial priesthood of the ordained, which von Balthasar called Petrine, and which is characterized by the masculine quality of service.[20] (But why is service masculine?)

The Marian dimension is 'antecedent' to the Petrine, which can be understood only in relationship to it. For the universal priesthood involves a call to holiness, to worship God with the gift of one's whole life. The Petrine dimension is secondary to the Marian, because the ordained priesthood exists for the sake of the universal: the authority of the ordained "has no other purpose except to form the Church in line with the ideal of sanctity already programmed and prefigured in Mary." It is at this point that the Pope quotes von Balthasar: Mary is "Queen of the Apostles without any apostolic powers: she has other and greater powers."[21] (We can see here one solution to the objection that to bar women from ordination is to confine them to an inferior status. On the contrary, women have other and greater powers.)

In the Person of Christ

Let us now give further thought to the idea of the priest acting "in the person of Christ" at the Eucharist when he pronounces the words of consecration. This is not a phrase that goes back to the time of the early Church, still less to the New Testament. The CDF is not fully justified in seeking confirmation in the Letters of St. Cyprian, for the latter did not exactly say that the priest acts in the person of Christ, but that he "truly acts in the place of Christ" (*vice Christi vere fungitur*), a phrase which does not imply an appeal to the importance of the priest as a symbol.[22] Cyprian's concern is rather to show that the priest must not say Mass with water instead of wine, because he must follow the example and the command of the Christ in whose place he acts. There is no evidence here for the idea that the priest is acting in Christ's person in speaking Christ's words of institution: "This is my body ...." The CDF can, however, claim the authority of St. Thomas Aquinas, according to whom "the priest also enacts the image of Christ, in whose person and by whose power he pronounces the words of consecration."[23] The first council to have followed Aquinas in this teaching seems to have been the Council of Florence in the fifteenth century: "for the priest, speaking in the person of Christ (*in persona Christi*) brings about this sacrament [of the Eucharist]."[24]

However the expression has never formed part of a dogmatic definition by the Roman Catholic Church, although it has gained common currency, and can claim to represent the Church's mind. For example, the Vatican II Decree on the Liturgy states that the priest presides in the person of Christ and prays in the name of the people[25]–a principle which reminds us that he also acts *in persona Ecclesiae*, in the person of the Church, as we have already seen in our investigation of *Inter insigniores*.

We can perhaps go a little more deeply into what action in the person of Christ means. According to the CDF, at the Eucharist the priest acts *in persona Christi* "to the point of being his very image, when he pronounces the words of consecration."[26]

The line of thought is that of Aquinas,[27] and also of St. Ambrose's explanation of the Real Presence to the newly-baptized of Milan towards the end of the fourth century: in the first part of the Eucharist the bishop prays on his own account, but when he recites the words of institution, he is speaking the words of Jesus Christ; so that since it is Christ who is saying "This is my Body", those words have power to bring about what they state, namely the presence of Christ.[28]

The logic of this position requires that the words of consecration be seen as an effective or declaratory formula, intended to bring about what it affirms. Other sacramental examples are easy to find: "I baptize you in the name ...;" "I absolve you ...." However this is neither the origin nor the function of the words of consecration within the eucharistic prayer as a whole, as is shown by the syntactical and logical connection between the words of consecration and the rest of the prayer. The words of consecration do not form a free-standing unit, but are linked with the rest of the prayer by a connecting word. For example, in the Roman Canon this takes the form of a relative pronoun: the Father is asked to ratify the gifts of bread and wine and make them acceptable, so that they may become the Body and Blood of Jesus Christ, "*who*, the day before he suffered took bread ...." In the Egyptian liturgy of St. Mark the words of consecration are introduced by a causal particle, which implies that the account of the institution gives the reason for what goes before, namely the invocation of the Holy Spirit on the offerings: "may the Holy Spirit make these offerings the body and blood of Christ *because* on the night before he suffered Jesus took bread ...."[29] In short, the words of consecration are not a unit in which the priest ceases to speak for the Church and instead speaks in the person of Christ, but are part of the overall prayer of thanksgiving ("Let us give thanks") which the priest speaks on behalf of the Church.

Thus, while it is certainly true that the priest at the Eucharist does represent Christ to the people, this does not seem to be by virtue of speaking the words of Christ like an actor playing a role. Perhaps it is as the one who *presides* at the Eucharistic assembly that the priest's representation of Christ is most evident. This seems to accord with the Vatican II Decree on the Liturgy, which (while discussing the prayers spoken at the Mass) speaks of the priest as the one who, "in the person of Christ, presides over the assembly."[30] The *General Instruction on the Liturgy of the Hours* uses similar terms in explaining that in the liturgical celebration of the Office the bishop and the priests united to him "represent the person of Christ."[31]

Other more recent documents confirm this view. Thus *the Catechism of the Catholic Church* makes no reference to words of consecration when it explains that

> Through the ordained ministry, especially that of bishops and priests, the presence of Christ as head of the Church is made visible in the midst of the community of believers.[32]

So too Pope John Paul's Apostolic Exhortation on the Laity *Christifideles laici* (written a few months after *Mulieris dignitatem*) speaks of the priest's action in the person of Christ without applying this action to the recitation of the words of consecration: ordained ministers receive from the Holy Spirit

> the authority and sacred power to serve the Church, acting *in persona Christi Capitis* (in the person of Christ the Head) and to gather her in the Holy Spirit through the Gospel and the Sacraments.[33]

The mention of the Gospel is a reminder that one of the essential ways in which the priest represents Christ is in proclaiming the Gospel and teaching its meaning and application.

Need Christ's Representative be Male?

After these considerations of the meaning of the priest's action in the person of Christ, let us reflect a little on the contention that to perform this representative function the priest needs to be male. Pope John Paul in *Mulieris dignitatem* suggested tentatively ("it is legitimate to conclude") that in linking the Eucharist with the Apostles, Jesus "wished to express the relationship between man and woman, between what is 'feminine' and what is 'masculine.' For it is above all the Eucharist which

> expresses the *redemptive act of Christ the Bride-groom towards the Church the Bride.* This is clear and unambiguous when the sacramental ministry of the Eucharist, in which the priest acts "*in persona Christi*", is performed by a man.[34]

Now the argument seems to be that what the priest signifies is not the maleness of Christ as such, but Christ's role as the Bridegroom of the Church. But does this act of signifying necessarily require sharing Christ's male gender? Indeed, might not a woman be an appropriate symbol of Christ's redemptive action, especially of his compassion and healing in the sacrament of reconciliation?

Priesthood or Ministry

One last observation–a cat among the pigeons?–before we try to draw our musings together. Almost invariably throughout these deliberations we have been speaking in terms of priesthood. However that is not the only possible terminology. It is well known that the New Testament, while freely speaking of a royal priest-hood shared by all the baptized, never refers to the ordained minister as a priest; it took several centuries for the term to be regularly applied first to bishops and later to presbyters. What

would happen to the argument if we spoke throughout of ministers rather than priests? Could this jog our imagination into
considering the possibility of an ordained ministry for women
which did not necessarily include the call to preside at the
Eucharist? The Canon Law Society of America has recently
explored the possibility of establishing or restoring a permanent
diaconate for women.[35]

Conclusion

So let me try to draw the threads of this rambling paper
together. My aim is not to question the teaching on the ordination
of women of any of the churches, but rather to consider the
relevance of gender-symbolism to the issue. We noted that in the
fullest official Roman Catholic exposition of the arguments, the
decisive appeal was to authority and tradition; considerations
derived from the symbolic force of gender were seen to provide
clarification and confirmation, but not proof. We have given
reasons for believing that gender-symbolism retains its validity and
its relevance even in modern society; and we have examined Pope
John Paul's innovative understanding of that symbolism. We also
recalled some of the ways in which the Old and New Testaments use
both male and female imagery to express the relationship between
Yahweh or Jesus Christ and his people. In this context, following
the lead of von Balthasar, we considered Mary as the Mother of the
Church and as its model in her feminine quality of receptivity,
which is complemented by the masculine, Petrine function per-
formed by the ordained priest. Finally we tried to identify the sense
in which the priest acts in the person of Christ.

Throughout I have been asking readers to do one thing: by
examining their own reactions to try to discover what symbolic
difference it makes to them whether the priest is male or female.
Does the argument from gender-symbolism really work for *you*?
To answer this question requires not only unprejudiced honesty
on the reader's part, but also considerable intellectual discipline.

One has to get down to essentials. Some reactions one may have to disregard: for example, if one sees the female priest as the vindication of the rights of downtrodden woman, or the pretentious claimant to powers to which she is not entitled, such feelings must be put aside; they are not at the heart of the matter.

There was once a woman whose son had died in a Japanese prisoner-of-war camp, and who could not find it in her heart to forgive the Japanese. One morning, while waiting in church for Mass to begin, she was kneeling with her head bowed, struggling with her emotions. When the bell rang, she looked up and saw that the priest was Japanese. At once the block to her forgiveness and peace of mind was removed.

That priest had a symbolic power for the woman in her effort to forgive: not because of his gender or his good looks, but simply by virtue of the fact that he was Japanese. I invite readers to make a similar effort of the imagination, and to pare down their attention to the one fact of the action of Christ in the liturgy, especially the Eucharist. What does it symbolize to you if the priest is a man? What does it symbolize to you if the priest is a woman? There are no correct answers.

Edward Yarnold, S.J.

Endnotes

1. An earlier version of this paper was given at a conference of the Ecumenical Society of the Blessed Virgin Mary. I am glad to have this opportunity of recalling Father Eamon's long association with this society and his regular reports on recent Marian studies. The headquarters of the ESBVM is based at 11 Belmont Road, Wallington, Surrey SM6 8TE, England; there is also an American branch based at the Oblate College, 391 Michigan Avenue NE, Washington DC 20017.

2. In in. *Declaration on the Question of the Admission of Women to the Ministerial Priesthood.*

3. In in, 4.

4. In in, 5.

5. *Ibid.*

6. *Summa Theologiae* III.83.1 ad 3.

7. *In IV Sent*, dist. 25, q.2, art. 2.

8. In in, 5.

9. *Ibid.*

10. *Ibid.*

11. *Ibid.* The CDF also refers to PO 2 and 6.

12. See *Origins* 24 (1994), 49-52.

13. *In IV Sent.*, dist. 25, q.2, art. 1.

14. MD *(On the Dignity and Vocation of Women).*

15. GS, 24. In this and in quotations from the writings of Pope John Paul II the italics occur in the original text.

16. MD, 18.

17. MD, 20.

18. MD, 18.

19. MD 27 and note 55.

20. See Paul McPartlan's helpful paper 'The Marian Church: Hans Urs von Balthasar and the Ordination of Women," *Mary is for Everyone* (edited by W. McLoughlin and J. Pinnock, Leominster, 1997), pp. 41-55.

21. MD 27, note 55.
22. Cyprian, *Epistles* 63.14; PL 4.397; CSEL 3.713, quoted in MD, 5.
23. *Summa Theologiae*, III.83.1 ad 3, quoted in MD, 5.
24. *Decree for the Armenians*, DS, 1321.
25. SC, 33.
26. In in, 5.
27. *Summa Theologiae* III.83.1 ad 3. D. M. Ferrara, "Represen- tation or Self-Effacement? The Axiom *In Persona Christi* in St. Thomas and the Magisterium," *Theological Studies* 55 (1994), 223, maintains that the CDF misunderstands St. Thomas' thought; he argues that when Aquinas says the priest acts in the person of Christ, he does not mean that the priest is like Christ, but that he serves Christ `as the instrument in whom Christ himself acts. However, I personally find Sara Butler's argument against this posi- tion convincing: see "Quaestio Disputata: In Persona Christi: A Response to Dennis M. Ferrara" in *Theological Studies* 56 (1995), pp. 51-80.
28. Ambrose, *De sacramentis*, iv.14.
29. See R. C. D. Jasper and J. G. Cuming, *Prayers of the Eucharist: Early and Reformed* (3rd edition, New York, 1987), p. 64.
30. SC, 33.
31. No. 28.
32. CCC, 1548.
33. CL. 22.
34. MD, 26.
35. "Canonical Implications: Ordaining Women to the Perma- nent Diaconate," *Origins* 25 (1995), 344-352. The report concludes that "ordination of women to the permanent diaconate is possible and may even be desirable for the United States in the present cultural circumstances," p.351.

Preaching on the Feasts of Mary

As Saint Ambrose taught, the Mother of God is a model of the church in the matter of faith, charity, and perfect union with Christ.
–Const. on Church, # 63

The Madonna is not happy when she is placed before her Son.
–John XXIII

Mary wants to get off the pedestal. She wants to be a vital human being.
–Kathy Denison, laywoman (interviewed in Time magazine)

When it comes to Mary, Mother of Jesus the Son of God, preachers are called to enter into an ongoing relationship. Next to Jesus, she is the most prominent person acknowledged in the liturgical life of the Church. We only encounter the various apostles, martyrs, virgins, mystics, holy men and women, once a year on their feast days, or perhaps as key figures during a particular liturgical season–John the Baptist in Advent and Peter and Mary Magdalene during Easter come to mind. But with Mary, the mother of Jesus, it is a different story, or, more accurately, there are many stories, events, and occasions that invite the community of believers to stop and contemplate this woman's unique role in salvation history and her special place in the affections of those who acknowledge her Son as Lord and Redeemer. Looking at the liturgical year, one finds fifteen days designated either as solemnities, feasts, or memorials of Mary, in addition to her strong presence during the Advent and Christmas

267

seasons, on Good Friday and Pentecost, and even on feasts redefined as celebrations of the Lord, such as the Annunciation and the Presentation in the Temple. So attention must be paid. It is fitting that we who preach occasionally reflect on how we present Mary, Mother of the Redeemer, to the community of the redeemed.

Furthermore, we are living at a time when interest in Mary appears to be undergoing a renaissance, and not only in Roman Catholic circles. In the last decade there have been works on Mary by notable authors, such as historian Jaroslav Pelikan's *Mary Through the Centuries*, theologian George Tavard's *The Thousand Faces of the Virgin Mary*, and liturgist J. D. Crichton's *Our Lady in the Liturgy*.[1] Sally Cuneen's personal quest has provided *The Search for Mary, the Woman and the Symbol*; storyteller Megan McKenna has given us *Mary, Shadow of Grace*; and poet-essayist Kathleen Norris has recently offered *Meditations On Mary*.[2] Most recently, "Mary, the first theologian" was the focus of the October, 1999, issue of the Protestant quarterly, *Theology Today*. Add to that cover stories in *Time* (Dec.30, 1991), *Life* (Sept., 1996) and *Newsweek* (Aug. 25, 1997), and even a 1999 television movie entitled "Mary of Nazareth." One can state with some certitude that there must be a market for Mary.

Yet, for all this, as a teacher of homiletics, I have found that the major feasts of Mary evoke little passion among preachers, often creating more apprehension than enthusiasm, especially among beginning preachers. There seems to be an uncertainty about what one should say about Mary. There is a questioning about the value and even credibility of much that has been handed down, whether it is believable in today's culture. How to make sense of such doctrines as the Immaculate Conception and the Assumption as well as the Queenship of Mary and the apocryphal Presentation in the Temple. To quote the old Rodgers and Hammerstein song, "How do you solve a problem like Maria?"

Within this article, I would like to do three things that might assist preachers: a) indicate five ways of relating to Mary that predominate among those writing and thinking about her today; b) review the criteria for a sound Marian devotion provided by Paul VI in his 1974 apostolic exhortation, "Devotion to the Blessed Virgin Mary" (*Marialis cultus*), as applicable to the preaching we do on Marian feasts; and c) propose four ways of presenting Mary within a homily on a Marian feast, ways that allow the preacher to fulfill the homiletic task as envisioned by the 1982 document, "Fulfilled in Your Hearing: The Homily in the Sunday Assembly."[3]

Images of Mary, Past and Present

Mary, Mother of Jesus

This is the biblical designation for Mary; it is the reason she will be honored and venerated until the end of time. This relationship is at the heart of all of the Marian feasts and is explicitly recognized in the opening prayers for these days. Mary is who she is for us because she is the mother of Jesus. As the mother of Jesus, she is the mother of the Son of God, the crucified Savior, the risen Lord, Emmanuel, in whom God has acted for our salvation. Because of this role in salvation history, she came to be designated the Mother of God (*Theotokos*; literally, God-bearer or "Forth-bringer of God") at the Council of Ephesus in 431. Because the biblical witness must lie at the heart of all preaching on the Marian feasts, let us briefly review it.

The first appearance of Mary in the Bible stresses the divine initiative. In Matthew 1:20-21, the angel tells Joseph not to be afraid to take Mary as his wife, "for the child conceived in her is from the Holy Spirit. She will bear a son, and you are to name him Jesus, for he will save his people from their sins."[4] In Luke 1:35 the angel tells Mary, "The Holy Spirit will come upon you, and the power of the Most High will overshadow you; therefore the child to be born will be holy; he will be called Son of God." These fundamental assertions place Mary in proper relationship to the mystery of the Triune God. Her unique role renders her "blessed among women" and "the Mother of my Lord" as Elizabeth proclaims (Lk 1:42). Thus, this basic affirmation of Mary as Mother of God is Christological. We identify her in terms of her relationship with Jesus, as the mother of Christ, mother of the Lord, Mother of God.

God's people have related primarily to this image of Mary over the centuries; it has engaged the imaginations of poets, artists, scholars and preachers. "This is the carnal rose that re-enfolds heaven into earth," quotes Geoffrey Hill in his poem to Our Lady of Chartres, delicately imaging her role in the mystery of the Incarnation.[5] Furthermore, in bearing Jesus, she became the mother of all who believe in him. While it was Paul VI who favored the title "Mother of the Church," this recognition is also discovered in the Patristic age when she was called the "new Eve," mother of all the living, an image itself rooted in her presence at the cross in John's gospel, from which tree came forth eternal life. Alongside the "new Adam," she ushered in the new creation and was henceforth considered the spiritual mother of all those united in the mystical body of Christ.

Mary, Model of Faith

Of the synoptic gospels, it is Luke who makes the greatest case for the ongoing imitation of Mary by all believers. Luke's presentation reveals her as one who hears the word of God and responds wholeheartedly to it: "Here I am, the servant of the Lord; let it be with me according to your word" (Lk 1:38). Her cousin Elizabeth's greeting reinforces this when she cries out, "Blessed is she who believed that there would be a fulfillment of what was spoken to her by the Lord" (Lk 1:45). Mary attentively listened to the shepherds' report of what the angels had spoken about her Son, and "treasured all these words and pondered them in her heart" (Lk 2:19). Luke's Mary witnesses the encounter between her infant Son and his people, represented by the wisdom figures of Simeon and Anna, hearing the words about her child's destiny as "a sign that will be opposed," and her own participation in that sword—like suffering (Lk 2:34-35). Eamon Carroll notes that, due to the Vatican Council's use of the so-called 'difficult sayings' from the public life—that is, the incidents of the true kinsman (Mk 3:31-35; Mt 12:46-49; Lk 8:19-21) and the enthusiastic woman (Lk 11:27-28)—texts which formerly some had interpreted as being critical of Mary, were now read as praise for the Mother of Jesus, applying them to her as one who does God's will (Mk and Mt), and who hears the word of God and keeps it (Lk).[6] Finally, there is Luke's final image of Mary that has her waiting once again on the Spirit (Acts 1:14), this time with the apostles and other disciples in the upper room in Jerusalem, joined with them in prayerful expectation, in readiness for that overshadowing that will bring to birth the new body of Christ, the Church. Mary's role is to be in their midst, praying and waiting with them for God's action through the Spirit.

John's gospel also offers us Mary as the woman of faith, presenting her at Cana as one whose request is based on a true intuition of faith, not merely on a biological relationship (2:1-11), and whose presence at the foot of the cross furthers this theme by presenting both Mary and the beloved disciple as representing the community of true believers (12:25-27). Pheme Perkins notes that Mary's position here is equivalent to that of the beloved disciple, not yet above it. Together they serve as the heart of that community Jesus came to establish, having perceived his "hour of glory" and responded to it in spirit and truth.[7] In the fourth gospel Mary is present at the beginning and the end of Jesus' ministry, both as faithful disciple and as a witness to "the hour" when the glory of God was fully revealed.

Mary, Prophet of God's Justice

The foundational text for honoring Mary as prophet is Luke 1:46-55, with her bursting into that great biblical aria, the Magnificat. Here she joins with all those prophetic voices in Israel's history which proclaimed Yahweh as the God who saves, who lifts up and does great things for the lowly, and who is the hope of the oppressed and the downtrodden. Whereas Matthew's genealogy (1:1-16) puts Mary in the role of an "outsider," chosen to play a pivotal role at a key moment in Israel's story—just as Tamar, Rahab, Ruth, and Bathsheba did. Luke's portrayal of Mary singing her canticle places her within the sisterhood of women of great courage and faith, alongside such figures as Miriam, Hannah, Deborah, Judith, and the Mother of the Maccabees. Mary of Nazareth, her heart and body having received the Word of God, moves out into the world to serve, attentive to the counsel of the Spirit. In this moment of proclamation she is the courageous herald of the power of God, faithful witness to the hope of fulfillment, and subversive agent opposing the unjust status quo of the rich and self-satisfied.

Both liberation theology and feminist biblical scholarship have taken up this image of Mary. Leonardo Boff writes that even though traditional Christianity "has rendered the critical, liberating content of the Magnificat impotent," today's Church must take up its urgent task and "develop a prophetic image of Mary— an image of Mary as the strong determined woman, the woman committed to the messianic liberation of the poor from the historical social injustices under which they suffer."[8] In a similar vein, theologian Sydney Callahan refers to Mary as "the mother of Christian feminism," who enlists us in the liberation of women because "in so many instances women remain the poorest of the poor, unjustly subjected to gender discrimination, sexual abuse, and violence."[9] The words of Mary's *Magnificat* confront any situation where social, political, economic, or sexual oppression remains. God is for the poor, especially for the poorest of the poor who most often are women in today's world.

Mary, the Female/Feminine Face of God

A further contribution of feminist theology has been to bring to the consciousness of the community how over the centuries Mary has done what the three persons of the Trinity were unable to do; she has functioned as the carrier of the "female face" of God. Elizabeth Johnson writes that "images of God as female, arguably necessary for the full expression of the mystery of God but suppressed from official formulations, have migrated to the figure of this woman."[10] The most radical expression of this is found in the work of Leonardo Boff who sees Mary as the embodiment of a hypostatic union with the Holy Spirit.[11] But while this is the most extreme example,[12] throughout our history there has been a tendency to attribute to Mary the divine compassion, mercy, and tenderness of God. Johnson concludes that the challenge in our age is to retrieve these divine aspects, lifting them from Mary, and directly attribute them to God as female. In this way God will be proclaimed in a fullness presently lacking, "letting God be imaged as a female acting subject," and Mary will be restored to her full stature as "a genuine woman whose life was a journey of faith."[13]

A similar approach is to speak of Mary as the feminine face of God, the one who "reveals to us the feminine dimensions of the Christian God."[14] One problem with this is that the meaning of "feminine" is so culturally determined. The justified complaint of feminist authors is that what is often referred to as "feminine" is the male idea of what constitutes femininity, that is, the "patriarchal feminine." Mary Gordon has written of her experience of Mary back in the 1960s when "Mary was a stick to beat smart girls with. Her example was held up constantly: an example of silence, subordination, of the pleasure of taking the back seat." Gordon's response was to reject this but found herself "denied a potent female image whose application was universal."[15] Johnson, again, calls for female images of God rather than speaking of feminine dimensions or traits, arguing that both male and female images are needed, that both are capable of imaging the holy mystery, neither able to exhaust it. Such female imagery that would constitute "ultimate metaphors" for the Divine Mystery could include God as Mother, as Divine Compassion, as Female Saving Power, as Immanent Presence, and as Recreative Energy."[16]

While I respect and agree with the need to make use of both male and female imagery when speaking of God, as Scripture itself does in both testaments, I do not think men and women will cease finding in Mary a glimpse of our God. When discussing the role of the saints in the life of the faithful, the *Constitution on the Church* states, "In the lives of those who shared in our humanity and yet were transformed into especially successful images of Christ (cf. 2 Cor. 3:18), God vividly manifests to men [sic] His presence and His face. He speaks to us in them and gives us a sign of His kingdom...."[17] Mary has been first and foremost in this role of manifesting God's "presence" and "face" for generations. Our challenge is to help others recognize whom we all are seeing when we marvel at her.

Mary, Woman

The earliest reference to Mary is found in Paul's Letter to the Galatians which refers to Jesus as "born of a woman" (4:4). While so much of even today's religious art presents an image of Mary as the 'Fairy Queen,' she is first of all a woman, born into a specific time, place, and culture. The gospels set this woman before us in a deliberate fashion: a young, unmarried woman invited to be part of God's plan for our salvation, who responded in a thoughtful, questioning, and finally decisive manner; a pregnant woman, touched and overshadowed by the Spirit, who traveled to attend to an aged, pregnant cousin, and responded to her words of greeting in a hymn of faithful confidence and radiant joy; a young mother who ponders both the child in her arms and the words spoken about him by shepherds, wise men and the pious elders of Israel; an exhausted fugitive who had to escape an enraged king and flee to a foreign land to protect her child; an anguished parent searching out a lost teen in a crowded city; a caring guest whose faith implored her Son to act out of the appointed time; a woman of sorrow who stands by her crucified Son as he endures a painful death; and, finally, a woman of prayer, sitting with the community, again waiting on the Spirit to bring about a new birth through wind and fire. Mary's life as portrayed in the Scriptures was a human life, an ongoing journey in faith. Before she was the recipient of the many titles given her over the centuries, she was the woman of Nazareth: virginal, married, child-bearing, widowed, sorrowing, aging, dying. Her seven ages correspond to the universal experience of humanity.

Marian studies today offer us many ways of thinking about Mary; the above are not exhaustive. They can help to focus on the one called "an icon of human possibility," and a "woman for all seasons."[18] To aid us in preaching about her, let us now attend to the contribution of Pope Paul VI in his exhortation on devotion to the Blessed Virgin Mary.[19]

Four Guidelines and a Principle: Paul VI and Marian Devotion

In *Marialis cultus* Paul VI places the renewal of Marian devotion within the context of the Second Vatican Council's liturgical reforms. The second part of his exhortation offers specific guidance "to help the development of devotion that is motivated in the Church by the Word of God and practiced in the Spirit of Christ." Such guidance is particularly helpful for the preacher. We find articulated first the key theological principle expressing Mary's relationship to the Trinity, to Christ, and to the Church, followed by four guidelines that develop the implications of this principle.[20]

Pope Paul begins by setting out the foundation for Mary's relationship with the Trinity: "In the Virgin Mary everything is relative to Christ and dependent upon him. It was with a view to Christ that God the Father from all eternity chose her to be the all-holy Mother and adorned her with gifts of the Spirit granted to no one else."[21] At the same time, devotion to Mary must recognize her unique mission in the mystery of the Church, helping us realize that "both the Church and Mary collaborate to give birth to the Mystical Body of Christ since 'both of them are the Mother of Christ, but neither brings forth the whole [body] independently of the other.'"[22] Mary serves as a model for the Church both in bringing Christ to bodiliness and to action in the world, and she serves as a sign of hope for sharing in the salvation made possible for all through Christ's death. To keep a proper balance in speaking of Mary in relation to both the Trinity and the Church, Pope Paul offers four guidelines that remind preachers of key areas of concern in our efforts to speak of Mary as the Mother of Christ and our Mother in the Communion of Saints.

The Biblical Guideline

Paul VI writes that it is not enough that Marian devotions make "diligent use of texts and symbols skillfully selected from the Sacred Scriptures" but also "the texts of prayers and chants should draw their inspiration and their wording from the Bible, and above all that devotion to the Virgin should be imbued with the great themes of the Christian message."[23] If the prayers and chants should make use of the words, symbols and themes of the Scripture texts, how much more the preaching? Mary's presentation there as one blessed because she heard the Word of God and kept it, and as mother and sister and daughter in the eschatological family founded in the saving death and resurrection of Christ and constituted Church by the descent of the Holy Spirit, is the resource for ongoing reflection and meditation by all preachers. Mary engages us from within these texts as one who is the recipient of God's grace, rejoicing in God her Savior and going forth to be of service. She is seen first and last as one waiting on the Holy Spirit; between the Annunciation and Pentecost she is presented always in relationship to her Son, never for her own sake. This is particularly important for those feasts of a more devotional nature that present her as standing alone. The biblical images keep her in proper relationship with the Father, Son, and Holy Spirit, and with the community of believers.

The biblical witness also keeps preaching in check by avoiding the excesses of either an overly sentimental approach that in the end only further removes her from contact with our lives, or an exaggeratedly relevant approach that tries to make her into something she was not, either by divinizing or humanizing her beyond the evidence at hand.[24] Pope Paul's call to root Marian devotion in the great biblical themes of the Christian message, such as God's initiative in the work of salvation and God's care for the lowly and the poor, is clearly pertinent to preaching on the feasts of Mary. A complementary resource here can be found in the world of artists and sculptors and their depiction of the biblical scenes and the various images of Mary. Such presentations can help to provide a fresh take on scenes that have become "frozen." I think of the differences between Lotto's and Tanner's paintings of the Annunciation, the various contemporary images of Mary by such artists as Meinrad Craighead and John Giuliani, and the controversial exhibit by Robert Gober which featured a traditional statue of Mary with a culvert pipe running through it. The work of artists can help to see her from a fresh perspective.

The Liturgical Guideline

Preaching on the Marian feasts should also be in harmony with the focus of the liturgical action and season, derive inspiration from it, and orient people towards it.[25] Preaching within the Eucharist functions as an *integral* part of the liturgy, that is, its purpose is to serve as the connecting link between the liturgy of the Word and the liturgy of the Eucharist. Keeping in mind the particular Marian feast and its relation to the paschal mystery, such preaching is grounded in particular scriptures and liturgical texts: it disposes the community to move from being attentive hearers of the Word of God to giving thanks and praise for what has been and is being done for them in Christ; then to participation in the reception of the Eucharist; and finally to ethical behavior that fosters the coming of the reign of God in our world. In this way preaching on the Marian feasts remains an integral part of the rite.

Preaching that is mindful of its liturgical setting will help make the community conscious that Mary stands with us as a member of the communion of the saints, as a sign of hope, and as one who intercedes for us as we pray the Eucharistic prayer to the Father: "Make us worthy to share eternal life with Mary, the Virgin Mother of God . . . ,"[26] and "May he [Christ] make us an everlasting gift to you and enable us to share in the inheritance of your saints, with Mary the virgin mother of God, with the apostles, the martyrs, ... and all your saints on whose constant intercession we rely for help."[27] Careful study of the liturgical texts proper to each Marian feast, especially the opening prayer of the day and the preface, can help provide focus for the preaching. That the liturgical prayers are addressed to God reminds us that Mary stands with us as a recipient of God's grace. These prayers situate Mary first of all as one in whom God has worked for our salvation and then recommend her as one who intercedes for us. Consider the alternate collect on the feast of the Annunciation, which addresses God who has "revealed the beauty of your power by exalting the lowly virgin of Nazareth and making her the mother of our Savior," and then concludes by saying, "May the prayers of this woman bring Jesus to the waiting world and fill the void of incompletion with the presence of her child." Such prayers realize the theological principle of keeping Mary in proper relation both to the Triune God and to the community of believers.

Preaching on the Marian feasts also can also help to lead the community more deeply into the celebration of the liturgical seasons in which they are placed; the feast of the Immaculate Conception falling during Advent, the feast of Mary, Mother of the Lord, during the Christmas season, and the feast of the Annunciation during Lent or Easter. Such events, celebrated with an eye to the season, also keep Mary's place in the life of the Church connected to the central mysteries of Christ: the Incarnation and the Paschal Mystery of his suffering and death.

The liturgical guideline, then, complements the biblical one by presenting Mary in relation to the great events and themes of salvation history: always first and foremost the recipient of God's saving grace.

The Ecumenical Guideline

As Marian devotion is to be "in accord with the deep desires and aims of the ecumenical movement," so too the preaching on Marian feasts. Paul VI notes how Catholics share Mary as a subject of devotion with the Orthodox and the Anglicans, and that we share her words of praise in the Magnificat with the Churches of the Reform. But he then goes on to warn that in fostering devotion to Mary "every care should be taken to avoid any exaggeration which could mislead other Christian brethren about the true doctrine of the Catholic Church."[28] For all Christians, Christ is the one mediator, the source and center of the Church's communion, the Lord and Savior. Mary must not be placed over and against Christ as was done during the medieval period with its attribution of the kingdom of justice to Christ and the kingdom of mercy to Mary. And there must be a proper understanding of Mary's spiritual motherhood of the faithful: "For Mary did not and cannot engender those who belong to Christ, except in one faith and one love: for 'Is Christ divided?' (1 Cor 1:13)."[29] Preaching does not hesitate to proclaim Mary as one who continues to love even beyond death, as she continues to behold new sons and daughters who have become part of the body of Christ, her Son in the flesh.[30] Mary does not cease to love the brothers and sisters of Jesus, nor to intercede for them as a mother would for all her children, "for she is inseparably linked with her son's saving work."[31]

The Anthropological Guideline

This last guideline keeps Mary within the circle of the community of believers as fully human, as one with whom we can identify. Mary as presented in some devotional literature, Pope Paul recognizes, "cannot easily be reconciled with today's life style, especially with the way women live today;" he notes such contemporary realities as women's equality and co-responsibility with men in caring for the family, and their achievements in the political, social, and cultural arenas of our day. In light of such factors, Mary's life may seem too constricted to have any contemporary relevance. But Mary is not to be approached as one to be imitated precisely in the type of life she led, but rather "for the way in which, in her own particular life, she fully and responsibly accepted the will of God (cf. Lk 1:38)."[32]

In her journey of faith, she listened, questioned, pondered, sang, worried, showed concern for others, and grieved. To keep sight of her humanity in no way shortchanges her unique role in God's plan, but rather makes her more accessible for those who experience the life of faith as a challenge. Paul VI asserts that the modern woman will find in Mary one who exercised decision-making power in "an event of world importance," who opted for virginity as a "courageous choice" made not as a rejection of marriage but as a sign of total love for God, and who was neither "timidly submissive" nor "one whose piety was repellent to others." Rather, Mary was "a woman who did not hesitate to proclaim that God vindicates the humble and the oppressed, and removes the powerful people of this world from their privileged positions (cf. Lk 1:51-53)."[33] Mary of Nazareth remains as a strong woman who knew poverty, exile, and suffering, a woman for others who is "the perfect model of the disciple of the Lord."[34]

How preachers speak about Mary can do much to counter the often sentimental and sometimes superstitious presentations of the past. Sound preaching offers a portrait of a biblical figure of heroic stature, who put her trust totally in the living God. She continues to stand in this new millennium as one worthy of honor and praise. She encourages all of us to hear God's call to bring Christ into the world in our bodies, to dwell in the awareness that together we form the body of Christ, and to participate in the continuing work of the liberation of the world from all that enslaves and destroys.

Paul VI has provided guidance for all preachers on the feasts of Mary. We will now consider several ways Mary can be presented within the homily, understood as a scriptural interpretation of the community's existence, leading them to praise and a life rooted in the gospel.

Preaching on the Marian Feasts

There are fifteen Marian feasts in the General Roman Calendar explicitly dedicated to Mary, the Mother of the Lord, and several others in which she plays a primary role. Some are clearly rooted in the biblical story, whereas others are grounded in a combination of theological, devotional, and historical factors. When preaching on her feasts, we do not put Mary in the place of Christ. Rather we attempt to discover how we can collaborate with her in the task of interpreting the community as the locus for God's ongoing work of salvation. Mary can function in a number of ways in the homily, as other saints do on their feasts. I would suggest four possible roles: Model, Mirror, Mentor, and Metaphor. I will briefly consider each heading, placing certain feasts under each one. This is not meant to limit a particular feast to that heading; Mary may be presented in various ways on the same feast, although I suggest choosing one in the interests of clarity.

Mary as Model

Jessica Powers' poem, "The Visitation Journey," contrasts the Mary that artists have frequently portrayed–Lady Mary in a blue silk gown, riding gently over hill and dale on a bright spring day, with birds singing and flowers bowing–with her own terse vision: "a girl riding upon a jolting donkey/ and riding further and further into the truth."[35] In the poet's view Mary's journey covers more than geographical distance. And, in this respect, it is one all are invited to make: to ride further and further into the truth of who God is, who we are, and what we are called to be. Mary is a model of responding to God's grace and the Spirit's good counsel on this particular feast.

The preacher can present Mary as a model of what it means to say "yes" to God, to become the vehicle of incarnation, on the feasts of Mary, Mother of God (January 1), the Annunciation of the Lord (March 25), the Visitation (May 31), and the Dedication of St. Mary Major (August 5), the commemoration of the church built by Pope Sixtus III to honor the Mother of God shortly after the declaration of Mary as *Theotokos* at the Council of Ephesus in 431. The core moment for our imitation of Mary as model occurs in her "yes" to God. In that moment Mary begins her growth into the image of the New Eve, woman of the new creation, mother of all the living. In her "yes" Mary accepted the unique vocation of being mother of the Lord. But this "yes" does not set her apart from the rest of us; rather it simply acknowledges that she was ahead of us. "Yes" is what we are all called to say, as the mystic Caryll Houselander reminds us, so that we might fulfill the universal vocation of bearing Christ in our bodies and giving him to the world. "Nothing but things essential *for us* are revealed to us about the Mother of God; the fact that she was wed to the Holy Spirit and bore Christ into the world."[36]

We can also present Mary as model on such feasts as the Immaculate Conception (December 8) and the Assumption (August 15); on both occasions she models what it means to be a recipient of the generous gift of God's grace. In her Immaculate Conception, Mary is the model of what has happened for all of us in baptism, the ratification of our being surrounded by God's love from the very beginning; and in her Assumption she is the model of our destiny in Christ, to be raised up into the communion of all the saints with Christ who reigns.[37] Preaching on these feasts call us to know more deeply the gift of God given in Christ and to make this gift more fully our own by choosing the path that will allow our own "riding further and further into the truth."

Mary as Mirror

George Tavard writes that the Mary of folk piety often is a "mirror of the attributes of God," especially of God's ubiquity and healing power. "Our Lady of Everywhere reflects the God who is everywhere by creative presence and power. Our Lady of Everything Good reflects the benevolent God who is at the same time supreme power and supreme goodness."[38] Such mirroring also can be found in feasts like the Immaculate Heart of Mary (the

Saturday following the Second Sunday after Pentecost, and the day after the feast of the Sacred Heart of Jesus), the mother's heart reflecting the compassionate love of her Son's. On the feast of Our Lady of Sorrows (September 15, the day after the feast of the Exaltation of the Holy Cross), Mary the suffering mother mirrors the suffering Son.

More problematic is the feast of the Queenship of Mary (August 22, the octave of the Assumption). It recently came into the calendar at the end of the 1954 Marian year, but as J. C. Crichton points out, the Church had long celebrated Mary as Queen, seeing in her exaltation "the dazzling 'reward', so to say, of Mary who gave herself totally to her Son and to his saving work."[39] We can see this as the culmination of the movement of Mary into full communion with her Son after death, given expression by the Assumption, taking her position where, as the Constitution on the Sacred Liturgy reminds us, she is "linked with his ongoing saving work."[40] The difficulty with this feast is that it could work in the opposite direction, encouraging a tendency to set Mary in isolation from the saving work of Christ, reinforcing the idea of a parallel kingdom where Mary dispenses mercy, while Christ dispenses justice.

Other feasts such as Our Lady of Lourdes (February 11) and Our Lady of Guadalupe (December 12) present Mary as a mirror of God's healing power and God's love for the poor. Here again, we can encounter the problem already mentioned. Interestingly, both feasts present her as the crowned Queen of Heaven, and both present her alone, (though in the latter she is pregnant). But the impression can be reinforced that she reigns in her own right, making it all the more important to emphasize Mary as participating in the ongoing work of her Son, not taking his place, and certainly not in competition with him.

Mary as Mentor

Certain feasts allow preachers to present Mary as one who guides us more deeply into the paschal mystery. As our mother, she is also our mentor, instructing us in the ways of her Son. As Our Lady of Sorrows she draws us into the contemplation of the suffering and death of Jesus, and as Our Lady of the Rosary (October 7) she calls us to ponder the saving mysteries that surround the incarnation, death, and resurrection of the Redeemer. The feast of Our Lady of Carmel (July 16), commemorating the origin of the Carmelites in the 13th century, presents her as the true daughter of Zion who calls us to silent adoration and to doing God's will. And on the feast of Mary's Birth (September 8), she teaches us through the Matthean genealogy and the annunciation to Joseph (Mt 1:1-16, 18-23) that God worked through the most broken circumstances to bring about the birth of the Messiah, empowering the weak and lowly, a pattern that continues in our own day. Mary as mentor calls us to ponder the works of God in the silence of our hearts.

Mary as Metaphor

Mary was made for metaphor. The litany of Loretto generously employs them: Mirror of justice, Seat of wisdom, Vessel of honor, Tower of David, Tower of ivory, House of gold, Ark of the covenant, Morning star. Throughout the ages, Mary has been greeted by preachers and spiritual writers in a manner worthy of impassioned troubadours. She has unleashed the Church's often prosaic tongue and freed it to speak poetically. Mary Gordon reminds us that we must continue to find isolated words and images to name her role in our own day, that "one must travel the road of metaphor, of icon, to come back to that figure ... who has moved the hearts of men and women...."[41] One feast in particular invites the preacher to play in its metaphorical field, the Presentation of Our Lady in the Temple (November 21), based on a legend found in the *Protoevangelium of St. James*. Originating in the East with the dedication of the church of St. Mary in Jerusalem in 543, it invites preachers to engage their imaginations, encouraged by texts that include Zechariah's speaking of God coming to the Temple, Mary's *Magnificat* as responsorial psalm, and the gospel where Jesus proclaims "whoever does the will of my father is brother and sister and mother to me" (Mt 12:50). Artists have portrayed the three year old Mary joyfully going to live in the Temple, leaving her parents without a backward glance. The image of this young girl, soon to be the temple of the living God, taking up residence in the temple made of stones, to be instructed in the law of the Lord, invites all the faithful to ponder their own identity as the temple of the Spirit and body of the Christ.

On the first anniversary of the beginning of the Second Vatican Council, Pope Paul VI prayed: "O Mary, make this church . . . recognize you as its Mother and Daughter and elect Sister, as its incomparable model, its glory, its joy, and its hope."
May our preaching help make this prayer a reality.

James A. Wallace, C.Ss.R.

Endnotes

1. Jaroslav Pelikan, *Mary Through the Centuries: Her Place in the History of Culture* (New Haven: Yale, 1996); George H. Tavard, *The Thousand Faces of the Virgin Mary* (Collegeville Liturgical Press, 1996); J. D. Crichton, *Our Lady in the Liturgy* (Collegeville: Liturgical Press, 1997).

2. Sally Cuneen, *In Search of Mary, The Woman and the Symbol* (New York: Ballentine, 1996); Megan McKenna, *Mary, Shadow of God's Grace* (Maryknoll: Orbis, 1994); Kathleen Norris, *Meditations On Mary* (New York: Viking, 1999).

3. See *Fulfilled In Your Hearing: The Homily in the Sunday Assembly* (Washington, DC: USCC-NCCB, 1982), 29 for its understanding of the homily as "a scriptural interpretation of human existence which enables a community to recognize God's active presence, to respond to that presence in faith through liturgical word and gesture, and beyond the liturgical assembly, through a life lived in conformity with the gospel."

4. All quotations are taken from *Holy Bible: The New Revised Standard Version* (Nashville: Thomas Nelson, 1989).

5. See *Upholding Mystery: An Anthology of Contemporary Christian Poetry* (Edited by David Impastato, New York: Oxford, 1997), p. 269.

6. Eamon Carroll, O.Carm., *Understanding the Mother of Jesus* (Wilmington: Glazier, 1979), p. 13.

7. Pheme Perkins, "Mary in Johannine Traditions," *Mary, Woman of Nazareth: Biblical and Theological Perspectives* (Edited by Doris Donnelly, New York: Paulist, 1989), p. 114.

8. Leonardo Boff, *The Maternal Face of God* (San Francisco: Harper and Row, 1987), p. 189.

9. Sydney Callahan, "Mary and the Challenges of the Feminist Movement, " *America*, December 18, 1993, p. 7.

10. Elizabeth Johnson, "Mary and the Image of God," *Mary, Woman of Nazareth*, edited by Doris Donnelly (New York:

Paulist Press, 1989), p. 26.

11. Boff, *op. cit.*

12. For a critique of Boff's position, see Tavard, *Thousand Faces of the Virgin Mary*, pp. 261-263.

13. Johnson, *op. cit*, p. 28.

14. Andrew Greeley, *The Mary Myth, On the Femininity of God* (New York: Seabury, 1977), p. 217.

15. Mary Gordon, "Coming to Terms with Mary," *Commonweal*, January 15, 1982, p. 11.

16. Johnson, *op. cit.*, pp. 48-54.

17. LG, 50.

18. Cuneen, *op. cit.*, pp. 307ff; Pelikan, *op. cit.*, p. 215ff.

19. MC.

20. MC, 17-29.

21. MC, 18.

22. MC, 20-21.

23. MC, 22.

24. On the divinizing side, Andrew Greeley has noted that the fourteenth century presentations of Mary which made her more important than Jesus or God were "often not the Mary of Mother-love but the Mary ... of enormous and dangerous spiritual power who could be especially punitive when she was offended." See "The Faith We Have Lost," *America*, October 2, 1993, p. 26.

25. MC, 22-23.

26. Eucharistic Prayer II.

27. Eucharistic Prayer III.

28. MC, 24

29. MC, 25.

30. Cf. Carroll, *op. cit.*, p. 57.

31. LG, 103.

32. MC, 26.; Carroll, *op. cit.*, p. 47.

33. MC, 27.

34. MC, 27.

35. Jessica Powers, *Selected Poetry of Jessica Powers* , edited by Regina Siegfried and Robert F. Morneau (Kansas City,

Missouri: Sheed and Ward, 1989), p. 67.

36.   Caryll Houselander, *The Reed of God* (New York: Sheed and Ward, 1944), p. xii.

37.   See Karl Rahner, *Mary Mother of the Lord* (New York: Herder and Herder, 1963), especially the chapters on the Immaculate Conception (pp. 42-52) and the Assumption (pp. 83-92.)

38.   Tavard, *op. cit.*, p. 248.

39.   Crichton, *op. cit.*, p. 87. This work is very helpful for preachers, providing comments on all the biblical and liturgical texts of the Marian feasts.

40.   SC, 103.

41.   Gordon, "Coming to Terms with Mary," p. 12.

42.   Quoted in Tavard, *op. cit.*, p. 205.

Our Lady of Mount Carmel
Pray for Us!
The Scapular Promise
and the Garbage Pickers
at the Nejapa Dump

Life at the Nejapa Dump

The road from Apopa to Quetzaltepeque follows the route of the waters that fall off the volcano of San Salvador on course to the Tomayate River. Road and river easily scar the volcanic soil, creating a natural pathway for the torrential rains that fall on El Salvador every winter from June until November. Midway between Apopa and Quetzaltepeque is the town of Nejapa and its two major industries: the garbage dump for metropolitan San Salvador and the Coca-Cola bottling plant.

The dump is new, replacing another antiquated and overloaded landfill, and it is considered a modern marvel of waste management. Garbage from greater San Salvador is brought in by commercial and municipal truckers, weighed and dumped in huge plastic liners. Citizens pay for this service with a tax on their electricity bill. The private company that manages the dump has committed a portion of its profit to social programs that benefit the poor. Their first demonstration of this commitment was to evict the fifty families that lived on the old dump and to bar them from sorting through the garbage at the new, modern facility.

Life at the older Nejapa dump was certainly a horror. The evicted families include a generation of young people who have only known life on the dump. They were born there; they have worked there since childhood; they first made love there and now are raising their own children in the same ambiance of offal and garbage. The garbage pickers' work consists of salvaging whatever can be re-sold. Salvageable items include electronic components, cardboard, metal, and scrap wood that can be used for firewood. But the major marketable resource of the Nejapa dump is plastic. Plastic sheeting, bottles, bags, hard plastic, molded plastic; any plastic whatsoever can be sold for recycling. The most adept at recycling plastic from the dump are children. The easiest part of the dump to scavenge is the unloading zone. There, the mixture of waste is loose, not yet compacted by the bulldozers, trucks and the tramp and tread of feet. The unloading zones are also the most dangerous and children frequently die under bulldozer tracks or the wheels of the garbage trucks.

By far the most precarious danger at Nejapa comes from the garbage itself. First, there exists the chronic problem of bacteria, viruses and parasites that permeate the garbage. Salvaging consists of running ones fingers through the garbage, feeling the plastic and yanking it out for resale. Hands pass to mouths and the children become hosts for whatever microbes are in the garbage. Recently, with increasing deposits of medical discharge from San Salvador's hospitals, additional dangers are present from HIV-infected hypodermic needles. Cases of AIDS from the dump have not been reported as such–death comes too quickly and anonymously for public health officials to take notice. But the causes of these deaths are known to the families whose children become ill, suffer without respite, and die.

Second, there is the danger of gas. The burrowing of children creates dips and pockets in the garbage where methane accumulates. Methane is odorless. It seeps undetected into cavities created by the garbage pickers. The children breathe the gas, they collapse, and they die. In one tragic incident, a small girl fell into one of these gas hollows and passed out. Her older brother attempted to rescue her. The gas overcame him as well. Another brother followed. All three died. The mother could not be consoled at the funeral mass held later in the day for her three children. The next day, work resumed. With each delay, more debris covers the valuable plastic.

Third, the water at the Nejapa dump is thoroughly contaminated. Studies by the Lutheran University show high levels of lead, arsenic, heavy metals, fecal matter and a wide range of biological contaminants in the water. The results are evident in the high incidences of undernourishment, skin diseases, bronchitis, intestinal diseases and chronic diarrhea evident in the children–the only population formally studied at the dump.

Finally, life at the dump attracts other-than-human scavengers. Nejapa is the end of the human-consumer chain in El Salvador. But the Nejapa dump has other scavengers, including large rats, which often bite the fingers of the children as they probe in the garbage. The rats have their natural enemies. Where there are rats there are python snakes. The pythons keep the rat population in check.

When the dump stopped receiving organic waste, the rat population dropped. Faced with a shortage of food, the pythons looked to other sources of nourishment.

Pythons can grow to twelve feet. The pythons at the Nejapa dump are smaller– averaging around six feet. They are too small to attack the child garbage pickers, but they are sufficiently strong to attack the infants left behind in the garbage pickers' shacks. One mother described in horror her attempt to force her nine-month baby from the gullet of a python. The child was eaten whole and by the time a group of men had caught the snake and cut it open, the baby was dead and partially digested by the acidic mucus lining the snake's stomach.

The garbage pickers live in the dump because they need to protect their salvaged property. The children do the scavenging while the adults are responsible for the classification and sale.

This work is completed at the edge of the dump where buyers arrive daily to negotiate prices and discuss terms of credit. If someone is not present to guard the family's pickings, the salvage will be stolen.

Not surprisingly, the economy of the Nejapa dump is subject to the forces of the international market. When pickings are low, the product is more valuable. If imports of plastic from Mexico are low, recyclable plastic receives a higher price. The pickers keep their ears to the ground and measure market trends. When a ship of scrap plastic from the United States was recently detained by customs for health reasons, the value of plastic from the dump doubled. When a large packaging company recently signed an agreement with a recycling company for pickup of scrap plastic at the factory, the value of Nejapa plastic fell dramatically.

In 1998 the Canadian-based multi-national SYMTEC–the new owners of the dump–decided to free their stockholders from responsibility for the families that live on the dump. They opted to prevent these families from sorting through the garbage. This is how multi-national corporations throughout the developing world express their social consciousness. The story is the same in the Philippines where the Carmelites labor among the urban poor. It is the same in Mexico, Peru and in the great urban slums of Brazil, all places served by Carmelites.

An Appeal to Carmel

In June, 1998, a delegation of the garbage pickers from the Nejapa dump appealed for help to the Committee for the Corporal Works of Mercy of the pastoral council of Our Lady of Mount Carmel in Canton Cabanas. Angelica, the elected representative of these families, explained things: "You have to be poor to work in garbage and live on a dump. But you've got to be poorer still to be thrown off the dump." Her plea was simple: "Help us, we have no place to go." Specifically, Angelica was asking for the support of the pastoral council to resettle on land owned by the Church in

Cabanas. This land was a former refugee camp that had reverted to parish ownership.

Canton Cabanas is part of the parish of Calle Real in the municipality of Ciudad Delgado, about five miles from the dump. The first Carmelites from the Province of the Most Pure Heart of Mary visited Calle Real in the summer of 1986. They were part of a fact-finding tour sponsored by a Texas-based organization, CRISPAZ, that the province had supported through the Human Development Fund, and a bequest from the family of J. J. McCarthy. This first group to visit Calle Real included Peter Hinde, Jerry Williams, Dave Walsh, Andy Skotnicki, John Jones and Marco Pardo. At the time of this visit, Calle Real was the site of the largest in-country refugee camp. Because of the camp, the population of Calle Real swelled from 5,400 in 1986 to 35,000 by the end of the war in 1992. When the refugees left the camp to resettle in Calle Real their status changed from refugees to displaced persons. Through various sources, including Catholic Relief Services, Food for the Poor, the Knights of Malta, and the Province of the Most Pure Heart of Mary, the Church was able to help establish 26 communities of displaced persons in this part of the Archdiocese.

The last community to receive this kind of support was Canton Cabanas. Cabanas is located on the top of a steep hill. By most reckoning in the community, the access road to Cabanas was built in the late eighteenth century. It had not been improved much in the last two centuries and was virtually inaccessible except by horse or on foot. In 1987 the community formed a pastoral council under the patronage of Our Lady of Mount Carmel. In the following decade, this pastoral council assumed two important burdens: it formed brigades of men, women and children to work from 8 PM to 2 AM to rebuild the road; it also constructed an eighty-bed retreat house dedicated to Our Lady of Mount Carmel.

The community pastoral council (*directiva*) meets bi-weekly. But the assembly, consisting of the whole community, meets only twice yearly–in December for the annual evaluation

and pastoral planning, and in July for the feast day of Our Lady
of Mount Carmel. For the past three years (1997-1999) the July
assembly has consisted of the following components: vigil procession from the northern extremity of the community to the retreat
house; scriptural rosary; reflection on assigned texts; feast of
tamales and other traditional foods to raise funds for the poor. It
has concluded with the celebration of the Eucharist on the feast
day. As part of its commitment to building the "spirit of Carmel"
within the community, the council has based the scriptural
rosary and reflections on "Carmelite" readings. In 1998 the needs
of the garbage pickers from the Nejapa dump entered these
scriptural reflections in a major way. Before describing the
consequences of these reflections, a minor digression is necessary to describe the basic methodology of scriptural reflection in
a base community of the poor, according to the practice of the
Church of San Salvador.

Reading Scripture from the Point of View of the Poor

Base Christian communities are not new to the Church.
They have existed in one form or another since the beginning of
the Christian era and have contributed to the Church's life and
ministry since then. A base Christian community is a voluntary
association of lay Christians who meet with regularity to read
scripture and ask, "What does this mean?" The base Christian
community seeks meaning from three sources: the intention of
the author of the text, the meaning of the text in light of the
experience of the community, and the significance the text in
terms of the pastoral *praxis* of the community.

1. Interpretation from the Perspective and Intention of the Author

One member of the community is assigned responsibility
for providing the others with an exegesis of the text from the point
of view of the intention of the original author. The sources used

by these "Delegates of the Word of God" are varied. They include simple, didactic materials available in the parish library. The most popular of these materials are the commentaries written by Carlos Mesters, O.Carm., and published by *Paulines Ediciones*. Numerous dioceses and religious communities have pirated Carlos' material and re-packaged it—often without reference to the original source. This material and similar workbooks are generally available. The Latin American Bible includes excellent footnotes and references. Other materials are available from the religious conference, the Archdiocese or from commercial bookstores.

The Delegate of the Word can easily yield to the temptation of preaching to the community. The Delegate's role is neither to preach nor to limit discussion to the material he or she has provided. It takes many years to train a good Delegate of the Word. They must share the information they have uncovered, as well as its source. They must be patient while the members of the community record these sources in their notebooks. But the most difficult component of the Delegate of the Word's pastoral work is to teach with authority, without excluding the participation of others. If someone has additional or contradictory sources of information, they must be encouraged and feel free to share it. The point of the exercise is, as much as possible, to understand what the author of the text meant by understanding his own audience and the concerns of the primitive Christian community. Typically this first exercise will last a half-hour with ten minutes devoted to exposition and twenty minutes to a larger discussion.

2. Interpretation from the Perspective of the Experience of the Community

The text is read once again as the community attempts to illuminate the text with reference to their own experience. Here, the Delegate of the Word is more of a facilitator than a teacher. The Delegate encourages the participation of the members and prevents domination of the group by individuals or sectors.

This process is essential to reading itself. As Paul Ricoeur writes in his essay "The Model of a Text, Meaningful Action Considered as Text,"[1] these two perspectives constitute the "worlds" of a text: the world "behind" the text (the historical-critical perspective) and the world "in front of" the text (the point of view of the reader). The act of reading invokes both worlds. A text "does not only mirror its time," writes Ricoeur, "but it opens up a world which it bears within itself."[2] In Ricoeur's terms, the importance of a text depends upon how far a text's relevance goes beyond its relevance to its initial situation.

For example, the writer of John's gospel describes a scene from the crucifixion (Jn 19:25-27) unknown to the Synoptics, where Jesus commends the care of his mother to John, and the care of John to his mother. Omitted are the mocking of Jesus, the scorn of the thieves, and the period of darkness. "Instead of this isolation, Jesus savors the proximity of those close to him: the mother of Jesus, his mother's sister, the wife of Clopas, and Mary Magdalene stand around the cross."[3] During El Salvador's twelve year civil war, the Committee of the Mothers of the Disappeared, Tortured and Political Prisoners identified with the suffering of Mary, found solace with her and adopted the feast day of Our Lady of Mount Carmel when this reading occurs, as their feast. Mothers of political prisoners read this text from the point of view of their experience and identified with the suffering of the Blessed Mother. Their understanding of the torture, imprisonment and death of Jesus was formed, in part, by their own experience. Without knowing any particulars of the economic structure of the Roman Empire, they assumed that the role of the Roman procurator was like that of the United States ambassador to El Salvador, and the troops under Rome served a function like that of the American military advisors to the Armed Forces of El Salvador. Local Palestinian collaborators included King Herod, tax collectors and priests; Salvadoran collaborators included the wealthy oligarchs, minor government officials and local clergy. Even the zealots had their parallel in El Salvador, likened to the Marxist revolutionaries who preached liberation but offered a suspicious substitute under the promise of a dictatorship of the masses.

When the war ended and United States military assistance also came to an end, the reading of this text changed as well. Now the Roman Empire is seen as an instance of multi-national capitalism, evidenced in El Salvador through the huge increase of sweatshops which provide El Salvador with a major source of foreign income. The presence of these multi-nationals is evident in the Korean and Chinese managers who run these factories, and in the paid, private security forces hired to protect them. The highest paid local collaborator is the Minister of Labor, aided by informants and union breakers in the sweatshops. The zealots are no longer armed guerrillas, but a new generation of union activists more interested in closing these factories than in securing better benefits and wages for the workers.

The reading from "in front of" the text includes more than socio-economic-political conditions. Popular religion is also part of the world of the base community. The manner in which a base community of the poor reads and understands the text of Mary at the foot of the cross is also influenced by the popular culture of the film industry. During Holy Week, Salvadoran television broadcasts a plethora of religious films, including *The Ten Commandments*, *The Robe*, *The Greatest Story Ever Told* and all existing versions of the life of Jesus. Salvadorans do not distinguish between documentary and fiction in the same way as North Americans. Even though they know the films are interpretations of events, they tend to give these interpretations a great deal of historical veracity. The films become part of the world "in front of" the text and this interpretation joins with other factors to interpret the gospel.

3. Pastoral Action as a Consequence of Interpretation

It is not enough to simply interpret the text. Base communities are formed to motivate pastoral action. Typically, a meeting of a base community will end with a discussion of needs evident in the community, and solutions proposed in light of the gospel. These problems and solutions are most often small concerns: the roof needs repair; the choir is out of tune; the elders' lunch needs more cooks; the retreat house needs help in the garden. But a few times in the course of the year, major problems surface that require attention. The fifty families of garbage pickers from the Nejapa dump presented one such problem.

They were being evicted. They needed a place to resettle. The Church had land in Cabanas and the Church wanted a recommendation from the pastoral council of Our Lady of Mount Carmel.

Mother, Behold Your Son: Social Responsibility and Solidarity

When Angelica and the people from the Nejapa dump asked for the support of the Cabanas base community, the implications of their request were immediately evident. More families living in the community implied greater strain on the already limited social services, particularly health and education. The community has very low electrical power and only a few wells. One concern expressed by the community was that the garbage pickers not "bring their work home" and create piles of garbage in the rural landscape. So great were the implications of helping the garbage pickers that the pastoral council decided to delay any decision until the community assembly met on the vigil of Our Lady of Mount Carmel.

The community of Cabanas includes 400 households. Of these, about two hundred families participate in two base communities. These communities are called the "Garden" and the "Retreat House" respectively, depending on where they meet. Typically each community has between one hundred and fifty and two hundred "members," with forty to fifty participating in each gathering. The participants in each gathering change greatly from week to week with different members attending or staying home to watch over the house while the others are away.

In July, 1998, the pastoral team in Cabanas proposed that each community dedicate two days before the vigil to reflect on one of two readings, and then share their reflections during the vigil of Our Lady of Mount Carmel. The "Garden" community assumed responsibility for the reading from John's gospel used for the feast day (Jn 19:25-27). The "Retreat House" community prepared the text from the Book of Revelation dealing with the woman and the dragon. Both these communities include members of the parish's Committee for the Corporal Works of Mercy. Each of the women who serve on this committee brought the story of the garbage pickers from the Nejapa dump to their reflections. Thus, as the communities met to reflect on scripture in anticipation of the general assembly, the women from the Committee for the Corporal Works of Mercy were advocating the cause of the dump families.

In 1998 the popular religious culture in El Salvador included fears about and anticipation of the change of the millennium. Both Catholic and Protestant radio stations seemed to play on the fears of the people with constant references to the end-of-times. The two figures that dominated the popular imagination throughout 1998 were those of the woman and the dragon from Revelation 12.

When the "Retreat House" community of Cabanas met to reflect on the scriptures assigned them for the vigil, the Delegate of the Word had prepared her exegesis of the Revelation text by using Carlos Mesters' text, *El Apocalipsis: La esperanza de un pueblo.*[4] Mesters' series on the bible was created for community reflection where there is a dialogue between the "worlds" of the text. His essays typically include the results of his own research into the world behind the text and the results of his pastoral practice with communities whose contributions are included in his book.

The Delegate of the Word who led the reflection in the "Retreat House" community is Marta Jimenez, a woman who has held community leadership positions for twenty years. Marta prefaced her comments on the reading from Revelation with seven counsels of Carlos Mesters on how to read scripture: read scripture together in community; do not add to nor detract from the text; use your intelligence; read the text with thirst for life and for the truth; be open to the Holy Spirit; allow the message of the text to be transformed in prayer; and finally, practice the Word in life. She limited her participation to ten minutes and three themes, all derived from Mesters' book. First she described the historical conditions of the primitive Christian community at the time of Revelation's origin. Second, she recounted Mesters interpretation of the principal symbols of the apocalypse. Third, she focused on Mesters' interpretation of chapter twelve and the struggle between the serpent and the woman.

Marta encouraged the community to distinguish, as does the author of Revelation, between good and bad government officials and the system within which they operate. "The question is not, 'Is the Minister of Education a good person or a bad person?' The question is, 'Does the educational reform law benefit all Salvadorans or just the wealthy?' Surely there are good and bad factory owners," Marta said, "but bad or good, the question remains: 'Do labor laws benefit the workers as well as the owners?'" Overriding all of these issues is the sense that the source of structural inequality involves forces far beyond the pale of the individual factory or the borders of El Salvador. Life and death in El Salvador are determined by global forces; the symbol of these forces–the Dragon.

The "Garden" community reflected on the text of the women at the foot of the cross. Its leader, Sonia Lopez, prepared her material from a simple, catechetical guide prepared by the Pastoral Concerns Office of the Archdiocese of San Salvador. During the war and the time of great persecution it caused, women tended to identify with the solidarity of the mother of Jesus with her suffering Son. Women whose sons and daughters had been captured, killed, imprisoned or tortured, saw in this text a model of solidarity between mother and child. With the advent of peace, however, and the diminishing memory of those hard times, women in base communities have begun to identify with the solidarity between themselves and the disciple John.

Although scholars tend not to accept Bultmann's interpretation that John means to portray Mary as a representative of Jewish Christianity and John as a representative of Gentile Christianity, this interpretation has appeared in some pastoral guides such as those published by the Archdiocese of San Salvador. Sonia's community took this point of view seriously and reflected on the importance of reconciliation in the face of hardship and suffering. The challenge to solidarity articulated by Jesus was seen as relevant for post-war El Salvador.

On the day of the vigil, the Delegates of the Word sponsored a general, pastoral assembly. The first part of the assembly was dedicated to a plenary session in which community representatives shared insights from the previous days' study groups. The process was simple. First, the persons designated as "secretaries" for the two groups provided a synthesis of the texts and the information provided by the Delegates of the Word. They then summarized the conclusions of the two groups and highlighted what each group understood as the contemporary relevance of the texts. When the secretaries had completed their reports to the general assembly, the two Delegates of the Word asked if anyone wished to modify or amend the conclusions of the secretaries.

This involved another half hour of discussion as members of the community made particular observations.

When the plenary session ended, the chairmanship of the meeting was turned over to the president of the community. Don Juan Jimenez instructed the secretary and treasurer of the communal association to read the minutes of the last assembly and to make a financial report on the status of the community bank account. He then announced the items for the agenda of the assembly. These were two: the petition of the dump pickers for help in resettlement in Cabanas, and the organization required to begin a project to introduce water to the community.

Juan Jimenez is the founding president of the community. He guided the community through the lengthy process of legalization, thus empowering Cabanas to request financial assistance from governmental and non-governmental sources. The

previous year he had withstood an intensive audit by the Salvadoran equivalent of the General Accounting Office, which was
investigating misappropriation of funds by the municipality.
Juan is also a crafty politician with strong motivation to remain
president. He began the discussion of the dump pickers' request
by asking the community to consider all of the negative consequences of responding favorably to their petition.

The negative factors came down to a simple formula. The
community of 400 families was struggling to introduce water and
electricity to the community. They had also requested an extra
day of service in the community clinic and two additional teachers
for the public school. Responding favorably to the resettlement of
50 additional families from the dump would eliminate any advan-
tages they hoped to gain with the public utilities and ministries
of health and education. The question remained a simple one: can
we afford to be generous?

President Jimenez then asked the Delegates of the Word to
address the petition of the fifty families from the point of view of the
texts that had just been considered by the general assembly.

Marta Jimenez spoke first:

> When the municipalities announced that
> they had signed an agreement with this Canadian
> company to allow pick-up and disposal of garbage,
> we all thought this was a good thing. We agreed to
> pay taxes for this service.
>
> Some of us were skeptical about allowing a
> large, foreign company to manage this dump
> because we felt that we would have little or no say
> in how things went if problems occurred. Now we
> are forced to confront one of these problems. Fifty
> families have no place to live and they are asking
> us for help. If we say yes to their request, we will
> surely share in their suffering, as they will share in
> the benefits that derive from living here. These
> families have felt the wrath of the dragon in ways

that most of us cannot imagine. Who can imagine what it must be like to lose three children in one day to the poisonous gases of the dump? What mother can imagine the terror of seeing her child eaten by a snake? Yet, this mother's pain is the pain of us all. What she has experienced in the dump, we have all experienced when our children disappeared, were imprisoned, or were taken away from us and tortured.

The early Church was clear in its collective response to the dragon of Imperial Rome. We must stand together in front of the dragon to protect the children of these mothers who have suffered. We will have to struggle hard to get medical attention and more teachers in the school, but we should regard these mothers as our allies and draw strength from their suffering.

Sonia's words were no less direct:

We are assembled for the vigil of Our Lady of Mount Carmel. Tomorrow, after the celebration of the Eucharist, we will all renew our scapular promise and enroll new members of the community in the confraternity of Our Lady of Mount Carmel. As we have learned from reading the text of tomorrow's gospel, Jesus has enjoined us all, in front of his suffering, to join together in acts of solidarity, in the face of the oppressor.

Jesus did not tell Mary and John simply to love one another. He instructed them to actually take care of one another, and John to take Mary into his house. How can we not do the same?

The assembly then addressed the strength the community would gain from assuming responsibility for these 50 families. The final decision of the community was to invite the fifty families to settle in Cabanas, on Church land, to offer them support, and to invite them to participate in the mass of Our Lady of Mount Carmel the next day.

Enrollment in the Scapular - Canton Cabanas, 1999

The invitation to participate in the Eucharist and receive the scapular was extended that same evening by the President of the community and two members of the Committee for the Corporal Works of Mercy.

In El Salvador there is a huge devotion to Our Lady of Mount Carmel. Dance groups, workers, sailors and construction workers frequently choose her as patroness. There exists a popular religiosity around the feast of Carmel and a set of beliefs regarding Mary's intercession for sinners and those who work in dangerous professions. It is interesting to note that Central Americans do not recognize the name of St Simon Stock nor do they associate the "scapular promise" with any particular historic or mythic event. The promise is thus regarded more as a general promise of protection from dangers (in this world or the next) and not with the same specificity that typifies Carmelite, popular religious culture in the United States and Europe. Salvadorans see the scapular itself as a totemic symbol of the confraternity of men and women who profess confidence in Mary's intercession.

The nature of this intercession is defined by Salvadoran religious culture. Salvadorans are serious about their faith and they place a great importance on the sacraments as a means to achieving salvation. But so important are sacraments in the life of the poor that they require great public displays: elegant dress, the invitation of many guests, great feasting and exchange of gifts. So great are the costs that many families delay confirmation and marriage. Living outside the church, though still active participators in its life, a large percentage of Salvadorans believes that if they die unexpectedly, they will not be part of the Reign of God in the afterlife.

It is possible to say that in most Catholic families the man and woman are active in the church but remain unmarried because they lack the means to marry in the way defined by their culture. They accept the Church's requirement of marriage and live in a state of peril. They also believe that if they die in circumstances that prevent them from confessing before they die, the mercy of God will save them. The scapular is the guarantor of this mercy.

For the Salvadoran, therefore, it is not St Simon Stock who receives the scapular from Mary. It is Mary who receives the scapular from Jesus on Calvary. She, as designated mother of us all, in turn gives the scapular to us. If we face the peril of death without the opportunity to reconcile with the Church, our reconciliation is pre-determined by means of the scapular. Salvadoran religious culture mixes religion and magic with ease. In the case of the scapular promise, however, magic is not invoked nor expected. The scapular holds no significance as a talisman with the power to protect. Rather it is a symbol of redemption already promised.

The mass for Our Lady of Mount Carmel was held the following day at 5:30 PM in the community's retreat house. Forty representatives of the fifty "dump" families were in attendance.

The entrance procession included a small, wooden statue of Carmen and sixty boys and girls from the last first communion class. The entrance song was a traditional folk song about Our Lady, *Cuando Carmelitas* (When Carmelites Are There). The offertory procession included gifts to be shared after mass by the whole community: tamales, beans, sauces, coffee and chocolate. The last gifts placed on the altar were two hundred and fifty scapulars for new members of the community and those whose scapulars had worn out during the year.

After mass, enrollment in the scapular took place. This was achieved in the simplest manner. All the new members of the community formed a line and approached the altar one at a time.

The altar was flanked by two members of the Guardians of the Blessed Sacrament (*Guardia Santissima*) dressed in white and holding large candles. The actual investiture was made by an elder of the Confraternity (*Confradia*) of Our Lady of Mount Carmel. After the investiture, the President, Don Juan Jimenez, concluded with a brief discourse.

> Well, you all know why we are here, and I can see that this year we have some more folks than last and I guess that is a good thing. On behalf of the *directiva*, I welcome you and especially the new families that will soon become a part of our community.
>
> What we are doing here, today, after this mass we have just celebrated, is something we have done since 1984 when we put the community under the protection of Our Lady of Mount Carmel. We are inviting you to become part of this community and so also to become one of her children and wear her sign.
>
> We wore her sign during the war when our lives were threatened by the army. Some of us remember having the scapular torn off our persons when the army invaded the community back in 1985. I asked a soldier back then, "Why do you do this?" and I remember what he said: "Because you are rebels and this thing is the sign of your defiance".
>
> I remember that soldier and I thank him today for his words because they were true. The scapular is the sign of our covenant. In the last week we have talked much about this covenant and we have decided to entrust, once again, our community to the care of the Blessed Mother. We expect no special power from this sign [the scapular] but we stand firm in our resolution of solidar-

ity with these families from Nejapa who have suffered so much.

I do not know how we will stand with ANDA [the public utility for water] or CAES [the public utility for electricity] or the ministries of health and education. I hope we can convince them that our added needs are real. But I know that the Virgin has not let us down in the past and I expect that she will be in solidarity with us in the future. Perhaps it is fair to say that by being in solidarity with you, we renew our confidence in her.

And finally, to our new community members, I encourage you to wear this scapular as a sign of faith, as we did in the war. Do not hesitate to demand justice, because justice is promised you. With this sign you show your defiance in the knowledge that your cause is just and your cause is also the cause of all the families of Canton Cabanas.

In August 1998 thirty-five families displaced from the Nejapa dump re-settled in Cabanas. The Committee for the Corporal Works of Mercy donated clothing and food. The Social Pastoral Council intervened on behalf of these families with USAID for a donation of lumber, tent canvas and porta-johns. While the conditions for these families are still primitive, they are much healthier than at the dump.

The reservoir of salvageable plastic at the old dump has all but dried up. Each of the families that settled in Cabanas was offered one scholarship for vocational training in industrial sewing, carpentry, welding or auto mechanics. When these courses conclude in December, 2000, the families will have alternative sources of income.

David S. Blanchard, O.Carm.

Endnotes

1. Paul Ricoeur, "The Model of the Text: Meaningful Action Considered as a Text", in *Hermeneutics and the Human Sciences* (Cambridge: Cambridge University Press, 1981), pp. 197-221.
2. *Ibid.*, 208.
3. Ernst Haenchen, *A Commentary on the Gospel of John Chapters 7-21* (Philadelphia: Fortress Press, 1984), p. 193.
4. Carlos Mesters, O.Carm., *El Apocalipsis: La esperanza de un pueblo* (Buenos Aires: Ediciones Paulinas, 1986).

The Ecclesial Presence of Our Lady and Our Alliance with Her

Following the Second Vatican Council's dedication of an entire chapter on the Mother of God to close its Dogmatic Constitution on the Church, Marian doctrine and devotion have undergone a significant renewal. Chapter VIII, following a special vote of the Council Fathers, was given a title signifying and defining its purpose: "The Role of the Blessed Virgin Mary, Mother of God, in the Mystery of Christ and the Church."[1] The Fathers of the Council chose to adapt a specialized treatise on Mariology and to integrate it into its doctrine on the Church. This integration made us aware of the need for ongoing adaptation of doctrinal expression in order to confront the many changes of our times. Similarly, Marian devotion has become more attentive to Mary's presence within the Church, allowing us to recognize an alliance or covenant with her in her own ongoing mission. Both factors, doctrinal development and devotional modification, demonstrate the openness of Christian understanding to the needs of our times.

I. The Presence of Mary in the Church

In a talk given at the Marianum on December 10, 1988, Pope John Paul II noted the renewal in Mariology and presented various new problems for study. Among them he mentioned

continuing research into "the presence of Mary in the Holy
Scripture" and intensified exploration of "the nature of the
multiple presence of Mary in the life of the Church."[2] The Holy
Father himself frequently uses the term "presence" to explain the
salvific influence of Mary within the Church. Father John A.
Schug, in his book *Mary, Mother*, provides some four pages of
quotations taken from John Paul II's writing on Marian presence.
From 1987 (the year of *Redemptoris mater* and the beginning of
the Marian Year) to 1991, Schug has counted some fifty explicit
mentions of her "presence" found in the texts provided by
L'Osservatore Romano.[3] Since then the Pope has continued to
invoke with fervor Mary's presence.

A. *Mary's Historical and Spiritual Presence*
    — the Plan of God and Its Unity

In his proclamation of the Marian year 1987-1988, the Holy
Father placed great emphasis on Mary's presence in the mystery
of Jesus and his Church. He said: "Now, following the line of the
Second Vatican Council, I wish to emphasize the special presence
of the Mother of God in the mystery of Christ and his Church."[4]
We can even say that *Redemptoris mater* is dedicated to Mary's
presence. The text speaks of two kinds of presence: 1) Mary's
historical presence in Israel, in Jesus' life, and in the life of the
primitive Church; 2) Mary's "maternal presence in the Church"
now, after her Assumption, "her active and exemplary presence in
the life of the Church." Noting that distinction, the Pope stresses
the unity of Mary's presence in the salvific plan of God. Both are
"the unique presence of the Mother of Christ in history, especially
during these last years leading up to the year 2000."[5] Our Lady's
presence in the Church, he states, is the continuation of her
historical divine motherhood: "She who is present in the mystery
of Christ as Mother becomes by the will of her Son and the power
of the Holy Spirit present in the mystery of the Church."[6] Mary's
presence is due to the will of Jesus and to the special operation
of the Holy Spirit in the mystery of the Incarnation.

1. It is the Will of the Son

The Pope overcomes the hesitation of the Council in its interpretation of John 19:25 ff. When Jesus from the cross said to his mother: "Woman, behold your son" and to the beloved disciple: "Behold your mother," he revealed Mary's spiritual maternity. The Pope refers to the teaching of Vatican II about Mary's cooperation in our birth and development as Christians. And he explains: "Here we perceive the real value of the words spoken by Jesus to his Mother at the hour of the Cross. . . . They are words which determine Mary's place in the life of Christ's disciples and they express . . . a spiritual motherhood, born from the heart of the Paschal Mystery."[7] Quoting the Pope, an important letter from the Congregation for Catholic Education explains: "The Mother of the Lord is a 'datum of divine Revelation' and a 'maternal presence' always operative in the life of the Church."[8]

John Paul II insists on the unity of this Marian presence. It is a continuous maternal presence embracing both the time of Christ's life on earth and the time of the Church. We have to believe in "the full truth of this motherhood. Since by virtue of divine election Mary is the earthly Mother of the Father's consubstantial Son and his 'generous companion' in the work of redemption, 'she is a mother to us in the order of grace'.[9] This role constitutes a real dimension of her presence."[10]

2. Mary's Presence—the Work of "the Power of the Holy Spirit"

Lumen gentium explains how the Holy Spirit inspires in the Church a filial love for Our Lady. "Instructed by the Holy Spirit, the Catholic Church with the affection of filial piety honors (Mary) as most loving mother."[11] The faithful "are moved to filial love toward our mother and to the imitation of her virtues."[12] Jesus' Spirit guides us to Mary's presence.

B. An Instrumental Causality?

How can we explain theologically the mystery of Mary as "maternal presence" who forms and educates us to our Christian life of union with Jesus and with God?

Schug explores the question of the nature of Mary's spiritual motherhood. How is she our mother in the order of grace? "Does she merely intercede for grace, or is she actually an instrumental cause of grace?"[13] For him Mary is our mother not only by her powerful intercession, but by some causal presence. Therefore, he discusses the kind of causality that Our Lady may exercise in the order of grace. We may hesitate to speak about such a Marian causality. God alone enables us to participate in his divine life. He is the only source of our divinization. We may say only that God shares with us, through his Son, Jesus, his loving power. We are, through his action, secondly, participated causes. God is the divine *principal* cause. He sent us Christ as our Mediator. Jesus in his humanity is the participating human cause of our birth to the life of God. The man Jesus is the united instrument, the *instrumentum conjunctum*, of his divine person for our regeneration. He is the only mediator. While he remains the only human principal cause of our divine life, he shares that power of life with Mary, with the Church, with us all, under diverse titles.

Mary, the Church, all people of good will, are instruments of the Holy Spirit and become sources of supernatural life in complete dependence on and subordination to God and Christ. We are, therefore, secondary causes. God changes our hearts as well as our personal and collective lives through many graces, especially a sanctifying grace which is permanent. In that sanctification we are instruments of the Spirit, but not merely material instruments. God, Christ, the Spirit arouse in us personal acts of faith, hope, and charity (divine love) which they use for the salvation of our race. In other words, the mercy and the charity of the Father, Christ and the Spirit expand, arousing and "using" our union of charity-agape with them. They use the maternal charity of Mary (and the agape of any good will) for a new creation, for our regeneration. Therefore, the mystery of Mary and of the whole Church, seen in the mystery of Christ-Head and his Mystical Body, is an expansion of the supreme salvific mercy of God. God, Christ, and the Holy Spirit justify, sanctify, and save our human race. They have their own ways, that are not our ways. As Cardinal Journet explains in his third volume of *L'Eglise du Verbe Incarné*, Mary was associated with her Son at the very time of our redemption through her maternal charity-agape. Such a role was unique.

C. *A Unique Presence in the Eucharist*

The abstract notion of causality is not the only explanation of Mary's influence in the Church and in our lives. Theologians have explored new possibilities.

The Eucharist is the great presence of God, of Jesus, of their Spirit. The Church secures and so is the presence of God, of Jesus, of their Spirit among us: through her ministries, sacraments, liturgical prayer or celebrations, and through the collective and personal prayers of the faithful. Already Chromatius (d. 407) observed that where the Church is, there Mary is.[14]

Father Ignacio Calabuig[15] noted a recent papal text on the presence of Mary. In his May 31, 1998, Apostolic Letter, "The Day of the Lord," John Paul II stated: "Without in any way detracting from the centrality of Christ and his Spirit, Mary is always present in the Church's Sunday."[16]

Why? The Pope reasons thus, a kind of argument *ad absurdum*. "It is the mystery of Christ itself which demands this: indeed, how could she who is '*Mater Domini*' and '*Mater Ecclesiae*' fail to be uniquely present on the day which is both '*dies Domini*' and '*dies Ecclesiae*'?" In Calabuig's analysis this is "a requirement delving from the mystery of Christ and arising from it," i.e., the mystery of "the person and saving work of Jesus." Calabuig also explains "the way of her being present," provided by the Pope: "exemplary presence. . . , presence of communion . . . , guiding presence from Sunday to Sunday . . . , prayerful presence (by) her maternal intercession."

1. A Virtual Contact?

Rev. James O'Connor, studying "Mary and the Eucharist,"[17] asks: "Can we speak of a direct and immediate contact of Mary with us?" In other words, what do we mean by a "presence of Mary?" O'Connor describes virtual presence as, for example, in a telephone conversation between two persons in love with one another; they find themselves not in physical, but virtual contiguity. "Mary's presence in the Eucharistic action . . . is what would be called virtual contact." Further, he concludes that in the Eucharist

> ". . . we are actually 'communicantes' with Christ, Mary and the angels and saints in a reality which is not earthly. At that point, more than any other time, our lives are already 'hidden with Christ in God' (Col. 3:3). Such is the truth as perceived by all those who insist that there is only one Eucharist, although the appearances are many. In that sense, Mary's presence in each Eucharistic action is real, physical (because, of all the saints, only her body is in heaven), and unique (as Mother and Associate) in this memorial of our redemption."[18]

We may retain for Mary's presence in the whole life of the Church the comparison with a virtual contact. We have to remember how many saints speak of their experience of Mary in their lives, of the gifts of her presence. We could say this is a "virtual presence." They experience the love of Mary for the Church, her maternal, virtual presence, through a mutual, shared love, charity/agape, gift of the Holy Spirit to the Communion of Saints.

D. The Holy Spirit Elects Mary to a Unique Presence in the Communion of All Saints

René Laurentin explains Mary's presence through the Communion of all Saints, the work of the Holy Spirit: "Thus Mary is present to us in the Holy Spirit. Her presence is not a transcendental presence, as God's presence is. She is present in God, through the Holy Spirit, in the Communion of Saints."[19]

1. Real Presence?

She is the most eminent member of the Communion of Saints, chosen by the Spirit to receive the fullest union with Christ and therefore to enjoy a maternal charity expanding into the most powerful intercession. Is this only a "moral" presence? The Pope speaks not only of her intercession, but of her unique, real presence. *Marialis cultus* indicates certain principles and guidelines of true Marian devotion, namely, its Trinitarian, Christological, ecclesial and Pneumatological aspects, as well as guidelines from Scripture, liturgy, ecumenism, and anthropology. It is in such a framework that we understand the presence of Mary in the Church and in our lives as a unique presence. We have cited the divine plan of salvation as God's loving will to reveal himself. The Triune God allows us to participate in his divine life through Jesus, who repaired our rebellion. Within that merciful design the Pope contemplates the divine gift of a continuous presence of Mary. Indeed, Mary is, after Jesus, the highest glorification of the Triune God, through her unique relationship with the three divine persons, Father, Son, and Spirit. We may describe this divine gift of a continuous presence of Mary at the level of God, at the level of Mary, and at the level of our faith.

At the ontological level of God's salvific action, the whole life of Mary, her whole existence and maternal presence pertain intimately to the decree of the redeeming incarnation of the Son of God seen in its transcendent unity. Mary was predestined and created only to be the mother of the Son of God in our redemption.

Mary's presence belongs to that climax of all the *mirabilia Dei* which are revealed by the Word of God.

At the level of Our Lady we contemplate her presence in revelation through a tradition which affirms her unique relation to the Triune God as real mother of the Son made man. Jesus was conceived by his mother, in her absolute virginity, through the intervention of the Holy Spirit. She entered into a new, unique state of life, which Father M. J. Nicolas analyzed as the integral concept of the divine motherhood.[20] By the generating action of Mary, mother and son enter into a relation from person to person. Since Jesus is from all eternity a preexistent divine person, Mary enters forever into her unique relation to God, a maternal relation with the divine person of the Son. Through the archangel Gabriel, the triune God asked the conscious, free consent of the Blessed Virgin of Nazareth. The Spirit inspired Mary "full of grace" more than the angel. She conceived the Son of God first in the loving faith of her heart and so in her womb. The Spirit formed in Mary a unique union with God as mother of his Son, so elevating her human person, soul and body, to the most intimate relationship with the divine persons. The Spirit had prepared her through a unique sanctifying grace. Her participation in the trinitarian life constituted her holiness from her immaculate conception onwards, with the result of her preservation from original sin. Henceforth, she was his most holy (*panagia*) temple for her whole life as his "kecaritw menh" fully graced, *plena gratiae* (Lk 1:28). At the Annunciation, he inspired her consent, her spiritual participation in the incarnation of God's Word, the Logos. Most eminent member of the Church, most intimate disciple of her Son and Savior, she also is, through her maternal relation to the Logos, the spiritual mother of the Church and of all Christians, the model for the sanctification of all our race, the New Eve.

At the level of our faith, of our experience, we believe and we experience one continuous presence of a mother given by God through his Son and his Spirit.

II. The Alliance or Covenant with Mary

Devotion to Mary through history took on a variety of forms and expressions. In the nineteenth century with Father Chaminade, and in the twentieth century with Father Kentenich, it became a covenant or an alliance with Mary.

A. *The Alliance with Mary in the Society of Mary*

William Joseph Chaminade (1761-1850) lived his apostolic life in France, especially at Bordeaux, during many political changes, the reign of kings, the French Revolution, Napoleon and the Restoration, with the short interruption of the revolution of 1830. At the age of fourteen, Chaminade offered himself to God taking for ever the vows of poverty, chastity, and obedience under the guidance of his brother, John-Baptist, sixteen years older and formed as a Jesuit before the suppression of that Order in France. Man of absolute faith in God, Chaminade was convinced that the Church lived in a time of trouble in which Divine Providence reserved to Mary the mission of a profound renewal. With a prophetic spirit he understood that the world needed not a mere restoration but a new evangelization. In 1800, having obtained from Rome the title "Apostolic Missionary," he began his "mission" with young laymen who came to his Oratory, the Madeleine, at Bordeaux. With them he revived a sodality by asking members to be apostles of Mary in the new evangelization. He told them: "The new sodalities are not only associations in honor of the Blessed Virgin, but they are a holy militia that advances in the Name of Mary and knows how to battle with the infernal powers under the guidance and obedience of her who is destined to crush the head of the serpent."[21] We recognize in our more recent time the militant language of Frank Duff. Chaminade called the Marian dedication of his sodalists an "alliance" or covenant with Mary. Despite political troubles, he developed that spirit in a marvelous way.

Writing the life of Father Chaminade, Simler counts in 1804 as members of the various sodalities three hundred young men, the same number of girls, sixty family fathers, and as many Christian mothers. The core of a zealous youth gave vocations to the religious orders and the seminaries, as well as founded solid Christian families. In 1869 the bishop of Bordeaux, Cardinal Donnet, could say: "The venerable Father Chaminade what an eminent man! Not only did we not know and appreciate him. We were not even aware of our indebtedness to him. And yet, if we trace back to their origins all our institutions in Bordeaux, we find the name of Father Chaminade inscribed at the origin of each one."[22]

To help sodalists whom he directed to religious life but who had to remain in their secular daily obligations, Chaminade began what we now call a "secular institute." He called it the "Etat" or State! That development ended in the creation of two religious orders: in 1816, the Daughters of Mary, and in 1817, the Society of Mary, whose members were later called Marianists. During a retreat preached in 1819 to the first members of the Society of Mary, Chaminade explained what he meant by the life of alliance with Mary.[23] He quoted Moses' declaration to Israel: "You today made this declaration about Yahweh: that he will be your God.... And Yahweh has today made this declaration about you: that you will be his very own people" (Dt 26:17-18). He added a commentary. "One could say the very same to us. But if we are in an alliance with God, are we not also in an alliance with Mary, and why should we not apply these words to this alliance? 'You are making this agreement with Mary; you are to be a family peculiarly her own.'"

The Founder made a remarkable comment, analyzing that mutual agreement on both sides. He said:

> Let us consider this alliance in the choice, in the commitment, in the society which constitutes it, whether on our part or on the part of the Blessed Virgin Mary.

First point: on our part.

1. We have chosen Mary for Mother; could we have made a more reasonable choice, or one that is better founded? Could we possibly have chosen a more powerful mother, a more tender mother, a mother more truly mother?

2. We have made a commitment to Mary; what is its nature? We have bound ourselves to all that a child ought to feel and do for a good mother: love her, respect her, obey her and give her assistance. Most of all we have bound ourselves to this last effect of filial love, assistance and active good will; we have bound ourselves to make known the name of Mary and to cause it to be held in honor everywhere.

3. We enter into close association with Mary, that is to say, we acquire rights to her merits, to her prayers, to her protection, to her glory, and to everything she has received from the limitless bounty of her Son.

Second point: Mary forms an alliance with us.

1. She has chosen us over so many others, that we might be her family and her cherished children. How have we merited this?

2. She takes upon herself obligations in our regard. What obligations? Those of a mother, to love us, to help us in all our needs, to defend us.

Third point: We enter into a life of close association with Mary, that is to say, we share with her all our goods. All our powers are at Mary's command; we have given ourselves to Mary with all our possessions and all the faculties of our being. May she do

with us whatever she pleases, for the greatest glory
of her Son.[24]

Chaminade wanted two signs of religious profession.

All the professed religious wear a gold ring on their
right hand; they also wear on their breast under
their garments a crucifix which is quite percep-
tible. The ring reminds them unceasingly of the
alliance they have contracted with Mary, their
Queen, and the crucifix keeps them always aware
that they should be crucified at all times to the
world and to themselves so as to be conformed to
Jesus crucified.[25]

The ring does not have a sponsal or bridal meaning of the
mystical order in imitation of some of the saints. The present
Constitutions, called *Rule of Life*, explain: "At the time of perpetual profession the religious receives a gold ring as a sign of the
commitment by which he places himself permanently at the
service of God in the Society of Mary."[26]

The Marianist commitment, which is essentially Marian,
is also expressed at the perpetual profession by a special vow of
stability. The vow manifests the official, public commitment to
fulfill the mission of the Society of Mary. It is a special union with
the Founder: to penetrate into the vision of Chaminade, i.e., to
love Mary in conformity with Jesus' own filial love, and to devote
his life to her mission in our times. Chaminade repeated frequently the lapidary motto: "You are all missionaries of Mary."
The letter written to the retreat masters on August 24, 1839,
explains in a remarkable way that missionary vocation. In the
Rule of Life the Marianists sum up the charism they inherit from
the Founder: "By our alliance with Mary, we seek to assist her in
her mission of forming in faith a multitude of brothers for her firstborn Son."[27]

B. The Alliance with Mary
According to Father Joseph Kentenich (1885-1968)

Father Joseph Kentenich was born in Germany on November 18, 1885, at Gymnich near Cologne. On April 19, 1914, as spiritual director of the Pallotine minor seminary at Schoenstatt near Koblenz, he founded a Marian Sodality. That same year, on October 18, together with some students he made what he called "a covenant or alliance of love" with the mother of God.

Having read how the Italian Lawyer, Blessed Bartolo Longo (1841-1926), had devoted his whole life to the pilgrimage of Our Lady of Pompei, at the worldwide famous shrine of Valle di Pompei, or Basilica of Mary, Queen of Victories, at Naples, he decided to transform the chapel of Schoenstatt into a place of pilgrimage. He prayed to Mary that she might make it a shrine of grace. The result was the International Schoenstatt Movement. Each member enters into his own personal covenant of love with our Lady, sealing it at the shrine of Schoenstatt. Therefore, each is incorporated into the historical covenant of Father Kentenich. We may imagine a mutual contract of promises. On the one side, "the Mother of God promises to dwell in the Shrine, to bring about and to lead a great movement of renewal or education from there, and to use [this] place and the bearers of this movement as instruments 'to reveal her glories to the world.'" On the other side, the members make their promise: "we promise to let ourselves be transformed by her [Mary] toward total self-giving, or to increase our efforts to the highest conceivable degree [and] to make ourselves available as her perfect instruments."[28]

Jonathan Niehaus published an anthology of texts concerning "Schoenstatt's Covenant Spirituality."[29] In the letter to Monsignor Schmitz quoted above, Kentenich explains his covenant of love in the perspective of the history of salvation. As for Grignon de Montfort, it is a consecration expressing the baptismal covenant made with God through Jesus, our Savior. Therefore, "much can be said of the significance about our covenant of love. It can be called the fundamental form and fundamental purpose, or final goal, the fundamental strength and fundamental norm of our family. Our family's history can be seen and explained as the historical unfolding of this covenant, as a genuine covenant history, as a triumph of mutual covenant loyalty."[30] We may add that the texts show how the "covenant of love" fulfills the principles given by *Marialis cultus* for a true Marian devotion. Though they already were mentioned, we repeat them: a true devotion must be Trinitarian, Christological, ecclesial, with prominence given to the Holy Spirit, and also biblical, liturgical, ecumenical, and anthropological.

Kentenich first of all preached a profound theological insight into the mystery of the Holy Trinity. Genesis 1:27 reveals that God created our humanity in his image. We have to know ourselves as the work and the image of the Triune God. We speak in all reality of God when we speak of his image: the image of the Father, the Son, the Holy Spirit. God is not vaguely God; he is Triune God.

The Christocentrism also is evident. Because we used our freedom to rebel, to sin, the Triune God sent his own Son as savior and redeemer. We are a new creation. In the movement of his pascal mystery through death to resurrection, Christ draws us into a new unity of creature with the Creator. On our own, we are lost, split into a mystery of good and evil. We are restored in Jesus through the mystery of divine grace. The Triune God is like a master tennis player. He is all-powerful, able to direct our whole game according to his eternal purposes.[31]

In that divine economy of a new creation, each of us is a new person in/for a new community, a whole new humanity. Mary, the New Eve, is that new human person who totally was attracted by and transformed into Christ. She is the model formed by the Spirit as the new presentation of Christ in a human person.

Theodore Koehler, S.M.

Endnotes

1. AAS, 57 (1965), 58.
2. *Marianum*, 138 (1988), 25-26.
3. John A. Schug, *Mary, Mother: A Theological Study of the Spiritual Motherhood of Mary* (Springfield, Massachusetts: St. Francis Chapel Press, 1992).
4. RM, n. 48.
5. *Ibid.*, n. 3.
6. *Ibid.*, n. 24.
7. *Ibid.*, n. 44.
8. "The Virgin Mary in Intellectual and Spiritual Formation," March 25, 1988.
9. LG, n. 61.
10. RM, n. 39.
11. LG, n. 53.
12. *Ibid.*, n. 67.
13. Schug, *Mary, Mother*, 121 ff.
14. Chromatius of Aquileia, *Sermo XXX*, 1, in *Sources Chrétiens*, vol. 164, p. 134. See Vincent Vasey, "Chromatius of Aquileia, Marian Ecclesiologist," in *Marian Library Studies* (new series), no. 10 (December, 1978), 28.
15. Ignacio M. Calabuig, "Letter from the President," *Marianum. Notizie-News*, 2/1998, p. 26.
16. John Paul II, *Dies Domini*, n. 86.
17. James O'Connor, "Mary and the Eucharist," *Marian Studies* 34 (1983), 64.
18. *Ibid.*, 64-65.
19. René Laurentin, "Presence of Mary in the Communion of Saints," *Marian Library Audio Tape* 090.
20. See M. J. Nicholas, "Le concept intégral de Maternité Divine," *Revue Thomiste* 42 (1937); "Essai de Synthèse mariale," in H. DuManoir (ed), *Maria*, vol. 1, pp. 707-741; *Marie, Mère du Sauveur*, Paris: Desclée, 1967. See also Bérulle, *Vie de Jésus*, ed. Migne.

21. William Joseph Chaminade, *Marian Writings*, vol. 2, translated by Henry Bradley and Joseph H. Roy (Dayton, Ohio: Marianists Resources Commission, 1980), 107.

22. Joseph Simler, *William Joseph Chaminade: Founder of the Marinanists*," translated by Joseph Roy (Dayton, Ohio: Marianists Resources Commission, 1986), 149.

23. See William J. Chaminade, "Retreat of 1819. Twelfth Meditation," in Chaminade, *Marian Writings*, vol. 2, nn. 751-753, pp. 299-300.

24. *Ibid.*

25. Constitutions of 1839.

26. *Rule of Life*, n.1.7.

27. *Ibid.*, n. 6.

28. "*Das Lebensgeheimnis Schoenstatts*," Letter to Msgr. Joseph Schmitz, 1952, II, 13. See translation in R. M. Isabel Naumann's doctoral thesis, "Cum Maria ad altare: Toward an Integration of Mariology and Ecclesiology," IMRI, Dayton, Ohio: 1998, p. xiii.

29. Jonathan Niehaus (ed), *Schoenstatt's Covenant Spirituality: Texts by Father Joseph Kentenich* (Waukesha, Wisconsin), 1992.

30. Niehaus, *Schoenstatt's Covenant Spirituality*, p. 117.

31. J. Kentenich, "October Brief," 1949, in Niehaus, *Schoenstatt's Covenant Spirituality*, 42-43.

The Biblical Blend
of Speech and Silence

According to the Hebrew Bible, an outstanding trait of the wise person is expertise with words in every sense, knowing when to speak and what deserves to be said, the right word at the right time. Wise words and thoughtful silence go together. This holds for any Carmelite aspiring to be faithful to the biblical roots of the tradition to which he or she is heir. Eamon Carroll has long been known for his sensitivity to words and language. He peruses a dictionary with a diligence even greater than he shows for airline schedules and prices. His feeling for words can be seen in the snappy characterizations that he has written for the Marian bibliographies over the last forty years. The present essay is the *primitiae* of a chapter in a book which I hope to entitle the "biblical heritage of Carmel," and it is offered here in tribute to Eamon for the goodly portion of that heritage that has been manifested in his speech and writings.

Speech

When we read of the "pleasing sayings" that Qoheleth wrote (Ecc 12:10), we dare not understand them as sweet nothings. His was a "tough love," in that his message is sharp and piercing concerning the "vanity" or absurdity of life. It is in this sense that we understand Ecclesiastes 12:11, "the words of the

wise are like goads." They are meant to spur the reader on. The
Israelite sages wrote in many different genres: the proverbial
saying or aphorism, the "better" saying, rhetorical questions,
commands and prohibitions, parables (Jesus distinguished himself by the depth and sharpness of his parables), alphabetic
poems (Sirach cultivated 22-line and 23-line poems), the debates
that characterize the Book of Job. I am limiting myself to the
wisdom literature, because it is here that the sages made a point
of reflecting on speech and silence. All will recognize that the
historical narratives (e.g., Elijah) and the words of the prophets
(e.g., Isaiah) contain masterful examples of the power of the word.
The deft paronomasia, assonance and alliteration–all the tricks of
the writing trade–can not be recognized and appreciated in
English translation. The parallelism between the lines of a verse,
generally considered to be characteristic of Hebrew poetry, opens
up tantalizing instances of ambiguity. Parallel lines are not simply
repetitious. The second (or sometimes third) line defines, or
specifies, or expands the first line. One has to marvel at the quality
and quantity of the literature produced by this *Winkelvolk* located
at the crossroads of the Fertile Crescent.

There are clear indications that the wise cultivated a
certain aesthetics of speech. They do not theorize about it; they
just do it. As Proverbs 25:11 indicates, "Like golden apples in a
silver setting is a phrase well turned." Although the translation is
difficult, it is clearly said that the "word is worded." Timing is as
important as style or content. "The wise remain silent until the
right moment, but a boasting fool ignores the proper time," wrote
Ben Sira a couple of centuries before Christ (Sir 20:7). The blend
of speech and silence is at the heart of the wisdom movement in
Israel. These two words make up a whole. One either speaks or
keeps silent, and both actions are fraught with meaning. That is
why one reads in Proverbs 26:4-5:

> Do not answer a fool according to his folly,
>   lest you too become like him.
> Answer a fool according to his folly,

lest he be wise in his own eyes.

Timing can be even more important than the saying itself in some cases:

> A proverb when spoken by a fool is unwelcome,
>> for he does not utter it at the proper time
>>> (Sir 20:20).

Sirach, in particular, has emphasized the appropriate moment of action: like a song in time of mourning is inopportune talk (22:6); "refrain not from speaking at the proper time" (4:24).

It has been estimated that about 20% of the sayings in the Book of Proverbs are concerned with *proper* speech, and this figure could be increased if other aspects were to be included. Probably the oral origins reflect the emphasis on words. When the sayings are assembled in a collection, and Proverbs is a collection of collections, they might seem to lose their individuality unless they are read closely and carefully. It has been said that proverbs in a collection are dead, presumably because the immediate context in which the sayings first arose is not available to the reader. That is not necessarily so. The proverbs can find new life in new applications, even if different from their original thrust. You can lead a donkey to the trough, but you cannot make him eat. This saying has been applied to human stubbornness, to disobedience, etc. The sayings are short and pithy, and often deliberately ambiguous, as we shall see. Moreover, they have to be understood in the light of the over-all goal of the sage, which is the moral formation of youths (although all ages and both sexes can profit). That does not mean that the sayings are always moralistic. They are often mere observations that do not have an immediate moral thrust; rather, they reflect on the human situation, the "way it is." The contrast between the just and the unjust is perhaps the most frequent in Proverbs 10-15, but there is a lot more to the book than the working out of good and evil in human action.

The Hebrews preferred to speak of the various organs of the body as expressive of words. Thus, it uses the concrete: mouth, lips, tongue, to express the word or whatever is said. Then there is another move: the word is closely associated with deed or action. Knowing and speaking are not theoretical; it is as if no word is without its effect, good or bad. The use of language is quite versatile, even paradoxical. Thus, "a soft tongue can break a bone" (Prv 25:15b) is a picturesque paradox that is parallel to the success that patience has when one is dealing with another. Words have power, for weal or woe. By definition, the words of the wise are to be remembered and assimilated. The intensity of the teacher is particularly evident in Proverbs 7:1-3, "My son, keep my word and make my commands your treasure. Keep my commands and live, and my teaching, like the apple of your eye. Bind them on your fingers, write them on the tablet of your heart." Such emphasis is reminiscent of the Deuteronomic insistence on the observance of the great commandment (Dt 6:6-9), and it was justified because the words of wisdom were the way to life, prosperity, a good name and immortality in one's children. These were the blessings that betrayed divine approval.

However, there could also be the opposite: the "smooth" tongue, the "double" tongue, the outright lie. In Proverbs 12:19 truthful lips are said to be forever, in contrast to the momentary life of the lying tongue. The tongue carries an ominous echo in Ben Sira:

> If you blow upon a spark, it quickens into flame,
>> if you spit on it, it dies out;
>> yet both you do with your mouth!
> Cursed be the gossiper and the double-tongued,
>> for they destroy the peace of many....
> A blow from a whip raises a welt,
>> but a blow from the tongue smashes bones;
> Many have fallen by the edge of the sword,
>> but not as many as by the tongue
>   (Sir 28:12-13; 17-18).

In a prayer, Sirach prays for a "guard" over his mouth, "that my tongue not destroy me" (Sir 22:27). It is no wonder that he could write:

> The root of all conduct is the mind;
>> four branches it shoots forth:
> Good and evil, death and life,
>> their absolute mistress is the tongue

Such power of the tongue is also familiar from the Letter of James (3:1-12), which is, as it were, the "wisdom book" in the New Testament.

One of the most profound insights into human nature is the "test" that Sirach puts to a person:

> When a sieve is shaken, the husks appear;
>> so do a person's faults when he speaks.
> As the test of the potter's work is in the furnace,
>> so in his conversation is the test of a person.
> The fruit of a tree shows the care it has had;
>> so too does a person's speech
>>> show the bent of his heart.
> Praise no one before he speaks,
>> for it is then that people are tested (Sir 27:4-7).

This is a superb insight into human nature. Though we reveal ourselves by our public actions, the best indicator is our speech. Over the long haul it betrays who we are. It may be double-tongued, but that too will become evident. And this is more than a test for honesty or integrity in actions, for it reveals the inner self, the depths of our being. Proverbs 27:21 puts it sharply:

> Crucible for silver and furnace for gold,
>> and a human being according to the praise.

The favorite examples for refining are silver and gold, as in Proverbs 17:3. But in 27:21 the test comes not from the Lord but from the praise that one receives. If this is genuine praise from others, it could be ennobling and encouraging (Prv 12:8a). But it has to withstand the rigorous scrutiny of fellow human beings. Even then praise from others is a two-edged sword. If merited, it might have an adverse effect, such as undue self confidence. If unmerited (flattery from the smooth-tongued?), it can lead to self-deception. There is a further edge to the saying; it is worth remembering that a crucible not only tests, it purges, and hence purifies.

Fundamental to the teaching of the sages is a remarkable reverence for the word, the care that one must take in speaking. Ben Sira put it this way: "Be quick to hear, but deliberate in answering. If you know what to say, answer your neighbor; but if not, put your hand over your mouth" (Sir 5:11-12). Proverbs excoriates those who answer before they have listened (18:13). Haste is scored in several sayings. It is contrary to the unruffled calm that is urged by the sages, and in particular: "You see someone hasty with word? There is more hope for a fool than for him" (18:20). That is a fierce judgment that is made several times. The saying is the more serious because it is applied to persons who think they are wise, but in reality there is more hope for fools than for them (Prv 26:12). In the wisdom tradition there is much talk about the "heated" man, an impetuous person who loses his temper, who speaks without thinking. "Whoever is slow to anger has great intelligence, but the quick-tempered exalts folly" (Prv 14:29). "An angry person stirs up disputes" (15:18); "Whoever spares his words is knowledgeable, and the cool of spirit is an understanding person" (17:27). The cool one is the diametrical opposite to the hot-headed or quick-tempered.

Silence

Is there any way of easing oneself into this careful frame of mind urged by the sages? Paradoxically, our speech is helped and protected by our silence. Thomas Merton once wrote that "Silence is the mother of speech."[1] He goes on to say, "Silence enters mysteriously into the composition of all the virtues, and silence preserves them from corruption." That is a rather extreme statement, but it finds support in the wisdom literature.

What relation does silence have to speech? Of its nature it gives a person time to think; it prevents a hasty reaction in word or deed. Anything marked by haste is tainted, even riches. Wealth acquired in haste may be quickly lost, and it will be definitely lost if unjustly acquired. You cannot take it with you (Ps 49). However, the most important contribution of silence is that it enables a person to *hear*. Wisdom is a question not only of what one says but of what one hears. In particular, the wise person must be able to hear the criticism which others voice. Receptivity to criticism means progress, because it is by means of such openness that one learns about oneself. The rebuke and the reprimand were sweet music to the sage because they became opportunities to improve. We learn from each other: "Iron sharpens iron; so one sharpens the face of a friend" (Prv 27:17). Hence the paradoxical sayings:

> Better an open rebuke
> than a love that is hidden.
> Reliable the wounds from one who loves,
> unwelcome the kisses from one who hates
> (Prv 27:5-6).

No man is an island.

Both the Book of Proverbs and Sirach recognize the ambiguity of silence, and Sirach is more explicit:

> One person is silent and is thought wise;
> another is talkative and disliked.
> One person is silent because he has nothing to say;
> another is silent, biding his time.
> The wise one is silent till the right time comes,
> but a boasting fool ignores the proper time
> (Sir 20:4-6; cf. Prv 17:27-28).

This attitude has been partially caught in the well-known saying: If you had kept quiet, you would have been taken as a philosopher. But Sirach has added to it an important factor, timing: "The wise remain silent until the right moment, but a boasting fool ignores the proper time" (Sir 20:7). Such sayings are quite true, but also difficult to observe. Timing is everything. The dilemma we face is caught in two contradictory proverbs:

> Do not answer a fool according to his folly,
>   lest you too become like him.
> Answer a fool according to his folly,
>   lest he be wise in his own eyes (Prv 26:4-5).

The editor has deliberately placed these contradictory proverbs together. They are contradictory only in appearance; the striking contrast is to force one to think about timing and about what to say. The first prohibition is not surprising. Throughout the wisdom literature one is advised to avoid the company of fools. Qoheleth warns his readers:

> Words from the mouth of the wise win favor,
>   but the lips of a fool destroy him.
> The words of his mouth start with folly;
>   his talk ends in dangerous nonsense
>   for the fool never stops talking (Ecc 10:12-14a).

Perhaps the most vivid warning is Proverbs 17:12: it is safer to encounter a bereaved she-bear than to meet up with a fool in his folly. Whatever fools might say is not worthy of mention, since they utter only folly, but it could be harmful (Prv 10:14, 21). Proverbs 26:5 goes in the opposite direction to verse 4. Answer the fool! Why? Lest the fool be "wise in his own eyes." Such a motive is ambiguous. Is it for the would-be wise person, or for the sake of the fool? Could it be a genuine concern for the fool to attempt to move such people to abandon their folly? That meaning is not easy to accept. In general, Proverbs is very explicit in warning youths to stay away from fools lest they become like them; they are infectious and hence to be avoided. Perhaps the most serious charge against fools is their inability to change. They seem to be hopeless cases (Prv 23:9), so incorrigible that you can crush them in a mortar without removing folly from them (27:22). However, more needs be said. What is the significance of the phrase, "more hope for a fool?" Thus: "If you see a man wise in his own eyes, there is more hope for a fool than for him" (Prv 26:12). Is there, after all, hope for a fool? Not really. The point of 26:12 does not have to do with improving the lot of fools. It is, instead, a threat against those who think they are wise. The real concern of the sages is to have integrity, an honest, clear vision, and a correct evaluation of self. Life is fraught with self-deception, and the worst deception is to think that one is wise. Nothing can help in that case. But one may ask why the editor put these contradictory proverbs back to back, and conveniently placed in the same chapter as verse 12. Did he favor one proverb over the other? Is there a time to answer a fool according to his folly? Could this be a deliberate contradiction to warn the reader about the ambiguities that characterize experience? Is the human grasp on wisdom all that tenuous–that if one is "wise in one's own eyes," one loses wisdom? Apparently so, because one possesses instead a specious, untrue self-understanding. Rather, one should have the integrity and insight of Qoheleth: "I said, 'I will become wise.' But it was beyond me. What happens is distant and very deep. Who can find it out?" (Ecc 7:23).

Some sayings have stated that there is "more hope or a fool than for ..." (Prv 26:12; 29:20). Whatever the point scored, the proverb raises the question: Is the incorrigibility of fools a deliberate exaggeration? It is true there are many proverbs that warn against associating with fools. The reason is that one may be persuaded to follow their bad example, their values. But is the incorrigibility, the impossibility of conversion a ploy, a means of persuasion that the sages used? Personified Wisdom addresses all people. This is quite explicit in Proverbs 8:4, and then in the following verse "fools" are specifically mentioned. In the book of Proverbs the simple or naive particularly are shown consideration. There is hope for them, if only they will listen. Proverbs 9 presents is a vivid portrayal of two women at work, Lady Wisdom and Dame Folly, who issue invitations to a banquet. Lady Wisdom addresses the "simple" and "those who lack sense," and the meal she prepares is life-giving. Dame Folly has the same audience in mind, the simple and those who lack sense. However, those who accept and follow her deceitful invitation ("stolen waters are sweet") will eventually discover that her guests are in Sheol. The rivalry between Wisdom and Folly indicates that conversion is possible, that the fool can be made wise. The whole thrust of the book is in that direction, even if the fool, *as fool*, is incorrigible.

The Carmelite Rule

By emphasizing silence and solitude the Carmelite Rule aims to preserve certain values in the biblical tradition. The Rule specifies that each friar is to stay in his own cell or nearby, pondering the Lord's law day and night (Ps 1:2) and keeping watch at prayer unless attending to some other duty.[2] Further on it becomes more specific:[3] "The Apostle would have us keep silence, for in silence he tells us to work [1 Thes 3:7-12]. As the Prophet also makes known to us: Silence is the way to foster holiness [Is 32:17]. Elsewhere he says: Your strength will lie in silence and hope [Is 30:15]." Hence the Rule lays down the period of the so-called "great silence," from Compline to Prime of the next day. Then it goes into greater detail: "At other times, although you need not keep silence so strictly, be careful not to indulge in a great deal of talk, for as Scripture has it and experience teaches us no less, sin will not be wanting where there is much talk [Prv 10:19], and he who is careless in speech will come to harm [Prv 13:3]; and elsewhere: The use of many words brings harm to the speaker's soul [Sir 20:8[4]]." There is also a reference to the words of Christ about careless talk (Mt 12:36). This number ends with composite quotations from Sirach 28:29-30[5] and Psalm 37(38):2, and it repeats Isaiah 32:17. The Carmelite Constitutions give a positive purpose to silence: "The silence of solitude which individuals and communities must cultivate makes us docile to the voice of the Holy Spirit. In all the houses of the Order, we must therefore create and foster an atmosphere of silence, recollection and solitude. This will enable us to engage more easily in personal prayer, and to make our study and other activities more fruitful."[6] Specific norms are to be determined in Provincial Statutes.

The above chain of quotations from Isaiah has been influenced by the pregnancy of the Latin phraseology. Thus, Isaiah 30:15 in the literal sense has nothing to do with silence; it refers to the need for Israel to abstain from foreign alliances made in the hope of defending itself. Its true strength and hope comes from reliance on the Lord who saved them in the first place from Egyptian slavery. This counsel is typical of Isaiah, and it is a commonplace also in the Psalms (Pss 20:8; 33:16-18; 147:10). The citation from Isaiah 32:17b is more intriguing. In the Latin Vulgate it is *cultus justitiae silentium*. The context of Isaiah is that of peace and security which will be provided for the people of God after their exilic trials. Moreover, Carmel is mentioned three times in Isaiah 32:15-16. It does not stand for the place name or the mountain; it refers to the flourishing farm land. Then in verse 17b, "the result of righteousness [will be] quiet and security," as the Hebrew text has it.

In the other citations one can single out certain basic theses relative to silence and solitude. Solitude is the "atmosphere," since the mode of life at the time was cenobitic. The cultivation of silence seems to be motivated by the stress on communion with God, "meditating on the Law." This is not an empty silence; it means that one's concerns are focused on what is perceived as the center of life. Moreover, the series of quotations from the wisdom literature considers silence a means to escape sin. An example of this is Proverbs 10:19 in its Latin form: *in multiloquio peccatum non deerit*, "in much talk sin will not be absent." In other words, there is the possibility that careless talk (more than is needed) injures one's spiritual life. The positive reason is featured again in the Constitutions.[7] The attitude is not silence for the sake of silence, but "to make us docile to the voice of the Holy Spirit; to engage more easily in personal prayer," etc.

Carmelites, and indeed all Christians, can profit from the vigor and creativity of the biblical views on speech and silence. A prayerful contemplation of Israel's wisdom is a first step.

Roland E. Murphy, O.Carm.

Endnotes

1. *A Thomas Merton Reader*, Doubleday, p. 459.
2. *Regula Ordinis Fratrum Beatissimae Virginis Mariae de Monte Carmelo*, 10 [Editors note: This was formerly referred to as Chapter 8; however, as of May 21, 1998, the General Councils of both branches of the Order decided it appropriate to refer to the various points of the Rule not by Chapters but by the agreed upon marginal numbers as found in the critical editions].
3. *Ibid.*, 21 [Editor's note: formerly referred to as Chapter 18].
4. This follows the Vulgate text; for a more exact version see NAB, 20:7, or NRSV, 20:8: Whoever talks too much is detested.
5. Vulgate numbering; cf. 28:24-26.
6. Const #67.
7. *Ibid.*

Carmelite Spirituality:
Enduring Themes

Introduction

This article identifies five fundamental themes in Carmelite spirituality which are present in people's lives now, and which we can assume will be present in the future. These realities all involve the spiritual hunger of humanity, and Carmel's articulation of that hunger and ministry to it.

I am addressing the article, in the first instance, to all who share Father Eamon Carroll's Carmelite heritage. But it is also hoped that the article communicates something of Carmel's wisdom to any interested reader.

The first theme or reality is the hunger of the human heart for God. The second reality is the capability of the heart to form attachments and create idols. The third reality is that God has already found and accepted us. The fourth reality is the ever-present experience of the tragic in people's lives. The fifth reality is that, in spite of all, and through all, the human journey is toward union with God, or as John of the Cross wrote, "We become God!"

These five realities–the hunger for God, the creation of false gods, God's acceptance of us, the sense of the negative and tragic in life, and the invitation to enter into a divinizing process which transforms us–are among the realities which gave rise to the Carmelite tradition, establishing it as one of the major spiritual paths for today and tomorrow. I would like to comment on each reality with a brief reflection.

The Hunger for God

"Our hearts are restless," wrote St. Augustine, and that truth seems fundamental to the human condition. Human restlessness, human desire, human yearning–none of it ever seems finally and fully satisfied. The baby beginning to crawl and explore the environment is an expression of human restlessness, and the first Carmelites leaving home to settle in a valley on Mount Carmel is also fueled by the same desire. We are truly pilgrims.

We humans never have enough because, with St. Thérèse of Lisieux, *we choose all.* And we will never rest until we get it. The Carmelite tradition recognizes this hunger in the human heart and says we are made this way. We are made to seek and search, to yearn and ache, until the heart finally finds something or someone to match the depth of its desire, until the heart finds food sufficient for its hunger. We name that food, that fulfillment, that goal of human desire, God. Carmelites have been intentionally pursuing that elusive, mysterious fulfillment for 800 years. "I wanted to live," wrote St. Teresa of Avila, "but I had no one to give me life ...."[1]

We believe that, named or not, every human being is on this quest. We can assume this: that every student in our school, every member of our parish, every candidate in our seminary has an openness to the transcendent mystery we name God. Time and time again the desire will be denied, the hunger temporarily satisfied, the yearning stifled, distracted, weak. But we know it is there and it will emerge in one form or another. Our tradition has the power, the language, the imagery to help illumine what people are experiencing in their innermost being.

The Carmelite tradition attempts to name the hunger, give words to the desire, and express the journey's end in God. The human heart will forever need this clarification of its wants.

Carmel has wanted the same thing and will walk with all we meet along the way. We cannot satisfy their hunger, but we can help them find words for it and know where it points. We can do it, and have done it, in art, in poetry and song, in counseling and teaching, in simply listening and understanding. And we can warn people that eventually all words fail and at times all we have is the desire itself.

In his book *The Holy Longing* Ronald Rolheiser observes that a serious problem in spirituality today is a naiveté about the desire or energy that drives us. Our God-given spiritual longing, which may be expressed in numerous ways, including creative, erotic energy, is dangerous for us if not carefully tended. Rolheiser thinks we are naive about this deep desire within us and are not alert to its danger. Without a reverence toward this energy and ways of accessing it and keeping it contained, most adults waver between alienation from this fire and therefore live in depression, or they allow themselves to be consumed by it and live in a state of inflation. Unable to handle this energy we either feel dead inside or are hyper-active and restless.

Rolheiser, a religious priest in Canada, believes that most people go to Mass on Sunday in order to be able to find a proper expression for this energy, this longing. Without that ritual they would either live in depression or live in inflation. In commenting on inflation, he says, "... we are generally so full of ourselves that we are a menace to our families, friends, communities, and ourselves." The challenge is to find a balance in a proper relationship to energy or desire, especially creative, erotic, spiritual energy, which he sees as the same thing. He writes, "Spirituality is about finding the proper ways, disciplines, by which to both access that energy and contain it."[2]

This dilemma would be understood by the saints of Carmel. They approached this flame found deep in their humanity and were burned and purified by it in their encounter. John of the Cross begins his poem "The Spiritual Canticle" by complaining, "Where have you hidden, Beloved, and left me moaning? You fled like the stag after wounding me; I went out calling you, but you were gone."[3] John's understanding of our humanity is that we wake up in the middle of a love story. Someone has touched our hearts, wounding them, and making them ache for fulfillment. Who has done this to us, and where has that one gone? Those questions haunt every human being's journey, and propel every step, from the crawling of a baby to a Pope's pilgrimage to the Holy Land, and all the human endeavor in between.

What do the men and women in our parishes, our retreat houses, in counseling want? Everything! Count on it, and minister to it. And we say to ourselves and them, that the hunger within us is so deep and powerful that, acknowledged or not, only God is sufficient food. When Jesus preached the present and coming Reign of God he was speaking precisely to the deep desires, the holy longing in the hearts of his listeners.

Recently I traveled with our provincial to visit one of our men serving in a parish in El Salvador. While there we visited the places associated with Archbishop Oscar Romero, including the chapel of the Carmelite sisters where he was assassinated. March 24, 2000, was the 20th anniversary of that assassination.

Romero's conversion from a rather traditional, professional cleric with a sincere but otherworldly piety, to an outspoken courageous shepherd of his people, came because he saw the longing in the faces of his people. As he celebrated the funerals of those killed by the powerful and read off the names of the disappeared, he found it was his duty more and more to give voice to these voiceless ones, to express their oppressed longings–to embody in his courageous presence the holy longing of the Salvadoran people.

To assist people in hearing and voicing their deepest longing is part of Carmel's continuing ministry.

The Heart and Its Idols

A second perennial theme in Carmel's spirituality is the need to decide which God to follow. Our tradition was born on

Mount Carmel, the scene of the struggle between the followers of Yahweh and the followers of Baal. Elijah encouraged the people to be clear about their choice of the one, true God.

The saints in our tradition know how hard it is to find and follow the true God, among the many gods offered us. On our human pilgrimage the heart grows weary awaiting the Lord and frequently settles down with lesser gods.

Even in talking about the good religious person, the person who has been converted to Christ, John of the Cross still finds deep flaws. His suspicion is that the human heart has the capacity to pervert anything, especially good things, and turn them into idols. For example, good religious persons are secretly proud of their humility, envious of the holiness of others, and gluttonous regarding books, conferences, and other spiritual activities. John leaves one no place to hide. A reader will have to acknowledge how easily we turn things into idols. The longing for God is now being poured into a lesser god, and we ask that lesser god to feed our hunger–an impossible task.

When our tradition talks about attachments, it does not mean that relationship with the world is a problem. We have to relate to the world. Our saints are talking to adults whose heart has been enslaved by someone or something in place of God. It is not the person or thing that is the problem, but the way we are relating to them, the disordered way our desire or longing is being expressed. And detachment does not mean withdrawing from life, but becoming free from enslavements so that we can engage the world healthily and for its well-being, and not for what we need it to be.

A contemporary theme related to our traditional theme of attachment is addiction. We are coming to realize that we are all addicted in one way or another, and that only God's grace can free us from our addictions. One can be addicted to obviously destructive things, but one can also be addicted to the church, addicted to the Pope, addicted to religious practices, even addicted to Carmel, and addicted to God as we create God to be. In other words, we can ask part of God's creation to be uncreated, to be the nourishment for the deepest hungers within us whether as individuals or as a people. We are asking from God's creation what only God can give. And our tradition insists that *nada*, no part of God's creation can be substituted for God. Only the one who is *nada* (no thing, yet everything) can be sufficient food for our hunger.

One writer opined that the Carmelite vocation is to be suspended between heaven and earth, finding no support in either place. That is a rather dramatic way of saying that ultimately our faith, our confidence and trust in God, will have to be its own support, and God leads us beyond all of our earthly and spiritual constructs. At the end of her life, Thérèse of Lisieux found her life-long hope for heaven mocking her. John of the Cross reminded us of St. Paul's observation: if we already have what we hope for, it is not hope; hope is in what we do not possess.

Does this suspicion of human intentions and constructs make Carmelites eternally curmudgeons? Or does it allow us to bring a sharp critique regarding the human heart and its idol-making propensity? Is it not actually a ministry of liberation, freeing us from all the ways we enslave ourselves and give ourselves away to idols? Is not the Carmelite critique a challenge to not cling to anything, to not make anything the center in one's life, other than the Mystery who haunts our lives. And in that purity of heart, really only achieved by God's spirit, are we able to love others well and live in this world wisely. The Carmelite challenge is to cooperate with God's love, often dark, which is enlivening and healing us.

This continual listening for the approach of God, in the middle of all the words and structures we have constructed, is a prophetic task for Carmel. Which God are we to follow? The gods of our addictions? The gods of ideologies and limited theologies? The gods of oppressive economic and political systems? The gods of all the "isms" of our time? Or is our God the God who transforms, heals, liberates, enlivens?

Archbishop Oscar Romero was a traditional, careful, studious cleric. He was a good man, reserved, pious, prayerful. But his conversion came when he saw another face of Christ, a face somewhat different from the Christ of his piety and prayer, a face somewhat different from his theology, a face different from the Christ familiar to the hierarchy of El Salvador. It was the face of Christ in the face of the people of El Salvador, it was the face of Christ truly incarnated in history and finding its outlines in the struggles of his people. The other bishops saw the same struggle, but their carefulness apparently blinded them to the face of Christ emerging in the people of El Salvador. Romero said,

> We learn to see the face of Christ–the face of Christ that also is the face of a suffering human being, the face of the crucified, the face of the poor, the face of a saint, and the face of every person–and we love each one with the criteria with which we will be judged: "I was hungry and you gave me to eat."[4]

The idols of our times are not just personal loves and possessions, but are especially the idols of power, prestige, control, and dominance which leave most of humankind looking in at the banquet of life. Romero commented:

> The poor person is the one who has been converted to God and puts all his faith in him, and the rich person is one who has not been converted to God and puts his confidence in idols: money, power, material things .... Our work should be directed toward converting ourselves and all people to this authentic meaning of poverty.[5]

Accepted by God

One of the most impressive messages from our Carmelite saints has been the realization that God loves us first, as we are. Thinking they were looking for an absent God and that life was a pursuit of God, they returned from their efforts testifying that God had been pursuing them all along. The story of our lives is not our search for God, but God's desire for and pursuit of us. God is the first contemplative whose gaze made us lovable and irresistible to God. Just one hair of our head, says John of the Cross, is enough to cause God to swoon.

One time Teresa of Avila heard these words in prayer: "Seek yourself in me!" She asked a number of her friends and directors in Avila the meaning of "Seek yourself in me!" Among the respondents were a lay spiritual director, Francisco de Salcedo, her brother Lorenzo de Cepeda, and John of the Cross. They met to discuss their responses but Teresa was absent. So they sent their replies to her.

In imitation of academic sparring sometimes practiced in the schools, Teresa playfully determined to find fault with each answer and gently mock it. We do not have their responses, but we do have her rejections of their answers.

One respondent, Francisco de Salcedo, quoted St. Paul frequently, and then closed his response with a humble statement about having "written stupidities." Teresa, then, chastised him for accusing the words of St. Paul to be "stupidities." She said she had a mind to hand him over to the Inquisition.

John of the Cross must have responded that "Seek yourself in me" meant that first she had to be *dead to the world* and then seek God. Her answer to him was a prayer to be saved from people as spiritual as John. His answer was good for members of the Company of Jesus, she said, but not for those she had in mind.

Life is not long enough if we have to die to the world before we find God. Teresa pointed to the gospels and observed that Mary Magdalene was not dead to the world before she met Jesus; nor was the Canaanite woman dead to the world before she asked for crumbs from the table. And the Samaritan woman had not died to the world before encountering Jesus at the well. She was who she was and Jesus accepted her. Teresa closed her response to John of the Cross by thanking him for answering what she did not ask![6]

Teresa's point is, God accepts us where we are in our lives. We have been accepted all along. The challenge for us is to accept the acceptance, and allow that accepting Presence to change us. The reality of that embrace is the basis for our prayer. To pray, then, is to step trustingly into that relationship as the foundation of our lives. It is easy to talk about, but very hard to live out day to day.

The Carmelite tradition can be misread. Carmel could easily appear to be saying to people that a rigorous asceticism will achieve union with God; that the idols of our lives can be toppled with our courageous efforts and isolated, rugged living. In fact, however, Carmel's message to people is the necessity for God's grace, and the good news that grace is always available. All we need do is open our lives to it.

The recent attention paid to Thérèse of Lisieux and her message reminds us that priority should be given not to our merits and efforts, but to living with confidence and trust. Thérèse begins her autobiography with St. Paul's words to the Romans: "So it depends not on human will or exertion, but on God who shows mercy" (Rom 9:16).

Theology today talks about grace as uncreated grace, the loving, healing presence of the Father, Son, and Spirit. And theology teaches that every human being is an event of God's self-communication. The gentle whistle of the shepherd from the center of Teresa's castle captures the reality of God's loving presence.

When we talk about contemplation to people, we are simply encouraging them to open their lives to and trust in this love offered them. God is continually coming toward us inviting us more deeply into our lives, into a wider freedom, and into a loving relationship. Contemplation is being open to that transforming love, no matter how it is approaching.

One of the recent developments in the understanding of the Carmelite charism has been the re-locating of contemplation among our priorities. We had always spoken about prayer, community, and ministry as the three corners of our charism. Contemplation was seen as a higher or deeper form of prayer, and at times in our history ministry and contemplation seemed at odds.

However, here is a description of contemplation from the Order's recent document on formation:

> ... a progressive and continual transformation in
> Christ worked in us by the Spirit, by which God
> attracts us toward Himself by means of an interior
> process which leads from a dispersed periphery of
> life to the more interior cell of our being, where He
> dwells and unites us to Himself.[7]

We are understanding now that contemplation is an activity which grounds and links prayer, community, and ministry. The door is prayer, but God's love is offered us in various ways in those realities of our lives; and one can enter into this contemplative openness to God–in other words live a life of authentic faith, hope, and love–through any of those three avenues. They are not pitted one against another, but they are windows and doors to the transcendent reality at the depth of our lives and offer contact with that Mystery.

I stress this perspective because Carmel has had 800 years of ministry in response to the Church and God's people, and, God-willing, will have many more centuries of unselfish service. And none of it is inimical to a contemplative living. Many a Carmelite has been transformed into a more loving person through engagement with people in various ministries.

Archbishop Romero was transformed and converted by God's love not only in the solitude of his prayer, but in his engagement with the Lord in history, in the messy efforts of the people to find their place at the banquet of life.

Our contemplative living, our openness to God's love coming toward us in good times and bad, is the gift we can give to others. What happened in the lives of Carmel's saints, what is happening in the lives of Carmelites today, is happening in everyone's life. We witness best by keeping a focus on who we are: a contemplative fraternity living in the midst of the people.

A young German Carmelite spoke to the Order's General Congregation in 1999 and stressed the contemplative charism :

> I strongly believe that our first task is to put quite
> a bit of our energy, time, and personal talents and
> qualities into this process of a growing relationship
> with the God of life and love. Our personal human
> and spiritual growth as well as our future as an
> Order depend on how much we as individuals and
> communities yield to and develop this intimate
> friendship with God so that he can transform us
> according to the image of Christ, acting through us
> for the sake of the Church and the world.[8]

The Dark Love of God

I have often thought that part of Carmel's appeal to people
is that it does not avoid the unpleasantness of life; Carmel deals
with it directly. When one presses into the life of Thérèse of
Lisieux, it is obvious how much suffering was present. The heavy
reputation of John of the Cross, his very name, and his image of
the "dark night" speak of a spirituality that is serious about
coming to terms with the dark side of life. And think about the first
Carmelites who went to the periphery of society and there,
without distractions, opened their lives to the inner warfare of evil
and good spirits.

Often, inexplicably, Carmel's saints have declared a special affinity to suffering. Thérèse of Lisieux expressed a life-long
desire to suffer. It had a mysterious attraction for her, which
would be suspect had she not related it to love. Teresa of Avila,
when describing her intimate union with God in the seventh
dwelling place of the castle said, while she was not as hard on
herself as in the past, she still trusted suffering more. Instinc-
tively, these women knew that the dark way is often the way to life,
and the easy, consoling way may end in deep disappointment.

John of the Cross' descriptions of the nights eventually
wear a reader down in their heaviness. If one is not having the
experiences John is describing, he seems extreme, overly dra-

matic. But, when compared with descriptions people give of their own sufferings, John's language is particularly expressive of the tragic. I do not think John is saying we must bring dark times down on ourselves; he is describing life as people often experience it. He is no tougher than life itself. The fact that he acknowledges these trying experiences and analyzes them from a faith perspective is an enormous contribution to contemporary spirituality.

In the debris of one's life, in the failure of one's efforts, in the evaporation of consolation and even of meaning in life, John testifies to a love which is present through it all and which will see the person through the dark waters.

John Paul II has amplified John's image of the dark night to include the modern world's sufferings:

> Our age has known times of anguish which have made us understand this expression better and which have furthermore given it a kind of collective character. Our age speaks of the silence or absence of God. It has known so many calamities, so much suffering inflicted by wars and by the destruction of so many innocent beings. The term *dark night* is now used of all of life and not just of a phase of the spiritual journey. The Saint's doctrine is now invoked in response to this unfathomable mystery of human suffering.

> I refer to this *specific world of suffering.* . . . Physical, moral and spiritual suffering, like sickness–like the plagues of hunger, like war, injustice, solitude, the lack of meaning in life, the very fragility of human existence, the sorrowful knowledge of sin, the seeming absence of God–are for the believer all purifying experiences which might be called *night of faith.*

> To this experience St. John of the Cross has given the symbolic and evocative name *dark night*, and

he makes it refer explicitly to the plight and obscurity of the mystery of faith. He does not try to give to the appalling problem of suffering an answer in the speculative order; but in the light of the Scripture and of experience he discovers and sifts out something of the marvelous transformation which God effects in the darkness, since "He knows how to draw good from evil so wisely and beautifully" (Cant. B 23:5). In the final analysis, we are faced with living the mystery of death and resurrection in Christ in all truth.[9]

The generals of the two Carmelite Orders called for a "new spirituality" to complement the "new evangelization." Will that new spirituality grow out of Carmel's ever-increasing awareness of the realities people are experiencing around the world? As the face of Carmel changes and new members enter the Order, especially from populous, poor countries, the situation of the world's masses is brought to our first-world doorstep. The internationality of the Order and the international bonds forged in the family of Carmel give us a unique opportunity to hear the Spirit in many diverse contexts, and the opportunity to be challenged to respond.

Union with God

Carmelite spirituality has frequently been presented as a "high" spirituality, a rarefied spirituality for the chosen few. It is often presented as soaring ecstatic unions, or dramatic sufferings more intense than the usual troubles in life. Images come to mind of Bernini's statue of Teresa of Avila's "transverberation," her experience of being pierced by a golden dart with all its ecstasy and agony. Or John of the Cross's drawing of Christ on the Cross, drawn from the perspective of the Father looking down on his crucified Son. Or one thinks of the drawing of John of the Cross showing the way up Mount Carmel. The paths of material and spiritual possessions do not reach the top; only the middle path of the *nadas* opens to the top where God is *nada* and *todo* (no thing, yet everything!).

Carmel seems to represent an heroic, even epic journey to God. And it is only for experienced mountaineers who dare scale its heights. If so, what are we ordinary Carmelites doing here? Do we sometimes feel we are guardians of a tradition we have never really experienced? Do we feel that we often are reporting second hand accounts of the land that is Carmel, but have never really been there ourselves? As a result of our transformation in love, "We become god!" John of the Cross boldly proclaims. How rare is this divinization our tradition celebrates?

John uses another image for the journey, besides traveling through a night or climbing a mountain. He writes that "The soul's center is God" and that our journey is to that center in our lives.[10] But, instead of envisioning a distant center requiring an arduous journey, John says that even with one degree of love we are in the center! I take that to mean one degree of desire, of yearning, of hope, no matter how inarticulate, we are in the center.

Our theology today reinforces John's observation. Strictly speaking, there is no natural world. It is a graced world, from the beginning: creation and redemption going hand in hand. In other words, our lives are permeated with the loving, enlivening, healing presence of God, uncreated grace. Instead of searching for a hidden center, the center has come to us.

So, what is the journey? The journey, said John, is to go deeper into God. But we are in union with God all the way; the divinizing process is continual. So the goal described by our Carmelite authors is one taking place in each soul who only feebly desires more.

A conclusion I draw is that many, many Carmelites and others reach the so-called "heights" of Carmel. The heights are approached, not when someone drops off their pew in a swoon, but when a life more and more is expressing God's will.

What is the purpose of prayer, and therefore the goal of her castle journey, according to Teresa of Avila? The purpose of prayer is conformity with God's will. The prayerful person is more and more in union with God, and this union is expressed in the individual more and more wanting what God wants. We do not get tougher ascetically and thereby wrestle our will into submitting to God's will. No. God's love lures us into a transformation of our desire so that we desire what God desires; we want what God wants. People can be so transformed that all ways of living can become expressive of God's will. If we may interpret Jesus as saying that God's will is the well-being of humanity, then the prayerful person is more and more living in a way which furthers that well-being. In other words, the transformed, divinized person is living in a way which cooperates with God's present and coming reign.

These people are hard to spot. Meister Eckhart warns us that someone living from their center very naturally lives in accord with God's will. He says while others fast, they are eating; while others keep vigil, they are asleep; and while others pray, they are silent. After all, what is the purpose of the vigil, the prayer, the fasting, if not to live out of the soul's center, which is God. Of course, he is exaggerating to make a point since our pilgrimage is never finished this side of death. The point, I take it, is the absolute humanness of the transformed person.

Teresa tells us that these people are not even continually conscious of their spiritual life. Interiority becomes less and less an object of focus. Not even God preoccupies them, because in all the ways they are living they are expressing their relationship with God.

In the conclusion of the Carmelite Rule, Albert, Patriarch of Jerusalem and the law-giver, writes: "Here then are a few points I have written down to provide you with a standard of conduct to live up to; *but our Lord, at his Second Coming will reward anyone who does more than he is obliged to do.*"[11]

Kees Waaijman of the Brandsma Institute in Nijmegen sees this statement as a clear allusion to the Good Samaritan story. The Carmelite is placed in the role of innkeeper. His plans and orderly house are upset when a stranger brings a beaten man to be cared for. The stranger asks the innkeeper to take care of the victim, and *if the innkeeper incurs further expense*, i.e., *does more*, the stranger will compensate him when he returns. The innkeeper dutifully takes care of the wounded person, perhaps without emotional investment or ego-involvement. Waaijman concludes that all real giving is essentially dark.

Friars need make no apologies for not being true Carmelites. Our spirituality is not about heroic asceticism; it is about God's all-conquering love, a love that has touched every heart and made it ache; otherwise we would not be here.

Realizing that we are naturally at home on the heights of Carmel, and still always in need of God's mercy, our spiritual ministry is to make available Carmel's tradition to help our brothers and sisters "see" and "hear" the presence of God in their own lives.

In order to tend this flame in others, it seems right that we will have come to terms with it in our own lives. If we listen to our hearts, we will know the hearts of the people with whom we live and minister. Dust off any Carmelite vocation and you will usually find a glowing ember waiting to be fanned into a flame, a flame that yearns for wholeness, peace, security, joy, and that finds its best expression in service of our brothers and sisters. That is why we came. That is why we stay.

John Welch, O.Carm.

Endnotes

1. Teresa of Avila, *The Book of Her Life* in *The Collected Works of St. Teresa of Avila*, I, translated by Kieran Kavanaugh, O.C.D., and Otilio Rodriguez, O.C.D. (Washington, D.C.: ICS Publications, 1987), 8, 12.

2. Ronald Rolheiser, *The Holy Longing* (New York: Doubleday, 1999), p. 27.

3. John of the Cross, "The Spiritual Canticle," in *The Collected Works of St. John of the Cross*, translated by Kieran Kavanaugh, O.C.D., and Otilio Rodriguez, O.C.D. (Washingon D.C.: ICS Publications, 1991), stanza 1.

4. Marie Dennis, Renny Golden and Scott Wright, *Oscar Romero* (Maryknoll: Orbis Books, 2000), p. 19.

5. Ibid., 28.

6. Teresa of Avila, *A Satirical Critique* in *The Collected Works*, III:359-362.

7. *Ratio Institutionis Vitae Carmelitanae*, #27 (as yet unpublished).

8. Günter Benker, O.Carm, "Open to the Future of God" in *The Mission of Carmel for the Third Millennium* (Melbourne: Carmelite Communications, 1999), p. 51.

9. *Master in Faith*, Apostolic Letter of John Paul II in *Walking Side by Side with All Men and Women* (Rome: Institutum Carmelitanum, 1991), pp. 22, 23.

10. John of the Cross, "The Living Flame of Love," in *The Collected Works*, stanza 1, number 12.

11. Rule, No. 24.

A Spiritual Reading
of the "Dark Night"

Fr. Eamon Carroll and I were classmates in the Carmelite seminary system from first year high school through novitiate to ordination and beyond (1935-1947). Both of us were lucky enough to be sent on to graduate studies in theology in Rome and to spend most of our lives in theological education. But our paths diverged along the way. Eamon stayed teaching in academe right to the end, retiring from Loyola University of Chicago in January, 2000. I left the confines of academic theology in the seventies to engage in what Bernard Lonergan called the specialty of communication. For me this meant speaking and writing in what I like to think has been what the French call *haute vulgarisation*, popularizing theology in adult education, retreats, seminars, and workshops. My tribute to Fr. Eamon is to share something of this experience, specifically my recent use of the poetry of St John of the Cross in retreats. I want to present a spiritual reading of the poem "Dark Night" as a way of leading into the experience of God.

John's poetry has come into prominence for its pastoral application only recently. Its literary excellence has been recognized at least since the middle of the 20th century through the discoveries of outstanding literary critics like Damaso Alonso and Marcelino Menendez y Pelayo. John is now regarded as one of Spain's greatest poets. The use of this poetry as the first and most important window into the Saint's mystical experience is another matter. This is a later development.

A sign of this new appreciation is in *The Collected Works of St John of the Cross*[1] in the translation of Kieran Kavanaugh. The earlier editions located the poetry at the end of the volume along with the letters and minor works. The 1991 edition places the poems in the front to remind the reader that the poetry is John's first statement of his experience; the prose treatises come afterward. The poetry is the first place to look for an understanding of the saint's teaching.

Poetry is a privileged entry into human experience. Great poetry captures profound and universal experiences that come from the deepest layers of the soul. It shares these experiences through primordial imagery that resonates with those depths. Great poetry is catholic, defined by James Joyce as "Here comes everybody," and it speaks with a universal ring. John's poetry is like that. It is exalted religious poetry and unequaled mystical poetry. One of my teachers, the great Hispanicist scholar, Helmut Hatzfeld, held the opinion that a poem is mystical in proportion as it reaches the heights (or the depths) of John's "Spiritual Canticle."

By definition mystical experiences are ineffable, i.e., they cannot be put into words. This quality refers to matter of fact prose. Poetry uses metaphors and symbols, "figures, comparisons, and similitudes" ("Spiritual Canticle," prologue 1) to evoke the deep experiences of the spirit. John chooses poetry as the primary medium to express and celebrate his experience of God. His poems are art-objects that represent the inexpressible. Later on and usually by request he unpacks some aspects of the poetry in prose commentary. Even then his commentaries are at their best when they are poetic themselves, as is the case of much of Sacred Scripture. Thus he waits for the right moment, when he is "deeply recollected" ("Living Flame," prologue 1) and moved with fervor to write about the outpourings of the spirit.

Our task is to familiarize ourselves with the poem "Dark Night," to read it over and over and let it speak to our own hearts, thereby drawing us into John's experience as well as our own of dark night (see Appendices A and B).[2] For those who do not know

Spanish, the English translation of Kavanaugh is recommended. Any translation, of course, is a limitation. Poetry is words and sound, the rhythm and sound being an important part of the communication. Even the literal transcription of Kavanaugh in blank verse or no verse at all loses the sound and has its own words. The substance of the poem is salvaged through the message and the images. Some translators of the poetry, like Roy Campbell, Willis Barnstone or Frederick Nims, create new images, hence equivalently new poems. This approach in my judgement is less helpful. One valid way of compensating for the loss of the melodious Spanish is to utilize a musical accompaniment along with the English translation, such as the work of John Michael Talbot who puts some of the Kavanaugh translations to music. Music connects us to the nuns and friars of John's day who sang the lyrics for recreation and devotion. Those with even a modicum of knowledge of Spanish will find it helpful to listen to readings or to read aloud the Spanish text.

The Poem as End and Beginning

St Teresa of Avila wrote that "it is one grace to receive the Lord's favor; another, to understand which grace or favor it is; and a third to know how to describe and express it." (*Life* 17.5) John illustrates this natural order. He is first a gifted mystic, then an insightful theologian who understands his religious experience especially from the Sacred Scriptures (see *Ascent*, prologue 2), and finally a great poet who can create a beautiful icon of his experience. The poetic quality of the Scripture helps him interpret his own experience and gives him a language for his poetry. The language of his greatest poems comes from the Song of Songs. Thus his own poetry is doubly indebted to Scripture in the second and third steps of the process.

The poem in turn is our door to the experience of God according to John of the Cross. We start with the poem and work our way back through the reflections to the experience. It is important not to circumvent the process, especially the first step, the mastering of the poem. We are tempted to go immediately to the commentary as if this would give us the full understanding. The poem gives a "feel," an intuition, and an emotional quality that escape the rational explanation. There is more in the poem than can be captured in a prose statement. A poem "is," and it represents an excess of meaning that is appropriated only by wrestling with the text.

John Welch has an excellent chapter on directives for unpacking the poetry in his book on John of the Cross, *When Gods Die.*[3] He follows Carl Jung's understanding of poetry as images and stories that arise from the collective unconscious and therefore from the common patrimony of humanity. The language of poetry is the language of the imagination, and therefore poetry will reveal its secrets by the same tools that interpret any work of the imagination. Welch applies Robert Johnson's four steps in dream analysis to the poetry. So the poem is to be (1) amplified by similar images and stories drawn from other sources such as Sacred Scripture; (2) related to one's personal growth; (3) interpreted in understandings and laws of life; and (4) expressed in a ritual, such as prayer. John of the Cross himself did this kind of analysis in his commentaries. We are invited to engage in this reflection, interfacing the poem and our own lives. The reader and the poet are in dialogue with each other, and who can predict the outcome of a conversation?

The Story of the "Dark Night"

We start with the story line and the images of the poem. This is the literal sense of the poem. The "Dark Night" is a human love story, a human drama involving lover and beloved, bride and bridegroom, that is a story all in itself. On another, second level, the bride is humanity or the individual soul; the bridegroom is Christ. A non-believer could appreciate the first level without any interest in the second, spiritual level. At times there is a breakthrough of the theological intent. Thus in stanza five of this poem the bride cannot contain herself and abandons the human metaphor in favor of a spiritual statement about God: "O guiding night!/ O night more lovely than the dawn!/ O night that has united/ the Lover with his beloved,/ transforming the beloved in her Lover." The indication of this exception in Kavanaugh's translation is the capitalization of "Lover." Elsewhere the personal nouns and pronouns are in lower case, because they refer to the human protagonists. Later in this paper I state that human love works a similar transformation in two human beings, so that the passage could be interpreted along the same lines as the rest of the poem. In any case it would be a mistake to skip this human story in favor of an immediate, spiritual reading, since the human love story is the vehicle for communicating the beauty of the love-relationship between Christ and the soul.

John wrote "Dark Night" after his escape from the prison cell in the Toledo monastery in August, 1578. Other poems preceded it, notably his longer and more famous "Spiritual Canticle," which was composed in large part during the incarceration. The memory of his liberating escape is still fresh in his mind: the exhilaration of taking the chance, moving out unseen in the pitch blackness, the rope ladder down the side of the building, scurrying along parapets and ledges, and finally freedom at last, "my house being now all stilled." These memories are the content of the first two verses. A hidden message of those two verses is the passage from "urgent longings" to "my house being now all stilled." We address this purifying experience later in the paper.

The inner experience of that wondrous night and the eventual encounter with the beloved make up the rest of the poem. This part too is full of excitement and joy. There is nothing lugubrious about this dark night, contrary to impressions associated with this night in the popular mind. The negative side is only one small part. The night is a joy, because of the inner light and fire that burn in the heart of the escapee (stanzas 3-5) and the term of this light and love, which is the uniting of bride and bridegroom in a magnificent encounter (stanzas 6-8). The whole poem is the bride's perspective; it is her monologue. The bride stands for the soul in its search for God, and as such there is usually no hesitation in men identifying with the feminine figure. Not only do men have a counter-sexual, feminine side, but before God, as the Fathers of the Church used to say, all souls are feminine.

The night is a cover that protects the bride from any outside interference, obstacle, or competition, and it allows full sway to the light within as guide to the beloved. Alone with each other the two embrace, and in an idyllic pastoral setting they express affection and consummate their union (stanzas 6-8). Here is the surrender of perfect human love, made possible in the story because of the external liberation and the release of profound inner life. Divine love follows the same pattern. Love for God finds its fulfillment when it passes through the three stages of the spiritual life called purification, illumination and union.

The Night as Symbol

The major symbol of the poem is the night. The whole poem takes place within the "one dark night" that goes from dusk to dawn. The symbol evokes the richness of darkness. Darkness makes possible the freedom *from* outside influence and inner weakness, and freedom *for* the pursuit of one's dream. The liberated bride describes her happy state in a series of epithets that indicate autonomy: she goes forth unnoticed, anonymous, concealed, disguised (stanzas 1-2), "in secret, for no one saw me/ nor did I look at anything " (stanza 3), all because her house is "now all stilled." The darkness allows her to attend to her heart's desire (stanzas 3-4), to pursue the encounter and absorption in her lover (stanzas 5-8). Her inner life takes over and thrives, transcending the constraints of the human condition. She is full of joy; the dark night is a glad night, because it brings bride and groom together.

The darkness has another function in the poem. It points up the fact that the journey is uncharted, like the path of the just man on the summit in John's sketch of Mount Carmel, for whom "there is no law, he is a law unto himself." In the darkness there is no need for maps or directives; other people do not get in the way, because they are either absent or they cannot see. There is no place for misguided opposition or human respect or envious competition. A whole new world is available by leaving the brightness of daytime and entering the night.

Some of John's poems are adaptations of secular verses that were being sung in the streets. John took them and gave them a religious turn, and the new poem was said to be *a lo divino*. We could convert the contemporary lyric, "Music of the Night" from the play "Phantom of the Opera," into a religious hymn to darkness *a lo divino*. The phantom, who has a disfigured face but a beautiful voice, is trying to lure the singer Christine into the darkness where music reigns. He portrays the riches of the darkness in these words:

> Night-time sharpens,/ heightens each sensation ...
> Darkness stirs and:/ wakes imagination ...
> Silently the senses/ abandon their defenses ...
> Slowly, gently/ night unfurls its splendor ...
> Grasp it, sense it–/ Tremulous and tender ...
> Turn your face away/ from the garish light of day,
> Turn your thoughts away/ from cold, unfeeling light
> And listen to/ the music of the night ...

The song continues in this vein, celebrating the beauty of life in darkness. A similar darkness with a different agenda is the environment for the love story of the "Dark Night."

Themes in the "Dark Night"

Various reflections are suggested by the different sections of the poem. The first two verses are particularly rich, enough to occasion the five books of commentary that make up *The Ascent of Mount Carmel* and the *Dark Night*. John got no farther than the first verse of the second stanza in these two commentaries.

"Love's urgent longings" in the first stanza represents unbridled desires for the beloved that are full of ego. They are beginning love or a new burst of love that gets one started on the pursuit and moves one into a new level of relationship. The love at this point looks perfect, but it is excessively emotional and impetuous. Romantic love has a long way to go before it is mature and integrated. The latter goal happens when "my house [is] all stilled" and there is peaceful possession of both the love and the object. This movement from imperfect to perfect love is the process of purification, the subject of John's two commentaries.

Others write their own commentaries. Jessica Powers, the Carmelite poet, muses on the "before" of the process in her poem, "The House at Rest."[4] In the brightness of daytime each part of the house looks for attention, causing a certain distraction, fragmentation and many-mindedness:

> How does one hush one's house,
> each proud possessive wall, each sighing rafter,
> the rooms made restless with remembered laughter
> or wounding echoes, the permissive doors,
> the stairs that vacillate from up to down,
> windows that bring in color and event
> from countryside and town,
> oppressive ceilings and complaining floors?

Darkness allows the shift from multiplicity to simplicity, from distraction to stillness, from noise to quiet. How does that happen? The darkness makes the parts invisible; it neutralizes them. But darkness is only a cover; real healing comes from within: "Virtue it is that puts a house at rest." Virtue does not destroy the parts. It integrates them, so that "when the call is heard," the tenant "is free to take his kindled heart and go."

Thomas Tyrrell makes *Urgent Longings*[5] the title of his excellent book on the passage from infatuation to contemplative love. Urgent longings mark the experience of infatuation that happens in young adulthood and often again in mid-life. The desires are good, but they need reordering. Desire is not taken away; it is shorn of self-serving. Romantic love becomes contemplative love, which loves people and God as they are, without projection. The love is still full of passion; it is more passionate in Teresa of Avila's view, more genuine and more profitable than lesser degrees, because "it is what love really is" (*Way of Perfection* 6.7 [Peers translation]). Contemplative love is surrender of the whole person, not the furtive search for indulgence and self-satisfaction. Covert selfishness is the basic enemy of both human and divine love. Tyrrell elaborates this truth in the light of contemporary psychology, while John's commentaries are more theological.

One final take-off from these two verses is the subject of violence. Violence, according to the famous French anthropologist Rene Girard, comes from mimetic desires, viz., desires born of competition and invidious comparison. Mimetic desires quickly become covetous. They are the root of violence toward oneself and others and come to term in murder as with Cain and Abel. More distressing still, violence, spawned by desires, is the foundational principle of human cultures throughout the world. The prophetic tradition of the Hebrew Scriptures and above all the life and teaching of Jesus Christ stand against this culture of violence. A popular presentation of these theses can be found in Gil Bailie's, *Violence Unveiled.*[6] A fruitful dialogue might occur between the teaching of the poem on personal autonomy as noted above–the bride proceeding in secret and by inner direction–and the theories of Rene Girard. In his teaching on love and desires John of the Cross offers the antidote to the destructive quality of mimetic desire.

The Middle Stanzas, Three to Five

The night as guide, darkness as cover for the inner light of faith, is the theme of these three stanzas (3-5). This "glad night" is "more lovely than the dawn," immensely more revealing and rewarding than human lights and resources, because the soul is participating in the light of God, which paradoxically is the bright darkness of human unknowing. The soul is experiencing enlightenment, illumination, and the source is living, loving faith, the faith "which expresses itself through love" (Gal 5:6). Such faith is God's work, beyond the possibilities of human imagining and thinking. It is the surrender that costs, as T. S. Eliot has said, no less than everything, and the reward is a new identity, expressed eloquently by St Paul in Galatians 2:20-21: "I live, no longer I, but Christ lives in me. I still have my human life, but it is the life of faith in the Son of God, who loved me and gave himself for me."

This participation in divine life has a human analogue. A Persian fable describes a young suitor going to the home of his beloved. He knocks on the door, and a voice from within asks, "Who is there?" He responds, "It is I." His beloved refuses to open the door, indicating that he does not love enough. He goes away, pines after her and returns a second time; the same conversation ensues: "Who is there?" "It is I." "You do not love me enough." The suitor becomes desperate. He spends months thinking and suffering in his great love. Finally he returns to the house and knocks. "Who is there?" asks the lady within. "It is thyself" is the response. The bride-to-be opens the door and says, "Now you truly love me." When the "other" becomes one's very self, when the alchemy of love transforms one's very being and gives a new identity, the love is perfect. So it is in this blessed night "that has united/ the Lover with his beloved,/ transforming the beloved in her Lover" (stanza 5).

Pure faith connects the person with the real God, not the God of one's own fashioning, one too small for the unspeakable Mystery that is Father, Son and Spirit. T. S. Eliot captures this thought in the following words from "East Coker":

I said to my soul, be still, and wait without hope
For hope would not be hope for the wrong thing; wait without love
For love would be love of the wrong thing; there is yet faith
But the faith and the love and the hope are in the waiting.
Wait without thought, for you are not ready for thought:
So the darkness shall be the light, and the stillness the dancing.[7]

These words are commentary on faith as a leap in the dark, a free fall that lands one in the arms of God. The God of true faith is not our own construction. The real God is not the answer to our questions, a God brought down to our own level. The prayer of the mystic is that God be God in her experience. The result is "transluminous obscurity," the darkness of God, the third night of St John of the Cross, which is eminently "more lovely than the dawn."

Final Stanzas, Six to Eight

The poem culminates in the intense exchange of love between bride and bridegroom. The transformation that is the goal of Christian faith is not a static condition, an ontological reality that just sits there. The transformation calls for expression and the nuptial imagery of the poem suggests contemplative presence of the two lovers one to the other. The picture is nuptial lovemaking, the bride caressing her lover in a setting of cool, refreshing breezes. The poem ends in the self-oblivion of a love that forgets everything other than the beloved; it is the ecstasy of abandonment, a going out of from oneself that "leav[es] my cares/ forgotten among the lilies."

The reader may feel that the exalted love celebrated in these last stanzas is matter for admiration but beyond imitation. This would be a mistake. Every person of faith is gifted with the same transformation in love, though not necessarily in the same degree. The least amount of grace achieves the divinization and participation in God's life that are the foundation for the lovemaking of this poem. Only the degree of that possession is different. The poem describes the fullest measure of new life in Christ. John of the Cross' experience is ordinary experience "writ large." Christian experience is the same in kind for all in the state of grace. We go to John to see the possibilities of grace, to be challenged and inspired to enter into loving conversation with God.

Prayer is not the only expression of this new life. The winning essay in a competition sponsored by *Spiritual Life* magazine was entitled "John's 'One Dark Night': Romantic, Political or Mystical?"[8] The author shows that the poem is both the celebration of mystical love and the story of romantic, human love. But it is more. Sophisticated hermeneutics and literary criticism expand the horizons and show how the whole life of John is involved in the poem. There is the dimension of suffering that culminated in the Toledo prison cell and the politics of struggle in living in a conflicted Order. There is also the whole venture of searching for the truth. All these factors are part of the drive to self-transcendence in the poem. Thus the poem is about community and ministry, about interpersonal relationships and societal commitment as well as contemplative union with God. The poem is about a whole life.

I end this essay in the way I began. I thank God with my classmate, Eamon Carroll, that we have been privy to these secrets and I ask the grace for both of us and for all who read this piece to be faithful to their inspiration.

Ernest E. Larkin, O.Carm.

Appendix A: Noche Oscura

Canciones de el alma que se goza de haber llegado al alto estado de la perfección, que es la unión con Dios, por el camino de la negación espiritual.

1. En una noche oscura,
   con ansias, en amores inflamada,
   ¡oh dichosa ventura!
   salí sin ser notada
   estando ya mi casa sosegada.

2. A oscuras y segura,
   por la secreta escala disfrazada,
   ¡oh dichosa ventura!
   a oscuras y en celada,
   estando ya mi casa sosegada.

3. En la noche dichosa,
   en secreto, que nadie me veía,
   ni yo miraba cosa,
   sin otra luz y quía
   sino la que en el corazón ardía.

4. Aquésta me guiaba
   más cierto que la luz del mediodía,
   adónde me esperaba
   quien yo bien me sabía,
   en parte donde nadie parecía.

5. ¡Oh noche que guiaste!
   ¡Oh noche amable más que el alborada!
   ¡Oh noche gue juntaste
   Amado con amada,
   amada en el Amado transformada!

6. En mi pecho florido,
   que entero para él solo se guardaba,
   allí quedó dormido,
   y yo le regalaba,
   y el ventalle de cedros aire daba.

7. El aire de la almena,
   cuando yo sus cabellos esparcía,
   con su mano serena
   en mi cuello hería
   y todos mis sentidos suspendía.

8. Quedéme y olvidéme,
   el rostro recliné sobre el Amado,
   cesó todo y dejéme,
   dejando me cuidado
   entre las azucenas olvidado.

Appendix B: The Dark Night

Songs of the soul that rejoices in having reached the high state of perfection, which is union with God, by the path of spiritual negation.

1. One dark night,
   fired with love's urgent longings
   –ah, the sheer grace!–
   I went out unseen,
   my house being now all stilled.

2. In darkness, and secure,
   by the secret ladder, disguised,
   –ah, the sheer grace!–
   in darkness and concealment,
   my house being now all stilled.

3. On that glad night
   in secret, for no one saw me,
   nor did I look at anything
   with no other light or guide
   than the one that burned in my heart.

4. This guided me
   more surely than the light of noon
   to where he was awaiting me
   –him I knew so well–
   there in a place where no one appeared.

5. O guiding night!
   O night more lovely than the dawn!
   O night that has united
   the Lover with his beloved,
   transforming the beloved in her Lover.

6. Upon my flowering breast,
   which I kept wholly for him alone,
   there he lay sleeping,
   and I caressing him
   there in a breeze from the fanning cedars.

7. When the breeze blew from the turret,
   as I parted his hair,
   it wounded my neck
   with its gentle hand,
   suspending all my senses.

8. I abandoned and forgot myself,
   laying my face on my Beloved;
   all things ceased; I went out from myself,
   leaving my cares
   forgotten among the lilies.

Endnotes

1. *The Collected Works of St John of the Cross*, edited by Kieran Kavanaugh, O.C.D., and Otillio Rodriguez, O.C.D. (Washington, D.C.: ICS Publications, 1991).

2. The Spanish text of the "Dark Night" and an English translation is reprinted with permission from *The Collected Works*, pp. 50-52.

3. John Welch, O.Carm., *When Gods Die* (New York: Paulist Press, 1990), chapter two.

4. *Selected Poetry of Jessica Powers*, edited by Regina Siegfried and Robert Morneau (Kansas City: Sheed and Ward, 1989), p. 122.

5. Thomas Tyrrell, *Urgent Longings* (Whitsunville, Massachusetts: House of Affirmation, 1980).

6. Gil Bailie, *Violence Unveiled* (New York: Crossroads, 1997).

7. T. S. Eliot, *The Complete Poems and Plays* (New York: Harcourt, Brace and World, Inc., 1958), pp. 126-127.

8. Mary Frohlich, "John's 'One Dark Night': Romantic, Political or Mystical?" *Spiritual Life*, 37 (Spring, 1991), 38-47.

Theotokos Yesterday and Today

Around the year 182, Irenaeus, the second bishop of Lyons, wrote *Adversus Haereses* to refute the Gnosticism of Basilides, Valentinus, and Marcion. Against the Gnostic separation between a heavenly, saving Christ and the earthly, crucified Jesus,[1] Irenaeus insisted for soteriological reasons that Jesus Christ is "one and the same," not "one and the other," and that this one and the same Jesus Christ is "truly God" (*vere Deus*) and "truly Man" (*vere homo*).[2] Irenaeus' insistence on one and only one subject in Jesus, of whom must be predicated all things divine and human, presages what will come to be known as the "communication of idioms"[3] as well as the notion of "hypostatic union."[4] This "one and the same" or "the same" will be repeated seven times, lest the point be missed, in the doctrinal formula of the premier Christological Council, the Council of Chalcedon held in 451. Likewise, it is this "one and the same" which will make possible, as we shall see below, that same Council's calling Mary the *Theotokos*, the God-bearer (*Deipara* in Latin) or "Mother of God" (the usual translation in Western languages)[5], a title affirmed of her twenty years earlier at the Council of Ephesus.

In this essay I would like to explore the Christological-soteriological significance of the title, *Theotokos*, especially as it is used at the Council of Ephesus, itself received and affirmed by Chalcedon. Having explored the basic Christological-soteriological affirmation or doctrine embedded in this title from Ephesus and Chalcedon, I would then like to consider its significance for the pluralist model of Christology-soteriology in vogue today, especially as represented by Roger Haight in his *Jesus Symbol of God.*[6] According to Haight, Jesus is normative for the salvation of all but constitutive for the salvation of none.[7] Thus he writes:

> A Spirit christology correlates with demands of the new consciousness of Christians regarding other religions .... On the one hand, it accounts for the normativity of Jesus for humankind generally. For Jesus empowered by God as Spirit offers a salvation that is true, universally relevant, and thus normative. On the other hand ..., God as Spirit has been present and at work in the world for human salvation from "the beginning," without a causal connection to the historical appearance of Jesus.[8]

I hope to show that Haight's Christology underlying this soteriological position can be maintained only at the price of rejecting the Christological conciliar tradition of the Church, in the first place the teaching of Ephesus, affirmed at Chalcedon, regarding the oneness of person of Jesus, of which everything divine and human (*vere Deus, vere homo*) must be predicated and which makes possible the affirmation, *Theotokos.* As a consequence of rejecting Ephesus, I believe that Haight likewise rejects not only Chalcedon but also Nicea's "one in being with the Father." Indeed did St. John Damascene (d. 749) exhibit that hermeneutical sense of "appropriateness" or fidelity to the tradition, rightly demanded in our day by David Tracy,[9] when he wrote: "This title (*Theotokos*) contains the whole mystery of the Incarnation."[10] Not to affirm it in its full Christological and hence soteriological significance will be tantamount to a denial of the incarnation and hence of salvation itself.

Although the *Theotokos* title has roots in the New Testament,[11] the first certain literary appearance of the title itself is found in a letter (c. 319) of Patriarch Alexander of Alexandria to his fellow Patriarch, Alexander of Constantinople.[12] At the end of this letter, written to alert Alexander of Constantinople of certain

Arians and their heresy, Alexander of Alexandria provides a summary statement of the faith, creedal in its tripartite structure of belief in the Father, the Son and the Holy Spirit, to which is appended belief in one, catholic, and apostolic Church and the resurrection of the dead. In this context are found the words: "... we know of the resurrection of the dead, the first fruits of which was our Lord, Jesus Christ, who in very deed, and not in appearance merely, carried a body, of Mary, Mother of God (*Theotokos*)...."[13] The obvious sense of the title here is an anti-docetic or anti-gnostic meaning, np. that Jesus truly was human.[14] The nonchalant use of the title "leaves the impression of everyday usage, long established and uncontroverted."[15]

Prior to Alexander of Alexandria's explicit use of the *Theotokos*, its equivalent is found in varied ways in Ignatius of Antioch, the Apologists, Irenaeus, Tertullian, Clement of Alexandria, Origen and others. Thus, Ignatius calls Jesus "Mary's Son," who is sprung both from Mary and from God. Justin can speak of God who became man by Mary, and Irenaeus can claim that if God's birth from Mary is unreal, our redemption is also imperilled.[16] In the insistence upon the true humanity of Jesus, because Mary is his mother, we can see in these pre-fourth century equivalents of the *Theotokos* the same anti-docetic, anti-gnostic meaning.

Of course, in these same second and third centuries, the title *theos* (God) was being applied more and more to Jesus, whose mother was Mary.[17] Obviously it will not take a great stretch of the imagination to begin calling Mary "The Mother of God," which after Alexander's use of the title comes to be more and more the case in fourth century writers such as Athanasius and the three Cappadocians. However, it is interesting and perhaps portentous to note with Burghardt that the title "is conspicuously absent from Antiochene literature."[18]

Athanasius' use of the title is instructive.[19] In his *Orations Against the Arians* the title does not seem to have a directly anti-Arian sense, i.e. as directly affirming against Arius that Jesus is truly divine. Rather, the literary contexts indicate that the primary significance of the term here remains anti-docetic.[20] However, according to Pelikan, in Athanasius an advance in the significance of the term is made.[21] This advance, quite apposite for my interest here, can be seen, for example, in *Orations Against the Arians*, III. 29. Here, Athanasius, having accused the Arians of misunderstanding the biblical texts, asks:

> What is the basic meaning and purport of Holy Scrip-
> ture? It contains ... a double account of the Savior. It
> says that he has always been God and is the Son,
> because he is the Logos and radiance and Wisdom of
> the Father. Furthermore, it says that in the end he
> became a human being, he took flesh for our sakes
> from the Virgin Mary, the God-bearer (*Theotokos*).[22]

Here we see Athanasius, as Irenaeus before him, stating the three conditions for salvation: the savior must be truly human; the savior must be truly divine, and the one who is truly human must be the same one who is truly divine.[23] But in stating these conditions, Athanasius here, in a *Theotokos* text, also provides not only the theological justification for the communication of idioms (namely, in Jesus there is only the one self-same subject, the Logos); he also thereby provides the rationale that Cyril will use to defend the *Theotokos* against Nestorius almost a half a century after Athanasius' death.[24] Athanasius' theological use of the *Theotokos* exhibits what soon will come to be known as the principle of *lex orandi lex credendi*, the principle that implicit in Christian worship is a normative doctrinal content which needs to be made explicit.[25]

On the basis of what has been said thus far, it may be instructive at this point, before moving on to the Nestorian controversy, to highlight that the following three theological concepts are intrinsically related: salvation in Jesus, the communication of idioms, and the title of Mary, *Theotokos*. Where there is one, there will be the other two. Where one is explicitly rejected, the other two also will fall.[26]

Use of the *Theotokos* continued throughout the fourth century in both the East and the West without controversy. And then came Nestorius, Patriarch of Constantinople, a "hammer of heretics,"[27] soon to be numbered among their ranks.

Nestorius, a monk from Antioch, became Patriarch of Constantinople in 428. He immediately found himself embroiled in a controversy involving the *Theotokos* title, which had been attacked by Anastasius, a priest brought from Antioch to Constantinople by Nestorius. The theological background for this controversy was a conflict between Apollinarians, whose use of the title suggested that Jesus lacked a genuine humanity, and the Arian followers of Paul of Samosata, the Photinians, who used the title to show that Christ was not truly divine, since God could not have a mother.[28] Nestorius, having been drawn into the debate, supported Anastasius' rejection of *Theotokos*,[29] and proposed as a compromise the title *Christotokos*, Mother of Christ. Both factions appeared content with the compromise.[30]

However, Eusebius of Doryleum, upon hearing of the *Christotokos* compromise, immediately charged Nestorius with the errors of Paul of Samosata, namely, the two sons theory and its consequent adoptionism. Soon word of Nestorius' *Christotokos* solution reached the Egyptian monks, "the shock-troops of orthodoxy,"[31] whose agitation caused Cyril, Patriarch of Alexandria, to join battle with Nestorius in 429.[32]

Cyril, being from the school of Alexandria, where the communication of idioms and hence the *Theotokos* were widely accepted, launched his attack on Nestorius by writing a letter to the Egyptian monks and two letters to Nestorius, the second of which will become the text of the Council of Ephesus, to be discussed below. In these letters Cyril warns Nestorius of the heretical implications of calling Mary "Mother of Christ" and not "Mother of God." As earlier with Eusebius of Doryleum, he sees in Nestorius' rejection of the *Theotokos* a revival of the third century theory of the "two sons" who are linked only by a moral union.[33] Although Nestorius clearly affirmed: "We know not two Christs or two Sons or Only-Begottens or Lords, not one and another Son ..., but one and the same ...,"[34] the fact is that he maintained not only the distinction of the human and divine natures but also the distinction between the eternal Logos, the Son of God (not Mary), and the man, Jesus, who is son of Mary. In other words, each nature had its own *hypostasis* (objective reality) and *prosopon* (concrete appearance).[35] Therein was the rub for Cyril, and so it was not without reason that Cyril accused Nestorius of teaching two sons who were "one and the other" and not "one and the same." Of course Nestorius believed that it was only by distinguishing the Son of Mary as one objective reality (*hypostasis*) from the eternal Son of God as another objective reality (*hypostasis*) that he could protect the genuine human reality of Jesus and hence salvation itself.[36] As Kelly notes:

> "... if the redemption was to be effected, the second Adam must have been a real man. Yet an authentically human experience would have been impossible if the Lord's humanity had been fused with, or dominated by, His divinity. Hence the two, divinity and humanity, must have existed side by side, each retaining its peculiar properties and operation unimpaired. Each was a concrete nature (*physis*).... He could not think of two natures except as each having its *prosopon* ... and its *hypostasis*....[37]

Nestorius feared Cyril's schema of "one nature" (*mia physis*) or "one hypostasis" (*mia hypostasis*) and hence "hypostatic union" (*henosis kath' hypostasin*)[38] for basically the same reasons he disliked the *Theotokos*. First, it was, in his opinion, tantamount to an Apollinarian mixing or confusing of the divine with the flesh resulting in the loss of the human soul of Jesus, and second, it resulted in the Word's becoming the subject of the God-man's sufferings.[39] Hence, he preferred a "conjunction" (*synapheia*) of the human and the divine to a "oneness" (*henosis*).[40] He employed the metaphor of "indwelling" (*enoikesis*) to explain this union by way of conjunction. The Word indwelt the man Jesus, as

God indwelt God's temple (Jn 2:19). And he characterized this indwelling as one of favor, grace or goodwill, analogous to the way God dwells in God's saints.[41]

Nestorius' preferred way of describing the unity of Jesus was through the notion of a "unity of *prosopon*" or "the *prosopon* of union." The *prosopon* of union was a "resultant," or an "additive subject," the outward form or manifestation *resulting from* the union of the human and divine natures.[42] *Whom* one saw in Jesus was one, but beneath this one *prosopon* were (seemingly) two "who's," two individuals, two *hypostases*, the Son of God and the Son of Mary.[43] This "resulting prosopon" was not, therefore, the eternal Logos, a title Nestorius eschews, but the Christ or the Lord.[44] "This 'prosopic union' thus becomes Nestorius' attempt to provide a metaphysical account of Christ's unity of person which did not involve the difficulties of 'natural or substantial' union...,"[45] i.e. a union by way of *physis* or nature , as Apollinaris, and Cyril, in Nestorius' judgement, maintained. It will be precisely with this 'prosopic union' that Cyril will find the tragic soteriological flaw in Nestorius, as we shall see.

Regarding the communication of idioms,[46] Nestorius maintained that the human acts of Jesus are predicated of the concretely existing human nature and hence of the human *hypostasis*, and divine acts are predicated of the concretely existing divine nature and hence of the divine *hypostasis*. In virtue of the *prosopon* of union, both human and divine acts can be predicated of the God-man, Jesus Christ. But in no way could human acts be predicated of the eternal Logos, which continually indicated to Cyril that indeed Nestorius' Christ lacked a single, underlying, grounding, person (*hypostasis*), i.e. a single bearer or possessor of all that is divine and human in Jesus. Again, Nestorius' "one person" or *prosopon* of union was merely a person which *resulted from* but did not *antecede* the union.[47]

In response to Nestorius' schema of two natures-two *hypostases* which are (seemingly) only loosely and extrinsically related by way of indwelling (*enoikesis*) or "conjunction" (*synapheia*), Cyril insisted for soteriological reasons[48] upon one

concrete nature (*mia physis/mia hypostasis*)[49] and therefore
hypostatic *union (henosis kath' hypostasin)*.[50] Summarizing the
contents of Cyril's letter of 429 to the monks of Alexandria, in
which he attacks Nestorius, Young writes: "You cannot sever the
one Lord Jesus Christ into two, separating what was from the
Holy Virgin from what was from God."[51] In Cyril's estimation, the
incarnation never truly occurred according to the Nestorian
indwelling-conjunction schema. It was nothing but an illusion.
The Word never truly *became* flesh, as John 1:14 demands. At
best the Word merely indwelt the man or was present to and
operative in the man.[52] Whereas for Cyril "God the Logos did not
come into a man, but he 'truly' became man, while remaining
God."[53] Not one and the other but one and the same.

For Cyril the terms nature (*physis*) and individual reality
(*hypostasis*) are used interchangeably.[54] In affirming one *physis/
hypostasis*, Cyril is not denying, as Nestorius charged, the
distinction and integrity of the human and divine aspects or
"natures" of Jesus.[55] Rather, he was affirming that Jesus was one
concrete reality, one concrete existent, one concrete individual,
one Son, the Logos, of whom everything human and divine must
be predicated. Therefore, the divine and human predicates may
not be divided between two persons.[56] Hence the basic meaning
of hypostatic union (*henosis kath' hypostasin*) in Cyril is clear.
The oneness (*henosis*) of Jesus with the Logos is not by reason of
or in virtue of (*kath'*) a oneness of will or good pleasure (*henosis
kata thelesin monen, henosis kath eudokian*), or by reason of a
conjunction (*kata synapheian*) or indwelling (*kath enoikesin*),
positions espoused by Nestorius.[57] Rather, this oneness is by
reason of or in virtue of (*kath'*) the one individual (*hypostasin*),
np., the Logos of the Father, about which one *hypostasis* must be
predicated everything human and everything divine.[58] Needless to
say, Cyril fully exploited the communication of idioms.[59]

Of course if Jesus is only one concrete reality, one
hypostasis, the Word of the Father, then to refuse to call Mary
Theotokos, an application of the communication of idioms, is to
reject the oneness of person in Jesus. For if she is Jesus' mother,

as Nestorius surely maintained, but not the Mother of the Word-God, then (seemingly) the concrete, existing individual (*hypostasis*) who is her Son and the concrete, existing "individual" (*hypostasis*) of the Word are not one and the same but one and the other. In which case salvation has not occurred. Heaven and earth, divine and human have not become one. There is no "at-one-ment," and thus sin and death have not been overcome, since the redemptive acts of Jesus would be those of a mere human being.[60] To affirm *Theotokos* is to affirm the communication of idioms, is to affirm the hypostatic union, is to affirm salvation. To deny any of the three is to deny salvation, for in that case John 1:14 never occurred. As Walter Burghardt poignantly states: "In the Nestorian controversy the Christian East was sundered ... by a word. With that word, *Theotokos*, 'Mother of God,' Cyril summed up orthodox belief in the Word Incarnate, the Son of God made flesh."[61]

After his letter to the Egyptian monks and his two letters to Nestorius, Cyril contacted Pope Celestine, as did Nestorius. Celestine held a synod in Rome in August of 430 which supported Cyril and the use of the *Theotokos*. Cyril was then entrusted to execute the decision of the Roman synod and Nestorius was given ten days to comply. Cyril, who tended to act in the superlative degree, went one better than the decision of Celestine and the Roman synod by writing a third letter to Nestorius to which he appended twelve inflammatory anathemas, which infuriated Nestorius and his supporters, the Antiochenes. Thereupon Nestorius, with the support of John, the Patriarch of Antioch, persuaded the emperor, Theodosius, to summon a general council which was to meet at Ephesus on Pentecost, June 7, 431. Prior to the arrival of either the bishops of Antioch or the papal legates, and against the protest of Candidianus, the representative of the emperor, Cyril opened the Council in the Church of St. Mary and assumed its presidency. Nestorius refused to attend.[62]

At this Council, with one hundred and thirty to one hundred and fifty bishops attending, Cyril's second letter to Nestorius was read aloud and unanimously accepted by the Fathers as being in agreement with the faith of Nicea. Nestorius' reply to Cyril's second letter, in which Nestorius rejected the *Theotokos*, was greeted with cries of 'Anathema,' and Nestorius was deposed. That evening the crowds chanted: "Praised be the *Theotokos*! Long live Cyril." It was this Council, with Cyril's second letter to Nestorius, which was accepted by Pope Celestine and later Pope Leo the Great, as well as ratified by Chalcedon.[63]

The pertinent sections from Cyril's second letter, which forms the text of Ephesus, read as follows:

> The holy and great synod (Nicea), therefore, stated that the only begotten Son ..., true God from true God ..., became incarnate, became man, suffered, rose on the third day and ascended to heaven. We too ought to follow ... these teachings and con- sider what is meant by saying that the Word from God took flesh and became man. For we do not say that the nature of the Word was changed and became flesh, nor that he was turned into a whole man made of body and soul. Rather do we claim that the Word in an unspeakable, inconceivable manner united to himself hypostatically (*henosas...kath' hypostasin*) flesh enlivened by a rational soul, and so became man and was called son of man, not by God's will alone or good pleasure, nor by the assumption of a person alone.... So he who existed and was begotten of the Father before all ages is also said to have been begotten according to the flesh of a woman.... The Word is said to have been begotten according to the flesh, because for us and for our salvation he united what was human to himself hypostatically (*henosas ... kath' hypostasin*) and came forth from a woman. For he was not first begotten of the holy virgin, a man like us, and then the Word de- scended upon him; but from the very womb of his

mother he was so united and then underwent begetting according to the flesh....

So we shall confess one Christ and one Lord.... If, however, we reject the hypostatic union (*kath' hypostasin henosin*) as being either impossible or too unlovely for the Word, we fall into the fallacy of speaking of two sons.... We ought not, therefore, to split into two sons the one Lord Jesus Christ.... For scripture does not say that the Word united the person of a man to himself, but that he became flesh (Jn 1:14)....

This is the account of the true faith everywhere professed. So shall we find that the holy fathers believed. So have they dared to call the holy virgin, mother of God (*Theotokon*), not as though the nature of the Word or his godhead received the origin of their being from the holy virgin, but because there was born from her his holy body rationally ensouled, with which the Word was hypostatically (*kath' hypostasin*) united (*henotheis*) and is said to have been begotten in the flesh.[64]

Grillmeier sums up the teaching of Ephesus in these words: "One and the same is the eternal Son of the Father and the Son of the Virgin Mary, born in time after the flesh; therefore she may rightly be called Mother of God."[65] And he goes on to explain: "Divine life with the Father, descent to the earth, incarnation and humanity must be predicated of one and the same subject, the Logos who is *homoousios* with the Father."[66] This "one and the same" teaching will be picked up in the 433 Formula of Union and in Chalcedon, where, as stated above, it is repeated three times, and "the same" four times.[67]

Ephesus is the triumph of Cyril over Nestorius, or at least Nestorianism. In the words of Pelikan: "The theology of hypostatic union had been vindicated when its (Ephesus') designation of 'one and the same Christ' as the subject of all christological predicates, including deity and crucifixion, had been acknowledged as *identical with the creed of Nicea.*"[68] Its basic doctrine is clear. It is the teaching of Cyril outlined above. There is in Jesus one Son, the eternal Logos now enfleshed. The incarnate Son cannot be divided into two, the man, Jesus, and the indwelling Logos who is present to and active in the man. Of this one Son, everything human and everything divine must be predicated. The predicates cannot be divided between divine and human sons. Two technical terms are used at Ephesus to express this soteriological-Christological doctrine, the two terms used by Cyril. These are hypostatic union (repeated four times either in nominal or participial form)[69] and the Marian title, *Theotokos.* Both terms express the reality of salvation which Jesus the Christ is and accomplished, i.e. the at-one-ment of the divine and the human. In Jesus heaven and earth became one. In that oneness is our salvation.[70]

Regarding Ephesus, Davis writes: "For the common people, Christ had defeated heresy; Mary, Mother of God, had triumphed over Nestorius."[71] A Mariological title had become "the ultimate test of orthodoxy."[72] But this should not be surprising, for, as Burghardt says: "... Our Lady's role at Ephesus is the spontaneous outgrowth of her role at Nazareth, of her role throughout history. Her deep significance has always been her relationship to Christ."[73]

Having considered the Christological-soteriological significance of the *Theotokos* in its historical setting, I would now like to consider the Christological-soteriological adequacy of the Jesus of Roger Haight as viewed primarily from the perspective of Ephesus but also Nicea and Chalcedon. Does Haight in effect present us in his recent work, *Jesus the Symbol of God,* with a neo-Nestorian or crypto-Nestorian Jesus who is not "one and the same" and, therefore, not reconcilable with Ephesus, and hence not with Nicea and Chalcedon, though he claims it is? And does he, therefore, present us with a Jesus who could not be the savior as that term has been understood in the Christian tradition sketched above?[74]

To understand Haight's ontological analysis or construction of Jesus Christ, one must first grasp his understanding of religious symbol, especially its dialectical character, on which it rests.[75] Haight introduces his treatment of religious symbol with reflections on religious experience. He rightly notes that all experience of God, "because it is tied to the world, is experience that is mediated by the world" (194), and "all religious responses to the (religious) question will themselves be mediated through some historical medium" (195). For the Christian, Jesus is "the central medium and focus for encounter with and faith in God (195). He is "the medium of God" (196). But "a religious medium is a symbol" (196). Therefore, for the Christian Jesus is the symbol of God. Hence the title of the book! But what is a symbol, how does it "work," especially a religious symbol?

"A symbol may be understood as something that mediates something other than itself. A symbol makes present something else" (197), unlike a sign which is merely referential but does not make present or reveal the other (197). A symbol of its very nature, therefore, has a dialectical character or structure. On the one hand, it is itself. On the other hand, it participates in, but *is not* that which it mediates. Hence in the case of a religious symbol or medium, "on the one hand, the medium (or symbol) participates in transcendence, in God so that God is *present to and within* the medium. Yet, on the other hand, the medium is not the transcendent itself, because it is a finite piece of the world, and thus must point beyond itself to God" (196 - italics mine). This dialectical character of the symbol is extremely important for the use of symbol in Christology since "the dialectical character of symbol allows one to assert contrary things about the symbol, because it is not the symbolized, and yet it makes the symbolized present" (201). This "tensive unity and difference between the sacred and profane within the symbol itself, is the key to formal christology" (202).

Thus Jesus is a religious symbol on the one hand because he makes God present. "... we are speaking of *the real presence of God to him*, and through him to the world, that is mediated by him" (198 - italics mine). So to call Jesus "symbol of God" means that *God*[76] is *present* to Jesus or *active* in Jesus (210 - italics mine). We have here what is often called an "indwelling" and "functional"

Christology, spelled out in even greater detail in chapter fifteen
through the analysis of Logos and Spirit Christologies.

On the other hand, since symbols have a dialectical
structure, we must also say that Jesus is a religious symbol
because he is not the God whom he mediates or makes present,
just as "a *sacred* stone remains a *stone*" (201).[77]

This dialectical structure of symbol as applied to Christ
results in a dialectical structure in Christology, which, in Haight's
opinion, accounts for the two nature formula of Chalcedon in its
insistence that the two natures are truly distinct. "The Council of
Chalcedon is precisely an attempt to preserve this tension between the finite and infinite in Jesus against the tendency of
monophysitism. The doctrine of two natures corresponds to the
dialectical structure of Jesus as symbol of God" (205).[78] The
importance of the dialectical structure of symbol, as understood
by Haight for his ontological analysis of Christ, is seen even more
clearly in the following statement.

> Finally one has the formal and narrow christological
> question of the humanity and divinity of Jesus.
> Here the dialectical character of a symbol becomes
> directly relevant to one of the most important
> questions in the history of christology. What does
> it mean to say that Jesus is consubstantial with
> God, and thus precisely not a human being, and
> consubstantial with us, and in that measure other
> than God, a creature? (206-207)

For Haight, therefore, the content or truth of the doctrine
of Chalcedon, as well as Nicea, which, however, lacks the dialectical balance of Chalcedon with its "two-natures symbolism"
(205), is to be accessed or grasped through the prism of symbol.
Symbol *à la* Haight becomes the "hermeneutic" or interpretive key
for interpreting Christological doctrine.

The result of the employment of this prism or interpretive
key to interpret Christological doctrine is precisely and *only* the

type of indwelling and functional Christology already signaled above.[79] Again and again throughout his book Haight understands the divinity of Jesus as God's presence and action in and through him. For example, he writes:

> When one asserts the divinity of Jesus with a dynamic Spirit Christology, this means that God, and not less than God, is really present to and at work in Jesus, and that this is so in such a manner that Jesus is a manifestation and embodiment of the reality of God. (462)

And again in reference to his Spirit Christology he states: "This should also be construed as more than a thin functional or 'adverbial' presence of God to Jesus, and truly an ontological presence, because where God acts, God is" (455). True. But ontological only in the sense of "present to, acting in/through." The same could be said of any prophet, mystic, or, for that matter, any human being. God him/herself, and not merely some created gift or representation of God, is present and acting through every human being. This is merely to assert something comparable to Rahner's position of the supernatural existential or the universal presence and power of the Spirit.[80] With this understanding of the divinity of Jesus, as God (or Spirit, or Logos) merely present to and at work in Jesus, it does follow that Jesus is only one revealer (=savior) among many other possible revealers/saviors.

Haight's own understanding of the "one in being with the Father" of Nicea is likewise reduced to and completely consistent with his indwelling-functional model, itself necessitated by his understanding of symbol as applied to Christ. "The meaning of Nicea is that no less than God was and is present and at work in Jesus" (284). Again, this could be said of Moses or Mother Teresa. Is *this* all that the Arian heresy, Nicea and its aftermath were about, i.e. whether God himself and not something or someone less than God was *present* to Jesus? Nicea's concern was with Jesus as savior from sin and death.[81] In order to save in *that* sense,

Jesus himself had to be "one in being with the Father," and not merely the one in whom the Father (or the Spirit, or the Logos) was *present* and *active*, for only God can save.[82] Since for Arius Jesus is the Logos incarnate, and the Logos is something or someone less than God, Jesus himself is not "one in being with the Father." And hence in Nicea's judgement, the Arian Jesus could not save.

The indwelling-functional Christology of Haight is pre-cisely the type or model of Christology presented by Nestorius, which the Christological conciliar tradition, as articulated explic-itly first at Ephesus in its condemnation of Nestorius, found inadequate for the soteriological reason stated above. Nestorius' Christ was found soteriologically inadequate not because some-one or something less than God was *present* to him. Quite the contrary. For Nestorius no one less than the eternal Son of God was present to the man Jesus. But Ephesus demanded more than this Antiochene indwelling or "God-bearing man" Christology, because in its judgement Nicea demanded more, as we have seen. Ephesus demanded not only that God-Son or God-Logos was *present to* Jesus, of which God-Son we could say "one in being with the Father." It also demanded that of *one and the same person*, the incarnate Son, Jesus Christ, we predicate everything human *and* everything divine, as Cyril of Alexandria demanded. It would be of no avail soteriologically to divide the predicates, to predicate divinity merely of God-Son who indwells or is operative in the man, Jesus, and predicate humanity of a distinct person, the man Jesus. No. One and the same must be human and divine. There is only one hypostasis or person which constitutes Jesus, and both humanity and divinity must be predicated of that one person. It is this faith conviction which is witnessed through the technical term "hypostatic union" and the affirmation *Theotokos*. This faith conviction is again witnessed at Chalcedon, with its clear teaching that humanity and divinity must be predicated of the one and the same *prosopon* (person) and *hypostasis* (indi-vidual) and its reaffirmation of the *Theotokos*. Chalcedon too saw itself as really teaching nothing new beyond Nicea: "in agreement, therefore, with the holy fathers, we all unanimously teach...." (DS 301).

I have limited my evaluation of Haight's challenging *Jesus the Symbol of God* to merely one issue: its claim to be faithful to the Christological conciliar tradition. In my judgement, I cannot see how it is. Because of its failure to predicate human and divine of one and the same individual, Jesus Christ, because it divides the predicates, as did Nestorius, Haight's Christology appears to me to be in the first instance a neo-Nestorianism or a crypto-Nestorianism, much as the Christology of Hans Küng. Because it is, it seems to me to be also adoptionistic or reductionistic. It does not affirm the divinity of Jesus Christ but only of God "*present to*" or "*active in*" him. If this were all we could say of Jesus, then the conciliar tradition, to which Haight wishes to be faithful, could never have affirmed Mary as the Mother of God.[83] Once again in our day the *Theotokos* becomes "the ultimate test of orthodoxy."

Donald W. Buggert, O.Carm.

Endnotes

1. See e.g. *Adversus Haereses*, I, 7, 2; I, 26, 1; III, 17, 1.
2. *Ibid*. III, 16, 2-3; III, 16, 8; III, 17, 4; IV, 6, 7.
3. The communication of idioms is "the principle that, as a consequence of the incarnation and of the union of the divine and human nature in the one person of Jesus Christ, it was (is) legitimate to predicate human properties of the Logos (or eternal Son of God) and divine properties of the man Jesus." Jaroslav Pelikan, *Mary Through The Centuries* (New Haven: Yale University Press, 1996), p. 58. Examples of the communication of idioms are: the Son of God suffers, dies or is born; Jesus, the man, knows all things.
4. For now, by "hypostatic union" I mean merely what the Greek says: *henosis kath' hypostasin*, i.e. that the oneness of Jesus is due to the fact that he is only one *hypostasis*, i.e. one individual of whom must be predicated all properties and actions, human and divine.
5. Pelikan, *Mary Through the Centuries*, p. 55.
6. See Roger Haight, *Jesus Symbol of God* (Maryknoll, New York: Orbis, 1999), p. 399. By "pluralist" model, I mean a Christological-soteriological model which maintains that Jesus is one savior among many.
7. *Ibid.*, 403-410, 456. Haight characterizes his soteriology as non-constitutive but normative and pluralist. See pp. 395-423.
8. *Ibid.*, 456. Haight goes on to say that Jesus is constitutive and cause of the salvation of Christians. But for Haight this is so only in the sense that he mediates an encounter with the divine or of life in the Spirit. "Jesus causes salvation among those who encounter him historically when he in turn mediates an encounter with God as loving creator and friend." *Ibid*, 421. As will be seen below, this soteriological position is consistent with his own ontological analysis of Christ.

9 See David Tracy, *Blessed Rage for Order* (New York: Crossroad, 1975), pp. 72-73.

10. See Walter J. Burghardt, S.J., "Mary in Eastern Patristic Thought," in Juniper B. Carol, O.F.M., editor, *Mariology* (Milwaukee: Bruce Publishing Company, 1957), II:125.

11. See, e.g., Lk 4:42-43; Mt 1:20-23.

12. Burghardt, "Mary in Eastern Patristic Thought," pp. 117, 119-120. As Michael O'Carroll and others point out, the precise origin of the *Theotokos* title is difficult to establish. A papyrus, which some date back to the third century, in the John Rylands Library in Manchester, England, contains an early Greek version of the medieval prayer, *Sub Tuum Praesidium*, in which is found the *Theotokos*. However, not all scholars are agreed on a third century dating. See Michael O'Carroll, C.S.Sp., "*Theotokos*, God Bearer," and "*Sub Tuum*, The," in Michael O'Carroll, C.S.Sp., *Theotokos: A Theological Encyclopedia of the Blessed Virgin Mary* (Wilmington, Delaware: Michael Glazier, Inc., 1982), pp. 342-343, 336. Pelikan claims that very likely the title originated in Alexandria in fourth century devotion to Mary as the mother of the divine savior prior to Alexander of Alexandria's use of it. See *Mary Through the Centuries*, p. 57.

13. See Alexander Roberts and James Donaldsen, editors., *The Anti-Nicene Fathers* (New York: Charles Scribner's Sons, 1899), VI:296.

14. Burghardt seems to suggest that Alexander uses the title in this letter in an anti-Arian sense, i.e. against Arius' rejection of the true and complete divinity of Christ. See "Mary in Eastern Patristic Thought," pp. 119-120. I do not believe that the literary context warrants this conclusion.

15. *Ibid.*, 120.

16. For references, see Burghardt, "Mary in Eastern Patristic Thought," p. 118.

17. For an overview, see Aloys Grillmeier, S.J., *Christ in Christian Tradition*, vol. I, *From the Apostolic Age to*

Chalcedon (451), translated by John Bowden (Atlanta: John Knox Press, 1975), pp. 85-149.

18.   Burghardt, "Mary in Eastern Patristic Thought," p. 121.

19.   While authors debate how frequently Athanasius actually used the title, its appearance in the *Orations Against the Arians* appears to be authentic. See Pelikan, *Mary Through the Centuries*, pp. 55-56.

20.   See for example *Orations Against the Arians*, III, 29, 33.

21.   Pelikan, *Mary Through the Centuries*, p. 59.

22.   Richard A. Norris, Jr., editor, *The Christological Controversy* (Philadelphia: Fortress Press, 1980), p. 87.

23.   See Jaroslav Pelikan, *The Emergence of the Catholic Tradition (100-600)* (Chicago: The University of Chicago Press, 1971), pp. 232-234. As Pelikan states: "If salvation was to be the gift of impassibility and immortality, the Savior had to be the Logos himself, not only a man assumed by the Logos." *Ibid.*, 234.

24.   See Pelikan, *Mary Through the Centuries*, p. 59. Pelikan believes that Grillmeier in *Christ in Christian Tradition* underestimates the role which Athanasius played in the development of the communication of idioms. I suspect Pelikan is correct. For example, in the *Orations Against the Arians*, III. 33, Athanasius, having eloquently stated in the previous paragraph that the flesh of Jesus and its passions truly must be predicated of the eternal Logos or Son and not of some other subject, asks: "Who will not marvel at this? Who will not agree that it is truly something divine? If the works of the Logos' Godhead had not been done by means of the body, humanity would not have been divinized. Furthermore, if the properties of the flesh had not been reckoned to the Logos, humanity would not have been completely liberated from them. Here we have a classic statement of the communication of idioms: divine things are predicated of the man, Jesus, and human things are predicated of the Logos; both are made possible because of the oneness of subject in Jesus, np. the Logos of the Father.

We see here again the three requisites for salvation: that Jesus is human, that Jesus is divine, and that the one who is human is the same as the one who is divine.

25. Pelikan, *Mary Through the Centuries*, p. 59.

26. That salvation demands the communication of idioms, an example of which is the *Theotokos*, see Pelikan, *The Emergence of the Catholic Tradition (100-600)*, p. 250.

27. Leo Donald Davis, S.J., *The First Seven Ecumenical Councils (325-787)* (Collegeville, Minnesota: The Liturgical Press, 1990), p. 139. In discussing Nestorius, I deal with the Nestorian heresy. Whether Nestorius was himself a "Nestorian" is another question. In view of the discovery in the late nineteenth century of a Syriac manuscript in Iran of Nestorius' apology, the *Book of Heracleides*, many scholars today claim that Nestorius was the victim of ecclesiastical politics and not guilty of the heresy for which he has been condemned, np. "Nestorianism." In this apology, written many years after the Council of Ephesus, Nestorius himself claims not to have changed his position regarding Christ, condemned by Ephesus, and that he was in agreement with both his successor, Flavian of Constantinople, and the *Tome to Flavian* of Leo the Great accepted at Chalcedon in 451. See P. T. Camelot, "Nestorius," *The New Catholic Encyclopedia*, 10:348, and Frances Young, *From Nicea to Chalcedon* (Philadelphia: Fortress Press, 1983), pp. 230-231. Regarding the question of whether Nestorius was a Nestorian, see the appendix of Grillmeier, *Christ in Christian Tradition* I, "The Nestorius Question in Modern Study." Grillmeier himself is very sympathetic towards Nestorius, as is Kelly. See *Early Christian Doctrines* (London: Adam and Charles Black, 1965), pp. 310-317.

28. Grillmeier, *Christ in Christian Tradition*, I:451-452; Young, *From Nicea to Chalcedon*, p. 234.

29. At this point Nestorius is willing to accept *Theotokos* if balanced by *anthropotokos*, mother of the man. Later he

would admit to both Cyril and Pope Celestine that the term could be accepted if used cautiously. Nestorius of course did have reasons for objecting to the *Theotokos*. His main arguments were a) the anti-Arian argument that a temporal creature could not bring forth the eternal God, b) mutability ("being born") could not be predicated of the eternal Logos, and c) the title could be interpreted in an Apollinarian way, i.e., as if Jesus were just divine and not also a human being. See Davis, *The First Seven Ecumenical Councils*, pp. 145-147. Kelly, *Early Christian Doctrines*, pp. 311-312. Young, *From Nicea to Chalcedon*, p. 235, believes that Nestorius, no matter what he said, remained a determined critic of the term.

30. Young, *From Nicea to Chalcedon*, p. 234.

31. *Ibid.*, 245.

32. Camelot, "Nestorius," p. 348.

33. Kelly, *Early Christian Doctrines*, p. 311; Camelot, "Nestorius," p. 348.

34. See Davis, *The First Seven Ecumenical Councils*, 146. Nestorius emphatically denied Paul of Samosata's two sons position. He states, for example, "God the Word and the man in whom He came to be are not numerically two; for the person (*prosopon*) of both was one in dignity and honor, worshiped by all creation, in no way and at no time divided by difference of purpose or will." See Young, *From Nicea to Chalcedon*, p. 237.

35. Davis, *The First Seven Ecumenical Councils*, p. 146. Young, *From Nicea to Chalcedon*, p. 237.

36. Here Nestorius reflects the Antiochene model of the incarnation often characterized as Logos-anthropos, or "God-bearing man," as distinct from the Alexandrine Logos-sarx schema or "flesh-bearing God." John Meyendorff, citing G. Florovsky, characterizes the Antiochene school as "anthropological maximalism" and the Alexandrine as "anthropological minimalism." See *Christ in Eastern Christian Thought* (Washington, D.C.: Corpus Books, 1969), p. 8.

37. Kelly, *Early Christian Doctrines*, p. 313. Kelly goes on to note by way of defense of Nestorius that by claiming that each nature had its own *hypostasis*, Nestorius was not saying that "each nature was an actually subsistent entity, but that it was objectively real."

38. It must be remembered that at this time the terms *ousia, physis*, and *hypostasis* were all used somewhat interchangeably to designate a reality and exhibited a wide range of meaning, much as with the English word "being." As of yet neither the school of Alexandria (Cyril) nor that of Antioch (Nestorius) had arrived at the Chalcedonian distinction between the notion of "person" (*hypostasis*) and nature (*physis*), much less the metaphysical notion of person as that which has "subsistence in se." See Grillmeier, *Christ in Christian Tradition*, I:458-460. I shall return to these terms below.

39. *Ibid.*, 459; Kelly, *Early Christian Doctrines*, p. 312.

40. Kelly, *Early Christian Doctrines*, pp. 312, 314; Davis, *The First Seven Ecumenical Councils*, p. 146.

41. Kelly, *Early Christian Doctrines*, p. 314.

42. Grillmeier, *Christ in Christian Tradition*, I:453. *Prosopon* here retains its primordial meaning of "countenance," that which is seen or manifest. *Ibid.*, 459.

43. Young, *From Nicea to Chalcedon*, p. 237.

44. Grillmeier, *Christ in Christian Tradition*, I:453; Kelly, *Early Christian Doctrines*, p. 315.

45. Young, *From Nicea to Chalcedon*, p. 236.

46. As Grillmeier points out, at this time the communication of idioms was in the stage of "careful examination and discussion." It had not yet reached the stage of ratification by the Church. *Christ in Christian Tradition*, I:453.

47. Davis, *The First Seven Ecumenical Councils*, p. 155. See also Wolfhart Pannenberg, *Jesus–God and Man*, translated by Lewis L. Wilkens and Duane A. Priebe (Philadelphia: Westminster Press, 1977), p. 290.

48.   As Meyendorff rightly notes: "Doctrinal conflicts between
       the various theologies from the fourth to the sixth century
       cannot be understood until their soteriological aspects
       are taken into consideration." *Christ in Eastern Christian
       Thought*, p. 4. For Cyril, only if the Word in its incarnate
       state were the subject of the suffering and death could the
       power of death and sin be overcome. *Ibid.*, 7.

49.   Cyril's complete formula is: *mia physis* (or *hypostasis*) *tou
       Theou Logou sesarkomene*, one incarnate nature of the
       God-Word.

50.   Hence Pelikan characterizes the conflicting Christologies
       of Alexandria and Antioch as representing accordingly the
       doctrines of hypostatic union and the indwelling Logos.
       The Emergence of the Catholic Tradition, p. 247. In all
       likelihood Cyril himself invented the phrase, "hypostatic
       union," a phrase which, because of its Apollinarian over-
       tones, was disliked by the Antiochenes and continued to
       perplex Nestorius many years later when he wrote the
       Book of Heracleides. Moreover, the Antiochenes perceived
       in the phrase a natural necessity, i.e. "if the union was
       natural (*kata physin, kath' hypostasin*), it was inevitable;
       it was not a voluntary act of God's love towards men."
       Young, *From Nicea to Chalcedon*, p. 224.

51.   Young, *From Nicea to Chalcedon*, p. 215.

52.   Kelly, *Early Christian Doctrines*, p. 318; Meyendorff, *Christ
       in Eastern Christian Thought*, pp. 7-8. As is reflected, for
       example, in his fifth, seventh, and ninth anathemas
       against Nestorius (DS 256, 258, 260), Cyril saw the
       Nestorian "God-bearing man" as just another saint or
       prophet, nothing but a temple of the Holy Spirit, an
       accusation to which the Antiochenes never responded.
       Young, *From Nicea to Chalcedon*, pp. 225-226.

53.   Grillmeier, *Christ in Christian Tradition* I:477. Grillmeier con-
       siders this formula to represent "the fruits which Cyril, along
       with Athanasius, was finally able to reap for the Church from
       the idea of the Logos-sarx christology." *Ibid.* We will see how

important this formula is in assessing the adequacy of Haight's Christological-soteriological proposals.

54. Meyendorff, *Christ in Eastern Christian Thought*, p. 8, and see p. 170, note 9; Grillmeier, *Christ in Christian Tradition*, I:481-482. For Cyril, *physis* as the principle of life needs to be "rounded off" by existence and reality, which provides the *physis* its basis. As rounded off by existence and reality or as given such a basis, the *physis* is a *hypostasis*. This is why for Cyril the human *physis* of Jesus is *anhypostatos*, without its own *hypostasis* which would make it an independently existing human being. Recall that the semantic center of gravity to the word *hypostasis* is "to stand under," *hyp-stasis*. *Ibid.*, p. 481.

55. Kelly, *Early Christian Doctrines*, pp. 319-320; Grillmeier, *Christ in Christian Tradition*, I:478. As a matter of fact, Cyril also used the term *physis* in the sense of "nature," i.e. the principle of life and action. Grillmeier suggests that if, at this point in the controversy, Cyril had abandoned his *mia physis* formula, much linguistic confusion would have been spared. See *Christ in Christian Tradition* I:476. It was not without reason that Nestorius saw Apollinarianism in the *mia physis* formula of Cyril, since the formula derived as a matter of fact from Apollinaris and not Athanasius, as Cyril had supposed. Meyendorff, *Christ in Eastern Christian Thought*, pp. 8-9.

56. Kelly, *Early Christian Doctrines*, pp. 318, 319; Meyendorff, *Christ in Eastern Christian Thought*, p. 12. It is this very point, the oneness of subject in Jesus, np. the Logos, which prohibits dividing the predicates, that Cyril is most influenced by Athanasius. Grillmeier, *Christ in Christian Tradition*, I:476; see p. 482.

57. Grillmeier, *Christ in Christian Tradition*, I:487; Kelly, *Early Christian Doctrines*, p. 320.

58. Grillmeier, *Christ in Christian Tradition*, I:487; Kelly, *Early Christian Doctrines*, p. 320. As Kelly points out, for Cyril, being an Alexandrine, the Christological problem was not

that of explaining the union of two disparate natures. Rather, Cyril understood the Logos as having "two phases or stages ..., one prior to and the other after the incarnation." In the incarnation the Logos remained what he was but added to his form of being God the form of a servant. Both before and after the incarnation, he was (is) the same person. For Cyril, the unity or oneness is presupposed from the start. Hence, we can speak of the *logos asarkos* (the logos apart from the flesh) and the *logos ensarkos* (the logos enfleshed). *Ibid.*, 319-320.

59.   Kelly, *Early Christian Doctrines*, p. 322.

60.   *Ibid.*, 318.

61.   Burghardt, "Mary in Eastern Patristic Thought," p. 125.

62.   See Kelly, *Early Christian Doctrines*, pp. 324-327; O'Carroll, *Theotokos*, p. 112.

63.   O'Carroll, *Theotokos*, p. 112. Kelly, *Early Christian Doctrines*, p. 327. Shortly after Cyril's Council, the Antiochene bishops held their own Council under John of Antioch and deposed Cyril. This Council is important in that it laid the framework for the Formula of Union of 433 in which the *Theotokos* is used. This formula was accepted by both Alexandrine and Antiochene bishops and presages to some extent the formula of the Council of Chalcedon. *Ibid.*, 327, 329.

64.   See Norman P. Tanner, S.J., *Decrees of the Ecumenical Councils*, vol. I: *Nicea to Lateran V* (Washington, D.C.: Georgetown University Press, 1990), pp. 41-44. Both the Greek and Latin texts can be found in Tanner.

65.   Grillmeier, *Christ in Christian Tradition*, I:486.

66.   *Ibid.*

67.   Besides the "one and the same" or "the same," Chalcedon will articulate the unity of subject in Jesus through two terms, *prosopon* and *hypostasis*, as well as through the *Theotokos*. Because the Antiochenes found the *phrase "henosis kath' hypostasin"* so offensive and smacking of both Apollinarianism and now Eutychian confusion, it

was not used at Chalcedon. But the basic teaching of hypostatic union is retained. At the next Council, Constantinople II, the phrase will be reintroduced. See DS 301-302; 424, 425, 436.

68. *Mary Through the Centuries*, p. 262 (italics mine).

69. "The phrase 'union by hypostasis' is merely meant to express the reality of the union in Christ in contrast to a purely moral and accidental interpretation which the synod presumed to be the teaching of the other side; it is thus contrasted with a *henosis kata thelesin monen* or *kath eudokian* (unity in will only or union by way of good pleasure) which is only achieved by the assumption of the external mode of appearance of another prosopon." Grillmeier, *Christ in Christian Tradition*, I:487.

70. Meyendorff makes an interesting soteriological observation regarding Ephesus. He states: "Its importance consisted not only of the assertion of a historical truth, that of Christ's unity, but also of the proclamation of a positive and theologically creative concept: that of a Christic humanity wholly human, wholly 'appropriated' by the Word, and constituting the principle of the deification to which all those who are 'in Christ' are destined. That is what the council of Ephesus intended to preserve in naming a dogma from the term *Theotokos* to designate the Mother of Jesus; for Mary could not be only the Mother of the 'flesh' of Christ, because this flesh did not possess an independent existence but was truly the 'flesh of God.' In this flesh (*kata sarka*) did the Son of God suffer, die, and rise again; with this flesh is the whole of redeemed mankind called to have communion with the Holy Spirit. The concept of 'participation' in God and of the deification of man could not be attained in a strictly Antiochene context." *Christ in Eastern Christian Thought*, p. 10. Meyendorff makes exactly my point. One of the effects of Christ's saving work in especially the Eastern Fathers of the Church, but also the New Testament (2 Pt 1:4) and

later in Thomas Aquinas is deification through Jesus
Christ. This deification was a major argument employed
by Athanasius and the Cappadocians against the Arians
for the divinity of the Son. Unless Jesus were one with the
Logos, unless he were in fact "the expressed Logos," as
certain of the Apologists were wont to say, he himself and
his redemptive work could not be the principle of salvation
and hence deification. Gregory of Nazianzus' axiom used
against Apollinaris is equally applicable to Nestorius'
indwelling Christology: what is not assumed is not healed.
Without *Theotokos* (the communication of idioms) or
hypostatic union, there is no assumption of the flesh by
the Word, and hence no salvation.

71.   Davis, *The First Seven Ecumenical Councils*, p. 156.

72.   Walter J. Burghardt, "*Theotokos*: The Mother of God," in
      Walter J. Burghardt, S.J., and William F. Lynch, S.J.,
      editors, *The Idea of Catholicism* (New York: Meridian
      Books, 1960), p. 171.

73.   *Ibid.*

74.   Aware of the radical implications of historical conscious-
      ness, Haight in this work makes a serious and praisewor-
      thy attempt to present a Christology which is faithful to
      the tradition, intelligible in today's postmodern world, and
      empowering of Christian life (47). I cannot here discuss
      and evaluate the whole of Haight's book of over five-
      hundred pages. While I certainly resonate with many of its
      concerns, especially to safeguard the truly human history
      of Jesus, and agree with much, though not all, of Haight's
      critique of neo-Chalcedonian Christology, I have several
      criticisms of this work. Here I can only deal with one,
      namely, its claim to be consistent with the Christological
      tradition. In fact, Haight deals only with Nicea and
      Chalcedon (e.g., chapter ten). Haight has only one line on
      the Council of Ephesus (286), in which he merely states
      that it condemned Nestorius. But he presents no analysis
      of what was at stake at Ephesus. Nor does he engage

Constantinople II held in 553. As should be clear from my treatment above of Ephesus, if one rejects Ephesus, one will not be able to do justice to either Nicea or Chalcedon. One cannot pick and choose one's Christological councils. They "hang together," as it were, as the Fathers of those Councils themselves were very much aware. Here I wish to show that Haight cannot do justice to the doctrine of one person as formulated at Ephesus through its notion of "hypostatic union" and its affirmation of *Theotokos*, a doctrine implied and required by Nicea and expressly reiterated by Chalcedon and Constantinople II. If one really accepts Nicea and Chalcedon, as Haight claims he does, then one must also accept Ephesus. Given Haight's understanding of Jesus, to be presented below, I am not surprised that he gingerly skirted it.

75.   Haight claims that his understanding and use of symbol in Christology is influenced by several individuals: John Smith, Paul Tillich, Karl Rahner, Edward Schillebeeckx, Paul Ricoeur. I do not believe that all these individuals mean the same thing by symbol. Certainly symbol as understood by Haight and Rahner's notion of *Realsymbol* are not the same. Nor is Rahner's understanding of Jesus as *Ursymbol* of God the same as Haight's understanding of Jesus as symbol of God. For Rahner, see "The Theology of the Symbol," *Theological Investigations*, vol. IV, translated by Kevin Smyth (Baltimore: Helicon Press, 1966), pp. 221-252.

76.   I stress that it is 'merely' God, not God-Father, God-Son, God-Spirit. Haight seems to have a somewhat unnuanced, generic monotheism, unlike especially the Eastern tradition, which tends to speak of God-Father, God-Son, God-Spirit, just as the creeds are expressions of faith in God-Father, God-Son, God-Spirit, and not just a generic God. In fairness to Haight, he does speak about the Logos and Spirit of God (see especially pp. 431-465), which are also symbols of divine immanence and empowerment. But it is

not clear that there really is within God, even the God of the economy, any distinction. In the final chapter of the book, Haight talks about "the Trinity," but I am unable to see how his "Trinity" escapes modalism or even Unitarianism.

77. At this point one begins to query as to what exactly might constitute the difference between Jesus as symbol of the divine and a stone as symbol of the divine, or Moses or Mother Teresa, who are also symbols of the divine. Recall Cyril's own challenge to Nestorius and the Antiochene theologians regarding how their Jesus, as God-bearing man, was any different from any other saint or prophet. See above, note 52.

78. For similar statements see pp. 205 (note 27), 262, 298, 328, 458.

79. It is interesting that on p. 327 Haight criticizes Küng's own indwelling-functional Christology, but not because it is *only* indwelling-functional, but because Küng provides no ontological analysis for his position, as does Haight through his ontology of symbol.

80. See, for example, Karl Rahner, *Foundations of Christian Faith*, translated by William V. Dych (New York: Seabury Press, 1978), pp. 116-133.

81. See my "Saint Jesus or Jesus Savior?" *New Theology Review* 11(1998), 20-31. I cannot here present and evaluate Haight's soteriology in any depth. I certainly agree with Haight that much of our biblical and classical soteriological language appears today as being mythological, which of course does not mean false but in need of serious hermeneutical retrieval. As for Haight's own soteriological retrieval, it is entirely consistent with his reductionistic Christology. Hence he says: "The formula identifying the salvation theory that is proposed here is the following: Jesus is salvation by being a revealer of God, a symbol for an encounter with God, and an exemplar of human existence" (pp. 357-358). Jesus is savior, therefore, merely because he reveals God or because God is encountered

through him, but not in any way because God-Father through him, his human history and freedom, and hence causality, can enact and realize God's own inner being as a saving God. For God to do what only God can do, salvation, it takes God. But God always works through secondary causes, in this case the human event and history of Jesus as the self-exegesis or self-expression of God.

82.   It was, of course, precisely *this* soteriological argument, and not that God himself was merely *present to* Jesus and can thus be *revealed* by Jesus, which was employed by Athanasius during and after Nicea and which convinced the bishops and others of the necessity of affirming "one in being with the Father."

83.   I wish to affirm again in this concluding note that Haight offers a challenging work, which must not be taken lightly. I fully agree, as do many contemporary systematic theologians, that patristic Christology and the conciliar Christological tradition are highly influenced by Hellenistic metaphysics and its presuppositions, which in my opinion make a logically consistent articulation of the incarnation impossible, as the pagan philosopher, Celsus, noted in the second century. Thus the Christologies of both Alexandria and Antioch, Cyril and Nestorius must be transcended. In my judgment, Haight himself has not sufficiently *transcended* Hellenistic metaphysics, especially in its various Platonic forms. It is his failure to do so which forces him into his crypto-Nestorianism and hence adoptionism. It is this metaphysics with its "bad infinite" (Hegel) or infinite antithesis between the world of being and becoming, divine and creaturely, infinite and finite, eternal and temporal, which gives rise to both a two nature model of Christology, within whose framework Haight still works, and a certain understanding of the pre-existing Logos, with which Haight rightly has difficulties. Without doubt, the Christological and trinitarian tradition must be

played in a new key. The "bad infinite" must be overcome, for it does not exist in the Semitic world-view which underlies both Testaments. Time and history must enter into "being" itself, even into God and the "event" of the incarnation. But in articulating a contemporary Christology for today or any day, in "dehellenizing" the classical Christological and trinitarian tradition, one must still, at the end of the day, predicate human and divine of "one and the same" and thus affirm Mary as the Mother of God in order to claim fidelity to the conciliar tradition. As to how one might overcome the "bad infinite," the antithesis of being and becoming, eternity and time, infinite and finite in Christology, I suggest beginning with a look at Pannenberg and Rahner, though not the Rahner represented by Haight. Pannenberg rightly claims: "The dilemma (between Alexandria and Antioch) is insuperable as long as we think that the event of the incarnation was complete with the birth of Jesus." Along somewhat similar lines, Rahner writes: "The incarnation ... is a divine movement which is fully deployed only in the death and resurrection of Jesus." See Wolfhart Pannenberg, *Systematic Theology*, vol. II, trans. Geoffrey W. Bromiley (Grand Rapids, Michigan: William B. Eerdmans, 1994), p. 384. Karl Rahner, "Salvation," *Sacramentum Mundi*, vol. V, ed. Karl Rahner et al. (New York: Herder and Herder, 1970), p. 428. Both Pannenberg and Rahner have overcome Hegel's "bad infinite" and have introduced time and history into God and the "event" of the incarnation. In doing so, they give us a Jesus whose true human history is safeguarded, a genuine concern of Haight, but of whom we can still predicate everything human and everything divine.

PART III

BIBLIOGRAPHY

Fr. Eamon at the International Marian Congress
Saragossa, Spain, 1979

Bibliography of Eamon R. Carroll, O.Carm.

This bibliography of Eamon R. Carroll's writings is limited to his books, monographs and articles. It does not include his book reviews or abstracts. The bibliography covers publications through the end of 2000. A list of abbreviations used in this bibliography and in the endnotes is found at the end of the bibliography.

1941

Mary's Niagara Shrine. *The Carmelite Review* 2:3-4.

1942

Father Cyril [Kehoe]'s Last Days. *Sword* 6:417-418.

1947

Land of Our Lady. *The Carmelite Review* 7:2-3,18-19.

Land of Our Lady. *Our Lady's Digest* 2:1-5.

1950

Arnold Bostius and the Scapular. *Sword* 14:342-355.

Dominic Savio Returns to Rome. *The Carmelite Review* 10:8-9,16.

1951

International Carmelite Marian Congress, Rome, August, 1950 (translation). *Sword* 14:355-366.

1952

Légendes mariales du Carmel. *Marie* 6:13-16.

Visit to Fisciano. *Sword* 15:467-473.

Visit to Germany. *Sword* 15:310-330,504-525.

1953

Arnold Bostius, Our Lady's Author. *Mary* 14:50-58.

Our Lady's Queenship in the Magisterium of the Church. *Marian Studies* 4:61-81.

1954

The Immaculate Conception and Carmelite Theologians. *Sword* 17: 120-145.

1955

Carmelite Marian Legends. *Sword* 18:359-365.

Mary Immaculate in the Magisterium since *Ineffabilis Deus*. *Carmelus* 2:3-53.

Mary in the Documents of the Magisterium. *Mariology* I. Edited by Juniper B. Carol, O.F.M. Milwaukee: Bruce, Pp. 1-50.

Mary's Mediation and the Popes. Dayton, Ohio: The Marian Library.

Mary's Scapular, Garment of Grace. *Our Lady's Digest* 10:44-48.

What You Should Know about Our Lady's Queenship. *Mary* 16:13-17.

1956

Carmel and Our Lady. *Sword* 19:151-156.

Editorial: Present, Past, and Future. *Sword* 19:93-94; 191-192; 315-316.

The Holy Father and the Scapular. *Sword* 19:95-112.

Mariology: A Waldensian View. *Aylesford Review* 1:103-107.

Mary Books. *Mary* 15:82-83.

Mary's Mediation and the Popes. Dayton, Ohio: The Marian Library.

Our Lady's Virginity *Post Partum. Marian Studies* 7:69-102.

Pius XII Speaks on the Scapular. *Our Lady's Digest* 11:63-71.

Queen Conceived without Original Sin. *Virgo Immaculata; Acta Congressus Mariologici-Mariani.* Roma: Academia Mariana Internationalis, 1954. Pp. 37-53.

A Waldensian View on the Virgin Mary. *American Ecclesiastical Review* 135:380-397.

1957

Editorial: Present, Past, and Future. *Sword* 20:5-6; 157-158; 277-278.

Mariology: A Waldensian View. *Our Lady's Digest* 11:403-408.

Mary, Co-redemptrix. *Scapular* 3:1-2.

Mary Prays for Your Family. *Marianist* 48:2-5.

Michael of St, Augustine and the Marian Life. *Mary* 18:72-76.

Pius XII and the Queenship. In *Queen of the Universe*. Edited by Stanley G. Matthews, S.M. St. Meinrad, Indiana: Grail, Pp. 203-211.

Queen Conceived without Original Sin. *Our Lady's Digest* 11:317-320.

The Scapular and True Devotion to Mary. *Our Lady's Digest* 12:65-69.

Scapulars. *Carmelite* 4:1-4.

1958

Apparitions of Mary. *Mary* 19:10-15.

Living Our Lady's Life. *Mary* 19:72-78.

Mary's Badge. *Mary* 19:28-31.

Mary's Garment. *Ave Maria* 88:20-23.

The Meaning of the Immaculate Conception. *Marianist* 49:2-6.

The Perfect Christian. *Mary* 19:4-7,

Sorrows of Mary. *Mary* 19:9-10.

1959

The Assumption, *The Mariological Institute Lectures.* Edited by V. Nugent. Jamaica, New York: 1959. Pp. 53-72.

Carmel and Our Lady. *Our Lady's Digest* 14:53-57.

Husband and Wife. *Mary* 20:4-5.

Mediatrix of All Graces. *Mary* 20:11.

The Mystical Life. In *With Mary in Mind: A Guide to Mental Prayer.* Edited by Howard Rafferty, O.Carm. Chicago, Illinois: Carmelite Third Order Press. Pp. 171-183.

The Mystical Life in Carmel. *Mary* 20:82-88.

Pope of the Assumption (Pius XII). *Marianist* 50:3-7.

Reflections on *A Complete Mariology* by G. Friethoff. *American Ecclesiastical Review* 140:159-167.

What Is Mariology? *Mary* 20:24-25.

1960

The Coronation of Mary. *Mary* 21:12-14.

Mary, Woman of Faith. *Our Lady's Digest* 15:175-180.

Our Lady and the Mass. *Mary* 21:80-82.

The Queenship of Mary. *Mary* 21:5-7.

A Recommended Reading List in Mariology. *The Marian Era* 1:94-99.

The Scapular and Saturday. *Our Lady's Digest* 15:53-57.

Ten Years of Mariology. *The Marian Era* 1:74-85.

The Virgin Birth. *Mary* 21:5-11.

1961

Four Score for Our Lady. *Marianist* 52:21-25.

Marian Congresses. In *Mariology* III. Edited by Juniper Carol, O.F.M. Milwaukee: Bruce. Pp. 295-325.

Mother of God. *Mary* 22:5-7.

Saint Therese, the Little Flower of Our Lady of Mount Carmel. *Our Lady's Digest* 16:43-50.

The Virginity of Mary. *Mary* 22:25.

1962

The Divine Maternity. *Mary* 23:48.

English Marian Literature, 1960-1962. *The Marian Era* 3:123-128.

The Marian Theology of Arnold Bostius, O.Carm. (1445-1499); A Study of His Work "De patronatu et patrocinio Beatissimae Virginis Mariae in dedicatum sibi Carmeli ordinem." S.T.D. dissertation, Pontifical Gregorian University. Roma.

The Marian Theology of Arnold Bostius, O.Carm. (1445-1499). *Carmelus* 9:197-236.

Mary and the Mass. *Our Lady's Digest* 17:27-30.

The Meaning of Mary to the American Catholic. *Our Lady's Digest* 17:63-71.

The Mother of Christ. With study-club questions. New York: Paulist Press.

Motherly Advice. *Mary* 23:5-9.

Reading about Mary. *Ave Maria* 95:10-11.

The Theological Significance of Mary's Virginity. *Marian Studies* 13:122-151.

1963

Arnold Bostius, Witness to Mary. *Spiritual Life* 9:112-122.

The Immaculate Heart of Mary and the Scapular. *Our Lady's Digest* 18:43-51.

Mary and the Church. *Mary* 24:7.

Mary, the Perfect Christian. *The Marian Forum* 3:18-32.

The Meaning of Mary to the American Catholic. *Sword* 23:2,7-14.

Midsummer Feast: July 16th, Scapular Feastday. *Soul* 15:19-20.

Scapular Feastday. *Mary* 24:45-51.

Will Mary Unite Christians? *The Lamp* 61:22-23.

1964

Mary and the Church. *The Marian Era* 5:18-22,107-110.

Mary in the Conciliar Age. *Our Lady's Digest.* 19:91-98.

Our Lady and the Council. *Mary* 25:5-8.

Recommended Reading in Mariology, 1962-1964. *The Marian Era* 5: 123-128.

Role of Mary in Christian Unity. *Our Lady's Digest* 18:226-233. (Reprint from *The Lamp.*)

Seat of Wisdom. *Queen of All Hearts* 15:6-8.

1965

Devotion to Our Lady after Vatican II. *Our Lady's Digest* 20:71-77.

The Faith of Mary. *Mary* 26:3-9.

María en el magisterio de la Iglesia. *Mariología.* A cura di Junípero Carol, O.F.M. Madrid: La Editorial Católica. Pp. 5-53.

The Mariological Congress in Santo Domingo. *Our Lady's Digest* 20:55-58.

Mary Most Holy. *The Marian Era* 6:25-27,100-101.

Our Lady and the Church in the Second Vatican Council. *Ascent* N. 2:66-75.

Preachers, Pulpits, and People. *Sword* 25:79-89.

The Second Vatican Council: Our Lady in the New Constitution on the Church. *Carmel in the World* 5:279-291.

1966

The Faith of Mary. *Our Lady's Digest* 20:251-256.

Mary and the Mass. *Our Lady's Digest* 21:133-136.

The Mother of Jesus in the Communion of Saints: Challenge to the Churches. Presidential Addresss. *Proceedings of the Catholic Theological Society of America* 21:249-265.

Our Lady and Vatican II. *Cross and Crown* 18:277-288.

Our Lady's Abiding Place in the Church. *The Marian Forum* 4:44-52.

Preachers, Pulpits, and People. *Sword*, 26:47-57,74-82.

Protestant Reaction to the Role of Mary in Vatican II. *American Ecclesiastical Review* 154:289-301.

The Question of Mary. *The Lamp* 64:22-23.

Recommended Reading in Mariology, 1964-1966. *The Marian Era* 7: 108-112.

1967

Albert of Trapani, St. *The New Catholic Encyclopedia.* Vol.1.

Aloysius Rabatá, Bl. *The New Catholic Encyclopedia.* Vol. 1.

Baptist of Mantua (Spagnoli), Bl. *The New Catholic Encyclopedia.* Vol. 2,

Blessed Virgin, Queenship of. *The New Catholic Encyclopedia*, Vol. 9,

Devotion to Our Lady after Vatican II. *Our Lady's Digest* 20:71-77.

Frances D'Amboise, Bl. *The New Catholic Encyclopedia*. Vol. 6.

Franco Lippi, Bl. *The New Catholic Encyclopedia*. Vol. 6.

Mariology. *The New Catholic Encyclopedia*. Vol. 9.

Mary, Blessed Virgin, Devotion to. *The New Catholic Encyclopedia*. Vol. 9.

Mary, Blessed Virgin, Queenship of. *The New Catholic Encyclopedia*. Vol. 9.

Mary Most Holy. *The Marian Era* 6:100-101.

The Mother of Jesus in the Communion of Saints - Challenge to the Churches. *The Catholic Theological Society of America Proceedings* 21:249-265.

Recapitulation in Christ. *The New Catholic Encyclopedia*. Vol. 12.

Reflections of a Dogmatic Theologian about Exegesis. *Maria in sacra Scriptura; Acta Congressus mariologici-mariani in Republica Dominicana anno 1965 celebrati* II,29-66. Romae: Pontificia Academia Mariana Internationalis.

Soreth, John, Bl. *The New Catholic Encyclopedia* Vol. 13.

A Survey of Recent Mariology. *Marian Studies* 18:103-121.

1968

The Mary-Church Analogy in the Ecumenical Dialogue: Agreements and Disagreements. *Acta Congressus Internationalis de Theologia Concilii Vaticani II, Romae, diebus 26 septembris-l octobris 1966 celebrati.* A cura di Adolfus Schönmetzer, S.J. Città del Vaticano: Typis Polyglottis. Pp. 245-264.

The Revolt against Mary. *The Lamp* 66:22-23,28-29.

A Survey of Recent Mariology. *Marian Studies* 19:87-108.

Theological Reflections on the Blessed Virgin's *Impeccabilitas. The University of Dayton Review* 5:21-31.

1969

January 1, Mary's Day in the Liturgy. *Ascent* No. 1:26-28.

La madre de Dios. Santander: Sal Terrae.

Mary and the Church. *American Ecclesiastical Review* 160:291-311.

Recommended Reading in Mariology 1966-1968. *The Marian Era* 9: 106-111.

A Survey of Recent Mariology. *Marian Studies* 20:137-167.

A Survey of Recent Mariology. *Our Lady's Digest* 24:68-85.

What Happened to Devotion to Mary? *Sword* 19:40-53.

What Happened to Our Devotion to Mary? *The Cord* 19:141-148.

Where Have All the Devotions Gone? *Carmel In The World* 9:93-106.

Where Have All the Devotions Gone? *Whitefriars* No. 3:3-9.

1970

Mariology and Theology Today. *Ephemerides mariologicae* 20:137-151.

Mary and the Church. *Sword* 30:54-74.

Report from the New York Convention. *Marian Studies* 23:113-132.

A Survey of Recent Mariology. *Marian Studies* 21:203-230.

Theological Reflections on the Blessed Virgin's *Impeccabilitas. De primordiis cultus mariani: Acta Congressus Mariologici-Mariani in Lusitania anno 1967 celebrati*, II:371-385. Romae, Pontificia Academia Mariana Internationalis.

Where Have All the Devotions Gone? *Ascent* No. 2:91-99.

1971

A Survey of Recent Mariology. *Marian Studies* 22:91-111.

1972

The Mother of Jesus. *North American Voice of Fatima*, May 15 and 18.

Preaching the Good News about the Mother of Jesus. *Homiletic and Pastoral Review* 73:11-16.

Report on the Zagreb Mariological Congress. *Marian Studies* 23:113-132.

What's Happened to Our Lady? *St. Anthony Messenger* 80:12-17.

What's Happened to Our Lady? *Whitefriars* No. 13:8-10.

Woman of Faith for a Time of Doubt. *Liguorian* 60:2-4.

1973

Behold Your Mother: A Pastoral Letter on the Blessed Virgin Mary. National Conference of Catholic Bishops, November 21, 1973. Eamon Carroll, Consultant. Washington, DC: United States Catholic Conference.

"Blessed Are You Who Have Believed": Devotion to Mary and Gospel Understanding Today. *The Lamp* 71:2-5.

Discussions after Major Papers. *Marian Studies* 24:83-99.

Mariology. *Chicago Studies* 12:295-303.

Mary and the Church. *The Marian Era* 11:44-48,138-141.

Report on 1973 Annual Convention of the Mariological Society of America (Saint Louis, Missouri, 3 and 4 January, 1973). *Marianum* 35:255-259.

A Survey of Recent Mariology. *Marian Studies* 24:100-125.

The Virgin Mary in Ecumenical Perspective. *The Cord* 23:305-310.

1974

Born of a Virgin - The Virgin Birth. *Presence* N.1:3-4.

Descent into Hell: A Forgotten Saving Mystery. *The Lamp* 72:6-9.

Mariology. *The New Catholic Encyclopedia.* Vol. 16:

Mary Immaculate, Most Modern of Women. *Our Lady's Digest* 28:101-106.

Rediscovering Mary in the Gospels. *Our Lady's Digest* 28:83-87.

A Survey of Recent Mariology. *Marian Studies* 25:104-142.

1975

Ecco la tua Madre! Una donna di fede. Lettera pastorale dei vescovi statunitensi sulla Beata Vergine Maria. Catania: Edizione Paoline.

How the Joint Pastoral, *Behold Your Mother,* Came to be Written. *University of Dayton Review* 11:9-19.

La Madonna e l'ecumenismo. *Presenza del Carmelo* No. 7:33-42.

Mariology. In *An American Catholic Cathechism.* Edited by George J. Dyer, New York: Seabury Press. Pp. 75-88.

La Virgen María en los Estados Unidos después del Vaticana II. *Enciclopedia Mariana posconciliar.* Madrid: Editorial Coculsa, pp. 237-242.

Mary, Mother of Mercy. *Carmel in the World* 14:233-248.

Our Lady in the Church Yesterday and Today. *Our Family* 27:38-42.

Preaching the Good News about the Mother of Jesus. *Homiletic and Pastoral Review* 73:11-19.

A Survey of Recent Mariology. *Marian Studies* 26:221-254.

Twenty-sixth Annual Convention of the Mariological Society of America. *Marianum* 37:87-90.

1976

"Behold your Mother, Woman of Faith": Maria. *Catholics United for the Faith, Newsletter*, 1-5.

For People Who Like To Read More about Our Lady. *Our Lady's Digest* 31:43-47.

Mariologia. *Ein Katholischer Katechismus.* München: Kösel Verlag.

Mariology. *The New Catholic Encyclopedia.* Vol. 17.

Mary, the Mother of Jesus: a Catholic View. *Our Lady's Digest* 31:77-85.

Our Lady and Ecumenical Hope. *Queen* 27:8-11.

Recommended Readings on Our Lady. *Our Lady's Digest* 31:14-15.

A Response to Donald Gray. *Proceedings of the Catholic Theological Society of America* 31:45-50.

A Survey of Recent Mariology. *Marian Studies* 27:110-143.

Theology on the Virgin Mary: 1966-1975. *Theological Studies* 37:253-289.

Twenty-seventh Annual Meeting of the Mariological Society of America. *Marianum* 38:33-38.

1977

Arnold Bostius: Flemish Exponent of Carmelite Devotion to Mary. *Sword* 37:7-20.

Down to Earth: New Protestant Books on Mary. *Our Lady's Digest* 32:16-18.

The Mariological Society of America, 1977 Convention. *Our Lady's Digest* 32:31-32.

Our Lady and the Church. *Our Lady's Digest* 31:138-142.

Our Lady in the Acts of the Apostles. *Our Lady's Digest* 32:34-35.

Pope Paul's Thoughts at Fatima. *Our Lady's Digest* 31:121-125.

Some Thoughts of Pope Paul VI to Pilgrims Honoring Our Lady. *Our Lady's Digest* 32:74-79.

A Survey of Recent Mariology. *Marian Studies* 28:148-180.

The Twenty-eighth Annual Convention of the Mariological Society of America. *Marianum* 119:274-276.

1978

The Gospels and Our Lady. *Our Lady's Digest* 32:101-102.

The Historical Image of Mary. *Our Lady's Digest* 32:155-156.

Mary in the New Testament. *Our Sunday Visitor* 67:8.

Mary, Mother of Mercy. *Presence* N. 22-23:21-24.

Mary Queen of Prophets. *Our Lady's Digest* 32:141.

Pondering the Joyful Mysteries: Reflections on a New Book, *The Birth of the Messiah. Our Lady's Digest* 32:145-150.

Recommended Readings in Mariology. *The Carmelite Review* 37:10,10.

A Survey of Recent Mariology. *Marian Studies* 29:93-133.

The Twenty-ninth Annual Convention of the Mariological Society of America. *Marianum* 40:182-184.

1979

The Blessed Virgin Mary in Catholic Payer-life. *Today's Catholic Teacher* 12:40-41.

Mariología. *Catecismo de la doctrina católica.* Barcelona: Herder.

Maryology: Recommended Readings. *The Carmelite Review* 18:1, 2.

Mary s Role in Plan of Salvation Discussed by Marian Theologian. *The Carmelite Review* 38:2,4.

The Mother of Jesus and Unity among Christians. *Our Lady's Digest* 34:71-77.

Our Lady and Ecumenism in the English-speaking World. *Marianum* 41:461-481.

Our Lady and the Church. *The Marian Era* 12:23-25.

Papal Infallibility and the Marian Definitions: Some Considerations. *Carmelus* 26:213-250.

Prayer and Spirituality: The Blessed Virgin Mary in Catholic Prayer-life. *Today's Catholic Teacher* 12:40-41.

Song of the Nations. *The Marian Era* 12:19-21.

A Survey of Recent Mariology. *Marian Studies* 30:140-180.

Understanding the Mother of Jesus. Wilmington, Delaware: Michael Glazier, Inc.

1980

Mary and the Spirit in the Prayer of the Eucharist. In *Mary, the Spirit and the Church.* Edited by Vincent P. Branick, S.M, Ramsey, New Jersey: Paulist Press. Pp. 55-64.

Mary in the Western Liturgy: Marialis Cultus. *Communio* 7:140-156.

Mary - the Mother of God. *Vision* 7:6-7.

New Developments about Our Lady: Signs of Marian Renewal. *Our Lady's Digest* 35:71-77.

A Survey of Recent Mariology. *Marian Studies* 31:111-154.

Thirtieth Annual Convention of The Mariological Society of America. *Marianum* 42:309-310.

Thirty-first Annual Convention of the Mariological Society of America. *Marianum* 42:334-336.

1981

Annunciation. *Abingdon Dictionary of Living Religions.* Nashville: Abingdon Press, p. 38.

Assumption. *Abingdon Dictionary of Living Religions.* Nashville: Abingdon Press, p. 71.

Arnold Bostius, Fifteenth Century Flemish Exponent of Carmelite Devotion to Mary. *De cultu mariano saeculis XII-XV.* Acta congressus mariologici-mariani internationalis Romae anno 1975 celebrati. Vol. V: *De cultu mariano apud sciptores ecclesiasticos saec. XIV-XV.* Romae: Pontificia Academia Mariana Internationalis, pp. 347-361.

Ave Maria. *Abingdon Dictionary of Living Religions.* Nashville: Abingdon Press, pp. 82-83.

Carmel - Mary's Own. *Presence* 43:4-7,10-13.

Critical Review of *Jesus: an Experiment in Christology* by Edward Schillebeeckx, *The Thomist* 45:144-150.

Immaculate Conception. *Abingdon Dictionary of Living Religions.* Nashville: Abingdon Press, pp. 338-339.

Magnificat. *Abingdon Dictionary of Living Religions.* Nashville: Abingdon Press, p. 448.

Magnifying the Lord: Mary's Prayer of Praise. *Vision* 8:4-5.

The Mariological Society of America, 1981 Convention. *Our Lady's Digest* 36:23-26.

Mariology and Christian Unity. *Ecumenical Trends* 10:129-132.

Mary. *Abingdon Dictionary of Living Religions.* Nashville: Abingdon Press, pp. 463-465.

Our Lady in the Mass. *Presence* N. 44:10-12.

Our Lady of Sorrows and the Holy Spirit. *Our Lady's Digest* 35:130-141.

A Survey of Recent Mariology. *Marian Studies* 32:113-141.

The Thirty-second Annual Convention of the Mariological Society of America. *Marianum* 43:271-274.

Virgin Birth. *Abingdon Dictionary of Living Religions*. Nashville: Abingdon Press, p. 796.

With Mary to the Mountain. *Mary* 42:2-7.

With Mary to the Mountain. *Our Lady's Digest* 36:49-58.

With Mary to the Mountain. In *With Mary to the Mountain: A Book of Instructions for the Lay Carmelite Order*. Edited by Alexis McCarthy, O.Carm., and Howard Rafferty, O.Carm., Aylesford, Illinois: Carmelite Press.

1982

Carmel and Our Lady. *Welcome to Carmel: a Handbook for Aspirants to the Discalced Carmelite Secular Order*. Washington, D.C.: The Teresian Charism Press.

Hail True Body Born of the Virgin Mary. *Our Lady's Digest* 36:113-126.

In the Company of Mary. *Modern Liturgy* 9:4-5,19-22.

Mary in Our Prayer Life. *Sword* 42:28-32.

Mary is Presence. *Presence* 45:10-11.

Nineteen Eighty-two Convention Report of the Mariological Society of America. *Our Lady's Digest* 37:54-57.

Saint Teresa of Avila: Daughter of Our Lady of Mt. Carmel. *Our Lady's Digest* 37:4-9.

A Survey of Recent Mariology. *Marian Studies* 33:165-201.

The Thirty-third Annual Convention of the Mariological Society of America. *Marianum* 44:181-183.

1983

The Mystery of Mary. *Mary* 44:3-5.

The Mystery of Mary. *Sword* 43:43-45.

Our Blessed Mother and the Blessed Sacrament. *Our Lady's Digest* 38:104-108.

Recommended Readings on the Blessed Virgin. *Our Lady's Digest* 38:91-96.

Recommended Readings on the Virgin Mary. *Ecumenical Society of the Blessed Virgin Mary Newsletter* (Surrey). N. 24,6-8.

A Survey of Recent Mariology. *Marian Studies* 34:91-126.

The Thirty-fourth Annual Convention of the Mariological Society of America. *Marianum* 45:325-328.

Thirty-fourth Annual Convention Report of the Mariological Society of America. *Our Lady's Digest* 38:12-16.

Woman of Faith. *Emmanuel.* 89:185-193.

Woman of Faith. *Our Lady's Digest.* 38:81-89.

1984

Mary After Vatican II. *St. Anthony Messenger* 91:36-40.

Mary as the New Eve. *Carmelus* 31:6-23.

Mary in Our Lives. *Our Lady's Digest* 38:106-110.

Mary's Brown Scapular. *Mary* 45:3-6.

Mary's Garment to Her Children. *Our Lady's Digest* 39:34-38.

The Mother of Jesus in Catholic Understanding. *The Catholic Almanac*. Huntington, Indiana: Our Sunday Visitor Press. Pp. 267-270.

Recent Recommended Readings on Our Lady. *Our Lady's Digest* 39: 93-96.

Recommended Readings on the Blessed Virgin Mary. *Ecumenical Society of the Blessed Virgin Mary Newsletter* (Surrey). N. 27:6-7.

The Saving Role of the Human Christ for St. Teresa. In *Centenary of Saint Teresa*. Carmelite Studies, Vol. 3: Washington, D.C.: ICS Publications. Pp. 135-152.

Supplement to Recommended Readings on the Blessed Virgin. *Our Lady's Digest* 38:125-127.

A Survey of Recent Mariology. *Marian Studies* 35:157-187.

1985

Agreed Statements at International Mariological Congresses. *Communications at the VIth E.S.B.V.M. Internatiional Congress*. Vol. I: *Post-Conciliar Agreed Statements on Mariology*. Wallington, Surrey: The Ecumenical Society of the Blessed Virgin Mary, pp. 2-7.

Homily at Celebration of Historic Marian Decree. *Our Lady's Digest* 40:12-15.

Mariological Society Meeting. *Our Lady's Digest* 40:87-91.

Mary: The Woman Come of Age. *Marian Studies* 36:136-160.

Patterns in Popular Piety at the Turn of the Century, 1400/1500. *De cultu mariano saeculo XVI. Acta congressus mariologici-mariani internationalis Caesaraugustae anno 1979 celebrati.* Vol. II: *Studia indolis generalioris de Maria in Concilio Tridentino, in liturgia et in arte christiana.* Romae: Pontificia Academia Mariana Internationalis, pp. 69-84.

St. Teresa of Jesus and the Humanity of Jesus Christ. *Carmel in the World* 24:188-206.

A Survey of Recent Mariology. *Marian Studies* 36:101-127.

The Thirty-sixth Annual Convention Report of the Mariological Society of America. *Marianum* 47:355-358.

1986

American Theologians Meet about Mary in Tampa. *Our Lady's Digest* 41:74-76.

Blessed Titus Brandsma, Carmelite Scholar of Our Lady. *Our Lady's Digest* 40:105-107.

Mary and the Church: Trends in Marian Theology Since Vatican II. *New Catholic World* 229:248-250.

Mary, Daughter of Abraham, Our Mother in Faith. *Our Lady's Digest* 41:3-4.

Recommended Readings on Our Lady: Latest List. *Our Lady's Digest* 41:89-93.

Rejoicing in the Feast of the Annunciation. *Our Lady's Digest* 40:99-102.

A Survey of Recent Mariology. *Marian Studies* 37:165-195.

The Thirty-seventh Annual Convention of the Mariological Society of America. *Marianum* 48:273-275.

1987

Blessed Be the Glorious Assumption of Our Lady. *Our Lady's Digest* 42:2-4.

Blessed Mary Ever Virgin. *Social Justice Review* 78:186-188.

The New Testament Charisms of the Blessed Virgin Mary. In *Mary and the Churches*. Edited by Albert Stackpoole, O.S.B. New York: The Columbia Press. Pp. 98-107.

The New Testament Charisms of the Blessed Virgin Mary. *One in Christ* 23:10-18.

Report of the 1987 Convention of the Mariological Society of America. *Our Lady's Digest* 42:94-95.

A Salute to the Marian Year. *Carmelite* 6:3-5.

Seventeeth-century Carmelite Marian Mystics. *De cultu mariano saeculis XVII-XVIII: Acta Congressus Maariologici-Mariani Internationalis in republica Melitensi, anno 1983 celebrati.* Vol. IV: *De Cultu Mariano apud scriptores ecclesiasticos saec. XVII.* Romae: Pontificia Academia Mariana Internationalis, pp. 499-518.

A Survey of Recent Mariology. *Marian Studies* 38:171-194.

The Thirty-eighth Annual Convention of the Mariological Society of America. *Marianum* 49:594-595.

A Tribute to the Marian Year. *Our Lady's Digest* 42:72-75.

1988

Behold Your Mother: Woman of Faith. (A Pastoral Letter of the United States Catholic Conference). Leesburg, Virginia: The Catholic Home Study Institute.

Blessed Mary, Ever Virgin. *Our Lady's Digest.* 43:5-13.

Holy Mary, Mother of God. *Our Lady's Digest* 42:99-102.

In Praise of Mary. *Carmelite* 6:7,10-11.

International Ecumenical Conference: Mary, Woman for All Christians. *Marianum* 50:567-568.

International Ecumenical Conference: Mary, Woman for All Christians. *Our Lady's Digest* 43:85-86.

International Mariological Conference at the University of San Francisco. *Ecumenical Trends* 17:155-157.

Mariological Society of America: Convention Report. *Our Lady's Digest* 43:87-88.

The Memory of Mary. *Mary's Shrine* 49:2-3,6.

The Mother of Jesus in Catholic Understanding. *The Catholic Almanac* [U.S.A.], 261-164.

Our Lady of the Book. *Our Lady's Digest* 43:66-73.

Reflections for Thanksgiving: Gratitude for Our Lady. *Our Lady's Digest* 43:41-43.

A Survey of Recent Mariology. *Marian Studies* 39:163-195.

The Thirty-ninth Annual Convention of the Mariological Society of America. *Marianum* 50:561-562.

1989

Blessed Be Her Glorious Assumption. *Our Lady's Digest* 43:104-111.

The Cardinal Wright Mariological Award. *Marian Studies* 40:50-53.

The Fortieth Annual Convention of the Mariological Society of America. *Marianum* 51:628-630.

The Holy Name of Mary. *Our Lady's Digest* 44:39.

Mariological Society of America Marks its 40th Annual Convention. *Our Lady's Digest* 44:89-92.

Mary, Cause of Our Joy. *Our Lady's Digest* 44:66.

Mary in the Apostolic Church: Work in Progress. *One in Christ, A Catholic Ecumenical Review*. 25:369-380.

Our Lady at the Visitation. *Our Lady's Digest* 44:7-11.

A Survey of Recent Mariology. *Marian Studies* 40:154-179.

1990

Advent Tribute to Mary Immaculate Patroness of Our Land. *Our Lady's Digest* 45:66-71.

Bartholomew M. Xiberta, Our Lady's Theologian. *Mansuetudine sapientiae (James 3:13): Miscellanea in honor of Batolomé Maria Xiberta, O.Carm.* Edited by Redemptus M. Valabek, O.Carm. Rome: Institutum Carmelitanum, pp. 259-273.

The Blessed Virgin Mary Mother of Reconciliation. *Our Lady's Digest* 44:108-109.

An Explanation of the Sabbatine Privilege. *Our Lady's Digest* 45:15-16.

Fr. Theodore Koehler, S.M., Secretary Emeritus. *Marian Studies* 41:163.

The Forty-first Annual Convention of the Mariological Society of America. *Marianum* 52:379-380.

Marian Spirituality. In *Spiritual Traditions for the Contemporary Church.* Edited by Robin Maas and Gabriel O'Donnell, O.P. Nashville, Tennessee: Abingdon Press, pp. 365-379.

Mary in the Apostolic Church. In *Mary in Doctrine and Devotion.* Edited by A. Stacpoole. Dublin: The Columba Press, pp. 145-157.

Mary in the Apostolic Church. *One in Christ* 25:369-380.

Must Catholics Believe in Fatima? The Place of Private Revelation in the Church. *Our Lady's Digest* 45:35-48.

Our Lady of the Bells. *Our Lady's Digest* 45:77-78.

Our Lady's Openness in the Oldest Parts of the Gospels. *Our Lady's Digest* 45:4-10.

Recommended Readings on the Blessed Virgin Mary. *Our Lady's Digest* 45:58-64.

Recommended Readings on Our Lady: Latest Suggestions. *Our Lady's Digest* 45:92-96.

The Sacred Memory of Mary. *Carmel in the World* 29:13-24.

The Special Significance of Mary's Assumption. *Our Lady's Digest* 45:24-25.

A Survey of Recent Mariology. *Marian Studies* 41:125-152.

Thérèse and the Mother of God. *Experiencing St. Thérèse Today.* Edited by John Sullivan, O.C.D. Washington, D.C.: ICS Publications, pp. 82-96.

Throne of Wisdom. *Carmel in the World* 29:107-125.

La "Virgo Purissima" y el Carmelo. *Congreso Mariano internacional, Roma, abril 1989.* A cura de Alberto Yubero, O.Carm. Madrid: Libreria Carmelitana.

1991

Ecumenical Roundtables and International Mariological Congresses. *Marian Library Studies* 17-23: 566-577.

The Forty-second Annual Convention of the Mariological Society of America. *Marianum* 53:261-262.

Mother of God, Protect Us in Danger. *Our Lady's Digest* 45:114.

Must Catholics Believe in Fatima? The Place of Private Revelation in the Church. In *Exploring Fatima.* Washington, New Jersey: AMI Press, pp. 1-13.

Our Lady of the Book. *Our Lady's Digest* 45:98-104.

Revolution in Mariology, 1949-1989. In *The Land of Carmel: Essays in Honor of Joachim Smet, O.Carm.* Edited by Keith Egan and Paul Chandler, O.Carm. Rome: Institutum Carmelitanum, pp. 451-464.

A Survey of Recent Mariology. *Marian Studies* 42:172-203.

1992

Forty-third Annual Convention of the Mariological Society of America. *Marianum* 55:374-376.

A Survey of Recent Mariology. *Marian Studies* 43:160-189.

1993

Forty-fourth Annual Convention of the Mariological Society of America. *Marianum* 55:657-659.

Mary Treasured All These Things in Her Heart. *Queen of All Hearts* 43:11-12,28-29; 44:28-30.

The Scapular of Our Lady of Mount Carmel: Mary's Garment. *Queen*, 1992, pp. 20-22.

A Survey of Recent Mariology. *Marian Studies* 44:106-139.

1994

Forty-fifth Annual Convention of the Mariological Society of America. *Marianum* 56:464-465.

A Survey of Recent Mariology. *Marian Studies* 45:250-271.

Thérèse and the Mother of God. Washington, New Jersey: AMI Press.

The Virgin Mary and Feminist Writers. *Carmelus* 41:49-62.

1995

Behold Your Mother, Woman of Faith: A Pastoral Letter of the United States Catholic Conference, November 21, 1973. Paeonian Springs, Virginia: The Catholic Home Study Institute.

The Blessed Mother in Ecumenical Perspective. *Sword* 55:47-62.

Forty-sixth Annual Convention of the Mariological Society of America. *Marianum* 57:387-389.

Queenship and Immaculate Conception. *Queen of All Hearts* 45:40-42; 46:40-41.

The Scapular of Our Lady of Mount Carmel. Middletown, New York: National Shrine of Our Lady of Mount Carmel.

A Survey of Recent Mariology. *Marian Studies* 46:145-163.

1996

Light on Our Blessed Lady: Chapter Eight of Lumen Gentium. *Catholic Dossier* 2:13-17.

Marking Thirty: Theology, Mary, and Christian Unity. *Hopes and Visions* N. 1:3-11.

A Survey of Recent Mariology. *Marian Studies* 47:118-143.

1997

Forty-eighth Annual Convention of the Mariological Society of America. *Marianum* 69:315-317.

Mary in Ecumenical Perspective. *Ecumenical Trends* 26:65-73.

Mary in Ecumenical Perspective. *Theology Digest* 44:345-349.

A Survey of Recent Mariology. *Marian Studies* 48:138-162.

With Mary His Mother: A Theologian Reflects on Recent Scripture Studies. In *Master of the Sacred Page: Essays and Articles in Honor of Roland E. Murphy, O.Carm., on the Occasion of His Eightieth Birthday.* Edited by Keith J. Egan and Craig Morrison, O.Carm. Washington, D.C.: The Carmelite Institute, 1997, pp. 219-234.

1998

Lady of a Thousand Titles. *Queen of All Hearts* 48:30-31.

Mary as Evangelizer: Reflection for Pilgrimages and Shrines. *Carmel in the World* 37:278-280.

Miscellany of Our Blessed Lady: In Joyful Praise of the Holy Virgin. *Queen of All Hearts* 49:12-13.

A Survey of Recent Mariology. *Marian Studies* 49:141-166.

'Vergine Madre, figlia del tuo Figlio,' (O Virgin Mother, daughter of your Son) from Paradiso XXXIII, the Divine Comedy by Dante Alighieri. *Sword* 58:37-44.

1999

Bartolomé María Xiberta, Teólogo de Nuestra Señora. Translation of Bartholomey Maria Xiberta, Our Lady s Theologian by Checa Arregui, O.Carm. <*Cerni Essentia Veritatis*> *(Miscelánea homenaje al P. Xiberta de la Región Ibérica Carmelita).* Barcelona: Región Ibérica Carmelita.

Evolution in Mariology, 1949-1999. Keynote Address to the Mariological Society of America. *Marian Studies* 50:139-145.

Recent Publications on the Blessed Virgin Mary in English for IMRI. *Queen of All Hearts 50:36-37.*

Reflections on Our Blessed Lady. *Queen of All Hearts* 50:28-29.

The Saving Role of the Human Christ for St. Teresa. *The Catholic Dossier* 5:21-29.

2000

Jottings on the Blessed Virgin Mary. *Queen of All Hearts* 50:35-36.

Mary in the Way of Beauty in Christian Art. *Queen of All Hearts* 50:28-29.

Recent Publications on the Blessed Virgin Mary in English. *Queen of All Hearts* 51:40-41.

Abbreviations Used in Bibliography
and in the Endnotes

AAS   *Acta Apostolicae Sedis*

CC or CCSL *Corpus Christianorum*, Series latina

CCC   *Catechism of the Catholic Church*

CDF   Congregation for the Doctrine of the Faith

CL   *Christifideles laici*, Apostolic Exhortation on the Vocation and Mission of the Lay Faithful in the Church and in the World

Const   *Constitutions of the Order of the Brothers of the Blessed Virgin Mary of Mount Carmel* (Rome, 1996).

CSEL   *Corpus scriptorum ecclesiasticorum latinorum*

DIP   *Dizionario degli Istituti di Perfezione*

DS   *Enchiridion symblorum, definitiorum et declarationum de rebus fidei et morum* (Denzinger-Schönmetzer)

GS   *Gaudium et spes*, Pastoral Constitution on the Church in the Modern World

In in   *Inter insigniores*. Declaration on the Question of the Admission of Women to the Ministerial Priesthood

LG   *Lumen gentium*. Dogmatic Constitution on the Church

MC   *Marialis cultus*, Apostolic Exhortation on Honoring Mary

MD   *Mulieris dignitatem*, Apostolic Letter on the Dignity and Vocation of Women

NSIC   Archives of the National Shrine of the Immaculate Conception, Washington DC

PA   *Pastor aeternus*. Doctrinal Constitution on Papal Infallibility.

PG   Migne, *Patrologiae Series graeca*

PL   Migne, *Patrologiae Series latina*

PO   *Presbyterorum ordinis*, Decree on the Ministry and Life of Priests

RM   *Redemptoris mater*, Encyclical on the Mother of the Redeemer

Rule   *The Rule of Carmel*, edited by Bruce Baker, O.Carm. And
       Gregory L. Klein, O.Carm., 2000.

SC   *Sacrosanctum concilium*, Constitution on the Sacred Lit-
       urgy

TMA   *Tertio millennio adveniente.* Encyclical

List of Contributors

David Blanchard, O.Carm. received his Ph.D. in anthropology from the University of Chicago. He is an adjunct professor in the Mission and Cross Cultural Program at the Washington Theological Union and director of a development project in Central America.

Emanuele Boaga, O.Carm. received his H.E.D. degree from the Gregorian University. He is president of the Institutum Carmelitanum, archivist of the Carmelite Order, and professor of history at the Marianum in Rome.

James Boyce, O.Carm. received his Ph.D. in historical musicology from New York University and has published a number of articles on Carmelite liturgy, particularly its office tradition. Ten of these have been published as *Praising God in Carmel: Studies in Carmelite Liturgy.* He is currently teaching at Fordham University in New York.

Donald W. Buggert, O.Carm. received his S.T.D. degree from The Catholic University of America in systematic theology. He is professor of systematic theology and the chair of the the department of systematic and moral theology at the Washington Theological Union.

Richard Copsey, O.Carm. received his Ph.D. from University College, Dublin. An expert in the medieval history of the Carmelites, he was a member of the Carmelite Institute in Rome and served as editor of its journal, *Carmelus.* Currently he is chaplain to the Catholic students in Aberdeen University.

Leopold Glueckert, O.Carm. received his Ph.D. in history from Loyola University in Chicago. He has taught at Loyola Marymont College, Los Angeles and DePaul University, Chicago. He is now teaching history at Lewis University, Romeoville, IL, where he also serves as university chaplain.

George Kirwin, O.M.I. received his S.T.D. from the Catholic University of America, where he wrote his doctoral dissertation

441

under the direction of Eamon Carroll. He was a professor of theology at Oblate College in Washington, D.C. and served as its last president. Twice president of the Mariological Society, he now is involved in seminary formation.

Theodore Koehler, S.M. received his doctorate in sacred theology at the University of Fribourg. He has served as Director of the Marian Library of the University of Dayton, the secretary of the Mariological Society and the editor of *Marian Studies*. In 1975 he founded the International Marian Research Institute. He is now retired.

Ernest Larkin, O.Carm. received the S.T.D. from St. Thomas University in Rome. After almost twenty years of teaching theology at Whitefriars Hall and The Catholic University of America, he became in 1970 a co-founder of the Kino Institute in Phoenix, AZ. Since that time he has been involved in adult education, seminars and retreats in the United States and abroad.

John Macquarrie, formerly of Union Theological Seminary, New York, is Emeritus Lady Margaret Professor of Divinity at the University of Oxford.

Patrick McMahon, O.Carm. received his Ph.D. in history from New York University. He is the Director of the Carmelitana Collection, Washington D.C., Provincial Delegate to the Carmelite Laity, and lecturer in Carmelite Studies at the Washington Theological Union.

Carlos Mesters, O.Carm. received the Licentiate in Sacred Scripture from the Pontifical Biblical Commission and the Doctorate of Sacred Theology from the University of St. Thomas. He is well known for his work of helping the poor of the base communities of Brazil interpret their lives in light of the Scriptures. Since 1978 he has been a member of the Ecumenical Center of Biblical Studies in São Paulo.

Roland Murphy, O.Carm. is the George Washington Ivey Emeritus Professor of Biblical Studies of Duke University, and now resides at Whitefriars Hall, Washington, D.C. His most recent book is *The Gift of the Psalms*.

Louis P. Rogge, O.Carm. received his doctorate in theology from Union Theological Seminary in New York. He resides at St. Elias Friary in Joliet, IL and is a member of the Carmelite Preaching Team and Mission Band.

Joachim Smet, O.Carm. holds masters degrees from the Catholic University of America and the University of Chicago and the H.E.D. from the Gregorian University in Rome. He was co-founder in 1951 of the Carmelite Institute (Rome), and for forty years editor of the Institute's journal, *Carmelus*. Author of a five volume history of the Carmelite Order, he continues to serve as an active member of the Institutum Carmelitanum.

Thomas A. Thompson is director of the Marian Library at the University of Dayton and associate professor of theology at the International Marian Research Institute. Since 1990 he has been secretary of the Mariological Society of America and editor of its journal, *Marian Studies*.

James A. Wallace, C.Ss.R. received his Ph.D. from the School of Speech at Northwestern University. He is a professor of homiletics at the Washington Theological Union and has lectured extensively to preachers in the United States, Europe and Africa.

John Welch, O.Carm. received his Ph.D. in religious education from the University of Notre Dame. He is a professor in the pastoral studies department of the Washington Theological Union. He teaches in the areas of Carmelite spirituality and human development.

Edward J. Yarnold, S.J. is a British Jesuit with degree in classics and theology from Oxford University. He is a visiting professor in liturgical studies at the University of Notre Dame, a member of the Ecumenical Society of the Blessed Virgin Mary, and former member of the Anglican-Roman Catholic International Commission.